AF825795

International Political Economy Series

General Editor: **Timothy M. Shaw**, Professor of Human Security & Peacebuilding, School of Peace & Conflict Management, Royal Roads University, Victoria, BC, Canada

Titles include:

Pradeep Agrawal, Subir V. Gokarn, Veena Mishra, Kirit S. Parikh and Kunal Sen
POLICY REGIMES AND INDUSTRIAL COMPETITIVENESS
A Comparative Study of East Asia and India

Roderic Alley
THE UNITED NATIONS IN SOUTHEAST ASIA AND THE SOUTH PACIFIC

Dick Beason and Jason James
THE POLITICAL ECONOMY OF JAPANESE FINANCIAL MARKETS
Myths versus Reality

Mark Beeson
COMPETING CAPITALISMS
Australia, Japan and Economic Competition in Asia-Pacific

Deborah Bräutigam
CHINESE AID AND AFRICAN DEVELOPMENT
Exporting Green Revolution

Shaun Breslin
CHINA AND THE GLOBAL POLITICAL ECONOMY

Kenneth D. Bush
THE INTRA-GROUP DIMENSIONS OF ETHNIC CONFLICT IN SRI LANKA
Learning to Read between the lines

Steve Chan, Cal Clark and Danny Lam (*editors*)
BEYOND THE DEVELOPMENTAL STATE
East Asia's Political Economies Reconsidered

Abdul Rahman Embong
STATE-LED MODERNIZATION AND THE NEW MIDDLE CLASS IN MALAYSIA

Dong-Sook Shin Gills
RURAL WOMEN AND TRIPLE EXPLOITATION IN KOREAN DEVELOPMENT

Jeffrey Henderson (*editor*)
INDUSTRIAL TRANSFORMATION IN EASTERN EUROPE IN THE LIGHT OF THE EAST ASIAN EXPERIENCE

Takashi Inoguchi
GLOBAL CHANGE
A Japanese Perspective

Dominic Kelly
JAPAN AND THE RECONSTRUCTION OF EAST ASIA

L. H. M. Ling
POSTCOLONIAL INTERNATIONAL RELATIONS
Conquest and Desire between Asia and the West

Pierre P. Lizée
PEACE, POWER AND RESISTANCE IN CAMBODIA
Global Governance and the Failure of International Conflict Resolution

S. Javed Maswood
JAPAN IN CRISIS

Ananya Mukherjee Reed
PERSPECTIVES ON THE INDIAN CORPORATE ECONOMY
Exploring the Paradox of Profits
CORPORATE CAPITALISM IN CONTEMPORARY SOUTH ASIA (*editor*)
Conventional Wisdoms and South Asian Realities

Cecilia Ng
POSITIONING WOMEN IN MALAYSIA
Class and Gender in an Industrializing State

Fahimul Quadir and Jayant Lele (*editors*)
DEMOCRACY AND CIVIL SOCIETY IN ASIA: VOLUME 1
Globalization, Democracy and Civil Society in Asia
DEMOCRACY AND CIVIL SOCIETY IN ASIA: VOLUME 2
Democratic Transitions and Social Movements in Asia

Ian Scott (*editor*)
INSTITUTIONAL CHANGE AND THE POLITICAL TRANSITION IN HONG KONG

Mark Turner (*editor*)
CENTRAL–LOCAL RELATIONS IN ASIA–PACIFIC
Convergence or Divergence?

Ritu Vij
JAPANESE MODERNITY AND WELFARE
State, Civil Society, and Self in Contemporary Japan

Fei-Ling Wang
INSTITUTIONS AND INSTITUTIONAL CHANGE IN CHINA
Premodernity and Modernization

International Political Economy Series
Series Standing Order ISBN 0–333–71708–2 hardcover
Series Standing Order ISBN 0–333–71110–6 paperback
(*outside North America only*)

You can receive future titles in this series as they are published by placing a standing order. Please contact your bookseller or, in case of difficulty, write to us at the address below with your name and address, the title of the series and one of the ISBNs quoted above.

Customer Services Department, Macmillan Distribution Ltd, Houndmills, Basingstoke, Hampshire RG21 6XS, England

---

Japanese Modernity and Welfare

State, Civil Society, and Self in Contemporary Japan

Ritu Vij
Lecturer in International Relations,
University of Aberdeen, UK

palgrave
macmillan

© Ritu Vij 2007

All rights reserved. No reproduction, copy or transmission of this publication may be made without written permission.

No paragraph of this publication may be reproduced, copied or transmitted save with written permission or in accordance with the provisions of the Copyright, Designs and Patents Act 1988, or under the terms of any licence permitting limited copying issued by the Copyright Licensing Agency, 90 Tottenham Court Road, London W1T 4LP.

Any person who does any unauthorized act in relation to this publication may be liable to criminal prosecution and civil claims for damages.

The author has asserted her right to be identified as the author of this work in accordance with the Copyright, Designs and Patents Act 1988.

First published 2007 by
PALGRAVE MACMILLAN
Houndmills, Basingstoke, Hampshire RG21 6XS and
175 Fifth Avenue, New York, N.Y. 10010
Companies and representatives throughout the world

PALGRAVE MACMILLAN is the global academic imprint of the Palgrave Macmillan division of St. Martin's Press, LLC and of Palgrave Macmillan Ltd. Macmillan® is a registered trademark in the United States, United Kingdom and other countries. Palgrave is a registered trademark in the European Union and other countries.

ISBN-13: 978–1–4039–1544–3 hardback
ISBN-10: 1–4039–1544–X hardback

This book is printed on paper suitable for recycling and made from fully managed and sustained forest sources. Logging, pulping and manufacturing processes are expected to conform to the environmental regulations of the country of origin.

A catalogue record for this book is available from the British Library.

Library of Congress Cataloging-in-Publication Data
Vij, Ritu, 1959–
Japanese modernity and welfare:state, civil society, and self in contemporary Japan/Ritu Vij.
p. cm.
Includes bibliographical references and index.
ISBN 1–4039–1544–X (alk. paper)
1. Japan—Social policy. 2. Civil society—Japan. 3. Welfare state—Japan. I. Title.
HN723.5.V55 2007
300.952—dc22 2007023326

10 9 8 7 6 5 4 3 2 1
16 15 14 13 12 11 10 09 08 07

Printed and bound in Great Britain by
Antony Rowe Ltd, Chippenham and Eastbourne

For my parents
Achala and Jindi Vij
and
my sister, Bindu Maira

Contents

List of Tables

Preface

This book examines the relationship between civil society and welfare in modern Japan. It does so, however, in pursuit of a theoretical project that, in an important sense, stands above the case itself and provides the frame within which alone its *mondai ishiki* (problem consciousness) can be understood: the normative question of re-thinking the notion and provision of welfare under conditions of late capitalism.

Contemporary debates about welfare and its reform elaborate competing claims for a recuperation of the besieged Keynesian welfare state, its privatization via full-scale marketized provision, or, alternatively, the return to an older historical epoch of welfare as voluntary, charitable provision. Missing in these discussions, however, is any systematic attention to the demands that modern notions of personhood or subjectivity make, and the limits they must inevitably place on any efforts to re-think welfare in our times. Insofar as modern subjectivity is principally shaped by, and in relation to, the institutions of political economy, the question of rethinking welfare must be seen pivotally as the question of re-thinking the *limits* of state and market in terms of how they enable or impinge on subjectivity. Repudiating the theoretical foreclosure implicit in the location of welfare in *either* state or civil society (as above), and the dualism that attends treatments of civil society in relation to individual well-being as either wholly enabling (the free-market ideal) or wholly disabling (the Marxian critique, for instance), the larger theoretical project that frames the investigation of Japanese modernity and welfare pursued here takes the tension inherent within civil society, its enabling *and* disabling function vis-à-vis modern conceptions of personhood as the starting point of a rearticulation of welfare in state and civil society. It is this larger problematic within which the issues explored in the case of Japan are located.

The book, then, is conceived as an attempt to anchor this larger theoretico-normative project in a substantive way, specifically to concretize the historicity of this claim. It elaborates via a discussion of the Japanese case the homologies that structure an historically specific institutionalization of civil society, the notion of personhood constituted in relation to its institutions and social practices, and the ideal of welfare that gains legitimation therein. Modern Japan's welfare system – rendered anomalous or 'hybrid' by the criteria set forth within comparative studies of social policy or, conversely, 'exceptional' via hegemonic culturalist/statist narratives that dominate Japan area studies – is re-interpreted here in relation to the normative structure of subjectivity constituted within Japanese political economy, specifically via the explicit recognition and institutionalization of the social limits of the market. Linking the distinctive pattern of welfare provision uncovered here – the generous provision of goods that serve production-related social ends and the relatively scarce provision of consumption-related goods that satisfy individuated wants – to the specifically modern notion of subjectivity that took shape in Japan, the book offers a re-interpretation of civil society and welfare in Japan as a step toward anchoring a larger theoretical project of rethinking welfare in relation to subjectivity in political economy.

Acknowledgments

This book bears numerous traces: of people, places, and times. I cannot name or thank them all but a few I must: David Levine, Jim Caporaso, Peter Van Ness, Alan Gilbert, and Jack Donnelly at the University of Denver, for sustaining and nurturing a sometimes inchoate intellectual quest; David especially, not only for the remarkable quality of his work but the generosity with which he has shared it, opening up a field of inquiry that will, I suspect, occupy me for years to come; I owe him much, not least the intensive year spent reading a single text, Hegel's *Phenomenology of Mind*; for that and much else, my profound gratitude.

John Clammer, Matt Davies, Stephen Gill, David Levine, Craig Murphy, Mustapha Pasha, Magnus Ryner, Mark Selden, Timothy Shaw, Masaru Tamamoto, Anna Yeatman, and Ross Zucker read and commented on various iterations of this project, offering both constructive critique and encouragement, and for that I am grateful. Although I have tried to respond to all the feedback I received from them, they will probably find much to disagree with here. For commissioning this project and for the level of sustained professional and personal support Timothy Shaw, the IPE series editor at Palgrave, has extended to me, I am extremely grateful. His team there, including Phillipa Grand and Hazel Woodbridge, has shepherded the publication of this book across many continents with diligence and care; my appreciation and thanks to them.

In Japan, the list is doubly long: my thanks to John Clammer, Kazuko Furuta, Tom Gill, Reiko Gotoh, Eiichi Hoshino, Takahashi Inoguchi, Go Ito, Makoto Katsumata, Yoichi Mine, Kinhide Mushakoji, Ito Peng, David Plath, Kimi Sakurai, Giorgio Shani, Toshimitsu Shinkawa, Takao Takahara, and Masaru Tamamoto for discussion, critique, introductions, and camaraderie; to Peter Van Ness and Anne Gunn for their support during our shared time in Tokyo; to all the women at 'Bilingual House' in *Kamishakuji,* especially Beth Asher, Beverley Monk, and Maryline Boulay, for sharing the everyday unconditionally and with humour, during the long months of fieldwork that became the basis of this project; more recently, the teachers and 'mothers' at *Kougai Yochien, Kougai Shogakko,* and *Nishi-Azabu Hoikuen* who enveloped my children in an ever-widening circle of belonging, providing a lifeline of support during our 2 years in Tokyo – especially Harada, Ukai, Hirai, Nakano,

Yuri, and 'Ya' *sensei* – and in a class all of his own Fuji san, of *Takatsukata Hoikuen* in Kyoto; Asako Sakimura, Naoko Nomura, and Momo Urashima in Tokyo for their warm hospitality; and Miwako Matsusaki and Naomi Kamijo at PRIME for making possible the sometimes impossible in Japan.

For enduring friendships and the certainties they bring, I must gratefully thank the late Tom Auer, connoisseur of books and friend exemplar, whose satisfaction at the completion of this project would surely have exceeded mine; Itty Abraham, Michiyo Arakawa, Nikhil Aziz, David Blaney, Robert Bosco, Farah Chaudhry, Joe Clapper, Minnoo Das, Matt Davies, Ambereen Ebrahim, Yuko Gamo, Lalitha Gopalan, Claudio Gonzalez, Sherry Gray, Edward Hawley, Gigi Herbert, Eiichi Hoshino, Naeem Inayatullah, Ahmad Kamal, Sabby and Surinder Kaur, Vandana Kawlra, Debra Kriesberg, Manjula Lal, Sakah and Lori Mahmud, Sangeeta and Amit Mehra, Kostas Messas, John and (the late) Sally McCamant, Marcela Mikkola, Maki Mizokawa, Ruki and Biren Nanda, Aditya and Sushma Narain, Punam Puri-Leger, Tom Rowe, John Rusk, Magnus Ryner, Emita Samuels, George and Shirley Shepherd, Henry Schwarz, Jeanne Simon, Savita Singh, Kamini Singh, Anita Vasudeva, Rob Walker, and Matt Wartell.

My parents, Achala and Jindi Vij, and my sister, Bindu, to whom this book is dedicated, along with Hari, Cabir, and Brahm Maira have anchored me in ways I cannot fully articulate; to them I owe what the Japanese call, and rightly so, *gimu on* – a debt that cannot be re-paid. This book and all that went into its making is a small measure of my gratitude to them.

My deepest debt though is to Mustapha Kamal Pasha, my most exacting and devoted critic, not only for his humour, intellectual engagement, and unremitting kindness, but also for sustaining an unshakeable faith in the merits of this project precisely at the times I needed it most. As for our children, Ayesha and Tariq, although they may never quite understand the significance of the issues that detain us – for surely theirs will be different – I can only hope that something of the meaningfulness of the struggle to both affirm and negate may one day convey itself to them via the pages of this book.

Research for this project was supported at different stages by grants from the University of Denver, the Ford Foundation, the Social Science Research Council (USA), and the Japan Society for the Promotion of Science via a Long-Term Post-Doctoral Fellowship (2003–2005), and, most recently, a Small Grants Award from the University of Aberdeen (UK) that permitted me to travel back to Tokyo for a brief period of research in the summer of 2006. Library staff at several institutions have been indispensable to the research conducted for this book; I thank in particular those at the Universities of Berkeley, Chicago, Denver, and Stanford in the United States; the International House, National Diet, and Japan Foundation libraries in Tokyo; and the collections at Hitotsubashi, Keio, Ritsumeikan, Sophia, Tokyo, Meiji Gakuin, and Waseda Universities in Japan, and at the University of Aberdeen in the United Kingdom.

Following convention, all Japanese names are listed by family name first.

1
Introduction: Civil Society, Welfare, and Japan in Comparative Studies

Introduction

In a curious reversal of orientalizing proclivities, Japan's productivist social policy has become emblematic of an emerging orthodoxy in the West. At a time when the turn from welfare to philanthropy, "community," or "work-fare," symptomatic of the erosion of social rights and citizenship on some accounts, and the individualizing new technologies of government on others, is emerging as the new orthodoxy of a conservative policy-making global elite, the claim that productivist social policy offers a better, more enduring, solution to the problems endemic to capitalist economy universalized now on a global scale bears closer scrutiny. To the extent that academic claims about the relative success of Japan's "alternative modernity," "productivist social policy," or its success in having "gotten civil society right"[1] help secure the normativity of this turn from welfare to family and community, if not work-fare, the case of Japan merits attention within the interdisciplinary study of comparative social policy.

From an altogether different starting point, however, and reversing the tendency of theory to travel from West to East (Said 1978; Brennan 2000), the cartographical vantage point of Japan serves to highlight the potentiality for a *general* rethinking of welfare and its relocation in civil society and state that challenges the presumed modularity of welfare states and civil societies in the West, including contemporary claims about the fast-policy global diffusion of strategies of welfare reform. Equally, and perhaps more ambitiously, it aims to show how the problem of reconciling the twin logics of individualism and community in modern political life, as refracted in the problematic of welfare state capitalism, may profit from a closer look at institutions and social practices that appear in another time and place. In this sense, the discussion of Japan pursued here repudiates the conventions of a comparative studies that preserve the dualism of Western theory/non-Western case in its method of inquiry, as well as the conventions of an area studies approach committed to thick description. It offers, rather, a two-part claim: a theoretical argument about relocating welfare within *both* civil society and the state, by treating the Japanese case as an illustration of the potentialities contained within precisely such a division; and a re-interpretation of the nature of welfare state capitalism in modern Japan. Insofar as the discussion of the Japanese case is oriented toward a theoretical critique of contemporary debates about welfare and its provision, close attention to its historicity – and the ambiguities and tensions contained within it – forecloses its classification as "merely cultural" (Butler 1997) or, alternatively, its resignification as modular. Its import here, rather, stems from how it helps illuminate, if in elementary form, an argument about the necessity of both state and civil society to rethinking the problem of welfare.

Within both comparative studies of social policy and Japan area studies, the status of Japan's welfare system remains anomalous. Among area specialists, culture and state-based accounts of Japan's welfare exceptionalism have conventionally drawn attention to Japan's family- and firm-based system of welfare actively fostered by a "developmental state," in the single-minded pursuit of economic growth. Within the discursive space of regime analysis that dominates comparative social policy literature, on the other hand, Japan's designation as "hybrid" – combining elements of liberal, social democrat, and corporate welfare – reworks claims about Japanese exceptionalism, resignifying social processes within Japan as beyond, or outside, theory. Within these dominant approaches, contrary assessments of Japan as a "welfare superpower," a "welfare laggard," or even as "anti-welfare state" are further complicated by internally variegated patterns of policy-specific social spending that defy these mutually exclusive characterizations: generous provisions for the elderly and a cost-effective yet universal health care system, for instance, in contrast to minimal commitments to providing unemployment benefits and housing. Whereas the former warrants Japan's classification as a social democrat "regime type," the latter suggests Japan fits better the residual (liberal) welfare state regime category. Similarly, the history of welfare state formation in Japan eludes comparative theoretical enclosure: whereas in the West, liberal pluralism and "power resource theory" (focusing on the power of class-based political parties) are seen as central to accounting for divergence between and among welfare states, in the case of Japan the creation, management, and reform of the welfare state has been largely deemed the work of politicians or bureaucrats, challenging both liberal-pluralist and neo-Marxian accounts of political life in democratic capitalist society. Reflecting the deep hold that liberal pluralism continues to have in the theoretical imaginary of the discipline of political science, efforts to make sense of these empirical "puzzles" of Japan's system of welfare provision have largely focused on proximate factors, the role of different ministries within the government (Health and Welfare versus the Labor Ministry, for instance) in accounting for differences between and among developments in distinct policy arenas. The larger question of the normative status of welfare and the sources of its legitimation, including the differential provision of welfare goods and the seemingly contradictory logic it betrays, however, remains unaddressed.

The normative status of "welfare" and its institutionalized provision in modern Japan appears to be quite distinct from that of its Western counterparts. In sharp contrast to the "golden age" of welfare in Western capitalist democracies, when the ideal of welfare as a marker of social rights and citizenship enjoyed wide currency, welfare as "entitlement," a right guaranteed by the state, has not taken a central place in the collective socio-political imagination in Japan, even as its institutionalized provision has expanded rapidly in the post-war era. Nor has it entered a period of ideological or economic crisis that characterizes contemporary Western welfare states, despite chronic economic problems and escalating individual needs (for income, housing, health care, etc.) in recessionary Japan. What accounts for this marked contrast in the experience of welfare state capitalism in the West and Japan? Is it, as several scholars have suggested, simply the smaller size of Japan's welfare state (measured as a percentage of GNP) that renders state-sponsored welfare comparatively inconsequential to the organization of society and economy?[2] Or is it because the social meanings attached to the ideal of welfare[3] place it in a relation to society and economy that is distinctive, with quite different consequences for its normative status and the socio-economic consequences of its institutionalized provision?

This book explores the anatomy of Japan's welfare provision within the larger context of the constellation of modernity and capitalism in Japan. Rather than offer yet another narrative on the proximate causes of welfare state growth/rollback, convergence/divergence, it takes as its theoretical object the task of uncovering, to borrow Charles Taylor's felicitous phrase in another context, the "sources of welfare" in Japan. What are the deeper sources of legitimation of welfare in Japan understood here not *qua* abstract ideal, but as the specific bundling of social provisions that comprise Japan's welfare system? What is the normative horizon within which the specificity of Japan's welfare provision – its consistent and generous provision of health care, education, or elderly care, for instance, in contrast to minimal unemployment benefits – gains legitimacy? Insofar as all social formations must be seen as historically specific, that is particular resolutions to general questions – of space and time, universal and particular, the mortal and transcendental, inside and outside to name but a few – entailing distinctive ontologies and related epistemological positions (of which, it must be noted, Western modernity and the form modern subjectivity takes therein is but one), the question of welfare in Japan can be understood as meaningful, (that is normative), only via attempts to recuperate the continuities/ruptures between its institutionalized provision and the form of consciousness enlivened within it in relation to the *general* forms of consciousness constituted as *modern* in Japan. To the extent that the problem of welfare emerges as a distinctly modern question, in the context of capitalist social relations and the emergence of the modern subject, it is in relation to the institutions of modern political economy and subjectivity that the question of welfare as a theoretical and historical object of study must return.

To this end, this book offers a theoretically driven historical reinterpretation of state, civil society, and subjectivity in modern Japan to ask, what are the continuities/ruptures between notions of personhood enlivened within the institutions and social practices of welfare and those wrought within and in relation to the institutions of state and civil society in modern Japan? What are the antinomies of the subject as constituted within civil society, understood here not in the widely popular Tocquevillean sense as associational life or in its conservative uptake in discussions of welfare as voluntarism, private charities, or revival of community (Murray 1986; 1988; Green 1993; Tanner 2003), but in its classical sense as entailing a specific (capitalist) organization of abstract labor, its accompanying system of needs, and the modern subject as constituted within capitalist political economy? This way of posing the question uncovers a distinctive pattern to welfare provision in Japan: a generous provision of production-related welfare goods in contrast to the relative paucity of the provision of goods that satisfy individuated want. The legitimation of this pattern of provision, I will argue, can be understood contra orthodoxy on the role of Japanese culture, the state's developmental role, or international policy diffusion, but rather in relation to the nature of the subject as constituted within the institutions of modern Japan's political economy.

Reflecting both the purposive nationalism within which capitalist organization developed but also the individuating logic inherent in capitalism, the notion of the modern subject that took shape in Japan, particularly during the Showa period (1926–1989), reworked the wide and deep traditions of personal consumption in Japanese society around the axis of a modern notion of individuality. Retaining emphases on kinship ties, personalized loyalty in the domain of work and reframing consciousness of the collectivity from the group to the polity, the institutionalization of civil society in early Showa clearly demarcated those zones of social life which were to serve as the means to the realization of the social good from those which could serve as the crucible for the fashioning of a distinctly modern subjectivity. Labour or work was seen in non-individuated terms primarily as enhancing the collective good, leaving consumption alone as a legitimate terrain of individuation. While many have noted the link between work and collectivism in modern Japan, I want to suggest that consumption is not a site of homogeneity (Ivy 1993; Watanabe 1991; Kumazawa 1996), but rather the terrain of individuation that is not a recent phenomenon (Miyanaga 1991, Yoda 2000), contingent on Japan's post-war economic affluence, or the result of a Western-style consumerism evident in the phenomenon of the *shinjinrui* (new breed), but rather consistent with the individuating logic of capitalism constitutive of modern Japan. The state has thus fostered a collectivist ideology which at the same time departs from pre-modern forms of collectivism by accommodating the hallmark of a distinctly modern individuated self.

The reasons for the distinctive pattern of welfare in modern Japan, the generous state provision of goods that meet production-related social needs and market-/family-based provision of goods that meet consumption-related individuated wants, anomalous within dominant frameworks of analysis, can be readily apprehended as reflective of the ordering principle of Japanese modernity itself. Because modern subjectivity as constituted within civil society uncouples labor from consumption in terms of individuation, the state's sustained reluctance to provide consumption-related goods in contrast to its consistent provision of de-individuated goods that are seen to enhance productivity (as in the case of health care) is normatively consistent with the notion of self in modern Japan. That individuals in need of public assistance in Japan tend to partake more readily of state-based free medical care than state-provisioned income support, in marked contrast to evidence on take-up rates in other advanced industrialized democracies, is particularly telling in this regard. In this, the welfare state reinforces the separation between the de-individuated realm of production and individuated realm of consumption that grounds modern notions of personhood within civil society. The welfare state thus creates, as much as it reflects, the notion of personhood writ large in Japanese society.

It is this, the rethinking of subjectivity in relation to the institutions and social practices of political economy under conditions of late modernity (some might say globalization) that arguably figures the present moment in the trajectory of welfare as a crisis, rather than claims about the fiscal overreach of the state. Insofar as the case of Japan throws into sharp relief the consequences of an alternative mapping and limiting of civil society for both subjectivity and welfare, it enables a vivification of a potential rethinking of welfare provision under conditions of late modernity, via a focus on the crucial question of the *social limits* of civil society and state in relation to subjectivity and well-being. The significance of the Japanese case to the larger project of rethinking welfare – not as a model, it bears repeating, but only as a theoretical instantiation of the idea of the limits of civil society – is elaborated in the concluding section of this book.

The rest of this chapter maps the theoretical terrain of civil society and welfare in debates about Japan to identify some of the faultlines in contemporary discussions, considers briefly the question of Japan's location within the larger intellectual project of comparative studies, and provides a brief summation of the organization and content of the five chapters that follow.

Civil society in Japan

Modernity, noted Takeuchi Yoshimi (1910–1977), one of Japan's foremost philosophers, "is subjectivity" (Calichman 2000). What then is the distinctively novel social space within which subjectivity is constituted? And what are its elementary conditions of possibility? In the narratives that dominate contemporary social theory, the specificity of time and place in the origin of modernity and the modern subject – in the West – renders it, on one account, normative, offering to those still enmeshed in the putatively illiberal structures of traditional ascriptive identities the promise of a better future. In this account, the universalization of the modern subject remains the project of history; liberal capitalism and procedural democracy the necessary and sufficient conditions to its constitution. On an alternative account, the presumed universalization of what is deemed an essentially particularistic resolution to the problem renders not only the notion of the modern subject, but also the conditions deemed necessary to its realization (democracy and capitalism), deeply suspect, generative of an "imperialism of categories," (Nandy 1983) whose imposition in non-Western contexts ensures the permanent and deeply disabling condition of "living comparatively" (Harootunian 1999), marked either by the excess of unreason, lack of autonomy, and a natural predisposition to illiberal modes of being that can be set aside only by "modernization" or "development" via the civilizing agency of colonialism or, in our times, by "preventive wars" aimed at "regime change."

There is, however, a third account that has recently taken hold within the humanities and to a lesser degree in the social sciences. Drawing on the de-stabilizing effects of post-structural, post-modern, and post-colonial scholarship on dominant categories of social theory (state, society, self), the attempt to recover coeval modernities in non-Western contexts has generated a voluminous literature on "alternative modernities." Marked by an ambitious attempt to recoup, as it were, the plurality of modern social life in other times and other places from the stranglehold of the Western story, the effort to "provincialize Europe" (Chakrabarty 2000) has generated a vast literature on the variegated and complex entanglements of colonizer and colonized; the indigenization of Western forms by modernizing "native" elites, and their effects, and an impressive armoury of concepts (mimicry, ambivalence, hybridity, self colonization, Occidentalism) that work toward de-centering the knowing Western subject, and developing non-Western "self-understanding(s), self-critique and reform" (Yang 1994: 29). While this is not the place to rehearse at any length the merits of this literature, suffice it to say here that an interesting consequence of this repudiation of the categories of Western social theory, and one not often remarked upon, is the attempt to reform European theory via a counter-discourse of modernity and post-modernity in non-Western contexts. Especially striking in this regard is the temporal relocation of categories associated with the emergence of modernity in the West, in a putatively non- (or pre-) modern non-Western tradition. Nowhere is this more acutely demonstrated as in the contemporary discourse on civil society in non-Western contexts.

With the collapse of the Soviet Union and the concomitant effort to democratize Eastern Europe, civil society deemed "*the* idea of the twentieth and twenty first century," in an influential collection of essays (Kaviraj and Khilnani 2001:11), has been used as a rallying cry to both rejuvenate political and social life and to analyze social movements, community building efforts, and civic expressions of political protest (Keane 1988; Havel 1985; Miller, 1992; Cohen and Arato 1992; Taylor 1990; Walzer 1991; Hall 1995). Variously deployed to give analytical purchase to the study of civility, social capital (Putnam 1993; 2000; Skocpol 1999), anti-state democratic dissent (Havel 1985; Keane 1988), the public sphere (Habermas 1996), political and commercial society, or, most widely, associational life (de Tocqueville), the "long and varied history of the idea" (Kumar 1993) offers a seemingly bewildering range of concepts: from Locke and Aristotle's notion of civil society as *societas civilis*, with its emphasis on citizenship and communal mores, the quite different focus of the Scottish Enlightenment theorists (Smith and Ferguson) on economic transactions and civic republicanism, to more critical conceptualizations of civil society as the constitutive terrain of subjectivity (Hegel), class conflict (Marx), hegemony (Gramsci), or bio-power (Foucault).[4] (See especially, Keane, 1988, Walzer 1991; Cohen and Arato 1992; Seligman, 1992; Hall 1995).

Attempts to deploy the concept of civil society in non-Western contexts have followed one of two paths: while some scholars have fastened on the critical/normative force of the concept to develop a counterdiscourse of modernity, others have argued strenuously against its analytical utility in non-Western contexts. In the former instance, for example, deploying a Foucauldian critique of sovereign power, Mayfair Mei-Hui Yang sees the roots of resistance to socialist state bio-power in the rhizomatic networks that constitute *minjian* (people's realm) or a sort of civil society in the practice of *guanxi* in contemporary China, a practice that dates back to the third century BC (Yang 1994). In the case of India, in another example, civil society is purportedly found in the villages and in the "submerged civilizations" of the poor and the marginalized inhabitants of a heterogeneous social space in which tradition and ascriptive bonds continue to provide the glue of social solidarities and community life (Kothari 1988; Nandy 1989). In the case of Africa, on the other hand, primary ethnic and kinship associations are seen along with "civic associations" as central to the effort of democratizing the state (Woods 1992; Comaroff and Comaroff 1999). For others, the critique of enlightenment thought has generated attempts to elaborate the limits of the categories of Western social and political thought in non-Western contexts. Thus, beginning with the observation that the system of rights, contract, the liberal self is largely absent in non-Western contexts, various scholars taking a normative critique of these categories (the autonomous coherent self or the state for instance) as their point of departure have repudiated claims about the universalization or portability of the language of civil society in non-Western contexts. Foremost among them are post-colonial critics (Chatterjee 1997; Chakrabarty 1994; Rajagopal 2003) for whom the absence of the unencumbered bourgeois individual of (Western) secular modernity in post-colonial societies precludes the analytical use of the concept in the non-West, entailing either the "imposition of a liberal limit on the nature of public action" (Rajagopal 2003: 260) or its restriction to the small minority of modernizing elites (Chatterjee 1998). For these critics, the swathe and sweep of civil society as democratic dissent, civility, or the public sphere is better captured via a vernacular idiom of local politics that escapes enclosure by the vocabulary and analytical reach of the categories of Western political thought.[5]

Two points are worth noting here: one is the displacement of the necessarily *uneven* nature of the transformative impact of capitalist social relations in Western *and* non-Western contexts; the other, the effective de-historicization of cultural identity seemingly at play here. If capitalist modernity in the West reworked relations between lords and peasants, church and state, reconstituting notions of family, identity, and well-being, it did so unevenly; indeed the legacy of the unevenness of this spatio-temporal "modernization" (in Eastern and Western Europe, for instance) is inscribed into the history of the development of civil society in the West. So too, capitalist modernity in Asia, Africa, and the Middle-East, albeit wrought through the violence of the colonial encounter, introduced radically novel forms of distinctions and desires, as the circulation of new commodities, new forms of production, and dispossession, inherently uneven in tempo and effect, bespoke the constellation of distinctly modern forms of subjectivity. "Vernacular" modes of being, pre-modern and/or pre-capitalist, did not remain "in tact" but were themselves refracted, re-constituted, and re-worked in relation to the new modes of being associated with colonial capitalism. To suggest that civil society in non-Western contexts can be recovered outside of the constitutive structures of capitalist social relations is then to posit, albeit inadvertently and, indeed, ironically, Western forms of modern subjectivity as modular, or render large populations in non-Western societies outside the constitutive frame of (colonial) capitalist political economy and modernity.[6] The specificity of civil societ*ies* and the varied modalities of modern subjectivities in the non-Western world may be better apprehended via an attempt to identify the particularities of capitalist social relations that obtain in different contexts. Uneven capitalist development, in other words, in its originary *and* colonial contexts, inaugurates the birth of modern ways of being in different parts of the globe.

It is perchance no accident then, that the contemporary effervescence of the concept of civil society has fastened singularly on its Tocquevillean version as forms of local voluntary activity and associational life. As an "empirical concept" (Marcuse), a catchall phrase that gathers together the heterogeneous groups and organizations that constitute the associational landscape of a specific social formation, the presumed equality of social life central to this conception is grounded in a strand of liberalism that dominates Western political thought and practice, that helps account for both its success in scholarship as well as its portability and extension in non-Western contexts. In an important sense, the repudiation of the concept in post-colonial scholarship briefly outlined above is propelled by a rejection of this quintessentially liberal claim about social equality. John Ehrenberg's statement that "it is precisely [by virtue of] its disregard of the material processes of civil society" that civil society as associational life "performs a normalizing function by making it difficult to see the economic roots of contemporary problems and blinding us to the political avenues for their resolution" (Ehrenberg 1999) captures well the limits of civil society *qua* associational life at issue here. That the contemporary turn to civil society was occasioned by the cataclysmic denouement of socialist/communist regimes in Eastern Europe and the full-scale embrace of capitalism, in its political (democratic) and economic (free-market) aspects, renders any critique of capitalism (contained, it bears noting, in Marxian, Hegelian, or Gramscian iterations of the concept) antithetical to the normative embrace of specifically Tocquevillean celebrations of associational life, and helps account in large measure for its universal appeal.[7] The central weakness of the Tocquevillean approach to civil society as associational life, then, unlike its Hegelian, Marxian, or Gramscian forebears elides not only in the Japanese case as we see below, but in general, the material and social inequalities endemic to capitalist social organization.[8]

A similar impulse inaugurates the rapid increase in investigations of civil society in Japan.[9] Since the mid-1990s, civil society has emerged as a new focus of political activism and academic research in Japan Studies. Defined as the social sphere consisting of the "sustained, organized social activity that occurs in groups that are formed outside the state, the market and the family" (Pharr 2003:xiii), civil society's capacity to "reimagine Japan's society" (Bestor 1999) has been widely embraced as a distinctly post-war phenomenon by activists and scholars alike. Because "there were no citizens in pre-war Japan – only subjects" (Garon 2003: 343), a prominent historian of Japan notes, the language of civil society can be legitimately deployed only in the context of post-war Japan, when the *shimin* (citizen) formally replaces *kokumin* (subject) within the discursive and political terrain of social life in Japan.

Once deemed peripheral to the social scientific study of modern Japan, given the colonizing reach of the "developmental state" in society, this consensus about the periodization and conceptual life of "civil society" in Japan stands in sharp contrast to the robust debates that have accompanied its entry into investigations of other non-Western societies, a sharp reminder of Harootunian's critique (examined below) about the relative absence of theoretical contestation in the Japan Studies field.[10] Within the self-standing community that has now developed around this theme, civil society as the "unrecognized element of the developmental state story" (Pekkanen 2004) is seen as the center point not only of a post-"developmental" state strategy of "management" of the social and economic problems endemic to recessionary Japan (via partnerships with civic groups in society as Estévez-Abe [2003] points out), evidenced in legislative and financial initiatives (including, tellingly, the funding of large "civil society" focused research projects), but also, and somewhat paradoxically, a surreptitious rehabilitation of a statist paradigm, given its central role in shaping civil society in Japan. At a time when talk of de-centralization/privatization/de-regulation has taken a firm hold in populist and political talk in Japan, this is no small irony.

By most accounts the vocabulary of civil society or its Japanese translation *shimin shakai* (a complex term attesting to the problems of translatability)[11] entered mainstream popular discourse in Japan with the unexpected outpouring of volunteer activity in the aftermath of the Great Hanshin/Awaji earthquake of 1995. Although corporate philanthropy had been embraced by business leaders (including *Keidanren*, the Federation of Economic Organizations, most notably in the setting up of the One Percent Club, modeled on its American counterpart), *borantia* (volunteer) activities took on a new significance as the state promulgated a series of laws geared to encourage charitable giving, community development, and citizen participation via non-governmental organizations such as neighborhood associations and citizens group, *shimindantai* (social groups). The Non-Profit Organization (NPO) Law of 1998 which made it easier for unincorporated groups to gain legal status and gain tax benefits heretofore reserved for the few incorporated NGOs (which in the Japanese context refer specifically to organizations that focus on international issues such as development or foreign aid)[12] has contributed significantly to the use of the term within popular and academic discourse as the terrain of voluntary associational life, virtually excluding other competing conceptions, especially the Marxian that dominated scholarly discourse and political practice in Japan in the 1960s and 1970s. Socialist scholars of this earlier period including Hani Goro, Kuno Osamu, and Sakamoto Yoshikazu deployed the language of *shimin* as a critical category arguing in left journals like *Sekai* and *Shiso* that a society of citizens could only develop in the context of a socialist not capitalist organization of social and economic life.

The erasure of the fundamentally critical idea of citizen that Marx, following Hegel, distinguished from civil society, the terrain *not* of citizen but simply the *burgher* (bourgeois), is pivotal to grasping the limits of a Tocquevillean conception that posits associational life *ipso facto* as a terrain of social (citizen based) equality. The conflation of the two terms, or the slippage between them, emanating in part from the semantic field constituted by the original Hegelian formulation in German as *bürgerliche Gesellschaft* (implying both citizen and bourgeois) has assumed axiomatic status in comparative studies of civil society, foreclosing its recuperation as a category of critique and enabling its uptake as "normal science." Careful attention to the development of the original Hegelian formulation is, however, singularly telling: in discussing civil society, Hegel abandons the language of the Germanic *bürgerliche Gesselchaft* and deploys instead the French *citoyen* and *bourgeois*, making an explicit distinction between the two which enables him to claim that in civil society the burgher is a bourgeois but *not* a citizen (Neocleous 1995: 399). The centrality of capitalist social organization, in other words, and its critique, in the original conception of "civil society" that contemporary discourse draws from selectively, asserting the necessity of conjoining citizen and burgher in civil society, while abandoning the concurrent demand to attend to the specificity of civil society as a fundamentally capitalist society economic domain, merits scrutiny.

The problem is further exacerbated in the Japanese case where the transition from the language of a society of subjects (*kokumin*) to citizens (*shimin*) took place via the agencies of the occupation authorities in the aftermath of Japan's defeat in World War II. Arguably, the Meiji Restoration of 1868, the event that marks Japan's passage to modernity, and the accelerated changes – civil, political, and constitutional – that followed in its wake, may be deemed equally significant from the vantage point of claims about social equality. Not only did the Meiji oligarchs officially end (in 1871) the hierarchialized rank-based social structure of Tokugawa Japan, but the constitution of 1889 formally remade Japan into a democracy. This is, of course, only the official story; not only did the panoply of changes in early Meiji lack depth, as is widely noted, but equally the constitution, "gifted" by the emperor to his people, served only the urgent task of representing Japan as a modern state, so as to preserve its autonomy in the face of Western imperialism in Asia. The effective mobilization of the *tenno* (emperor-based) ideology in the period up to 1945, no doubt, rendered claims about citizenship-based social equality moot in the pre-war era, its official replacement by the new post-war constitution ostensibly marking the birth of citizenship and therefore civil society in Japan.

The discontinuities between pre- and post-war Japan central to modernization narratives of Japan, in which the putative move from *kokumin* to *shimin* serves as a significant boundary marker, however, must be put in context. Several scholars have drawn attention to the gap between the language of citizenship, rights, and democracy in place since the 1947 constitution, and their realization (see especially Takahashi 2006; Tamamoto 1994) suggesting that continuities rather than rupture offers a more nuanced grasp of the meanings at play in political and social life in contemporary Japan. Here, the conjoined aspects of state and religion (and consequently emperor-based identifications) are seen as never too far from the politics of nation and state. Insofar as citizenship discourse in (or about Japan) relies heavily on assumptions of a clean break from the past (the shift from *kokumin* to *shimin* for instance), it may be at the expense of grasping the intangible but vital connectivities, including memory, that structure state–society relations in contemporary Japan. On this account, the death of Emperor Hirohito in 1989 may deservedly be seen as the more pivotal boundary marker, signifying the end of the Showa era that spanned both pre- and post-war periods in Japanese history (Smith 2002). As some scholars suggest, the restraints imposed by the legacies of pre-war Japan preserved in institutional and generational memories that impeded expressions of dissent were released as the emperor's death marked the substantive end of the *tennosei* (the emperor system) and the "beginning of new opportunities to speak out" (Smith 2002: 39). Others draw attention to the atemporality of *tennosei* due to its fundamentally transhistorical character as a "symbolic emperor system" (Fujitani 1992). The official declaration of the end of imperial subjecthood in 1946, in other words, marks not the death, but the re-mobilization and re-location of the meanings associated with *tennosei*, problematizing claims about a neat rupture between pre- and post-war Japan.[13] Finally, the provocation that "the emperor remains the Japanese state's main source of legitimation" (Ollman: 2001) signals the need to locate the emperor not merely, or only, within a symbolic register of meaning, but rather as germane to the stabilization of political order of capitalist Japan.[14]

Unlike the critical discourse of civil society in Japan in the 1950s and 1960s, which retained a single-minded commitment to Marxian critiques of the material inequities endemic to capitalist social organization, the current hubris in discussions about civil society in Japan centers on its promise of enabling dissent and individual expression in Japan, while recognizing its limits as essentially a state-crafted social sphere. Celebrated in the West for limiting if not challenging state power, in Japan, the state's role in structuring a "quiescent" civil society is widely acknowledged, if not widely embraced. Thus, one author notes, "NGOs are needed to focus individual interest and initiative. Without this institutional focus, the unrestrained growth of individuality will cause chaos in Japan" (Chanin 1999). Deguchi (1999) draws attention to the "dual nature" of non-profit activity in Japan dominated by grass-roots civil groups without legal status.[15] Robert Pekkanen (2004; 2006), likewise, writes about Japan's "dual civil society," made up of a large number of social capital enhancing small groups but a relatively small number of advocacy groups, suggesting that Japan "has gotten civil society right in supporting groups that sustain social capital, while limiting advocacy groups" (Pekkanen 2004: 224). The state's role in shaping a tax and regulatory environment that discourages the formation of large advocacy groups while facilitating small groups that it can partner with in delivering public services (clean up of parks, disseminating information, support for migrant populations, etc.) accounts, Pekkanen suggests, for Japan's quiescent civil society. Thus, for Tsujinaka (2003) and Pekkanen (2004), leading exponents of this notion, the distinctiveness of Japan's civil society is to be found in the small local civil society groups, neighborhood associations which are seen as "Japan's most widespread groups which enjoy high participation rates, and are actively supported by the government" (Pekkanen 2004: 232). Nominal membership levels are over 90 percent nationwide, Pekkanen writes, making neighborhood associations "by far Japan's leading voluntary associations" with participation rates as high as 72 percent in 2000 based on survey data (Pekkanen 2004: 232). Activities of these groups include facilitating communication among residents, organizing sports events, local neighborhood watch patrols, and the local festival. Insofar as these neighborhood associations constitute "members but not advocates", they provide a crucial avenue for generating social capital without de-stabilizing political life, and may, Pekkanen speculates, have enabled Japan to get civil society right.

This view of community life as the source of social capital in Japan, remarkably, fails to address the constitutive role of *ethnie* and race underpinning assumptions of shared belonging in these seemingly civic neighborhood associations, and by implication the problem of ethnic and racial discrimination, long in place against minorities like the *Ainu, burakumin,* and Koreans, but considerably exacerbated now with the influx of foreign and *nikkeijin* workers following the Immigration Reform Act of 1990. Activists advocating on behalf of the rights of legal and "undocumented" (non-Japanese) workers in Japan tend to work outside their local (ethnically Japanese) communities in promoting their cause (Shipper 2002). A sensitivity to the widespread existence of *minzoku sabetsu* (racial discrimination) – little acknowledged and much less publicly discussed in Japan, given the premium placed on "thick" communal identity that very much shapes social life in present-day Japan – has led radical critics like Mushakoji Kinhide to declare that only NGOs in Japan, engaged in development, human security, or human rights issues in the *international* arena on behalf of the (non-Japanese) stranger (not domestically oriented NPOs), truly count as citizens in Japan insofar as they alone inhabit a cosmopolitan self-consciousness and orientation to the world. Yet another prominent critic Kang, Sangjung (2001) foregrounds the urgent need to create a "disaporic space" in Japan suggesting that social capital mobilized by thick communities may be inherently self-limiting as an avenue for civil society development in Japan. A similar critique, it bears noting, can be made against conservative arguments in the West advocating the return of welfare provision to faith- or community-based Tocquevillean associations and voluntary charities (Tanner, Green). Bearers of thick identifications, these associations are inherently limited in their capacity to revitalize increasingly multi-ethnic and multi-cultural societies. In the case of Japan, these *chienshakai* (literally "community society") and their related *chounaikai* (neighborhood meeting group) typically entail a thickness of shared identities in service of community life. Bearers of social capital they may indeed be but hardly open to the plurality and diversity of identities that many scholars celebrate as the distinctive hallmark of a Tocquevillean civil society (Janner 2003; Green 1993).

The literature thus highlights the distinctiveness of Japan's associational landscape as, first, a fundamentally social but a-political sector with little power to effect policy-making, and, second, dominated by small social groups (neighborhood associations primarily) oriented to local communal life. The promise of a mature civil society – ostensibly one where members will also be politicized advocates, the creation of better-funded, more assertive, and explicitly political NGOs (mirroring civil society elsewhere) – is seen as a potentiality yet to be realized. While no doubt effective in mapping the landscape of associational life in Japan, the reasons for its quiescence and the nature of subjectivity constituted within Japan's "dual civil society" remain to be explored.

The search for the distinctiveness or particularity of forms of modern sociability in non-Western contexts (that propels critics [Chakrabarty 1994]) to reject the language of rights and civil society as inherently limited in recuperating forms of sociability in post-colonial contexts) cannot stop at a simple mapping or enumeration of the multiple spaces in which it occurs. It must instead seek to recover its distinct shape and texture, limited not simply to an ethnographical retrieval of voice that Brian McVeigh (2005) calls for, but rather via Alasdair MacIntyre's provocation that (theoretical) objects do not behave the same in different contexts. Here, Hoshino Shinyasu's assertion that "a claim to social equality has not always been available to individual Japanese" (Chanin 1999) in the face of deeply entrenched corporate hierarchies precludes any simple equivalence of social equality and associational life (central to the Tocquevillean enterprise) in the Japanese context. More tellingly, as Imata (1999) goes to some length to point out, unlike the West, where civil society's virtues are largely related to its shoring of the social deficit generated by an individual rights-centered ethos (the communitarian critique), the virtues of participation in associational life in Japan stem from its potential in opening up possibilities for the expression and exercise of individual rights that remains, for the most part, overshadowed by the privileging of the social whole in contemporary social life. Others have seen the contemporary turn to civil society less as reflective of a real response to domestic interests but rather as a modernizing trope (Conrad 1999) inflected by the pursuit of "esteem concerns" (Reimann 2003) in the international arena, and as the result of specific distillations of discourse that characterize area studies as a particular kind of intellectual endeavor. In conjunction with influential claims (Maruyama 1982; Tamamoto 1994) about the long legacy of translation in Japan, and the related capacity to embrace novel ideas based on the usefulness of the concept without any deep commitment to its underlying ideal (Tamamoto 1994), the seemingly wide embrace of the rhetoric of civil society *qua* associational life must be treated with some caution. Having said that, claims about the specificity of civil society in Japan must be taken seriously. That the texture and substance of sociability within associational life in Japan is distinct, quiescent, constitutive, and expressive, suggests Pekkanen (2004), of a subjectivity that escapes enclosure by Western notions of personhood (specifically the utilitarian variant of individualism that serves implicitly as the counterpoint to claims about civil society's role in building social capital) is the implicit, if unexplored sub-text of extant literature[16] on civil society as associational life in contemporary Japan.

With few exceptions,[17] linear narratives of modernization theory shadow currently influential claims about the birth, development, and trajectory of civil society as associational life in Japan; as it matures, one is likely to see, we are told, the development of a larger, professionalized NGO sector, comparable to those of the West as "the reimagination of Japanese civil society as a dynamic process... by a growing federation of NPOs and NGOs"[18] (Bestor 1999). The "NGOization of civil society" latent in this formulation implicity treats the liberal, autonomous self of Western civil society as modular, its coming-to-be in Japan signaling a progressive maturization of democracy and subjectivity, as the late-developing civil society of Japan grows fully into an advocacy sector. This not only precludes recognition of what Nancy Fraser has referred to as "subaltern counter-publics," outside the liberal framings of the public sphere as an inherently rights-based legally sanctioned social arena, but also forecloses recognition of modes of resistance that repudiate not only dominant political agendas in the state, but also capital.[19] Indeed, the quiescence attributed to the functioning of civil society in Japan can be seen at play within discussions of it. Unlike earlier materialist discussions of Japan's class-riven civil society by Japanese scholars, or theoretical contestation about its applicability in non-Western contexts within post-colonial scholarship, civil society *qua* associational life arguably domesticates opposition, securing the parameters of where and what politics is deemed to be within an inherently liberal discourse of pluralism. In the case of Japan, especially, this domestication is especially evident in the near uniform focus on civil society's social-capital-building potential which helps explain, in large measure, its appeal within official circles at the present historical juncture.[20] That the neoliberalizing strategies of governance in Japan, at once dependent on increasing partnerships with social groups in society (hence, the rapid increase in the numbers of associations formed) and reluctance to cede any autonomy to them, may in fact militate against the development of a "mature," oppositional civil society is but one consideration. The other, and one more immediately the concern of this study, the crafting of subjects for an allegedly mature civil society, remains a tenuous proposition at best, not because Japanese culture precludes autonomy, individualism, and self-reliance, as some might argue, or because the state's regulative function vis-à-vis citizen-subjects has "moulded Japanese minds" to serve statist ends, but precisely because the strategies of pastoral care specific to Japan – *bokuminkan*[21] – within which modern Japanese subjectivity has been shaped by both state and market – may prove tenaciously resistant to neoliberal restructuring practices, drawing attention to the contradiction at the very heart of civil society *qua* associational life in Japan. Signifiers of voluntarism and/or independence, the subjects of Japan's civil society appear to be crafted within the theoretical space of Tocquevillean associational life by pastoral/neoliberal strategies of government that preclude the selfsame autonomy. The missing middle, the modern Japanese subject of civil society, autonomous in some ways and not quite others, remains to be accounted for.

Civil society: An alternative view

It is the distinctiveness of the nature of sociability in modern Japan's political economy that this book seeks to recover. Because the conditions of possibility for Tocquevillean associational life described by scholars of Japan's civil society are to be found in the theoretically prior constitution of the subject *within* the system of capitalist exchange relations, it is capitalism and its constitution of modern subjectivity that provides the framework for this study. To this end, following a tradition within Japanese (Marxian) scholarship that treats the question of civil society as one inherently of *capitalist* society, this book builds on the classical foundations of the idea as developed in G.W.F. Hegel's *Philosophy of Right.*

For Hegel, civil society is the realm of self-seeking, the distinctive social space of modern subjectivity. In the commercial society that develops with the capitalist organization of economic life, the relations of production and consumption within its sphere of market-based exchange create a "system of complete interdependence," in which the individual's pursuit of subjective desires, "universal egoism" on Hegel's terms, takes shape within a system of self-seekers. Linked by the web of social meanings and inter-dependencies that underpin a capitalist division of labor, modern individual subjectivity is, nonetheless, Hegel suggests, deeply social. The mediations and inter-dependencies generated by participation in the system of exchange, specifically through the production of goods, needs, desires, and identities, and their satisfaction via work and consumption are central to a process that is both self and socially determined (Levine 1995). It is in this sense that Hegel's civil society is "fundamentally linked to the modern notion of labor" (Hardt 1995: 27), characterized by the subsumption of the particularities of what Marx called "use-value" and concrete labor by the universality contained in exchange-value and abstract labor in capitalist social organization. It is this "economic medium" of civil society within which modern subjectivity emerges that gives the Hegelian notion of civil society its distinctive form. More strikingly, however, his non-economistic understanding of the economy as a constitutive and expressive terrain of subjective freedom repudiates utilitarian approaches to property, labor, and as we will see, welfare, emphasizing their expressive rather than instrumental significance in relation to individual subjectivity. Participation in relations of exchange, work, production, and the consumption of goods is central, on Hegel's view, not principally as an avenue for the satisfaction of material needs, but as necessary to the achievement of the normative ideal of self and social worth constituted within political economy. The structure of inter-dependence and mutualities within which individuals pursue their private interests generates, Hegel suggests, a dynamic of mutual recognition, rendering the self social in a double sense: dependent on the social recognition of identity, self-worth, or individuality, and required to extend in turn social recognition to another. By virtue of these necessary connections, the economic realm and its associated features – property, contract, labor, and commodities – contain within them the elementary structure of modern subjectivity.

Hegel's affirmative view of civil society and its enabling role vis-à-vis subjective freedom is, however, qualified by his critical recognition of its limits, specifically the hierarchies of wealth and want generated by the vicissitudes of a capitalist organization of economy. For Hegel, one crucial product of this systemic tendency in capitalism is the production of poverty as a distinctly modern form of debilitation; poverty (and, as we will see, welfare) implies a violation of personhood, not simply on the grounds of material deprivation but principally by virtue of the denial of self and social worth that is its defining feature.

In this respect, civil society's *disabling* role vis-à-vis individual well-being and welfare is also key, rendering the necessity of market-based exchange relations to self-seeking *and* its capacity for impingement a recurrent tension in modern social life. In acknowledging the simultaneity of both, a neo-Hegelian approach to welfare insists on the state's role in ensuring public social conditions that facilitate individual participation in civil society, while also directing attention to the necessity of participation in the social relations of exchange to individual well-being.

On Hegel's account, then, modern subjectivity is anchored in the mediating institutions of state and market, making political economy, *because constitutive*, the "external structure of subjectivity" (Levine 1995). The question of demarcation between state and market, the "boundary question in political economy," thus emerges as pivotal to shaping (and re-shaping) subjectivity. In accordance with the criteria of subjective freedom (or social individuation) and in view of the market's enabling *and* disabling role vis-à-vis welfare,[22] Hegel's social philosophy enjoins the state's role in optimizing public social conditions facilitative of the individual's participation in relations of exchange and a recognition of the social limits of the market.

From the point of view of grasping the sources of both the singularity and the differentiation of civil societies, the recuperation of a distinctly Hegelian conception of civil society leads in a direction not heretofore explored. If civil society is, at core, fashioned out of the fabric of capitalist social relations, specifically the social relations of production and consumption, it is to a historicized understanding of these relations in their particularized materializations in distinct social formations that one must turn so as to recover the "sources of civil society." The radical alterity of different life-worlds that the critique of enlightenment foregrounds, in other words, can profit from an approach that recognizes the coevalness of capitalist modernity in different place, but seeks to recuperate differences between and among alternate forms of modern subjectivities in relation to the meanings, rhythms, and dynamics of the social relations of production and consumption. Like Harootunian, whose attempt to recuperate difference within the coordinates of a universal capitalism focuses on the "everyday," the spectral presence of temporalities outside "nation-time," providing the source of difference that "makes a difference," the attempt here to recover the specificity of civil society in modern Japan is anchored in an account of how the institutions, social practices, and meanings contained in the system of capitalist exchange, specifically production and consumption, gave shape to a particularized (i.e. Japanese) modern subjectivity. The modes of being associated with *modan* (modern) consciousness, in other words, that shaped ideals of personhood and well-being, generating a distinctive life-world associated with the social formation named "Japan," can be understood only in relation to the specificity of capitalism. The pursuit of private self-interest, rather than positing the European self as universal, can thus be differentiated in specific historical social formations based on the nature and boundaries of the zones of life subject to mediation by exchange relations. Modern sociability, in other words, is recuperated here via an investigation of political economy as the external structure of subjectivity, specifically in relation to the social limits of the market.

Welfare in Japan

Mirroring in broad terms the trajectory of the welfare state in other advanced capitalist countries, welfare programs initiated at the time of the founding of the modern Japanese state during the Meiji period (1868–1912) have been consistently expanded by post- World War II administrations in Japan.[23] Following a period of rapid welfare state growth in the late 1960s and early 1970s that rendered Japan's welfare spending comparable to other OECD countries by the late 1970s, Japan has undergone a period of welfare state retrenchment commensurable with that observed in the West.[24]

The Japanese case merits special attention in any attempt to rethink the welfare question by virtue of the widely held view that Japan's welfare state has succeeded in circumventing the problems that have besieged its Western counterparts. That is, the indicators of welfare state failure that typically appear in Western welfare states seem to be notably absent in the case of Japan. Contrary to the experience of other advanced capitalist welfare states, Japan does not appear to have experienced an ideology of resistance to welfare states despite a significant retrenchment in specific areas of welfare state policy following a rapid spurt in welfare spending in the early 1970s. Unlike the United States and Britain where welfare statism has been more or less under consistent political attack since the 1970s, a populist anti-welfare state rhetoric has been notably absent in Japan. Despite fiscal deficits of the state, especially since the bursting of the "bubble economy" in the early 1990s, discussions of the "failure" of welfare statism have been limited in Japan. Moreover, unlike the experience of some Western states, the so-called "welfare backlash"[25] developed amongst bureaucrats and policy-makers in Japan as opposed to the general populace. Sentiment against further welfare expansion often expressed as fear of the "English disease" accompanied projections that by the turn of the century Japan would have the most rapidly aging population among the world, placing an excessive burden on the welfare state. Changes in state-sponsored welfare programs (particularly health care and social security schemes) have been ongoing since the late 1980s. Most strikingly, however, unlike efforts to roll back welfare provision in significant areas in the West, social spending in specific policy domains (child care and on the elderly especially) has increased, reflecting efforts by bureaucrats and policy-makers to pursue welfare renewal rather than retrenchment as an alternative strategy of dealing with socio-economic and demographic changes in twenty-first-century Japan.

Dominant approaches to understanding Japan's welfare state experience reinforce widespread views of Japanese exceptionalism. Given its low level of welfare spending and distinct institutional forms, scholars contend, Japan cannot legitimately be seen as a welfare state. More often seen as a "welfare society" with its emphasis on the private provision of welfare via the family and firm (Vogel 1979; Reischauer 1988; Hoshino 1988; Shiratori 1985), Japan's "creative conservatism" (Pempel 1989) is seen to have resulted in the creation of a welfare super-power (Nakagawa 1979) or, more critically, "a divisive and controlling" welfare state (Gould 1993). And finally, that Japan's "developmental state" (Johnson 1982) has made economic growth rather than welfare its *raison d' etre*. A second line of argument concedes that Japan, though a "welfare laggard," merits classification into the liberal welfare regime type and shares institutional characteristics with other welfare states of a liberal hue.[26] Japan's apparent success is simply due to its underdeveloped welfare state; as it matures, it is likely to face problems similar to those confronting Western welfare states.

In taking institutional similarity or difference (between the West and Japan) as their point of departure, these accounts erroneously take a particular (Western) form of institutionalizing welfare as emblematic of a universal idea of welfare (Goodman and Peng 1996).[27] Consequently, the question of welfare (the idea and its institutionalized form) in any given society is measured against this *a priori* ideal-type: states that do not provide a similar basket of goods are seen to be lacking a welfare component. This method of universalizing welfare results in two difficulties: first, construction of these ideal-type limits the conceptual boundaries of the idea of welfare; and second, closes off theoretical inquiry into different conceptions of welfare. Although recent scholarship has attempted to identify variations in provision by developing a typology of welfare states (liberal, conservative, corporatist, etc. as in Esping-Andersen's [1990] work), the demarcation between these regime types is determined by the amount of goods provisioned by each (the social democratic regime type characterized by a more generous provision, and at the opposite pole the conservative regime type by its relatively scarce disbursement of welfare goods). Quantitative distinctions in the amount of welfare goods provisioned (in terms of both the level of spending and the type of goods), however, are seen as emanating from an identical notion of welfare. Indeed, Kasza (2006) has suggested that there is intrinsically no difference between Japan's welfare provision and those of other advanced industrialized countries, when examined from the vantage point of comparable stages of industrialization.

The question, however, is not one of degree, a higher or lower level of the welfare state, but rather about the constitution of society which gives birth to a specific notion of welfare. How do different societies conceptualize the well-being of individuals? Which goods are seen to be sufficient to ensure the well-being of individuals? What is the notion of personhood that prevails in a given society in relation to which the conception of welfare specific to that society may be fully grasped?[28]

Japan area studies scholars, on the other hand, have pursued the issue of Japan's welfare exceptionalism somewhat differently. Some have suggested that Japan's institutional distinctiveness with regard to welfare – family and firm, not primarily state based – can be explained in terms of culture, specifically the enduring legacy of Confucian thought with its emphasis on familial obligations as the basis of social and moral order in Japan.[29] The claim that the particularity of Japanese culture with its alleged emphasis on harmony and cooperation accounts for the lack of an anti-welfare ideology in the face of fairly severe fiscal shortfalls and welfare state retrenchment and may, therefore, be ill suited to probe the explanatory power of theory, begs the very question it purportedly answers. Why has social policy in Japan not had a transformative normative impact in times of both welfare expansion and retrenchment, unleashing a tide of anti-welfare state discourse common to other advanced capitalist democracies? Why does the retrenchment of welfare statism elicit discussions of failure in some advanced capitalist democracies and not in others? A common argument is that the conservative nature of regimes accounts for the ideological rhetoric against welfare, whereas a radical tradition of social democracy (in Scandinavian countries for instance) its absence. Yet, Japan presents a contrast: its dominant conservative Liberal Democratic Party put in place the structures of welfare statism, but has not taken a significant anti-welfare stance in periods of financial or political crisis.

Others, challenging culture as the primary explanatory variable, have delineated an account of the policies of Japan's "developmental state" (Johnson 1982) that has prioritized wealth creation at the expense of the provision of welfare goods: because the animating logic of the Japanese state is developmental, it has shortchanged or privatized welfare. Much of the scholarship on Japan's social policy has adopted a variant of statist analysis. Stephen Anderson (1993) has examined the development of social policy in the post-war era in terms of political leadership, challenging Johnson's notion of the dominance of the bureaucracy in Japan's "developmental state." In the same vein T.J. Pempel (1989; 1990) attributes the creation of social policy in the 1970s to the "creative conservatism" of political and bureaucratic elites; Kent Calder (1988) striking a slightly different note suggests that welfare policy is part of a pattern of compensatory strategies deployed by the dominant conservative party to appease its opponents in times of political crisis.

Statist accounts of Japan's welfare system emphasize its single-minded pursuit of economic development to the exclusion of all other goals, including welfare.[30] In separating the state's developmental goals from its related welfare concerns, the concept of the developmental state assumes somewhat problematically a simple dichotomy between the two. Only to the extent that "welfare statism" is defined descriptively can the state's developmental and welfare roles be seen as rigidly distinct, the one denoting accumulation strategies, the other the state's ameliorative function vis-à-vis its citizenry. However, specific development strategies have latent within them a welfare function, discernable in their distributional outcomes and the ideal of societal or individual well-being they embody. The question is not whether the developmental state can be a welfare state but if (and how) developmental states structure welfare in ways that may be distinct from regulatory states. Rather than probing the distinctive idea of welfare that the capitalist developmental state might indeed engender, Johnson's dichotomization of development and welfare impedes a potentially fruitful inquiry into the relation between the two implicit in his own formulation.

Moreover, the notion of the capitalist developmental state while successful in capturing one end of a social process (the state's role in setting developmental goals) fails to provide a full account of its legitimation in society.[31] The role of state bureaucrats, though vital to the study of Japan, needs to be contextualized to explain the ready acceptance within civil society of statist projects. Since civil society is an arena of competition among privately pursued goals, the state's directive role vis-à-vis civil society requires theorization. How has the state's developmental project been enlivened within the institutions and social practices of civil society?

In the absence of a theorization of how both state and civil societies have pursued "developmental goals," the developmental state thesis rests implicitly on one of two claims: it must either implicitly incorporate culturalist arguments about harmony, cooperation, or loyalty as enduring features of the state–society relation in Japan; or, alternatively, attribute agency only to state actors, assuming an automatic translation of the state's agenda within the realm of civil society. The state can, however, achieve only that which is in some meaningful way latent within society. By its institutionalized embodiment of specific ideals, the state articulates and shapes society by laying emphasis on particular aspects of it, but it cannot, with any measure of success, impose on society ideals or norms that are in any significant sense external or alien. Here, Sheldon Garon's (1997) notion of the state's role in "moulding the Japanese mind" is more attentive to the demands of an account of legitimation.

Arguably, the limitations of Johnson's framework may be seen as the limitations of state-centered work more broadly considered. In an effort to overcome the shortcomings of society-centered approaches, state-centered work, by working with a notion of a state as a positivized "thing-in-itself" rather than along more Durkheimian lines as a "structure of thinking together," goes too far in the opposite direction in assuming an unproblematic "legitimation" of state goals and policies within society. While providing an important corrective to society-centered views, extant state-centered approaches in taking a voluntarist view of state action and a unidimensional focus on state elites render the actualization of state goals problematic. Both culture and state-based accounts of modern Japan's welfare system, although helpful in understanding aspects of Japan's welfare state capitalism fall short of accounting for it, not so much by misconceiving welfare in relation to Japan's institutional structure or social milieu, but rather, by offering, at best, a partial understanding of its animating principle. Institutions, including states and markets, must be properly seen as cultural, operating within, not outside of, specific social milieus. As a particularized instance, welfare in Japan is already manifestly cultural; culture as a category can only provide access to the meanings associated with it. It cannot, however, serve as a conceptual tool for uncovering its logic. Second, the failure to attend to the institutional context within which social meanings are produced results in a treatment of culture that is both a-historical and essentialist.

A small group of scholars have pursued a political-economy approach to the study of welfare in Japan. Shinkawa Toshimitsu (1990) has argued that the development of social policy in the 1970s was the result of a "crisis of social integration" in the late 1960s that compelled the state briefly to shift its focus from the needs of capital accumulation to social integration. Employing an orthodox Marxian approach, Fujita (1982) locates the emergence of welfare policy in Japan in the crisis of accumulation and in working-class struggle; similarly Rob Steven (1983) and Maruo (1982) emphasize the class nature of the Japanese welfare state in accounting for its late development and success.[32] The Marxian/neo-Marxian thrust of these arguments, while helpful in identifying the structural conditions under which social policy emerged prove less conducive to identifying the reasons for the apparent success of the welfare state in modern Japan. On Marxian readings, the capitalist nature of the welfare state necessitates a contradiction between its accumulation and legitimation principle, leading to either a fiscal or a legitimation crisis (or both). The absence in Japan of either a political or an economic crisis stemming unequivocally from its welfare provision raises questions about the theoretical and empirical validity of structural Marxian claims about welfare state capitalism in Japan.

Gosta Esping-Andersen's (2007) attempt to demonstrate that Japan is a "hybrid" case, combining elements of the three dominant welfare regime types he identifies – conservative, liberal, and social democratic – while useful as a description of several different elements of Japan's social policy, falls short in identifying the core thematic or organizing principle of Japan's welfare system. Japan is examined on the basis of the three ideal types that represent the historical experience of other (mostly Western) welfare states. Rather than apprehending the particularity of the Japanese case, Esping-Andersen's conclusion that Japan combines elements of each simply sees in it traces of other welfare state types, reducing Japan to a residual category on the one hand, without being able to specify theoretically how its putatively liberal, conservative, and social-democratic elements relate to one another and with what consequences.[33]

More recently, Japan's "uniquely unique" welfare state (Miyamoto 2003) has been incorporated in welfare state regime theory as a prototype of an "East Asian welfare regime." Rejecting culturalist accounts of East Asia's Confucianism as the bedrock of welfarism (Jones 1993) as an instance of "welfare state orientalism" (White and Goodman 1998), some authors have emphasized the need for explanations that center on the political and economic conditions required for achieving rapid development (Deyo 1992; White and Goodman 1998). In this context, a new line of research (Peng 1995, 2002; Ezawa and Fujiwara 2005; Schoppa 2006) has drawn attention to the heavily gendered nature of Japan's welfare provision. Gregory Kasza (2006) rejects all claims about welfare state exceptionalism in the Japanese case, suggesting rather that Japan's welfare system must be understood within the broader context of industrialization and global policy diffusion, as Japanese policymakers have consistently deployed Western models as pedagogical tools for developing policies suited to the Japanese context. In deploying a familiar theme in Japanese historiography, Japan's famous predilection for "borrowing from the West," in the welfare domain, Kasza's thesis targets the process of welfare policy-making. However, the question of the context within which the distinctive pattern of Japanese welfare provision gains meaning, (how do policy-choices garner societal legitimacy?) remains a problem that shadows claims about policy diffusion in general.

A note on comparative studies and "Japan"

At the high point of Japan's "miracle economy" in the 1980s, the influential scholar, Chalmers Johnson, bemoaned the lack of theoretical pluralism in the disciplinary study of economics in the United States which he held bitterly responsible for resisting a systematic study of Japan's political economy.[34] Writing almost two decades later, Harry Harootunian and Naoki Sakai (1997) offered an equally withering critique of the disciplining practices of the Japan Studies field (Reader 1998), which had fetishized linguistic competence as the sole criteria for "getting Japan right," contrasting the theoretical closure in Japan Studies with the effervescent theoretical landscape of other area studies – South Asia, Africa, and Latin America – all of which have made significant contributions to social theory in their own right. As if to prove the point, the near concurrent publication of books by John Clammer (1995; 1997), Samuel Eisenstadt (1996), and Johann Arnason (1987) (all three non-Japan specialists in the traditional disciplinary sense of the term) on social theory and Japan, although well received among comparativists interested in incorporating the historical experience of Japan into their work, were left in relatively benign neglect by the mainstream in the Japan field (Reader 1998). Harootunian's (2000) claim that Japan Studies has become a veritable "enclave of knowledge" with its own disciplinary and disciplining practices which has patrolled its hermetically sealed border against the de-stabilizing effects of heterodox approaches, including post-structural, hermeneutic, Foucauldian, and Lacanian theories, has once again generated a heated debate about the status of "area studies" in a post-Cold-War world.

This debate within Japan Studies bears comment, insofar as it tends to polarize into one of two extreme positions, theory *or* linguistic competence, each in itself untenable given the necessity of both to understanding the social object of inquiry that is "Japan." Insofar as the knowledge-producing industry related to Japan, like most other fields, continues to be dominated by mainstream thinking (what Thomas Kuhn terms "normal science") across the disciplines (political science, sociology, and economics especially), Harootunian's critique can be seen as valid. To the extent, however, that all data is theoretically coded (Gordon 2004), albeit in some instances in ways more reflexive than others (Tansman 2003), arguments by those on the other (language) side of the debate may, arguably, be seen as equally valid. There is, however, another way to approach this issue, in relation to the key issue underlying the theory/language divide: the question of Japanese "exceptionalism."[35] To the extent that the specificity of Japanese social life in all its myriad forms is accessed principally through the Japanese language (*Nihongo*) not simply as a matter of linguistic access (*qua* method) but *Nihongo qua* theory, the reproduction of the notion of Japanese exceptionalism is all but assured. The nuanced attention to locality that language enables without which, arguably, one cannot access the range of meanings and social practices specific in this case to Japan risks appropriation in thought as the merely local, that is bereft of any principle of immanent universality that would alone enable a "translatability between systems of thought" (Charkabarty 1994) such that it could take shape as anything other than an problematic encounter between Western theory and local practice, or residually, a juxtaposition of (theoretically) incommensurable localities. Investigations, however, conducted via the conceptually driven categories of comparative social theory enable access to the particularity of Japan's social, political, and economic life that is not "merely cultural" (Butler 1997) but located (and locatable) within the broader remit of social inquiry, and generative of understandings of Japanese *particularity* rather than exceptionalism.

This book is conceived primarily as an endeavor of theoretical reinterpretation. Its attempt to understand the logic underpinning Japan's welfare provision in relation to the meanings attributed to a distinct classification of welfare goods (meeting social needs or individuated wants) vis-à-vis modern subjectivity in Japan draws on the rich archive of cross-disciplinary scholarship on Japan, statistical data generated by governmental and non-governmental sources, and an ethnographically focused 2-year period of research in Japan.[36]

There is, however, a larger problem that complicates comparative macro-historical or sociological study. Critiques of eurocentrism and orientalism have called into question the very idea of self-contained geographical/cultural areas as their status as spectral constructions or objects of colonial desire has gained increasing currency. In this context, Benedict Anderson's methodology in recuperating the creation of nationalism as a product of a novel form of collective imagining is instructive. Beginning with the notion of homogeneous empty time that provides the medium for both theory and empirical (geographic/cultural) areas of studies, Anderson's proposal to begin with theoretical considerations (in his case of nationalism) in general, "move downwards to empirical studies out of which they grew, and finally to return to the more rarefied atmosphere" (Anderson 20), is instructive. Not only does beginning from the non-West repudiate a teleological vision of Europe, but in viewing nationalism in Europe through the prism of the "inverted telescope" (i.e. through a series that begin outside Europe), Europe is miniaturized, estranged, and stripped of its privileged normativity as the original ground of theory and comparison. More strikingly, the universality inherent in the notion of serialization (via newspapers especially), whether in the West or non-West, renders the "imagined nation" as one among many in a singular world. Because serialization structures the "grammar" of every nation, it provides the basis of comparability.

A similar undoing of the conventions of comparison is proposed by Harry Harootunian, whose focus on the "everyday" as the quotidian universal of capitalism renders it a legitimate ground of comparison. Capitalism destroys existent cultures of reference everywhere to remake societies "look like every other place" in keeping with the homogenized rhythms of capitalist work time, production cycles, incessant movement in an exchange economy, and the fetishism of commodities. Nonetheless, the encounter between the new and the old is disparate, uneven across space in different geographical and cultural areas and the resultant mix of "coeval temporalities" that structure the everyday of Japan/Brazil/China/India, distinct and yet the same. What is misconstrued as the hallmark of an incomplete modernity by native and Western observers alike, Harootunian contends, is simply a sign of modernity itself; the uniformity of cycles of work and consumption mediated by their mingling with vestiges of the past, coexisting "often uneasily and unhappily with older forms of production and their own preferences for social identity" (Harootunian 2000: 115). The everyday for Harrootunian thus offers the best hope for reconstituting the grounds of comparison, since it is capacious enough to accommodate a simultaneous account of sameness and difference. The very distinction between utopian and real time, in other words, that Chatterjee finds prohibitive in any deployment of Western theory in a non-Western context, Harootunian rejects as a futile, if romantic attempt, to construe any social space as "outside" modernity, capitalism, or clock time.

Taking the logic of capitalism as its starting point, this project sees it's particularization in different areas "inflected" not by pre-capitalist cultural forms, or spectral presences, as Harootunian would have it, but in a political-economy context, by the historically constituted limits placed on the market-based civil society. The institutions and social practices associated with different resolutions to this question are seen, in turn, as central to the forms of consciousness and subjectivities that are constituted in relation to them. Autonomy, agency, and subjectivity, in other words, are not self-standing, fully formed as it were, tropes of an essentially Western theory and experience, but rather shaped and moulded, as I want to argue here, by the limits placed on specific constellations of institutions and social practices that constitute the system of capitalist exchange. Variations across time and space in the limits placed on the principle of exchange enable a simultaneous account of sameness and difference, without presupposing a hierarchy of forms that renders some, *a priori,* superior to others. Unlike the "varieties of capitalism" (Hall and Soskice 2001) approach, however, in which institutional variability is deemed significant due to its effects on market *behavior* (movement of prices, distribution of resources including capital and labor, rates of growth, etc) and efficiency, the basis of comparability of the performance of variants of capitalism, the approach developed here attempts to recuperate *non-economistic* interpretations of the moral economy of the market, particularly as it shapes forms of consciousness and subjectivities wrought within and in relation to specific institutionalizations of the market. Differences, in turn, are understood not in foundational terms of discursive, ontological, of structural fixities, but as the outcomes of historical contestation reflecting normatively distinct understandings of personhood, autonomy, and agency. Neither outside capitalism as Chatterjee would have it, nor distinctively interpellated due to the variegated vestiges of pre-capitalist "spectral" pasts, as Harootunian suggests, variations in seemingly cultural registers of meaning (distinct from the logic of commodification) must themselves be re-worked into the narrative of the commodifying logic of capitalism, the outcome foreclosed not by assumptions of an *a priori* totalization of the principle of rationality (as the Frankfurt school theorists insisted), but rather via the spaces created within and in relation to the varied institutionalizations of the commodification principle. Against a theoretical mapping of the social limits of the market vis-à-vis the contradictory logics contained within its dominant commodification principle, namely freedom and unfreedom, wealth and want, a historicization of the optic of the social limits of the market enables a comparative understanding of capitalism that neither betrays its universal logic (as the varieties of capitalism approach inevitably suggests), nor dismisses its variability as a second-order phenomenon, reducible to the "merely cultural."

Organization of the book

The books are organized as follows: Chapter 2 maps the theoretical terrain of the relationship between welfare and civil society and provides a critical discussion of conservative, Marxian, post-Marxian and post-structural theories. The second half of the chapter draws on Hegel's non-economistic conception of welfare and civil society to sketch an alternative theoretical framework for the comparative study of welfare that takes as its focus the constitution of self in political economy.

Chapter 3 centers on the distinctive form civil society takes in Japan and on the status of the person in relation to the system of needs, specifically labor and consumption. It engages dominant conceptions of self and subjectivity in modern Japan to argue that the situational or relational self widely seen as distinctive to Japan is neither culturally unique as posited in most anthropological treatments, nor does it exemplify claims about hybridity central to post-structural critiques of subjectivity in recent scholarship on Japan. Rather, in Japan, as elsewhere, the constitutive role of the institutions and social practices within political economy help to illuminate the nature and distinctiveness of modern subjectivity. The domestic and international contexts within which the institutions of state and civil society shaped the idea of the person historically are highlighted in the last section.

Chapter 4 traces the pattern of welfare provision in pre- and post-war Japan via a conceptually driven analysis of the goods and services provisioned by the state. Specifically, it demonstrates that what is distinctive about Japan's welfare system is not, as commonly argued, its level of spending or its enterprise-based welfare system. Its distinctiveness, rather stems from how the notion of the modern self constituted within civil society grounds a particular division of labor between state and civil society in meeting welfare needs: the generous state provision of social needs geared to meeting the production-based needs of the collectivity and the provision of consumption-related individuated wants within the market.

Chapter 5 shows how reforms undertaken in the recessionary decade (1990s), specifically changes in unemployment benefits and public assistance provision, resist interpretation in terms of contemporary neoliberal formulations about the efficacy of "work-fare" and a productivist social policy. Rather, welfare reform in Japan continues the pattern of separating social and individuated ends in its attempt to grapple with the socio-economic contingencies of enhanced global competitiveness and demographic change.

Chapter 6 assesses the "neoliberal turn" in recessionary Japan in light of the thesis developed in this study, namely the link between the normative structure of subjectivity and the social limits of the market in modern Japan.

2
Theoretical Contestations: State, Market, and the Individual

How do states and markets contribute to individual well-being? Are individuals better off when markets are left untrammeled? Or does placing limits on the market better enable individuals to pursue their own ends? If so, by what criteria should states and markets be limited? Dominant thinking, grounded in conservative, Marxian, post-Marxian, and post-structural theories, tends to locate the problematic welfare and individual well-being in either state or civil society, taking one of the two poles of civil society – its enabling or disabling role vis-à-vis individual well-being – for the whole. Advocates of the free-market position idealize the market's enabling function by denying its equally powerful potential for impingement. Critics, on the other hand, view the market in primarily negative terms thereby denying its significance to individual well-being. In advocating state-based welfare as the only effective antidote to the vicissitudes of the market, critics of the market ignore the damaging effects of the lack of participation in exchange relations for self and social esteem vital to individual well-being.

The first part of this chapter critically maps this theoretical terrain to suggest that the tension inherent in civil society, rather than denied, must be made central to the question of welfare. The second part elaborates an alternative conceptualization of the relation between civil society, state, and welfare, rooted in G.W.F. Hegel's *Philosophy of Right*, which serves as the theoretical backstop for the subsequent discussion of the Japanese case. Specifically, Hegel's claim about the constitutive role of political economy vis-à-vis subjectivity renders both the state and market, within limits, necessary to welfare or individual well-being. Insofar as the Japanese case concretizes the claim about the necessity of political economy to the normative structure of subjectivity, while exemplifying, albeit in an attenuated way, the claim about the necessity of both state and civil society to individual well-being, it directs attention to the crucial question of the social limits of the market in rethinking welfare under conditions of late capitalism.

Conservative thought

The conservative position on welfare straddles, on one extreme, the libertarian view associated with the ideal of the "free-market" most famously advocated by Milton Friedman and the "New Right" it has inspired (Friedman 1962; Gilder 1981; Glazer 1988). The free-market vision advocates an extension of the market mechanism (contract) on the grounds that it unequivocally enhances liberty and therefore individual well-being. Others (Murray 1986; 1988, for instance) suggest the state's role be kept to a social minimum, not on the grounds of efficiency or liberty *per se*, but because its intervention is counterproductive not only for those whose problems it was designed to solve, but also for the rest whose natural communal proclivities are impinged upon by an activist state resulting in the enervation of community life. I consider each in turn.

For advocates of the free-market, liberty trumps all other goods as the basis for individual well-being, providing the *raison d'etre* for advocating "the widespread use of the market" (Friedman 1962: 24). At stake in making individual well-being contingent on liberty is the individual's freedom to make the choices that best satisfy her wants and preferences: as rational beings who know what they want individuals are seen as motivated by the desire to satisfy subjective desires. Markets play a pivotal role in this conception of individual well-being. First, because economic transactions are wholly voluntary involving neither a sense of obligations to others (as in family life) nor coercion, they are particularly well suited to the task of promoting liberty. Second, as the arena of competitive self-interest, markets are also particularly well suited to enhancing liberty: as markets grow they not only make available an exponentially increasing menu of goods thus expanding the horizon of choice, but by offering individuals greater opportunity to engage in contractual transactions markets enhance individual liberty and therefore well-being. It follows then that the wider the scope of the market mechanism the greater the possibility for individual freedom and well-being. Thus, the conservative critique of welfare focuses on the need to limit states to their proper "night-watchman" role guaranteeing property rights, formulating and implementing rules pertaining to contract, and putting in place the juridical and administrative structure necessary for the functioning of a market economy. The state's role is limited to protecting the individual's right to pursue private ends.[1]

For the libertarian, political decisions, because based on majority rule which requires that the minority submit to decisions not of their own making, should be kept to a minimum. In Friedman's words,

> The characteristic feature of action through political channels is that it tends to require or enforce substantial conformity. The great advantage of the market, on the other hand, is that it permits wide diversity.... Each man can vote, as it were, for the color of the tie he wants and get it; he does not have to see what color the majority wants and then, if he is in the minority submit.
>
> (Friedman, 1962: 24)

Accordingly, for free-market liberals the welfare state undermines individual well-being on two counts: by restricting the scope of the market mechanism it curtails liberty; and far more dangerous, however, it violates the principle of neutrality central to liberal thought. By institutionalizing welfare as social right the welfare state imposes a public end on private interests thereby restricting liberty and undermining the well-being of recipients and non-recipients alike. By being subjected to ends not subjectively determined non-recipients have their freedom restricted. Recipients, on the other hand, are also victims by virtue of having their status as autonomous beings jeopardized by the "nanny state."

The conservative solution is to restore traditional values of family, promote a work ethic, and encourage behavioral modification (e.g. deferred gratification), savings, and "wise" investment. The emphasis is on the creation of a "social minimum" so that the use of the market may be maximized. Any social shortfall is to be picked up by mediating structures, churches, neighborhoods, ethnic groups, in sum, "voluntary associations," or Tocquevillian civil society (Green 1993; Tanner 2003).[2]

That public ends be seen as fundamentally inimical to private ends is not, however, simply a question of ideology, as many critics of the free-market position are wont to argue. Rather, it stems from the conception of personhood that undergirds both the ideal and the institutional form a market designed around the ideal of the free-market takes. Because private interests are viewed as wholly subjective, stemming from needs and desires that bear no relation or connection to others, individuals can have no common ends with others. As such, they have no need for others nor any obligations to them; self-interest is neither contingent on nor requires any objective validation.

On this view, alienation, the necessary condition for the pursuit of self-interest, is transformed into a sufficient condition: rather than a realm that enables the freedom to pursue ends of one's own making distinct from the communal ends that bind persons in the realm of family or state, the free-market creates a realm in which the pursuit of self, because predicated on the denial of any connection to others, becomes a realm in which the private ends of each are threatened by the private ends of all. The market can be constitutive of self-worth, however, only if it is implicated in the construction of personhood. In the absence of the recognition of the self-in-the-other, and consequently selfhood in general, individuals contend only with the self-repudiating task of satisfying desires that fail to make them real in the world.

It comes as no surprise then to note that civil societies designed and enlivened by the free-market conception of personhood strain to accommodate even the most minimalist welfare state. Less obviously, because welfare states that emerge within such a milieu rest on prevalent notions of personhood, welfare, rather than exemplifying a genuinely public end, is simply the terrain for an aggrandizement of private interest, never quite making the transition from being a matter of law to one of right (i.e. embedded in social life). Thus, distinguishing between the deserving and the un-deserving poor, different social policies are viewed more as the successful *extension of private interests*, and therefore an imposition of the interests of some over the interests of others. It is no accident then that resistance to the idea of the state sponsorship of public services (health care for instance) would persist even as other demands on the state (as expressions of private interests, social security, pensions, for instance) grow. In this sense, the pluralist account of welfare may indeed hold but only in contexts where the free-market ideal dominates: because states have no ends of their own, their actions providing simply a vector of competing private interest groups, welfare in this context, rather than an accomplishment of social right, can only be an extension of the realm of private interest accounting for both its responsiveness in some arenas and its reticence in others.

Similarly, it is worth noting the internal relation between the notion of welfare dependency and the free-market conception of personhood. Some have advocated the dismantling of state-sponsored welfare programs for working-age persons on the grounds that they foster dependency as a mode of life, rather than providing short-term support that enables those in need to overcome temporary setbacks. Thus, food stamps, workmen's compensation, Medicaid, unemployment insurance, and so on are seen to have contributed to an uncoupling of the system of rewards and constraints that, in a pre-welfare era, served to motivate self-reliance particularly among those threatened with poverty. The "pathologies" of dependency including teenage pregnancies, drug and alcohol abuse, violence, and so on, stem, critics suggest, from the lack of accountability that state-sponsored welfare programs institutionalize. Even though designed to target specific social problems (unemployment, hunger, etc.), welfare states tend to make "bad" (dependent) rather than "good" (self-reliant) behavior into a whole mode of life; for instance, programs giving aid to families with dependent children, rather than supporting parents unable to provide basic needs, simply encourage further "irresponsibility" (to have more children), thereby exacerbating the problem.[3]

While it may be true that state-sponsored welfare appears to more readily sustain rather than actively negate self-destructive dependency, it is less clear why it should be the cause. That is, why does dependence on the state for a specific need (food, housing, medical care, etc.) take over, as it were, the whole individual, making dependency a whole mode of life?[4] The welfare state's alleged role in sustaining self-repudiating dependent behavior becomes explicable once its link to dominant conceptions of personhood is recognized.

If self-reliance in the market entails a form of subjectivity that is wholly subjective, that is bearing no relation or connection to others, the only recourse available to those unable to fulfill this ideal of selfhood is to abrogate the self altogether. Because its conception of selfhood rests on an absence (indeed denial) of the self-in-the-other, and therefore selfhood in general, individuals who fail to sustain this ideal in the everyday practices of the market can no more lay claim to being a self than the multiple others they encounter as non-selves within relations of exchange in the market. Put differently, the reason for the loss of self-worth on the part of welfare recipients (resulting in dependency on the welfare state) stems from the same source that stigmatizes welfare recipients as unworthy of social regard: the absence of the recognition of selfhood in general. That welfare states "fail" (to solve social problems or garner the support of private citizens for public ends) in countries where the free-market ideal structures conceptions of personhood is thus consistent with the organizing principle of the free-market institutionalization of civil society.

Thus, the pathologies of dependency often attributed to the welfare state can be understood as having a deeper root in the ideal of selfhood associated with the free-market vision. Only when the dominant societal ideal of selfhood includes connection with the self-in-the-other as a vital component of self, with the recognition of mutual regard and interdependence it entails, can specific social problems targeted by welfare states be construed, both by those in need and by those administering to that need, as relating to simply a part of rather than the whole self.

Current efforts to revitalize voluntary associations in civil society as a means of provisioning help to needy individuals must be recognized for what they are, a means of decreasing welfare dependency perhaps without, however, enabling self-determination. In the absence of state support individuals in need can either take recourse to the charity of strangers or rely on personal networks of support in family and/or communities in which conformity or sameness is the precondition for membership. In both cases material help comes at the risk of the denial of self; charity exalts the selfhood of the donor vis-à-vis that of the recipient; communities reward sameness. Only communities that enable the mutual regard of difference can, in principle, provide networks of support and facilitate self-determination.[5]

Second, the market, to which conservatives would return the question of welfare, is enabling of self-determination to the extent that its equally powerful capacity for impingement is mitigated. We can be assured that participation in the market will more likely than not enhance well-being only so long as the market does not institutionalize contractual forms and modes of behavior that violate individual integrity and personhood. In the absence of any recognition of the need to place limits on the market, the conservative prognosis appears only to resolve the question of welfare dependency, not the problem of the need for welfare. As such, leaving individuals to their own devices in the market, including the able-bodied poor and those most vulnerable to the rapacity of existing markets (single mothers with dependent children, the sick and elderly, etc.), can only serve, sooner rather than later, to re-create the conditions that necessitated welfare in the first place.

The creation of "work-fare" in lieu of welfare offers, many would counter, a way out of this dilemma. By engaging those previously on welfare in productive work the creation of new jobs can help foster and inculcate the habits of mind necessary to sustaining self-reliant modes of life. In an ideal market, where all jobs paid a living wage, "work-fare" might indeed offer a way out (although it would still raise problems having to do with the issue of self-determination). But in instances where the working poor constitute a large proportion of the disadvantaged, unable to afford the basic necessities that welfare states characteristically provide (health care, unemployment protection, social security, education, etc.), work-fare *per se* cannot suffice. That work is enabling of autonomy only insofar as it entails a process of acquiring the habits of mind and skills that fulfills some objectively determined need, given the social division of labor, "work-fare" insofar as it entails the close monitoring of clients being inducted into the realm of work may still prove inadequate to the task of fashioning self-reliant, autonomous individuals from those enmeshed in welfare dependency. The conservative solution to the problem of welfare dependency via the dismantling of social policy programs thus misdiagnoses the problem. The error lies in seeing the welfare state, rather than the institutionalization of civil society along the free-market ideal, as the source of the problem.

Marxian thought

Class-centered Marxian theory's[6] treatment of welfare state capitalism centers on the objective location of individuals in the realm of production (as workers or capitalists) that determines the horizon of well-being (Gough 1979; Corrigan and Leonard 1978; Ginsburg 1979; Wright 1978; Esping-Andersen 1990; Piven and Cloward 1983). Because, however, the market and the relations of exchange that are constitutive of it are conceived as inherently exploitative (the capitalist controls and profits from the surplus value produced by workers), the effort by workers to increase their share of the social product via class struggle bears an objective compulsion. The market's intrinsically debilitating impact on the worker's well-being, in other words, necessitates class struggle not only to improve the terms of exchange within the market (increase wages, terms of employment, etc.), but also to obtain extra-economic compensation via the welfare state (health care, education, disabilities and unemployment benefits, etc.). As such, individual well-being, within both the market and the welfare state, is conceived in material terms (Gough 1975; Corrigan and Leonard, 1978; Westergaard, 1978; Wetherly, 1988).

Three interrelated issues have dominated class-based analyses of welfare. One draws attention to the facilitative impact of welfare statism on workers: as the outcome of class struggle, welfare states embody a victory of the working class and an improvement in their social wage or material condition. By providing welfare (housing, medical care, and worker re-training) the state bears the costs of providing a skilled (healthy, trained, etc.) labor force to capital. Another draws attention to the stabilizing role of the welfare state vis-à-vis capital. Although they represent a significant gain in "social rights" on the part of workers, the short-term effects of welfare statism are seen as being essentially "market-supplementing" gains for capitalist development. Inherent in this view is the subordination of the political into the economic. Much like Marx's analysis of the Factory Acts, the welfare state is both a victory for the working class and serves the interests of capital by preventing the hyper exploitation of labor. A third, taking as its emphasis the alienating and oppressive nature of heavily bureaucratized welfare states faults the institutions and social practices of existent welfare states for their de-humanizing effects on recipients.

The implications of all three accounts for understanding the varied trajectory of welfare, including its success or failure in different contexts, in relation to their core conceptual category, class, is by no means clear. How does the welfare state impinge on class consciousness? Does the creation of a welfare state, understood as the victory of the working class, invite its own failure? Does the state provision of a means of livelihood enervate class consciousness to the point that the working class ceases to be a "class for itself"? Because, for Marxists, well-being and agency are class based, the key question turns on how welfare states class agency. This is by no means an easy issue to unpack, not the least because the very terms of a class discourse impede a fruitful conception of the individual as self-determined.[7]

For Marx, the location of individuals in the process of production determines their "class position": the division within the "relations of production" between the owners of the means of production and those who "have nothing to sell but their labor-power"[8] creates two types of individuals, the capitalist and the worker. To the extent that they are motivated by distinct goals, the capitalist defined by the purpose of wealth accumulation and the worker by the compulsion to satisfy needs,[9] differ in fundamental ways. Capitalists, in the pursuit of wealth, pursue interests that drive them into competition with each other. As each capitalist is driven by the profit-motive to gain either larger market share or greater profit margin, each must necessarily compete with others in pursuit of similar goals.

Workers, on the other hand, "due to the cooperative form of the labor-process," necessitated by the technologically determined rationalization and collectivization of capitalism, share the same objective conditions. Because the "expenditure of identical human labor-power"

(Marx 1976: 129) creates an objectively universal condition for workers, the worker *qua* individual (as in artisanal labor) is replaced by a class of workers. The increasing immiserization of the working class over a period of time standardizes the (worsening) conditions of labor, thus creating in objective terms a collective interest between workers. This creates a class-in-itself,[10] in which workers share a strikingly similar objective position.

Although capitalists and workers can have no ends in common, workers by definition share not only a common end (against capitalists), but also a set of values and mode of life associated with the fixity of need exemplified by the idea of subsistence that structures working-class life. The worker, as class-determined being, fails to constitute a particularized identity.

Crucial to this view is Marx's idea that the labor process in capitalism tends to collectivize and homogenize workers. The specific work done (auto-worker vis-à-vis computer-assembly worker) does not distinguish one worker from the other since there is an "expenditure of identical labor-power" in all cases. The idea of identical labor-power is tied to Marx's notion of abstract labor in which the distinguishing aspects of the laboring activity are subsumed resulting in an undifferentiated laboring activity. Negating all differences between types of laboring activity, however, eliminates much that is central to the idea of an individual.

Unlike the capitalist who is theoretically free to determine the nature of her consumption (thereby allowing the realization of a particular mode of being), the worker's life is circumscribed in fundamental ways by the idea of "subsistence." Briefly, this means that the variable cost of the capitalist (i.e. cost of labor) is historically fixed such that it provides the minimum wage bundle or a basket of goods to ensure the reproduction of labor (the cost of maintaining the worker and her family). The idea of subsistence, in other words, ties the worker's income to a wage-floor that is set independently of the "scarcity and productivity of labor" (Levine 1998).[11] Since income serves only to meet the necessities of life (sufficient to reproducing labor-power), the worker's money wage is treated as the means of purchasing a bundle of necessities or subsistence goods (food, housing, clothing, etc.).[12]

The idea of subsistence congeals a specific notion of the worker *qua* individual. Despite Marx's claim that his "...point of departure is the particular, real individual," Marx's implicit notion of class-determination deprives the worker of any basis for particularity. If what it means to be an individual entails differentiation of a significant sort (differences between the wants of individuals that lead them to pursue different sorts of activities/labor yielding different modes of being, and the multiplication of wants consistent with a dynamic view of individuality), then the notion of undifferentiated need-based consumption coupled with undifferentiated (abstract) labor leaves no room for particularization.

The capitalist, on the other hand, although a member of a class, does not become part of a "class-for-itself."[13] As such, capitalists as a group, despite being a class-in-itself, remain individuals or at least persons with the capacity for individuation. The idea of "private" interest that is associated with the capitalist although strictly "economic" in nature (via the pursuit of wealth) retains an emphasis on the individual aspects of private interest. The capitalist is free to invest, for instance, in any given market, given her assessment of the prospects for accumulating wealth. The capitalist is also free to determine the use of wealth between investment and consumption. The idea that the capitalist can individuate in contrast to the worker who cannot is also implied in Marx's idea that "in capitalist society, free time is produced for one class by the conversion of the whole lifetime of the masses into labor-time" (Marx 1976: 667).[14] In other words, although capitalists are conceptualized primarily in terms of their economic drive to accumulate wealth, there is implicit in Marx's theory the notion that the capitalist is an individuated being, free to use spare time and wealth in a manner that is self-determined.

From this vantage point, the Marxian defense of the welfare state's provision of basic needs can be seen as adequate, but only vis-à-vis a conception of individual well-being that does not incorporate self-determination as its principal element. If access to "enough" food, housing, and so on alone could assure individual well-being (sidestepping the thorny question of how or who determines what is enough), analysts would arguably be celebrating the unequivocal success of welfare. For, if a subsistence-based provision of welfare were enough to enhance the worker's individual well-being, her propensity to challenge the capitalist order, the capitalist class would stand to benefit as well. The difficulty with this line of argument is, of course, that the opposite appears to be case: not only does subsistence-based welfare prove inadequate to the task of enhancing the worker's well-being (if well-being depends on self-determination and an individuated mode of life), but also the challenge to the welfare state has been advanced by the class that ostensibly stands to gain the most from it.

Given this materialist class-based notion of subjectivity and agency, then, what bearing does the welfare state have on the individual?

Specifically, does welfare contribute to a material improvement in the lives of individuals or not? If so, does it reconstitute class identity? And with what consequences for the welfare state? To the extent that welfare states ensure (even improve) the material conditions of workers, welfare states can work to weaken class consciousness. This is, indeed, what class-based accounts of welfare state failure suggest.

Contrary to Marxian theory's axiomatic claim about the revolutionizing potential contained in "moments" of crisis for capitalists, the so-called embourgeoisement of the working class (Goldthorpe *et al.* 1969) effected by, among other things, increasing welfare benefits has worked to depress their revolutionary potential, reducing rather than enhancing the polarization between classes. The welfare state's material effects on working-class subjectivity, in other words, has ironically contributed to integrating the working class into the institutional structure of capitalism. This in turn has spearheaded a weakening of class struggle and thereby further entrenched the power of the capitalist class. Indeed, one can reasonably conclude, based on the weakening of trade unionism in most democratic capitalist welfare states and the diminished appeal of internationalism as seen in the renewed faith in protectionism and nationalism by workers, that the welfare state has indeed contributed to the effective creation of hegemony (in the Gramscian sense), thereby strengthening the class position of capitalists. In this case, the "failure" of the welfare state represents a new moment in the historic opposition between capital and labor.

But two issues remain: if Marxian theory's notion of subsistence need, central to its conception of class agency, holds, then the provision of welfare by states must be also seen as being inherently self-limiting (i.e. structured to meet only subsistence need). Indeed, this is what much of a Marxian-inspired empirical sociology of welfare documents. Not only are existent welfare states overly bureaucratized, critics allege, the delivery of welfare services minimal and de-humanizing, but welfare state benefits fall notoriously short of meeting the basic needs of those in need.

Post-Marxian theory

Post-Marxian theory's account of the sources of welfare state failure turns on the contradictory nature of the properties of the capitalist state. Theorists whose work falls within this genre include Jurgen Habermas, James O'Connor, Andre Gorz, and, most notably, Claus Offe, whose influential thesis on the "contradictions of the welfare state" (1984) warrants an extended engagement in any effort to rethink the relationship between welfare, state, and market-based civil society, and is, therefore the focus of discussion in this section.

Offe's purpose is to specify analytically the "internal limitations of the state" in an effort to problematize the "stabilizing activities of the state."[15] Unlike conventional Marxian economic theories of capitalism's crisis-prone tendencies, Offe locates the crisis in the *political* domain, one that he succinctly describes as the "crisis of crises-management."[16] The state's stabilizing activity ("crises-management strategies") characterized principally by its dual compulsion as a democratic capitalist state is, Offe suggests, inherently contradictory, its one pole negating the other, resulting in an irresolvable (and therefore fundamental) *instability*.

The democratic capitalist state is compelled to pursue the twin goals of capital accumulation and legitimation. Under conditions of late capitalism, however, the logic of state action in pursuit of its goal of accumulation necessarily undermines the logic of state action in pursuit of its goal of legitimation. The root of this tension, Offe suggests, is structural: whereas capital accumulation entails continued processes of "commodification," democratic legitimation under conditions of late capitalism inevitably (albeit inadvertently) generates "de-commodification." This structural dilemma stands at the center of Offe's theoretical formulation.

Of the two terms, "commodification," at least in the way Offe deploys it, can be quite readily understood within the conventions of a Marxian political economy to refer to the centrality of exchange in capitalist relations of production. In a capitalist economy the private appropriation of wealth renders the use of objects contingent on exchange. Only those objects that can be exchanged can be valorized. The "commodity form" refers thus to exchange value: "commodification" to the centrality of exchange in valorizing both capital and labor.[17] Echoing Marx's dictum that employment is the "absolute foundation of capitalist production,"[18] Offe suggests that economic growth is contingent on the continued commodification (employment) of labor. The state is compelled to intervene not only to offset the "paralysis of the commodity form" but also, more crucially, to prevent future disturbances. The state's institutional self-interest (stemming from its need for democratic legitimation) requires that the state step in to "recommodify" labor by providing infrastructural components such as health, housing, education, training, and so on. The strategies undertaken by the state to offset the "paralysis of the commodity form" are strategies of crisis management or, in his words, "administrative re-commodification." These include strategies to enhance

> the saleability of labor power (via) measures and programmes directed toward education, training, regional mobility and improving the general adaptability of labour power.... the saleability of capital and manufactured goods is enhanced through the transnational integration of capital and product markets, research and development policies, regional development policies etc.
>
> (Offe 1984: 124)

Because state action is necessitated by the need to circumvent actual or anticipated impediments to the accumulation process, the entire range of the state's activities under conditions of late capitalism effect its transformation into a "welfare" state. In other words, for Offe, the welfare state is not a narrowly conceived descriptive term, specific only to certain public policies (such as income support, education, housing, health, social security, etc.). Instead, it is a concept that refers to the transformation of the liberal (minimalist) state of the non-political economy to one whose dual structural determination necessitates "intervention" in the productive relations of the market. The state's re-commodifying strategies are, he suggests, self-defeating in that *crises management* strategies inadvertently generate new and more serious forms of crisis. Meant to foster the effective working of the principle of exchange by creating conditions conducive to it, the welfare state ends up effecting changes at both the objective and the subjective levels that undermine the normative appeal of exchange relations, subverting rather than augmenting processes of capital accumulation. Motivated by an effort to preserve and maintain the principle of exchange, the state's re-commodification strategies have de-commodifying outcomes.[19]

De-commodification is the result of a twofold process. The objective material conditions of labor change once the state provision of welfare goods frees labor[20] from the compulsion to exchange its labor-power for wages. With recourse to an alternative source of livelihood, workers become independent of the wage contract and, therefore, independent of the compulsion to bring its labor-power as a commodity into the realm of exchange. To the extent that a needs-based, state-sponsored welfare system operates outside a market system motivated by self-interest, it provides a source of livelihood for workers other than the wage contract mitigating "the disciplinary effects" of the "reserve army of labor" mechanism. In Offe's words,

> I speak of certain organizations as decommodified because their provision of use-values is no longer guided by the form of rationality appropriate to market behavior... If we consider the "products" of hospital workers, for instance, it is evident that it is not sold on the market and that its quantity, quality, timing and geographic distribution are not directly determined by market criteria.... [T]he continuous growth of decommodified organizations such as hospitals tends to weaken and paralyze market rationality.
>
> (Offe 1984: 264–265)

Key here is Offe's contention that elements of social life not directly subject to the logic of exchange relations bear a necessarily antithetical relation to a market system. To the extent that the provision of goods and services via the welfare state is not determined strictly according to market rationality, it negates the market principle. The welfare state's putatively stabilizing activities unintentionally generate greater instability since welfare statism "challenges the dominance of the central principle" of exchange of capitalist social relations. De-commodification[21] entails a serious erosion of the normativity of exchange as the organizational principle of capitalist society. He writes,

> If the dominant organizational principle of the social process of every capitalist society is that of exchange, a theory of the crises of capitalist society can identify those processes which challenge the dominance of this central principle. Not the self negation of the exchange principle but its restriction and questioning.... would serve as the criterion of crisis processes.
>
> (Offe 1984: 38)

The "restriction and questioning" of the dominance of the exchange principle constitutes the challenge to the normative order of capitalist societies. In the first instance, the principle of a non-interventionary democratic state is belied as the welfare state violates the "boundary between the political-administrative realm and that of the economy" and employs increasingly bureaucratized decision-making processes in response to an ever-spiraling "demand overload." As state decisions come increasingly to be the result of "negotiations between state planners and the elites of powerful social interest groups," they become more and more inaccessible. In this context, mass loyalty to the existing system of administrative and political power tends to disintegrate to a serious extent. The normative rules and resources necessary for the functioning of the system of state power are not produced in sufficient quantities by the existing processes of socialization "The more state policies close in on systems of socialization and economic life, the more they tend to be regarded by various actors as illegitimate." The welfare state, in other words, calls into question the democratic source of legitimation.[22]

At the center of this formulation is the claim that the "contradiction" between the competing logics of exchange (commodification) and citizenship (de-commodification) manifests itself primarily in relation to the individual: the principle of exchange constitutes individuals in particular ways; the principle of citizenship reconstitutes the individual, with negative consequences for both the process of capital accumulation and state legitimation. Offe's theses rest on the claim that the class of ostensibly de-commodified persons undergoes a radical transformation once reliance on the welfare state comes to stand in for reliance on the wage-contract. In this sense, Offe rejects the false consciousness thesis of classical Marxist thought in which the functional requisites for capital accumulation (based on exploitation of one class by another) are "produced" more or less unproblematically, due to a dominant ideology that legitimates both state power and capitalism such that the former may proceed unimpeded or unchallenged.

Pivotal to an assessment of Offe's theoretical formulations are two related issues: how and why (and under what conditions) "decommodified" individuals "choose" reliance on state-provided welfare as opposed to self-reliance on the market; and whether "exchange" (or commodification) and de-commodification are indeed mutually exclusive. Offe can only substantiate his claim that welfare statism has the unintended consequence of undermining both capital accumulation and legitimation of state power if he can substantiate his prior claim that de-commodification is antithetical to exchange relations.

Although Offe is categorical about rejecting a merely quantitative notion of state welfare (based on estimations of state expenditures, more or less spending, etc.) his claim that in light of the availability of state welfare, individuals would "choose" reliance on the state rather than self-reliance via the market rests (albeit implicitly) on some idea of what reliance on the state entails in terms of the "basket of goods" it provides.

If the basket of state-provisioned welfare goods is more than can be procured by workers via exchange in the market, Offe can arguably account for why individuals would choose reliance on the state as opposed to self-reliance in the market. If this is what Offe has in mind, several difficulties arise. First, the underlying assumption that work offers no non-pecuniary awards is questionable. Work is not simply a means to an end (of procuring a livelihood) but, inasmuch as it provides an important avenue for self-expression and social connectedness, an end in itself. When work is seen as meaningful, dependency on the state can be corrosive of self and social worth. In this context, even in instances where state-based welfare hypothetically provides a value in excess of subsistence wage, individuals would conceivably still prefer work to dependency.

If the state provides substantially more than the basket of goods available via exchange (assuming "more" satisfies the individual correlatively), then the state, to use Marcuse's phrase, "delivers the goods" and can only be legitimate. Offe, however, clearly does not think that the welfare state offers a basket of welfare goods that is abundant relative to the subsistence-based wage procurable via the market. If, on the other hand, state-provided welfare is either equivalent to or less than that provided via exchange in the market, Offe's suggestion that individuals would choose dependency on the state rather than self-reliance on the market is not self-evident. Unless the individual's relation to market-based work is assumed to be purely instrumental, neither expressive nor enabling of self-seeking, there can be no simple equation posited between state- and market-based compensation that does not deprive the individual of a fundamental need for self-realization and self-expression.

If state welfare either replaces a subsistence-based way of life provided by market-exchange (or provides less), it is not clear why individuals would perpetuate their reliance on the state in lieu of self-reliance on the market. The objection that it is precisely the absence of opportunities for exchange on the market that creates a cycle of dependency on the state, rendering the above-mentioned cases moot, is met by noting that Offe wants to explain the transformation of a temporary reliance on state welfare into a permanent (and self-reproducing) attribute that has de-commodifying outcomes.

It must be kept in mind that Offe can only claim that the legitimacy of both state power and exchange are undermined after he has established the claim that individuals once favoring self-reliance on the market choose reliance on the state as a way of life. On the other hand, if state welfare provides a value that is less than that which can be procured via exchange relations in the market, it is unclear why individuals would choose to perpetuate dependency on the state in lieu of improving their material circumstances via exchange in the market. If people choose to work, for instance, as the case of Japan vividly illustrates, state-based reliance would prove unattractive. Without implicitly assuming the disutility of work, Offe cannot offer a determinate account of long-term reliance on the state. In this case he can only assert that welfare is prima facie a desired "good" leaving open ended the question of why individuals would settle for less. Lastly, if the state provides welfare goods that are equivalent in value to what is potentially available via exchange in the market, several issues arise. On this account there is no objective (or material) basis for a change in consciousness of the individual: a subsistence-based way of life provided via exchange is replaced with a subsistence-based way of life provided by state welfare.

Offe's argument about the contradiction inherent in the accumulation and legitimation goals of the state hinges on a second crucial claim that the welfare state becomes an "unlimited liability insurance company,"[23] failing, as it inevitably must, in meeting an ever spiraling set of demands (to extend the de-commodified realm). This makes the question of increasing expectations pivotal to Offe's theory. Drawing on James O'Connor's notion of fiscal limits of the state, Offe argues that the increasing expectations of the state and the concomitant increase in the fiscal burden on the state have the effect of rendering the state incapable of meeting these expectations and leads, therefore, to the delegitimation of state power. It begs the question, however, as to why expectations of the state should necessarily increase. What underlying assumptions make the multiplication of needs and the demands on the state associated with it so compelling? Does the state's inability to meet rising expectations have to do with the state's fiscal constraints (as commonly argued), or does it rather have to do with the nature of demand? Can the state in fact meet certain kinds of demand, while it may, in principle, be incapable of satisfying others? In assuming that it is the state's fiscal capability that is principally in question, Offe fails to inquire into the nature of demand itself and what it may reveal about the limits of welfare.

Does the notion of de-commodification accommodate the idea of spiraling demand? Offe's assumption of rising expectations of the welfare state stands in tension with his notion of subsistence need. Staying within the parameters of Offe's claims, if the individual replaces "survival" in a market economy with survival via reliance on the state, it does not necessarily follow that demands should increase over and above the level associated with subsistence need. The claim that the welfare state is self-expanding (in that it is required to meet an ever-increasing set of needs) is predicated on an a prior account of the multiplication of needs it is required to cater to. A compelling account for why the welfare state must fall short of meeting an increasing set of needs and suffer a demand overload (an argument Offe wants to make but cannot substantiate) can be made by connecting the idea of a multiplication of need to the ideal embodied in de-commodification as an alternative to the way of life instantiated in civil society.

The notion of multiplication of need challenges the idea of subsistence need (which is historically and culturally fixed and consequently static). It points to an idea of personhood in which being a person implies having a way of life that is associated with a particular but dynamic set of needs. That is, individuals develop a pattern of consumption that enables and expresses an individuated mode of life. The multiplication of need thus stems from the activity of self-seeking that forms the life projects of individuals. On this account then, the claim about spiraling demand introduces a conception of individual well-being that stands in tension with Offe's subsistence-based conception.

To the extent that a de-commodified mode of life, grounded in the fixity of subsistence need (determined by the state on behalf of individuals), cannot but contradict the dynamic notion of personhood associated with the multiplication of need within civil society, Offe's claim that de-commodification undermines commodification may be deemed correct but not on the grounds he suggests. Rather, de-commodification, to the extent that it places individuals outside the system of exchange relation, deprives them of the opportunity to pursue an individuated mode of life, thereby diminishing personhood. So far as a meaningful notion of what it means to be a person is inextricably tied to the freedom to determine and express one's particular needs, any attempt to root personhood in a structure of set or fixed, externally determined needs must be self-negating.

The de-legitimation of state power that results as a consequence of "welfare statism" may be better understood not as the result of the state's inability to meet a "demand overload" due to fiscal constraints or administrative incapacities, but due to the contradiction contained in the very ideal of de-commodification. If the way of life implicit in the idea of de-commodification undermines rather than affirms personhood (by de-linking the individual from the social relations specific to civil society within which alone she is free to develop and gain objective affirmation of her sense of self), not only the "failure" of the state but, in fact (theoretically), even the state's possible success in actualizing this ideal will generate a contradictory outcome – the de-legitimation of state power – instead of its opposite. Insofar as the individual's need for both self and social worth necessitates relating self to the self-in – the-other within the system of needs made possible only within civil society, the total negation of civil society (implied by successful de-commodification) entails also the de-legitimation of the state.

If the state risks losing loyalty, it is not because it suffers a demand overload but because it cannot meet the real needs of subjects for an individuated mode of life. The significance of making self-determined individuation key to the conception of individual well-being is evident in the widespread discourse of the "failure" of the welfare state even, or especially, when its mandate is to provide subsistence need. The point here is that Offe's claim that welfare states effect de-commodification by freeing individuals from the necessity of entering relations of exchange ignores a vital aspect of both the nature of the "help" states extend and, more crucially, the non-pecuniary rewards that exchange brings, that is the satisfaction of self-seeking in relation to other self-seekers.

If individuals do not choose reliance on the state (in the long term) but are compelled into reliance via objective structural constraints, then de-commodification cannot be conceived as a "desired good" from the point of view of welfare recipients. If welfare dependency is not inherently desirable (as opposed to commodification in the market), it need not produce passivity and disengagement but could also elicit struggle against the perpetuation of a self-enervating dependency in an attempt to develop capacities necessary to self-determination in the market. That for Offe reliance on the state is not voluntary must mean that the system of exchange relations in the market is not (as Offe previously assumes) wholly negative. If individuals are forced into reliance on the state, then de-commodification appears as less "meaningful" than self-reliance via the market.

In anchoring his claim about the consequences of de-commodification to the claim that de-commodification is an outcome of factors other than human consciousness (individuals do not explicitly want to rely on the state but are driven to by forces beyond their control), Offe undermines his prior claims about the nature of de-commodification, and seems to take recourse to the idea of false consciousness.

If, however, Offe wants to claim both that exchange is predominantly a realm of exploitation and that individuals do not voluntarily or consciously "choose" reliance on the welfare state, then he must, in order to account for the individual's long-term reliance on the state, take recourse to the idea of false consciousness. Although reliance on the state is not self-chosen by individuals, this perpetuates a long-term dependency on the state due to the lack of consciousness of their true self-interest.

In this, Offe shares in a long tradition of critical scholarship that views the system of exchange relations as irredeemably corrosive of human dignity, freedom, and creative self-realization. Indeed, Marx's critique of political economy had as its end a deeper realization of social individuation; freed from the de-humanizing brutality of capitalist social relations, the potential of human capacities could be fully actualized. To the extent that the emergence of the individual was, on Marx's view, contingent on the eradication of capitalist exchange relations, Offe's claim about the erosion of possessive individualism and the normative dominance of the principle of exchange may be viewed as a reiteration of the classical Marxian critique.

What Offe appears to overlook, however, is the paradox that the de-commodified realms of social life he sees as so promising of an oppositional and ultimately emancipatory politics are in fact made possible by a co-existing realm of commodity relations that alone enable the pursuit of the very same de-commodified activities. To the extent that the new social movements bear upon the normativity of exchange, they tend to emphasize the limits of exchange (the negative impact of certain technologies of production for the environment; the environmental consequences of a rampant consumerism; and the democratic deficit of international economic institutions) or, at best, a more equitable distribution of wealth. The demand is of humanizing capitalism (debt relief to Third-World nations, a fair-trade regime, and protecting culturally specific understandings of needs and rights) as opposed to replacing the system of commodity-relations altogether. While being critical of existent institutions and practices of market activity, they do not radically question (as orthodox Marxists do) the principle of exchange itself. The new social movements may be more accurately seen as critical of a particular organization of exchange relations rather than as repudiating the principle of exchange *per se*.[24]

The absence of a fundamental challenge to the principle of exchange (contra Offe), in what many consider to be the epitome of contemporary critical political expression in advanced capitalist democracies, does not bear witness to the resuscitation of an uncritical neoliberal normativity, but provides a telling manifestation of the two-sided nature of exchange relations as they bear upon individual welfare, which, it bears recalling, informed also Marx's original conception.[25]

On the one hand, capitalist exchange relations tend to generate hierarchies of wealth and power given the unequal distribution of wealth spawned by what is inherently an uneven process of capital accumulation that relegates some to the drudgery of alienating and mind-deadening labor to meet minimal survival needs, while others amass wealth far in excess of what is needed for survival. On the other, the private ownership of property enables the constitution and expression of socially self-determined individuality through creative labor and the use of objects that embody freedom. Marx's unequivocal recognition of the progressive nature of capitalism (viz-a-viz feudalism, for instance) informed his attempt to overcome its limitations so as to liberate the dynamic of creative human purpose and capacities potentially contained in it. By advocating the extension of de-commodified zones of social life, Offe mistakes what may be better seen as an internal critique of capitalism for a challenge that repudiates the system of exchange relations altogether.

The implications of replacing exchange relations in their totality should be clear. Along with the eradication of the seemingly intractable problems it generates, the complete erosion of commodity relations also promises what Keane succinctly refers to as an "obedient forgetting of the image and substance of the bourgeois individual," whose realization in a richer, more concrete form Marx had sought (Keane 1984: 72) with a concomitant loss of freedom and social self-determination. Similarly, an uncritical celebration of the de-commodified realms created by the welfare state ignores the consequences of the rationalization of state institutions vis-à-vis the individual, especially its de-humanizing objectifying social practices.[26]

While existent institutions in advanced capitalist democracies must be faulted for being only partially capable of realizing the promise of modernity (especially in existent organizations of civil society whose extreme polarities of wealth and want impede the welfare of many), to claim that those elements that embody its non-economic moment defy its logic is to misunderstand the nature of capitalist social relations taken as a whole. Attempts to delineate a theory of the limits and potentially self-destructive elements of existent capitalist economies[27] identify its non-economic realms as the source of its internal subversion, mistaking the apparent "autonomy" of non-economic (de-commodified) realms as manifestations of an alternate logic or dynamic of social life. To the contrary, the de-legitimating potential of the non-economic realm (art or literature, for instance) is always circumscribed by (or contained within) the animating spirit of its particular social milieu and, as such, cannot be conceptualized as somehow "outside" it.

The critique of the welfare state should point, then, not to the celebration of the de-commodified realm and the eradication of exchange relations *per se* but to the reconstitution of the institutions of both state and civil society such that they might offer then a more promising path of a fuller realization of individual freedom in the context of social connectedness.[28] This entails the preservation of exchange. However, contrary to the full-scale marketization advocated by many, the argument developed here points to the necessity of placing limits on the market.

To conclude, by the conceptualization of de-commodification as a whole mode of life that contains emancipatory possibilities for individuals and society alike, due to its alleged promise of social justice, Offe fails to recognize what Charles Taylor refers to as the "necessary structure" of civil society's relation to individuation. Keeping in mind civil society's capacity to both facilitate and impinge on individual well-being, an alternative would be to attempt to identify those aspects of social life that would merit de-commodification while preserving those commodity (market-based) relations necessary to the social purpose that markets serve, that is individuation. By taking a one-sided view of the market, Offe forgoes the opportunity to address the potentially illuminating question: what are the appropriate limits of de-commodification in the welfare state and correspondingly the appropriate limits of commodity relations in the market?[29]

Post-structural theory

Unlike approaches in the social sciences that have concerned themselves with the question of why the social compact institutionalized by the welfare state has failed to live up to its promise – of reducing poverty, inequality, and humanizing the social conditions under which national wealth creation takes place – post-structural analyses of welfare have drawn attention to the inherently exclusionary and divisive character of welfare states. Challenging the very idea of citizenship, ostensibly the legitimating ground of welfare states, post-structural critics have attempted to show how the exclusionary practices of centralized welfare states serve rather to inscribe a notion of self, subject, and citizen that is necessarily predicated on the performative and discursive practices of technologies of power, of which the welfare states is but one instance. Welfare thus appears as one technique of governance or mode of "subjectification."

Key to this formulation is the crucial idea that selves are socially, specifically discursively, constructed. Rejecting a-historical and a-cultural notions of the autonomous and rational individual, and the self as the locus of will and agency, post-structural critics emphasize the inherent heterogeneity of the self, understood both intra-psychically and inter-subjectively. In the former instance, at least since Freud, the view of the self-contained, ego-centered, sovereign self has been called into question. Determined by competing and contradictory subtexts involving several meaningful others, unconscious desires and memories locate the self in a psychosomatic context of dependency with a host of others with or against whom the self's attempt at self-mastery can only be seen as an impossibility, its pursuit the effect of an oppressive, even ideological, myth of coherence. Intra-psychically then the self can only be a series of never-ending encounters with internal others, rendering the notion of stable identity, subjectivity, or self-actualizing agency suspect.

However, post-structural thought views the self as also the product of the capillaries of power, the overlapping networks of norms, conventions, or discourses that together contribute to the coordination of social life and thus the "regulation of conduct." First, as a linguistic construction, the self is seen in anti-essentialist terms as "performativity," an effect of the iteration of the norms and conventions within which it is located. Contrary to the rationalist view in which the self exists, so to speak, prior to language (or speech-acts), post-modern critics emphasize the narrative and dialogic determination of identity. The self as discursively constructed can only be properly seen as the effect of power, insofar as the norms, conventions, and discourses within which the self is located are constituted by hegemonizing and normalizing social practices.

Power is understood to be de-centered, working not through a central authority located in the government or state, but rather, following Foucault, as "a total structure of actions brought to bear on possible action." In recent scholarship, this link between government and subjectivity has been further specified as the "conduct of conduct." Governmentality (the expertise, knowledge, information, and calculation that are the conditions of government) is seen as the direction or regulation of human conduct. In short, rule or the practices of government come to depend upon and operate through the "practices of the self" (Dean 1995: 562).

Drawing on this Foucauldian thematic about the relation between techniques of government and the subjectification of the self, post-structural theorists view the trajectory of welfare in terms of a refiguration of the process of self-formation via the deployment of new political rationalities. Central to this new techne of government is the attempt to reconfigure the axis of self-formation. As Mitchell Dean notes, the Keynesian welfarist model

> took as (its) object of governance constructs of "the Social," envisaging rule as being most appropriately or effectively achieved by working through collective or aggregate properties and processes rather than in terms of individuals. Social classes, housing supply, the national economy, social disorganization and economic cycles became crucial concepts for thinking about objects of government. Individuals were still vested with a degree of responsibility, but this was extensively conditioned and vitiated by the operation of social forces.[30]

On this view then the "social" constituted the "imagined territory" upon which political strategies could act.[31] The social practices of the welfare state contributed to this construction of the social via their formation of recipients as passive dependents on, and recipients of, public assistance. As an important site for the representation of the "public" the welfare state was crucial to creating the population of subjects that could then be effectively regulated, managed, classified, and documented.[32]

In contrast to this earlier mode of governance, post-structural critics suggest, the new techne of governance constructs the individual as the primary locus of conduct.

> one defined as a self-governing actor replete with a repertoire of choice, and free subject, one whose subjection works through the promotion and calculated regulation of spaces in which choice is to be exercised.
>
> (Dean 1995: 562)

This new subject is located now in a new imagined territory, the community. Once a site for resisting the alienating practices of bureaucracies, the discourse of community has now been deployed as a new technique of governance. Communities made up of privatized, self-governing individuals "each of whom (have) unique, localized and specific ties to their particular family and to a particular moral community" are now mobilized in the practice of governance itself.

Welfare then is seen not as a normative ideal denoting the progressive nature of political and social/economic development, but rather as a social practice among an array of others meant to stabilize identity so as to better enable the working of the capillaries of power. The emphasis on the individual as an

> active agent in their own economic governance through the capitalization of their own existence is paralleled in a whole new set of vocabularies and devices for managing individuals.
>
> (Rose 1996: 339)

The creation of an active society through the creation of new autonomized subjects of government thus represents an emergent field of governmentality. In so far as the welfare state was key to constituting an earlier object of governance, the change currently underway represents an important shift in the government of subjectivity.

At the heart of this argument is the claim that the governance of aggregates (nation-state, economy, etc.) is now being replaced by the governance of an array of discrete, localized, "micro-sectors" (drug addicts, single mothers, mentally disabled, and job-seekers), each subject to the intellectual technologies of separate agencies and experts.

On this view, the logic underpinning the shift in the social practices of welfare is neither economic nor ideological in nature, nor for that matter a simple issue of "policy failure" or welfare state regime type. It signifies rather a change in the techne of government that has as its primary object a change in the axis of self-formation. Consistent with the discourse of the "enterprise culture" in which the individual as consumer or customer is central, the new work-fare state provides an important site for the creation/regulation of a new subject. Thus, unlike neoliberal and Marxian explanations of the challenge to welfare states that focus on the economic dimension of welfare and its transformative role vis-à-vis individuals, post-structural analysts are almost exclusively concerned with elaborating the political conditions of possibility that have occasioned the shift from a Keynesian welfare state to the new work-fare state.

Although post-structural analyses of discourses of poverty and welfare have done much to draw attention to the ubiquitous effects of rationalized and centralized attempts to coordinate social life, they encounter some difficulty in accounting for the varied trajectory of welfare, including its success and failure in different contexts. First, insofar as the shift from the Keynesian welfare state to the "active society" of "autonomized" individuals is explained in terms of discursive practices that provide the basis for self-formation, the construction of a new subject is seen to be central to this shift in governmentality. The reason for this transformation has to do with the creation of new processes of "subjectification," or new modalities of self-formation.

However, in taking discursive practices to be wholly determining of subjectivity, post-structural theory unwittingly treats discursive practices as subjectless practices. Insofar as the idea of a subject implies agentive capacities, the ability to "make a difference" by resisting or accepting discursive practices, Foucauldian analyses deprive their theoretical account of "subjectification" of subjectivity altogether.[33] Without an account of why the individual is so easily constituted in discourse, that is in the absence of an account of the negation of specific discourses, post-structural accounts of subjectivity remain open to question.

Accordingly, post-structural analyses of the constitutive role of welfare (in its Keynesian or neoliberal guise) vis-à-vis subjectivity are particularly vulnerable, especially when coupled with the underlying notion of power that undergirds Foucauldian social theory. Simply put, they leave no way, to borrow R.B.J. Walker's phrase, "to get from here to there." That is, if governmentality is emblematic of a specific form of subjectivity (a form of knowledge/power consciousness that is deployed via discursive practices in the construction of a specific kind of subject), the shift from one form to another (one mode of regulation to another) is rendered inexplicable in the absence of an account of agency. Introducing a notion of agency, on the other hand, would undermine the discursive determinism which grounds post-structural accounts of governmentality.

This tension is further exacerbated in light of post-structural understandings of power. Rejecting realist understandings of power as located in the state (which arguably allows an account of state management of society and hence an account of how to get from here to there – from one mode of governance to another), post-structuralists insist that power works through multiple channels. As Mitchell Dean puts it,

> government is not identified with the operation of the constitutional state or its executive and legislative arms. It is rather a general term to encompass all those agencies, practices, techniques and discourses that provide the means and conditions of administration and rule.
> (Dean 1995: 569)

In this sense, power pervades all dimensions of social life; lacking a center, its manifestation in every aspect of life renders both collective and individual consciousness subject to its working. This notion of biopower when coupled with the first tenet of post-structural theory – a discursive determinism that repudiates any notion of agency – renders post-structural theory unable to account for social transformation in general, and the institutions and social practices of welfare in particular. More specifically, it is unable to identify the sources and agents of transformation. If the state is neither the locus of power nor a collective agent (in the Durkheimian/Hegelian sense), it cannot be seen as the originator of change. On the other hand, since subjectivities are wholly determined by prevalent discursive practices that embody a specific form of governmentality, subjected (or abjected) selves, to the extent that they lack the (theoretical) capacity to resist, cannot be seen as the agents of change. In sum, the transition from one mode of regulation to another remains unexplained.

This brings us to the third and final disjuncture between the epistemological tenets of post-structural theory and its specific claims about the varied trajectory of welfare. In part the result of an antipathy to materialist analysis, but also due to their central emphasis on the discursive construction of social reality, post-structural theory has strenuously resisted addressing the question of the link between discursive and material power relations. As such, it has been committed to an examination of regulatory and disciplinary practices on a discursively constituted identity, without examining how the market is implicated in disciplinary practices, and the systematic linkages that may exist between material and discursive means of subjectification. As Tim Newton points out, a focus on

> the material is of interest to the extent that its use may reflect power relations which have a stability, deriving from repeated patterns in their social construction and reproduction over the medium to long term. . . . Such stabilities are significant to the extent that they condition the way in which discourses are established.
>
> (Newton 1998: 418)

In failing to connect discursive practices with existent material conditions, post-structural theory fails to recognize that changes in discourses (or modes of governmentality) may indeed be deeply connected to changes in material stabilities.

And yet, in attempting to account for the demise of the Keynesian welfare state, to delineate what has prompted this change from the government of the social to the government of the individual, post-structural theorists repeatedly invoke changes in material reality. Economic processes of globalization, to the extent that they are seen as undermining the nation-state's capacity to maintain the fiction of "national economies," "citizenship," or the territorialization of space (and hence order), are seen to have occasioned the move to a new techne of government in which the death of the social is heralded by the creation of the self-governing individual as the new object of government. I quote at some length from Nikolas Rose:

> An economy is no longer so easily imagined as naturally co-extensive with the realm of a nation-state with different "national economies" inhabiting a wider common field.... the economic problems of governments are being re-thought in terms of a revised image of economic space and the means by which it can be acted upon. It appears that, while national governments still have to manage a national population, the economic well-being of the nation and of its population can no longer be so easily mapped upon one another and governed according to principle of mutual maximization. Government of the social in the name of the national economy gives way to government of particular zones – regions, towns, sectors, communities – in the interests of economic circuits which flow between regions and across national boundaries. The economic fates of citizens within a national territory are uncoupled from one another, and are now understood and governed as a function of their particular levels of enterprises, skill, inventiveness and flexibility.
>
> (Rose 1996: 338–339)

Ironically, the above quote, as a defining statement of post-structural explanations of welfare state failure, repudiates all three of the central tenets of post-structural analysis discussed above: the notion of decentered power, the alleged immateriality of "material interests," and the wholly discursive construction of subjectivity. If states are reconfiguring "subjects" in response to changes in the global economy which mandate a new form of govermentality (or conduct of conduct), then the discursive practices deployed in the process of subjectification must be seen as embedded in material conditions. The market, in other words, is implicitly recognized as being central to the construction of subjectivity.

Further, post-structural theory's antipathy to class-based Marxian analyses of how the market bears upon individuals has sought to replace productionist accounts of the individual's location in the market with a focus on the significance of consumption in constituting subjectivity. Consumption, however, is seen not in conventional terms of the use goods provide, the social meanings they embody, or their role in particularizing identity, but principally as the consumption of the de-contextualized significations attached to them. This emphasis on the "consumption of signs" thus enables an account of a series of constantly changing identifications which becomes then the ground upon which the notion of a de-centered hybrid form of subjectivity may be elaborated.

But what of the overlapping and conflicting claims state and market make on subjectivity? How does the welfare state's ostensible colonization of interiority mesh with the consumption of signs in the market and its constitution of the subject? Is the subject as constituted in relation to state power hospitable to the forms of subjection determined within the realm of market relations? If not, how are these alternative processes of subjection negotiated? And with what socio-economic consequences? Do the varied processes which produce the conditions which enable consumption (labor and income) bear on the allegedly arbitrary array of signs consumed?

Post-structural theory's focus on "hybridity" as the hallmark of a post(anti)-modern, de-centered subjectivity emphasizes the negotiated character of identity. It is not very helpful, however, in specifying analytically the dynamics of negotiation, and, more crucially for our purposes here, the sociological and economic consequences of identity politics. Insofar as the welfare state bears on both the material and ideational aspects of identity, post-structural theory's emphasis on the significance of the latter in contrast to Marxian theory's exclusive concern with the former reproduces the one-sided nature of analysis it purportedly overcomes. Simply put, the post-structural claim that the market's role in self-formation must be understood principally in ideational terms (the consumption of signs, not goods) ignores two central issues: the role of production in constituting identity, specifically how different kinds of labor (work) bear upon identity formation; and the materiality of identity. Finally, by rendering subjectivity wholly determined by the context (linguistic, cultural) in which it is embedded (resulting in the repudiation of the very idea of a self-determined willing subject)[34] attempts to assess the market or state's role vis-à-vis individual well-being become problematic.

Since differentiation between and among those embedded in identical institutions cannot be accounted for without a theory of agency[35] (in turn necessary for an account of "difference"), a view that repudiates the very notion of agency making subjectivity derivative of context can only produce and sustain an assertion about the putatively homogenizing effect of the constitutive role of particular institutions. It comes as no surprise, then, that proponents of this view critique institutions like the state as being "totalizing," hostile to diversity and intolerant of difference, when in fact "homogenization" turns out to be a necessary product of this view's theoretically prior repudiation of agency. The strong relativism inherent in this view, although promising of emancipation from socially constructed hierarchies, turns out, ironically, to be unable to account for, much less overcome, the very same hierarchies. A theory that can do no more than name a matrix of constitutive categories (gender, race, class, ethnicity, and so on) that comprise the "inter-subjective" ground of subjectivity renders subjectivity not only incoherent but also derivative.

Given the present objective of determining the transformative impact of social institutions vis-à-vis individual welfare, the above conceptions fail to provide any determinate criteria by which we could meaningfully speak about the "welfare" of the individual, much less evaluate the impact of social institutions (state or market) on individual welfare. That is, if individual welfare is simply the product of "local narratives" then there can be no objective basis for evaluating the well-being of one individual vis-à-vis another, much less any action to improve the well-being of one group of persons vis-à-vis another.[36]

In sum, by analyzing the welfare state's regulating/disciplining effects on welfare recipients specifically, and on questions of governmentality more generally, independently of considerations of market-based processes of subjection, post-structural theory can do little to shed light on the boundary question: by what criteria should states and markets be limited?

An alternative

The previous sections have drawn attention to some of the ways in which current thinking about the question of welfare depends on a one-sided view of the relation between civil society and individual well-being. Consequently, welfare has been seen as either inimical to the working of the market or as a necessary antidote to the market's debilitating effects on individual well-being, constraining efforts to account for its varied trajectory. This section outlines an alternative approach. Drawing on two interrelated claims in Hegel's *Philosophy of Right*,[37] I develop first his conceptualization of the two-sided relation between civil society and the individual. Hegel's view is two-sided in a double sense. First, because, for Hegel, civil society's centrality to individual well-being stems from its role in enabling individuation, whose content nevertheless is deeply social, civil society incorporates alienation and connection, both necessary for well-being. Because, however, the reciprocity of exchange renders individuals dependent on the actions of others, civil society cannot guarantee the security of all participants; the polarities of wealth and want characteristics of civil society impede the well-being of many. Thus, for Hegel, the market can imperil individual well-being even as the modalities of exchange render it necessary for individuation.

Insofar as this is correct, the boundaries placed on civil society as well as the social meanings that inform its practices (production and consumption) shape societal ideals and norms of personhood. Because it is within relations of exchange that the individual both pursues her own end and encounters others similarly engaged,[38] the limits placed on exchange relations shape societal understandings of the self in relation to the other. To the extent that welfare concretizes societal understandings of the relation between the self and other, the nature of civil society is understood as crucial to welfare.

Second, because civil society takes shape only in the context of a state that, through its system of rights as well as the legal, administrative, and judicial system, provides the framework within which civil society operates, state and civil society are understood as mutually constituted. That is, both are necessary to and constitutive of a shared ideal of personhood. Welfare as social right accords equal recognition of personhood to all who are citizens; differences in welfare can therefore be fruitfully understood as reflective of different underlying conceptions of personhood. Because, however, the state contributes to, works with, and is limited by the ideal of individual well-being enlivened within civil society, differences between welfare states can be understood in relation to differences in the ideal of personhood exemplified by the limits (or absence thereof) of respective civil societies. The social meanings exemplified in exchange relations are deemed crucial to understanding personhood.

The idea of welfare as social right grants to all individuals the right to equal treatment by virtue of their citizenship in the state. By what measure, however, can citizens be deemed equal? Dominant conceptions of the individual point in different directions. For libertarians, for whom individuals are wholly subjective beings, equality necessarily violates liberty. Welfare as public end, or as the imposition of the private ends of some over the private interests of others, undermines liberty. For Marxists, on the other hand, for whom the equal provision of subsistence need points to a conception of individuals as wholly objective (class-determined) beings, to disregard equality is to jeopardize social justice. Finally, for post-structuralists, for whom individuals are bearers of socially constructed identities, equality via citizenship implies subjection and the suppression of difference.

Paralleling the one-sided view of exchange, current accounts can be seen to falter due to their one-sided conceptions of the individual. In splitting apart the subjective and objective elements of subjectivity, dominant conceptions tend to treat either one or the other as determinate. For those for whom subjectivity is wholly subjective, exchange is understood as unequivocally good; for those for whom subjectivity is wholly objective, on the other hand, exchange carries only a negative meaning due to its debilitating effects on the individual, particularly those who can only bring their capacity to labor for exchange.

But equality violates liberty only when the individual is construed as a wholly subjective being.[39] Insofar as connection with the other undermines any claim to radical self-subsistence, the individual whose subjectivity carries an objective content (i.e. connection with others) need not see welfare as an external imposition. Similarly, the equal provision of subsistence need is deemed just on the grounds that it enables an objectively determined class-based subjectivity. This makes sameness rather than differentiation the basis of subjectivity. Insofar as the individual's desire to be recognized as a particular (i.e. individuated) being militates against any objectively determined mode of life (based on merger with the group/class), the loss of self-determination implicit in the radically objective notion of subjectivity makes welfare (and exchange) more than simply a means of fulfilling material need.[40]

Restoring to subjectivity its objective content (and vice versa) potentially subverts dominant theoretical understandings of the relation between state, market, and individual, and, consequently, substantive analyses of welfare that are informed by these frameworks. Hegel's conception of the individual – to the extent that it elaborates the objective, that is social moment of self-determination – one that takes alienation and connection as its ground, offers an altogether different starting point for the study of welfare including the key questions: what ends to individuals hold in common and by what measure can citizens be deemed equal?

For Hegel, the end that individuals hold in common, by virtue of which alone welfare can be construed as an authentically social right, is the end that all individuals equally but in different ways pursue: the end of self-seeking. Through the course of their lives, via the activities they engage in, and the needs they attempt to satisfy, individuals seek to sustain an enduring sense of self that makes them real in the world: "self-consciousness is desire" (Hegel 1977: 109). To the extent that to be a self implies a particular way of being a self, the ends that individuals hold in common is the desire to make their particular way of being real in the world real.[41] The self that is the object of desire for all selves is thus an abstraction, a "striving for" that defines the life projects of different individuals. However, for Hegel, individuals discover and actualize their ideals of personhood only in the process of social engagement. The self, then, properly conceived is essentially a seeking after self.[42]

It is not enough, Hegel suggests, that individuals simply have an inward sense of their selves. For this subjective sense of self to gain actuality (which alone can secure self-boundaries), the individuated mode of life pursued must be recognized by others who in turn are recognized as different, but equal selves. Mutual recognition, however, assumes connection by which the self can recognize the self-in-the-other.

The basis of connection is, on the one hand, the self as abstraction, the "striving for" that makes humans into purposive beings, by virtue of which all may be seen as equal though different selves.[43] But it is also, for Hegel, due to the social meanings that individuals hold in common, or the world that endures independent of their respective subjective experience of it, that individuals are connected. To the extent that it is only by taking in and making their own what already exists in the world that individuals make their subjective way of being real in the world, persons are connected to each other by virtue of the social meanings they partake of and incorporate, albeit in different ways. The social meanings that attach to activities and things, so to speak, are vital to understanding the selves individuals can become. It is with this claim that we begin to approach the relevance of Hegel's social philosophy to the consideration of welfare.

Hegel's emphasis on the social renders the state vital to individual well-being. Insofar as Hegel places welfare within civil society, it is the administrative state that must create the conditions facilitative of welfare. Unlike the theories of welfare discussed thus far, in which the state's remedial action vis-à-vis welfare implies a means of provision that takes recipients out of civil society (via the state provision of basic needs, for instance), Hegel's view locates attempts to mitigate the problems generated by civil society within civil society itself. Any remedial action that does otherwise must, on a Hegelian understanding of welfare, be self-repudiating. We will see further on what this entails.

Self-seeking and civil society

Unlike others for whom the significance of market relations stems from their role in satisfying subjectively determined material wants, for Hegel it is civil society's role in enabling individuation within a system of mutual recognition that makes participation in exchange vital to individual well-being. Whereas within the realm of family and state the individual's subjective purpose is subordinated to the purpose of the larger whole, within civil society the individual is free to pursue ends that are wholly her own. The end the self pursues, however, is the end of self-seeking.

The virtue of the market[44] is not simply that within it individuals can make the satisfaction of self-seeking their primary end, but that as a system of self-seekers it makes mutual regard the ground of self-seeking. It is, in other words, the social component entailed in reciprocity that distinguishes the value Hegel places on the activity of self-seeking within civil society. We might say then, following Hegel, that civil society and the system of needs within it demarcates self-seeking as a distinct realm of activity. Within it, the pursuit of an individuated mode of life makes self-seeking contingent on reciprocal acts of exchange. The mutuality of self-determination, in other words, renders the activity of self-seeking within civil society thoroughly social.

To grasp then the ideal of personhood that both informs and takes shape within distinct institutional arrangements of civil society, the properties of civil society that enable alienation and connection need consideration. For Hegel, these consist of property, contract, and the system of needs within civil society. Because each entails both sociality (connection) and the investment of particular will (alienation), they enable individuation that is nonetheless social. I briefly consider each in turn.

Property, for Hegel, is "the first embodiment of freedom" (Hegel 1967: 42). Through the private ownership of objects, will, an inward property of mind, is externalized and therefore recognized as particular will. It is, however, in the use of the things that individuals make their own, that the personality of the individual gains actuality. Replacing the independence of things by incorporating them (via ownership) must be followed by the use of objects that invests them with subjective will. Via the ownership and use of things, individuals place their mark on objects that by virtue of being recognized as theirs (and theirs alone) attains objective affirmation of their particular beings.

If property is an embodiment of will, contract, which entails the reciprocal agreement entered into by two or more parties, embodies common will, by virtue of which alone individual will gains security. That is, in participating in a mutually agreed upon exchange of property (labor or goods), contracting parties recognize each other as persons and property owners: the other is both self-same and different. Contract and property thus enable the externalization of self and its recognition by others, thereby providing objective affirmation of the self's existence.

Property relations, however, do not simply secure the person's physical existence, but rather enable the formation and recognition of personality. The system of exchange relations facilitates social self-determined individuality to the extent that it makes possible the individual's pursuit of self-chosen activities and the use of self-chosen goods. It thereby provides an opportunity for satisfaction of the self. The two principal activities of the market that are necessary to social individuation are labor and consumption.

Hegel's conception of the role of labor in facilitating self-seeking, to be properly understood, must be seen in the context of his attempt to specify the logical relations between things, rather than their historical forms. That is, to view any existent civil society as a full realization of its immanent logic is to misread Hegel.

His point is that it is only within the structure of civil society that the logic of individual freedom finds expression. Labor (or work) entails the transformation of matter in accordance with an idea; by transforming objects[45] "into instruments and expressions of human will" the significance of work, for Hegel, is that it enables the expression of a creative quality of consciousness. Moreover, because objects embody human will, they enable an objectification and consequently recognition of the self. As creative will, labor "overcomes the otherness of the material world" and the givenness of brute matter.[46] He writes,

> In the course of work I make myself into a thing, to a form which exists. I thus externalize my existence, make it into something alien and maintain my self in it.[47]

Through labor, the individual imposes her will on the external world and thus objectifies it (since she recognizes in what she has produced a reflection of her will)[48] as well as realizes a substantive identity. A self-chosen form of labor is thus crucial to the process of self-seeking. Work, however, is not simply an avenue of self-expression. Insofar as individual labor takes shape only within the context of a social division of labor, work manifests in concrete form the inter-connectedness of the social world which makes connection in alienation possible. That is, by meeting objectively determined needs through the work we do, the individual's subjectively determined ends carry objective significance. Because enabling of mutuality, participation in exchange relations through self-chosen activities is vital to the task of self-seeking. Hegel's understanding of the non-pecuniary rewards of work is thus distinctive. Recall the utilitarian conception of work in conservative thought in which the significance of work stems from its role in providing a means to the satisfaction of material wants; and the materialist Marxian conception in which labor, unlike work, does not embody the subjectivity of the worker and is therefore alienated. Because subject to exploitation, labor is conceived in de-individuated terms as abstract labor. For Hegel, in contrast, the significance of the market and exchange is not that it provides a source of livelihood but that in so doing it enables self-expression and social recognition vital to self-seeking. Of course, it was Marx's critique that capitalism uncouples the creative aspect of work for the vast majority who as factory workers bring to work only the mindless repetitive quality of alienated labor.[49]

The point here is not whether the Hegelian or Marxian conceptualization of labor more accurately apprehends the present conditions of capitalist societies, but that the Hegelian view provides a critique of existent insitutionalizations of civil society without jettisoning private property altogether and along with it its centrality to individual well-being. To the extent that for Hegel the significance of work stems from its relation to self and social worth, work that remains disconnected from the subjective expression of the worker can fail to realize the ends of self-seeking. Accordingly, work-fare, to the extent that it is grounded in a pecuniary conception of work, where work does not need to provide any *intrinsic* satisfaction by virtue of its connection to the subjective life of the worker, cannot fulfill the demands of Hegel's conception of well-being. In sum, Hegel's conception establishes the necessity of work to individual vitality, not only because it enables self-expression, but also due to its role in connecting the self to the self-in-the-other which provides the only authentic ground for the satisfaction of self-seeking.

A second element of social individuation within the system of exchange relations is the individuated pattern of consumption expressive of a particular mode of life.[50] Through the goods it makes available, markets provide the individual with the opportunity to develop a pattern of consumption that both realizes and expresses a particular mode of life and sense of self. Because objects are not only produced by creative human labor, but produced to meet a need generated within a particular social context, the particular need for and consumption of objects must be properly seen as having a social origin. Because the use of objects is socially generated, every object is "bound up in a web of social uses and meanings."[51] The use of an object thus makes manifest the individual's identification with the set of social practices associated with it.

The capitalist production process[52] thus makes available goods that embody a socially specified meaning and practice, but whose use makes manifest only the personality of the consumer, not the producer's. By tying consumption to personality associated with a particular mode of life, abstract personhood, "the source from which possession springs," takes a substantive form since it is in the act of externalizing her socially self-determined self that the individual both recovers and makes her own[53] the meanings and social practices that comprise the cultural content of the world outside her as well as gains objective validation of her self-conception.[54]

The ownership and use of goods that are expressive of, and hence necessary to, individuation make a measure of wealth necessary to individual well-being. To the extent that it is only within the social relations of exchange that individuals can find and acquire the things that express their sense of self by following a line of work suited to their talents and capacities and self-expression, civil society is seen as vital to individual well-being. The individual's welfare then resides in having the means and capacities to realize and express an individuated mode of life based on her sense of self.

Civil society and the social limits of the market

Hegel's emphasis on social self-worth as the ethical underpinning of civil society constitutes a profound rejection of economistic understandings of the market. As such, it provides a powerful critique of the market's debilitating consequences for individual well-being based not on its failure to provide the basic means of subsistence to all, but rather on its capacity to deny social and self-worth to those unable to participate in exchange.

Because within civil society, livelihood is dependent on exchange which results from the voluntary actions of independent agents, the market can fail to secure a means of livelihood for all. Some may lack the capacities (physical or mental) that are valued in the market; others though suitably skilled may be unable to procure employment due to the vagaries of the business cycle. Contrary to those for whom the market's dire consequences follow from the lack of basic needs the loss of employment entails, Hegel's critique of civil society addresses its consequences for self and social worth.

For Hegel, the central problem of poverty is not that it renders "the penurious rabble" unable to have access to means of subsistence or livelihood (as in conventional justifications of subsistence-need-based provision by welfare states), but that, in the absence of the capacity to pursue self-chosen activities and self-chosen wants that make possible the private ownership of property, those without property are denied recognition of their self-worth in accordance with societal notions of personhood. Harry Brod puts it eloquently:

> For Hegel, the problem of poverty is not fundamentally that one group of people does not have the economic goods allotted to another group, but rather that by the standards of self-worth generated by civil society, one group is denied access to a conception of selfhood and independence deemed necessary by that society.
>
> (Brod 1992)

The problem of poverty is thus not simply a deficiency in the fulfillment of "basic needs," but the absence of those capacities deemed necessary to personhood given the standards of civil society. As Raymond Plant observes,

> In Hegel's view, the level of poverty is not fixed by some neutral or objective standard based on a notion of absolute or basic need but rather by some notion of need relative to what is necessary to be a functioning and integrated member of a particular society, with a specific standard of living and a pattern of consumption.... It is also clear that by welfare Hegel does not just mean the consumption of

> consumer goods but also the realization of those powers and capacities which [he] regards as being threatened by an unconstrained system of needs.
>
> (Plant 1983: 231–233)

Since private property is necessary to individuation, its lack impedes the process of self-seeking. Not only due to its role in expressing personality, but equally because the process of acquiring it is an essentially formative and educative process, participation in the system of needs is vital to individual well-being.

The limits appropriate to the market, accordingly, are those of self-seeking. Only those needs that satisfy the individual's pursuit of an individuated mode of life are appropriate to have satisfied via exchange. These include the freedom to choose a particular avenue of work (when work does not violate integrity) and the freedom to own and consume objects whose social meanings enable us to make our sense of ourselves real in the world. However, it also includes the right to own some property without which the individual can neither gain actuality nor develop an individuated mode of life. Above all, however, it requires limiting civil society in accordance with this criteria.

Minimally, this entails keeping out of exchange those transactions that violate integrity by reducing the self-in-the-other to simply an instrument of gratification, thereby denying personhood. More importantly, however, it requires instituting exchange such that it enlivens an ideal of personhood that takes qualitative differences between persons, not quantitative differences in wealth that create hierarchies of personhood as the basis for the mutual recognition of the self-in-the-other.

Civil society thus poses a dilemma for individual well-being. On the one hand, it affords the means to satisfy the need for individuation. By helping to secure self-boundaries and the recognition necessary to make the self real in the world, civil society enables the freedom of the self. However, it also promises freedom from the limits associated with being a particular self. Because in civil society the pursuit of both wants and wealth takes on a relentless quality – the acquisition of some wealth and the satisfaction of some wants lead to the incessant desire for more – wealth, rather than providing the means of satisfying the need for individuation, becomes the measure of personhood. Hierarchies of wealth thus translate into hierarchies of personhood where those with less are not simply different but lesser selves.

This then, for Hegel, is the root of the dilemma that civil society poses for individual well-being. By incorporating the desire for the freedom of the self as its locus and engine, it promises both the freedom of subjective self-expression and realization, and at the same time unleashes the desire of particularity to be the universal. The pursuit of wealth in other words brings with it a struggle for mastery over selfhood itself: the desire to be the one, rather than one among many ways of being a self.[55]

Welfare state and personhood

Civil society's relation to the individual makes exchange fundamental to individual well-being, where the latter is understood as social individuation. However, as seen in the delineation of this relation above, the modalities of exchange as well as the social arrangements by which it is instituted have consequences for individual welfare. Where no limits are placed on exchange, that is when contract is premised on the violation of personal integrity, exchange can imperil well-being. When also the social meanings attached to production and consumption measure hierarchies rather than qualitative differences in personhood, civil society jeopardizes individual well-being, injecting into the social order a quantitative ranking of personhood.

Insofar as this line of thinking is correct, distinct institutional arrangements of civil society can delimit the ideal of personhood in specific ways. Where civil society institutes exchange as an all-encompassing modality of social life, as in the free-market ideal, discussed earlier in this chapter, it violates the principle of mutual regard that is the basis of personhood. In this instance, the denial of the self-in-the-other becomes the objective basis for social relations within civil society. Insofar as the state takes on a welfare role, its actions are seen as an imposition of liberty, and recipients subject to both self and social disregard. According to the standpoint outlined here, the free-market solution to the "problem" of welfare – the dismantling of welfare support, especially to those most vulnerable (children or the mentally disabled) – and the instituting of work-fare are inadequate to the task of creating a civil society based on mutual regard.

On the other hand, the primacy placed on the need for mutual regard and civil society's failure to secure this for all becomes the basis for limiting exchange such that it represents collective, not individual, will. The attempt to substitute private property rights with centralized planning and the collective ownership of property violates the fundamental basis of individual well-being, the right to self-determination.

By denying citizens "the right to a private sphere,"[56] the state becomes, what Hegel calls, an "external state," alien to its citizens and therefore unable to create within them a sense of identity with the state.

An alternative solution to place limits on exchange by a state guarantee of the provision of subsistence need to all, on the other hand, although promising an immediate remedy to the material deprivation that plagues many in the wealthiest countries, proves to be inadequate to the task of overcoming the deprivation of self and social regard. While many would perhaps agree with the claim that subsistence-need-based state provision diminishes social self-worth, they would, more likely, defend the state provision of subsistence need on the grounds that subsistence is a basic need[57] that is prior to social individuation. The latter would be, on this view, a "luxury" the poor and destitute can ill afford.

Hegel's view challenges the claim that there can be a developmental relation posited between notions of personhood based on subsistence and social needs. To the contrary, it provides a powerful argument about the impossibility of getting from the one to the other: the progression assumed in the developmental view is overturned since the former not only impedes the realization of the latter, but denies its very essence. On this alternative account, the failure of subsistence-need-based welfare states is neither anomalous, contingent, nor simply an unfortunate ideological turn to the right, but is indeed immanent in the underlying conception of welfare institutionalized in the state itself.

This, then, may be the very heart of the matter and the major fault line in current debates between conservative, Marxian, and communitarian diagnoses of the problems of welfare statism in advanced capitalist societies. Arguably, each provides a one-sided (and therefore inadequate) focus on either the state or the market as the source of the problem. Whereas conservatives focus wholly on the negative effects of dependency on the state, they remain blind to the inequities of the market. The Marxian solution on the other hand, while correctly focusing on the debilitating effects of private capital, goes too far in subsuming private property to the private ownership of capital. In uncoupling the historically progressive link between wealth (*qua* private property) and individual freedom, the Marxian solution undermines the very notion of individuality even as it seeks to preserve and extend it. Lastly, the communitarian solution, much like the Marxian, in advocating the "community" as the end or goal that all individuals in an ethical order should strive for, misunderstands the significance of community. The idea of community resonates not because it suggests the subordination of individuality, but precisely because it is seen intuitively to be facilitating of it. To the extent that the communitarian solution subsumes individuality, and the differentiation entailed by self-determination, it encounters some of the same problems as Marxian social theory.[58]

On the view developed here, then, what has been commonly understood to be the epitome of a radical solution to poverty, the guaranteeing of social rights via entitlement to a social wage and basket of subsistence goods, turns out to be self-defeating. Ostensibly created to recognize the equal worth of all citizens, the mode of conception underlying welfare states turns out to be a profound repudiation of the very principle that comprises equal worth, namely social individuation.

To the extent then that civil society instantiates a specific ideal of personhood consistent with the kinds of limits it places on exchange, including the social meanings attached to production and consumption, the provision of welfare by the state that creates the juridical administrative and legal framework within which civil society operates is informed by this self-same ideal. It is in this sense, then, that Hegel's claim about the mutual constitution of state and civil society constitutes a powerful rebuke to those whose project of redress advocates solutions that require of those not in need only that they extend material sustenance to those in need, not the more difficult and more complicated project that begins with the recognition of the need to place limits on civil society. That is, only in the context of a limited civil society can the state's efforts to support, as opposed to only facilitate, the activity of self-seeking gain actuality.

The following chapters illustrate the argument developed above by showing how the apparently anomalous nature of modern Japan's welfare state can be readily apprehended in terms of the normative structure of subjectivity constituted within modern Japan's political economy. The distinctiveness of Japan's welfare state, the logic underpinning its pattern of welfare in other words, can be grasped in its totality only by linking it to the nature of the state and the ideal of personhood that has taken shape within the institutional arrangements specific to civil society.

3
Self, State, and Civil Society in Modern Japan

Personhood in modern Japan

With the publication of Maruyama Masao's celebrated work on the absence of individuation in Japan, the question of the "individual" and Japan's modernity moved from traditional anthropological treatment to the domain of Cultural Studies. From modernization theory's concern with how a technologically sophisticated, industrially advanced country had succeeded in maintaining putatively "traditional" mores of group identity and collectivism to the detriment of individuation, recent scholarship has been vexed by the question of whether personhood in Japan must be understood within the context of post-modernity, or a post-modernity that is also pre-modern. Has Japan circumvented the pitfalls of modernity, including its central tension of reconciling individuated ends with the social good by bypassing it altogether? Is its economic prowess and rampant consumerism an anachronistic result of its continued reliance on "traditional" forms of social life, including hierarchy, kinship, and status? Or is it suggestive of an internally riven society in which dissent, pluralism, democracy, and, most crucially, individuation have been putatively sacrificed at the altar of economic success?

Conventional anthropological treatment of the category of the person in Japan takes as its point of departure a rejection of the self-determined subject of Western modernity, with its emphasis on interiority, separateness, and self-interest. The work of Maruyama Masao, political theorist and historian, has been especially influential in this regard. Maruyama characterizes "social relations within the village community as affective and particularistic and therefore as fetters to the development of modern subjectivity." As Fujitani, summarizing Maruyama, puts it,

> The village community, he said, precluded the development of the individual and produced the personality type that supported the oppressive imperial regime – a personality type characterized by the lack of a unified, free, and responsible subjectivity.
>
> (Fujitani 1998: 307)

Insofar as an emergent modern subjectivity is deemed possible in Japan, Maruyama locates it "not in the mental life of the people but rather in a line of heroic intellectuals."[1]

A somewhat different slant on Maruyama's formulation is found in the "culture and personality" approach that became influential in the post-war decade. This approach draws attention to Japanese culture's emphasis on emotion, relation, and context that results in the group taking precedence over the individual (Benedict 1946). The social context in which individuals are located is seen to give rise to group-oriented subjectivity. Constituted within hierarchical "circles of obligations," the individual as a category gains salience only as a trace of specific group affiliations,[2] rather than as a self-governing, autonomous entity. Embedded within the *ba* (frame) of one group (Nakane 1970)[3] within multiple social contexts such as *ie* (household), *kaisha* (firm), and so on, the individual in Japan is, on this view, "group centered."

Because culture is seen as the unchanging essence that shapes society/institutions and in this case individuals, the claim about the absence of individuation in Japan fails to take account of changes in the social milieu that necessarily accompany historical and institutional transformation. The group-oriented self of twentieth-century capitalist Japan appears no different than the *ie* (household)-based person of feudal Japan. In this instance, the "perpetuation" of group loyalties in the face of the individuating logic of capitalist exchange relations demands explanation.[4] Further, the contrast between a putatively group-centered Japan and the individual-centered West betrays a modernization theory bias (individualism is recognizable only to the extent it takes on a Western form). As Alasdair MacIntyre has convincingly argued, this distinction is not a "culturally neutral distinction" as it purports to be, but rather one "already drawn from the point of view of modern American individualism."[5] Instead, MacIntyre suggests, it is the metaphysical of the self that is distinct in Japan. Unlike Western understandings of the self as "substantial soul" or psyche,

> in a Japanese understanding, there is that in the individual which is manifest.... facial expression and spoken words and actions, all of them to significant degrees conventionally ordered and there is by contrast, that which is concealed, what belongs to the heart, the sphere of unspoken thought and feelings. The former is not only what is socially presented, it is what in and through its conventional orderings constitutes social life. There is not the individual with inner and outer aspects and then, independent of these in some way the institutionalized social order. The outer aspects of the individual are the social order. Or, to put the same point in another way, the individual without and apart from his or her social role is not yet complete, is a set of potentialities waiting to be achieved, just as the social role is empty until brought into actuality by a particular person's self completion through it.
>
> (MacIntyre 1990: 493–494)

Although MacIntyre is correct in drawing attention to the recognition duly accorded the constitution of the individual in relation to the social roles assumed by the self in Japan, and the problematic privileging of Western individual*ism* in comparative studies, the notion of social individuation developed in the previous chapter provides a different way of thinking about the individual/group distinction so crucial in the comparative study of Japan. The theory of personhood elaborated here suggests that self is always and can only be constituted in relation to and in accordance with social roles that are self-chosen. On this view, there is no substantialized (qualitative) difference between the self as understood in Japan and the self as understood in the West; the difference, rather, is one of degree. As Donald Richie, an astute observer of Japan, notes, "the structure of Japanese society is visible, little is hidden." What is different about Japan is that its social life appears to be built on an explicit recognition of the social basis of personhood.

Taking a more historical view, scholars like Carol Gluck and Fujitani Takahashi have drawn attention to the *minshushi* or "people's history" project that calls into question some key assumptions in Maruyama's and the "culture and personality" school's emphasis on the absence of a "modern subjectivity" in Japan. In the 1960s and 1970s, the attempt to restore political and historical agency to the *minshushi* or subaltern in Japan, otherwise represented in orientalist discourse as inert and passive objects of elite manipulation, showed how *shutaisei* (self-management) and *nodosei* (activism) transformed the everyday life of the people during the Meiji era. The attempt to construct a new subjectivity originated:

> in the common people's desire to overcome their economic distress....The new popular thought gave rise to a sweeping transformation of the practices of everyday life, that ranged from the denial of magic to the disciplining of sexuality and festive activities, the reduction of extravagances and leisure, and the control over drinking and gambling....this conventional morality constituted an entirely new and dynamic subjectivity that became the human foundation of Japan's modernization.
>
> (Fujitani 1998: 312)

This attempt was discernable in the peasant uprisings and the popular right movements of early Meiji. It was this already active effort to construct a new self that the state would later harness, beginning in the late nineteenth century to reconstitute the people as "actively self-subjecting and self-disciplining subjects"(Fujitani 1998: 317).

Taking a different approach, some scholars have suggested that the individual in Japan is better understood as embedded in, though not fully merged with, group identifications. In an influential formulation Doi Takeo (1981) has argued that group cohesion does not result in the psychic annihilation of the individual. Because vertical relations of hierarchy are mediated by *amae* (the desire to be passively cared for by another), the fear of separation occasioned by the loss of merger in the primary relation (mother-child) is replaced in part by relations of *amae* thereby constituting awareness of self but only as part of the whole. What is crucial is the way in which the individual relates to society in different contexts. Distinguishing between the *soto* (outer) or *omote* (frontal) contexts in which expression is restrained and disciplined with the more spontaneous realm of *uchi* (inner) and *ura* (back) contexts, Doi's formulation has provided the springboard for recent scholarship on the relational self in contemporary Japan.[6] "Individuation" is thus conceived in terms that are not inimical to society (in the form of societal constraints implicit in the social contract metaphor underpinning liberal thought) but rather in tandem with society. The social embeddedness of individuals, rather than the total absence of individuation, provides a second strand of theorization about the ideal of personhood in modern Japan.

In a related formulation, Takie Lebra[7] draws attention to the situationally specific construction of the self in Japan: as socially situated actors, individuals orient action in accord with changes in context. David Plath (1980), Robert Smith (1983), and Harumi Befu (1980) variously contribute to a notion of the "relational self" showing how the individual takes shape only in the context of relations with others. The meanings attached to "self," "individual," or person in Japan are relational: individual subjectivity reflexively situated in relation to the other. Unlike those who deny the existence of individuated selves in modern Japan, these scholars do not see the self as merged with the group, but rather as embedded in social relations. Employing a conceptualization of the self as the center of consciousness and agency as constituted in relation to others, these scholars emphasize the "visibility" of the social basis of self-construction in Japan. As such, the contrast posited is not in dichotomized terms (Western-individual versus Japanese-group self), but rather about the level of awareness of the social basis of individuation that informs the organization of social life in Japan.

The idea of the "situational" or "relational" self has, however, also been utilized to illustrate post-modern claims about de-centered, hybrid subjectivity against the modern, essentialized self of modernity in the West (Kondo 1990; Tobin 1992; Bachnik and Quinn 1994; Rosenberger 1994; Ohnuki-Tierney 1987). Contra modernist notions of the subject as self-grounded in consciousness, the self in Japan is seen as hybrid in that its locus, or agency, is viewed as indeterminable, since the varied capacities of individuals (say for political action, religious belief, or sexual conduct) are constructed by multiple, often conflicting cultural and historical factors. Making much of the fact that the "Japanese language has no equivalent to the invariant English I: Japanese personal pronoun equivalents linguistically create an ever-shifting field between self and other" (Mathews 1995: 720), Western post-structural theory has eagerly embraced Japan as empirical substantiation of its epistemological and ontological claims. The Japanese expression *jibun ga nai* (I have no self) specifically has been taken as evidence of the "absence" of the individual.

For both cultural anthropologists and post-modern students then, the category of the self in Japan displays a remarkable continuity; the self remains curiously resilient to historical, institutional, and social transformation; there is an underlying continuity in the notion of person from pre-modern to post-modern times in Japan. Where one approvingly sees the resilience of traditional social structures (including the structure of the self) to the onslaught of modernization, the other rejects this periodization of Japanese history (pre-modern, modern, and post-modern) as the hegemony of Western epistemology, preferring to view the Japanese self as inherently de-centered. For both, the claim of continuity in notions of the self poses a problem. For the cultural anthropologist, the problem emanates principally from the emphasis on culture seen independently of other (historical, socio-economic, and political) factors; for the post-modern student, however, the problem is an inconsistency in argument. Post-modern approaches to personhood in Japan, while emphasizing relationality in the construction of identity, have little to offer by way of accounting for changes in the content or meanings attached to different ways of being. If inter-subjectivity as the ground of subjectivity is treated as a substantive rather than processual claim, the range of social meanings that constitute the realm of inter-subjectivity requires specification.[8] While it may be accurate to say the identity of self is always constructed in relation to many others, this in and of itself does not tell us anything about the substantive meanings or identifications that make up the social milieu within which the self and the other relate. Nor does it offer any account of changes in these meanings that result from historical and institutional transformation. To the extent that capitalism engenders new ways of being that fundamentally transforms the ways in which people relate to one another, post-modern attempts to locate an account of subjectivity in an a-historical processual claim about inter-subjectivity renders its claim about the social construction of persons formalistic, insofar as the "social" remains untheorized. Both the meaningful ways of being and the contexts within which these meanings are produced must be addressed.

On the one hand, post-modern arguments favor historicist readings of social phenomenon; most crucially, subjectivity. Because self-formation is viewed as constructed by the rationalities and techne of a variety of agencies, historical change must bear heavily on substantive changes in subjectivity. Inadvertently, however, post-modern accounts tend to reinforce an a-historical orientalized vision of Japan either by grafting a post-modern conceptual schema on conventional anthropological views of Japanese culture or by failing to take into account the role of social institutions, especially those of political economy, in the constitution of personhood in Japan. The de-centered, hybrid self is thus rendered *a priori*, not theorized in relation to the social institutions within which it is constituted. That is, post-modern conceptions historicize forms of hybrid subjectivity while treating the substance of subjectivity a-historically. Both succumb to a-historical treatments of the self in Japan. If subjectivity must be understood in relation to its social conditions of possibility, then the burden of analysis is to detect how changes in the latter bear upon the former. At specific points in time, how is a certain kind of subjectivity sustained/fostered/created, or transformed?

Based on the formulation *jibun ga nai* (I have no self), some scholars have suggested that the Japanese denial of self should be interpreted as a rejection of the modernist conception of personhood. But *jibun ga nai* makes sense only when due recognition is accorded to the significance of context in constructions of selfhood. In Japan, *jibun ga nai* is simply a way of rejecting the possibility of a pre-social, de-contextualized, self-referential notion of personhood, an acknowledgment of the emphasis placed on the relational dimension of selfhood. (The significance of related terms, *kosei* (individuality) and *jinkaku* (humanity), is discussed further along this chapter.)

The idea of the person in Japan, accordingly, must be understood as bearing the distinctive stamp of the vicissitudes of Japan's emergence as a modern capitalist nation-state. Replacing the idiom of familial ties with those of the collectivity, while at the same time facilitating the creation of a modern subjectivity, the ideal of personhood that emerged in modern Japan rested on a separation of the ends production and consumption were to serve. As members of the national polity, the individual's labor was seen as valuable, not because it served individuated interests but, to the contrary, because it contributed to the national goal of economic development. Often seen only as state-sponsored ideology meant to foster Japan's rapid transformation into a self-reliant capitalist economy, the collectivist ends production was meant to serve also laid claim to emergent notions of personhood in modern Japan.

The social inter-dependence only implicit in civil society where each pursues her own end became the explicit premise of Japan's modernity, shaping its collective and individual consciousness such that the production-related activities of civil society came to be seen as the legitimate terrain of the state in pursuit of the preservation of the polity. The state's claim to the production-related activities of civil society was, however, not simply constitutive of the state's "developmental" orientation, as Chalmers Johnson has shown, but also served to delimit the emergent ideal of a specifically modern subjectivity. By emphasizing the social ends production was to serve, the market's individuating consequences were circumscribed to consumption-related activities alone.

Here Pierre Bourdieu's notion of *habitus* may prove helpful in specifying how this seemingly contradictory principle (de-individuated work coupled with individuated consumption) animated social practices. For Bourdieu, the everyday social practices that are both constitutive of and constituted by individuals embody both the structural and the agentic forms that exist in specific societies at a given point in time. He writes,

> Structures tend to reproduce themselves by producing agents invested with the system of dispositions which engender practices adapted to these structures and thus contribute to their reproduction.
> (Bourdieu 1973: 78)[9]

Because the structural principle of Japan's modernity, in its ideal and institutional arrangement, was characterized by a de-individuated productivist vision coupled with individuation consumption, the everyday social practices of the people reflected this dual, seemingly contradictory, principle as normalized and meaningful ways of being. As Bourdieu pointedly notes, "It is because subjects do not, strictly speaking, know what they are doing that what they do has more meaning than they know" (Bourdieu 1973: 79). The antinomies of the tension contained in the principle of Japanese modernity, on the other hand, became periodically explicit: in the fascist attempt in the 1930s to hegemonize the collectivist vision by stamping out the individualistic strain; the attempt by post-war intellectuals to remake Japanese into modern democratic citizens via the promotion of *shutasei* (individual autonomy); Prime Minister Ikeda's "Income Doubling Plan" in 1960 that attempted to bind the polity even closer by reclaiming consumption as the terrain of a nationalist, rather than individual project; the ANPO riots in the same year that sought to resist the statist productivist ideology by espousing the democratic potential contained in individualism and rationalism.

That the welfare state reflected this principle as well was no accident of history, rather it served as a powerful mechanism of instituting this ideal of personhood within society at large. In this sense, attention to the institutional context of subjectivity in modern Japan serves to augment the notion of the "situational or relational self" understood now as referring to clearly demarcated zones of individuated expression: production-related activities are expressive of the corporate or state-oriented self, consumption constitutes the socially legitimate terrain of the individuated self. In recovering analytically the emergence of individualism in Japan, the market's constitutive role in crafting a modern subject in Japan must be understood in the context of Japan's transition to capitalism. The individuating thrust of consumption is not contingent on Japan's post-war economic affluence, or the result of Western style consumerism evident in the phenomenon of the *shinjinrui*, as many have suggested, but rather the very basis of the creation of a modern subject in Japan's emergent capitalism in the late nineteenth and early twentieth centuries.

The remainder of this chapter attempts to substantiate the claim made here. Rejecting essentialist understandings of the idea of the person in Japan as group oriented, or as the effect of determinations by the state, I attempt to show how the parameters of the self, the social meanings and forms of life that make individuated meaning possible (or social self-determination), were de-limited by the specific institutional form modernity took in Japan. The domestic and international contexts within which the institutional arrangements of Japanese modernity, specifically civil society, were crafted gave rise to a distinctive view of the person. Correspondingly, the idea of welfare too bore the imprint of Japan's particular arrangement of modernity. It is within this specification of the self in political economy that the normative and institutional structure of modern Japan's welfare state is more readily understood.

State, civil society, and the individual: An historical sketch

This section begins with a brief sketch of Japan's passage to modernity, focusing especially on the nature of the reforms undertaken by the Meiji leaders beginning in 1868. The objective here is to map briefly the historical circumstances, domestic and international, that help account for the nature of Japan's modern state and civil society. I then take up the question of how the newly institutionalized state and civil society promoted and shaped a distinct view of the subject in accordance with the productionist drive that animated Japan's vision of modernity. The next chapter discusses the pattern of welfare in Japan to show how it is both reflective and constitutive of the concept of the modern subject developed here.

Japan's passage to modernity in the mid-nineteenth century was the result of processes already at work during the latter part of Tokugawa (1603–1868), the feudal era immediately preceding the advent of Japan's modernization with the Meiji Restoration (1868). Specifically, the growing marketization of the economy, the development of proto-industrial enterprises, the unraveling of the rigid social structure put in place by the *shogunate* evidenced in the increasing strength of the merchant class, and the spread of education during the Tokugawa regime, most scholars concur, had created the conditions necessary for the emergence of a differentiated socio-economic structure.

The nature of the modern state and civil society that took shape in the late nineteenth/early twentieth centuries marked neither a simple continuation of old patterns nor a total rupture with the *ancien regime*. Rather, as Najita (1993) has argued, although the leaders that crafted Japan's modern institutions were products and bearers of the epistemologies of the Tokugawa era, many of the old epistemologies were in the process of being radically reworked by the end of the Tokugawa era.[10] Key among these included state, economy, and personhood.

By the end of the Tokugawa period, new notions of *kuni* (country), *kokka* (state), and *kogi* (public realm) denoted an emergent consciousness of Japanese collective and cultural identity, the construction of clear geographic boundaries of the state, and the relation of state boundaries to those of the Japanese ethnic or national collectivity.[11] This emergent sense of Japan as a national collectivity was developed in a specific direction by Meiji leaders, which enabled it to crystallize into a pragmatic program of modernity in a relatively short span of time.

It was, however, the forced opening of Japan in 1853 that provided the immediate catalyst for change. Ending over 250 years of seclusion, Commodore Perry's arrival on the shores of Japan in 1853 activated latent discontent with the Tokugawa Shogunate. A broad coalition of social groups led by the *samurai* (warrior aristocracy) successfully ousted the *shogunate*, leading to the imperial restoration of 1868. Faced with an impending military threat, its sense of vulnerability heightened by a sensitivity to the fate that had befallen neighboring China, the new leaders of Japan quickly attempted to put in place processes that would generate rapid industrialization and militarization. The motto of early Meiji was, "save the emperor, expel the barbarian," the latter being an urgent call to arms for modernization. Key to achieving rapid military and economic self-sufficiency was the need to mobilize people by fostering a distinctive national consciousness.

It was in this context that a series of reforms were undertaken, patterned in part on Western models, with the aim of achieving *bunmei kaika* (civilization and enlightenment) and transforming Japan from a centralized feudal society to a seemingly modern industrialized democracy. The *daimyo* (nobles) voluntarily surrendered titles to their *han* (fiefs), the *samurai* relinquished their elite status, with the result that as early as 1871 the formal structures of feudalism were dismantled; a democratic constitution drafted in 1881 and implemented by 1889 created a citizenry equal in the eyes of the law, divesting all social classes of their markers of relative status. The "abolition of almost all the ascriptive hierarchical social restrictions that had prevailed in

Tokugawa society"[12] created the conditions for the fashioning of the modern subject. In addition, the establishment of a national police system, universal military conscription, and a national educational system provided the channels by which the "values and ideology" of the new regime with its strong emphases on nationhood and progress could be instilled in the people.

It is no coincidence that the constitution reflected the Germanic and Austrian sacralization of the state that had so impressed Ito Hirobumi, the key figure in the Commission assigned the task of drafting it. Consistent with the norms of Japanese thinking promoted at the time, which attributed all moral and spiritual authority to the *Tenno* (emperor), the idealization of the state in Germany and Austria was quickly adopted as the rationale for the creation of a modern state. In its emergence as, what James Fulcher (1988) has called, a "bureaucratized state" the principles undergirding the modern state were premised on an explicit recognition of the moral authority of the state.

Within two short decades, Japan had taken the form of government recognizable to the West: a parliamentary democracy that recognized the equality of all by construing members as citizens. That the new constitution was bestowed as a gift by the emperor whose divinity continued to be upheld by the new form of government is indicative of the tensions contained in Japan's bid to recreate itself, within a very short period of time, in the image of the Western powers.

The transformation of Japan's economy is a more contentious issue. Its transition to a capitalist form of organization was already ongoing: Perry's arrival simply accelerated a process already underway. With a money economy in place since the early thirteenth century, Japan emerged from its feudal phase with roughly 80 percent of its working population employed in agricultural activity, and about 5 percent in manufacturing.[13] As Rozman has shown, the urban population of Japan grew almost 400 percent over two centuries of Tokugawa rule with roughly 30 percent (of about 32 million) in urban areas (towns and cities) by the end of the Tokugawa period.[14] Osaka, as a thriving center of commerce, ranked as one of the largest cities in the world in the early nineteenth century, Edo (Tokyo), the most populous by 1800.[15] Although a commodity economy was already in place, along with a money and credit system, Japan lacked an industrial base.[16]

With the change in the legal bases of ownership of property instituted by the Meiji oligarchs, the private ownership of land and the full legalization of private property completed a process already underway. All local barriers to trade were eliminated and property rights in land open to all without discrimination. The revision of the land tax *chiso-kaisei* (land tax) created a uniform (3 percent) tax rate and legalized the holdings of the peasantry.[17] The commoditization of land coupled with the relatively high levels of agricultural productivity reached by the late Tokugawa period resulted in strengthening the ownership rights of peasants, either as tenant or as proprietors, despite a rise in taxes as the Meiji state turned to the peasantry as its source of primitive accumulation. As a result, as Moore, citing E.H. Norman's classic work, observes,

> there was no huge exodus to the cities...the continuing rise in agricultural productivity was vital in making the whole transition bearable...one consequence...was that there was no great hunger in the towns to produce plebeian(s)...the advent of the market actually gave landed property to the poorer ranks of the peasants.
>
> (Moore 1983: 272–273)

The creation of conditions for the emergence of an urban proletariat and competitive capitalist enterprises was further accelerated by the Meiji state's initiation of economic activities. Ex *samurai* and *daimyo* received state subsidies to begin industrial ventures; entrepreneurship by "politically privileged"[18] merchants and ex-*samurai* was encouraged via state loans; state-owned enterprises were created in railways, postal services, telephone and telegraph, and iron and steel production; basic industries were set up by the state and then sold to what would come to be known as *zaibatsu* (Kawasaki, Sumitomo, and Mitsui); state subsidies were provided for heavy industry such as shipping; a national banking system was devised in 1872, and several private banks and finance companies increased rapidly until 1884;[19] and the creation of joint-stock companies was encouraged leading to the creation of new *zaibatsu* (Nissan, Nisao, Mori, and Riken).[20] By 1902, Japan had 8612 companies, 84 percent of which were founded in the few years following the Sino-Japanese war in 1894–1895[21]. Imperialist wars of expansion within the first two decades of the *Meiji Ishin* not only served to place Japan in the ranks of imperialist great powers, but more importantly served as a significant source of revenue.[22]

The *daimyo*–merchant–*samurai* coalition that had led the *Meiji Ishin* now became the key players in the government–business nexus upon which the industrial edifice was built. By the 1890s, Japanese finance and industrial capital had developed enough to begin competing successfully with Western industrial powers at least in some areas, most notably textiles, resulting in a major expansion of the workforce (the vast majority of Japanese factory workers were employed in textiles before World War I). The nationalist motivations that propelled the industrialization drive meant too that war-related machinery and tool-making industries were given priority.

The overarching principle that animated both the emergent state and civil society, however, was elaborated not in terms of individualism, as had been the case in Europe, but rather in the service of the national collectivity. Even as Meiji intellectuals debated the virtues of adopting Western ideas, those whose views prevailed in shaping public policy emphasized the link between modern notions of patriotism, education, the achievement principle, and so on, and the greater good of the social and political order. As Eisenstadt notes,

> Modernization, especially of the economy was of paramount importance, with its accompanying emphasis on diligence, fortitude, and achievement, not due to the expressive individualism it unleashed, nor because it provided the means to a transcendent universalism but due to its "functional contribution" to the collectivity.
>
> (Eisenstadt 1996: 34)

Labor and the sacralized work-ethic that accompanied it became the centerpiece of a productionist ethos which placed labor in service of neither the capital, or a divine being, nor, for that matter, the individual himself, but in service of the collectivity.

At the heart of the notion of collectivity was the emperor – extolled as the very embodiment of the Japanese nation. Drawing from the nativistic schools of the Tokugawa period, the emperor-centered *kokutai* was neither a natural progression of past thinking nor wholly new. It represented rather the crystallization of a modern ideology, a way of thinking that allowed Japan to contain, and therefore manage, the Western threat such that the promotion of national identity would not just provide a xenophobic, reactionary response, but would rather enable the articulation of a dynamic program of modernity. As Ikegami (1995) has so convincingly shown, this ideology did not emerge immediately, marking an unproblematic continuity between past and present, but culminated as a series of responses to competing visions and protests that the Meiji leaders had to negotiate.

In the face of an imminent Western military threat, the compulsion to modernize required not only economic and military self-sufficiency, but the institutionalization of laws along Western lines, specially those that recognized property rights within the framework of a modern legal and judicial system. The newly sacralized *tenno* system was meant to evoke a commitment to the collectivity, the "spiritual component of nationhood," distinct from its political form (*seitai*) which, because it was subject to change, could not be made the repository of national feeling needed to mobilize the people to the hard work of building a modern nation-state.[23] While institutionalizing egalitarian laws modeled on those of the "modern," (so as to better facilitate the creation of a conscripted army and a labor force), the new constitution of 1889 replaced the term *kokumin* (citizen) with the term *shimin* (subjects) in an attempt to ground national identity in relation to the *tenno*. The tension between the newly enfranchised citizenry of Meiji Japan and the *tenno* system was embodied in the juridicial creation of the individual as the subject of the modern Japanese state, even as the interest the individual was meant to serve was a predominantly public one. This tension became the centerpiece of Japan's passage to modernity: as its structural principle, it informed both the emergent state and civil society, giving shape to a modern Japan whose contradictions would later appear to elude analysis.

The alignment of production to the greater social (and political) good of the collectivity generated a discourse in Meiji (1868–1912) and Taisho (1912–1926) Japan that was predominantly state centered. This program of modernization was accompanied by "the development of new conceptions of man, woman, the human body, the family, and gender relations... all grounded in the distinctly modern legitimation of the State."[24] The private individual, as understood in the West, was not recognized as the subject or agent of modernity in Japan. Rather, in occupying the social roles especially valorized by the state (especially labor), the individual's predominant orientation was to the state. This is clearly discernable in the way gender roles were defined in Meiji Japan, "not as in many Western countries with a strong emphasis on the private family as against the public order, but as agents of the state. This was manifested in the strong orientations of women's movements to the state."[25]

The Meiji state thus attempted to craft a modern nation by channeling society's primordial communal identifications toward the state via an ideology that imbued economic development with moral fervor by virtue of its link to the polity. This effort, however, was fraught with contradiction. It sought to inculcate a collectivist ethos by promoting a form of economic development – capitalism – whose inherently individualistic logic, however, threatened to subvert the very ideals it was meant to foster. This tension began to surface during the Taisho period (1912–1926), with Japan's increasing economic prosperity visible in the consumption of luxuries. The state launched a campaign to foster National Strength (*Minryoku Kan'yo Undo*) attempting to reform the habits of "luxury and self-indulgence" that developed as a result of Japan's rapid economic expansion during World War I. Meiji leaders emphasized the virtues of "practability" as an antidote to the materialism and principled individualism they equated with the egotistical orientation that characterized Western societies.

The individuating logic unleashed by the transformation of Japan's political economy, however, could not be fully contained. Scholars of early Showa note the rising expression of individualism in art, literature, sports, and most of all consumption. The dominant literary form of prose fiction changed from *gesaku* (playful writing) to the *shosetsu* in the Meiji era. From about 1890, the appearance of the "I" form of novel, whose protagonist was typically a "superfluous man, alienated and introspective," marked a change in consciousness. As Miyoshi Masao notes, "unlike the hero in Edo fiction, the later hero is not just a name, but an interior space that reflects on itself."[26] Futabatei's *Ukigumo*, Natsume Soseki's *Kokoro*, and Dazai's *The Setting Sun* heralded the emergence of a self-declared *shutaisei* (individuality) in the face of an overwhelming attempt by the state to mold subjectivities in keeping with its agenda. While some have interpreted the *shotesu* or I novel as a formal insistence on the "I" in contrast with the ideological suppression of the self by the state, its widespread popularity at the time testifies to the expressive individualism at play in Japanese society at the time. The simultaneous emergence of a consumerist ethos and the "I" novel was not simply coincidental, a superficial imitation of Western culture and trends, but was rather symptomatic of the individuating logic of capitalism at work in Japanese society.[27]

Nor was this logic as effectively managed or suppressed by the state as many scholars are wont to argue. Although the state strenuously attempted to mitigate what it perceived to be the behavior that undermined its agenda to foster a state-/collectivity-centered consciousness, arguments that focus on its pragmatic efforts to manage and circumscribe this expression tend to attribute an undue prescience to the state, while making an essentially functionalist argument. Rather than viewing the simultaneous existence of a productivist state ideology and the flourishing of this highly commodified consumer culture as a "tension"[28] that needed resolution via either state management or societal resistance, it may be more fruitful to view one as necessitating the other. Different elements of a collective consciousness at a given moment in time incorporate a specific logic, a constitutive principle that provides the underlying link between seemingly disparate and opposing elements. Accordingly, the two different elements stand in a necessary not contingent relation to one another. In this case, to treat the state's productivist ideology and the expressive individuation related to consumption as inherently (i.e. logically) opposed phenomena is to misunderstand the connection between the two.

The relation between the productivist ethos fostered by the state and the individuated expression via consumption can be thus understood to be constitutive of the structural, institutional, and behavioral logic of capitalism in Japan. What is distinctive about capitalism in Japan is not, as in conventional accounts, that it has been crafted by a "developmental state," nor that it is, equally remarkably, an instance of a hyper "exploitative and manipulative" system, but rather that it is structured around the identification of specific zones of social life with collectivist ends and others with individuating ends. It is this dual determination contained within the logic of Japanese capitalism that gives it both its dynamism and its complexity.

The Meiji state indeed took on a developmental orientation but within the confines of the historical agentic and structural forms existent in Japan at the time. Tokugawa Japan was proto-capitalist, displaying at least in incipient form the logic attendant on the production of a surplus, urbanization, and a vibrant commercial economy. An individuating logic of consumption was already latently at work within the social fabric of Japan at the time of the *Meiji* Restoration. The *Meiji* state did not then simply create the institutions and social practices of civil society out of thin air, as it were, in accordance with their wholly productionist ideology, which individuated consumption threatened to undermine. Rather, the state's role may be better understood as drawing upon an existent communal ideal of personhood and deploying it in service of a productionist ideology, legitimated in nationalist terms, but at the same time leaving an emergent subjectivity related to consumption as a circumscribed zone of individuation within civil society. As the following chapter shows, welfare is but one congealed expression of this logic.

The civil society that emerged in the *Meiji* (1868–1912) era and crystallized in the *Taisho* (1912–1926) and early *Showa* (1926–1989) periods, exhibited two distinct, though related, aspects. On the one hand, the state's economic plans, discourses about labor and production, and the organization of the workplace all combined to foster a subjectivity that linked work to the polity. On the other, the newly created realm of a specifically capitalist form of consumption became the realm within which an individuated mode of being could be constituted and expressed.

Capitalist production as initiated by the Meiji oligarchs was in its very inception an enterprise that hinged on collective will and a consciousness of the primacy of the collective over the individual. What distinguished first the Meiji and then the post-war enterprise, however, was the attempt to foster capitalist development on de-individuated terms. In this context, Peter Duus and Daniel Okimoto (1979) note,

> The Meiji oligarchs had pursued economic growth through the initiative of private capital (with government assistance and direction, to be sure) while promoting an anticapitalist ethic through the educational system. The strains of this cultural dissonance produced the rampant "Japanist" and "restorationist" movements of the 1920s and 1930s, and to a large extent facilitated the downfall of the business-dominated party regimes.
>
> (Duus and Okimoto 1979: 69)

However, the Meiji oligarchs' primary emphasis was on ensuring that capitalist production fostered a collectivist ethos; an individuated expression in non-production-centered activities, while not explicitly fostered, was not actively suppressed. This is corroborated by the attempt in the 1930s (the fascist period) to temper the individuating impulse unleashed by capitalism. Duus and Okimoto (1979) continue,

> The intellectuals of the 1930s proposed to deal with this contradiction by creating a social order that modulated the profit-seeking impulses of the capitalists (and the wage-seeking impulses of the proletariat) by simplifying the social structure, and by eliminating the market mechanism as the principal means for the allocation and distribution of goods. They wished to achieve social harmony and consensus with institutional reforms that *contained and redirected individual materialistic motives in the name of higher collective purposes rather than through appeals to traditional "collectivist values"* (emphasis added). A consistent intellectual theme of the late 1930s stressed the virtues of *kyodo* – cooperation, and the suppression of individual needs or wants to further the goals of the collectivity.
>
> (Duus and Okimoto 1979: 69–70)

This structuring principle, de-individuated work oriented to the collectivity and individuated consumption, was further entrenched in the post-war era as the state attempted to negotiate labor militancy in the 1940s and 1950s. The claim that capitalist development, specifically production-related activities, constitutes the centerpiece of Japan's modern collective consciousness[29] has long been seen as foundational to the study of modern Japan. It has provided the subject of sustained commentary in the field of Japan Studies ever since the economic "miracle" of the 1960s and 1970s. Without rehearsing at length all the various ways in which this claim can be historically and empirically borne out, I will simply highlight here some of the more striking ways in which the link between production and the national polity, rather than individuated consciousness, has been fostered in modern Japan.

The creation of a collective consciousness that linked work to the national/collective interest was, in large part, the result of specific measures undertaken by both state and firms (Vogel 1963; Dore 1973; Rohlen 1974; Kondo, 1990). Firms provided a system of permanent employment, seniority wage, and enterprise unionism, often dubbed "the three jewels of Japanese management," which together constituted an effective institutional mechanism for creating subjectivities in which consciousness of the collectivity – corporate and state – predominates. I will explain each of these only briefly, since their role in generating company and national loyalty in relation to productivity is well known and widely accepted in the Japan field.

Of the three, the most effective means of coupling self-interest and work to the collective interest of corporation and state was the *shushin-koyo* or lifetime employment practice that became dominant in the 1950s. Permanent employment (the practice of recruiting employees from high school or university every spring and retaining them until retirement at between 55 and 60 years of age) (Clark 1979; Abegglen 1958), although formally guaranteed to only about 35 percent of the (predominantly male) workforce, has worked to produce a general climate in which even the second tier of the workforce, (mostly in a subcontracting role), although vulnerable to market forces, enjoy longer tenures on average than in other OECD countries. Initiated as a way of defusing militant labor strikes and trade unionism, the benefits of permanent employment are not formalized via contract but provide the basis for the conventions of the relationship between labor and capital. The system of permanent employment has minimized involuntary turnover for all workers in Japan,[30] and enhanced in-group solidarity within corporations. Also, as Harcourt notes, "a high degree of insularity is reinforced through policies of welfare capitalism, whereby some firms provide their employees with special medical, recreational, and housing facilities" (Harcourt 1996: 187). The reluctance to undo the lifetime employment system even during the recessionary decade of the 1990s is also instructive (see Schoppa 2006 and Ono 2005). I take up this point in Chapter 5.

The sense that corporations constitute an intermediate form of *ie* between the actual familial unit (the original *ie*) and the collectivity as the overarching paternal *ie* is inscribed in the social practices of life within corporations.[31] In part the product of the length of tenure of employees, group solidarity is further entrenched as the result of the nature of inter-personal relations characteristic of the workplace. Bound by relations of *amae* or what may be loosely translated as "benevolent hierarchy," the rigid recognition of situational hierarchy between seniors and juniors is mediated by an expectational structure that the former will act benevolently toward the latter. Because of this, the ethos of the workplace works first and foremost to engender a consciousness of the primacy of the collectivity (corporate and state). Indeed, there is a Japanese expression, *marugakae*, which means "totally enveloped," indicating that employers do not hire a man for his labor alone, they hire the total man.[32]

The seniority wage system (*nenko*) in which increases in salaries are tied to the number of years an employee has been with a firm, rather than individual talent or merit (a system that began in the pre-war years as a means of ensuring worker loyalty), also contributes to curtailing labor mobility. Since workers have to begin at the bottom of the pay structure if they choose to switch jobs, employee retention is high, rewarding the investments made in human capital by companies at all levels. Moreover, enterprise unionism, another distinctive feature of Japanese management, based on vertical rather than horizontal integration within, not across, firms, includes white- and blue-collar workers, and minimizes the differences among employees of different status and category while simultaneously serving to create an internal labor market within firms resulting in a corporatist relation between employer and employees. Enterprise unions contribute significantly toward producing a climate that emphasizes the notion of the well-being of the collectivity (in this case the firm) as opposed to individual self-interest. Seen as critical to the improvement of workers' material status, via the annual *Shunto* (Spring wage offensive) negotiations, enterprise unionism is often credited with redistributing some of the firms' wealth to employees.[33] The Japanese company, in other words, large and small, was set up as "a community of people who share a common destiny (*unmei kyodotai*)" (Kondo 1990: 161).

These three "jewels" of the Japanese employment system have been alternatively seen as the result of naturalistic Japanese culture, with its emphasis on familism or, in economistic/functional terms, rationalism on the part of industrialists who voluntarily enacted employee-welfare measures in a bid to counteract the challenges posed by the militant trade unionism and labor strife that characterized industrial relations in Japan in the 1940s and 1950s. However, as Linda Weiss[34] has shown, key to understanding the development of these measures was the state's role. In keeping with the dictates of its objective needs of industrialization and militarization, the state, ever since the Meiji Restoration, played a direct role not only in orienting a public discourse about production in service of the collectivity but rather by shaping the institutional arrangements of civil society so as to serve better its nationalist/military agenda. Included in its various efforts, some of which are documented above, was the development of novel labor management schemes through what came to be known as company welfare, first instituted in state-held companies as early as the 1920s, and subsequently transmitted to the private sector by (a) the privatization of state-held companies; and (b) the enforcement of state legislation regarding the universal provision of company-based benefits to all workers alike in the post-war period.

The nationalist cast capitalist development necessarily took, in light of which the state's direct hand in organizing market processes can be more fully grasped with a cursory look at some key indicators. Japan's industrialization drive took place in a span of some 50 years when it fought four major wars: the Sino-Japanese War of 1894–1895, the Russo-Japanese War of 1904, the Sino-Japanese War beginning in 1937, and the Pacific war of 1941–1945. Weiss notes,

> By the end of the Russo-Japanese war, more than two-thirds of the work force employed in the nation's engineering works was located in the state sector. By the end of the nineteenth century, almost 70 percent of industrial output and employment was concentrated in ship-building, iron and steel, and weapons manufacture, metals mining and processing, silk weaving and cotton spinning.
>
> (Weiss 1993: 334)

Concerned with the high turnover rate (as much as 200 percent in the 1880s), the state-run enterprises, especially in shipbuilding and armaments, began to offer inducements to a core group of technicians, including long-term contracts, a length-of-service reward system (the origin of the *nenko* – seniority wage system), and non-wage benefits conditional on length of service to the firm (what would come to be recognized as non-statutory enterprise welfare); the first major union was developed in the Tokyo Armaments Works, a state-run enterprise. These measures were transmitted to the private sector mostly by state legislation beginning with the Factory Law of 1911 and 1923 (discussed more fully in the next chapter) and the Health Insurance Law of 1922, but also by the sale of state-owned enterprises whose employment practices "were very likely carried over into private industry" (Weiss 1993:336). The Retirement Fund Law enacted in 1937 required all companies employing over 50 workers (roughly covering two-thirds of the nation's workforce) to establish funds for retirement-cum-severance pay. This measure, one of the largest components of company-based welfare, in effect extended company welfare privileges that were typically reserved for white-collar workers (in common with the practice in several OECD countries today) to the majority of blue-collar workers as well, a feature that is indeed distinctive to Japan. The impulse came largely from the new sense of urgency brought on by the beginning of the Japan's incursion into China in 1931. The Pacific War further heightened Japan's need for a skilled and healthy workforce, leading (as we will see in the next chapter) to the creation of the Ministry of Welfare in 1938 with General Koizumi, the former chief of the Army Medical Bureau, as its new Minister.

This brief overview of the state's role in mandating company welfare schemes is thus illustrative of the close nexus between Japan's military/national and industrialization needs in the late nineteenth and early twentieth centuries, key to understanding the form and structure that civil society took. That the institutions and social practices of civil society did not simply foster an ideology of collectivism but indeed objectively reflected this disposition is of vital significance. By locating the firm and all (not just the elite, white-collar) workers within a universally applicable discourse of collectivism, the productionist ethos that was thereby inculcated was a remarkably inclusive one, incorporating all social classes. The continuation of this collectivist ethos in the post-war period was ensured not only by the adoption of these employment practices by the majority of firms, large and small, but also by the state's indirect influence through the courts. Again, as Weiss paraphrasing the Japanese economist Kazutoshi Koshiro notes, "both the civil law and labor standards law make it virtually impossible to terminate an employment contract without notice. But even with such notice, court decisions, based on legal theory, have tended to restrict enormously the employer's right to dismissal" (Weiss 1993: 348). In addition, non-statutory company benefits have been made tax deductible, including retirement funds, commuting, and meal allowances. In sum, the institutions and social practices of civil society in modern Japan have been constructed so as to foster a collectivist ethos resulting in a milieu in which work appears predominantly as a de-individuated realm of activity, oriented to the firm/state (and until its constitutional revision during the occupation years), the *tenno*, and the collectivity.

Yet another indicator of the deliberate attempt to foster a collective productivist ethos not only by government officials but also by agents within civil society is the New Life Movement that originated in 1953 as an attempt to rationalize family life to enhance productivity in the workplace. Geared specifically to the creation of efficient, modern housewife, valued as household manager and consumer, to enhance her husband's status as producer in the workplace, the New Life Movement was, Andrew Gordon[35] notes,

> a chapter in the history of the ascendancy of the "enterprise society" (*kigyo shakai*) in Japan. By this term, I mean, a society where meeting the needs of the corporation is "naturally" understood to be social common sense and to be congruent with meeting the needs of all society's inhabitants.
>
> (Gordon 1997: 247)

This movement had its antecedents in the interwar era in the campaigns organized by both women's associations as well as government agencies to "improve daily life" (Gordon 1997: 248). What is striking about this effort was that it solicited not just support at the grassroots level in villages and prefectures all over Japan, corporations, but also the active support of several ministries, including the Education Ministry, the Ministry of Agriculture and Forestry, and the Health and Welfare Ministry, indicating the society-wide attempt to rationalize both the household and the industry such that the former might better facilitate the national productivist agenda.

This state–society-wide attempt to orient all activity toward the urgent task of nation-building, primarily by focusing the collective will and energy to production, is further highlighted by the following quote:

> It found expression even in the most mundane practices. Thus the eating of beef was publicly promoted in order to "create energy for the performance of patriotic duties and strengthen the national

> physique." Even the adoption of Western-style trousers in place of flowing robes was prescribed for official occasions, with the injunction that "people must not be soft, but must strive to build up a martial state."
>
> (Weiss 1993: 333)

This emphasis on the nexus between the collectivity and the workplace has been well documented in Dorinne Kondo's (1990) work on *Crafting Selves*.[36] Arguing that the ideologies surrounding labor and production have tended to emphasize the group, Kondo attempts to show how the *soto* (outside), *tatemae* (outer), and *omote* (front) contexts of the workplace are subverted by the insertion of *uchi* (inside), *honne* (inner), and *ura* (back) type behaviors, enabling the crafting of an individuated self in the de-individuated realm of work in modern Japan. For Kondo, it is precisely the association of labor with the collectivity, with its concomitant norms of formality, self-restraint, and discipline, against which informality and expressions of selfhood appear as the assertion of self. On this account, the self does not express or realize itself in the concrete labor it engages in on a daily basis; rather self-expression necessarily entails resisting the normalizing practices of the workplace that mark labor explicitly as a de-individuated realm in service of the collectivity. Kondo's work thus serves as a preliminary substantiation of the broad claim made here about the social meaning attached to production vis-à-vis personhood in modern Japan.

Within the realm of consumption, on the other hand, the expressive individuation at work within society was both widely recognized and accepted. This is evident in the mass culture that emerged as well as the state programs crafted to desist individuated expression within civil society because it threatened to undermine its collectivist project.

The industrialization that began in the first two decades following the *Meiji Ishin* quickly created a consuming class. By the end of World War I, white-collar consumers comprised 10 percent of the population, although small shopkeepers and factory workers also made up a significant proportion of consumers, especially between 1919 and 1922, as actual wages rose and the level of consumption increased by 160 percent.[37] Drawing from Ishikawa Hiroyoshi's cultural history, Silverberg notes the emergence of "social, cultural desires" for the "skilled laborer who enjoyed such forms as leisure, sports, travel, and reading from the 1920s onward."[38] Although a vibrant popular culture based on consumption was already evident in the urban centers of Tokugawa Japan (1603–1868, especially in Edo and Osaka),

> the creation of a large-scale consumption society as early as the 1910s and 1920s paralleled developments in the United States, as much of an emergent global culture of consumption was patterned on American developments (indeed America was the prime exporter not only of industrial production techniques and goods but also of technologies of desire and consumption, mass marketing techniques, and forms of display).
>
> (Ivy 1993: 242)

That the advent of industrial capitalism would give rise to a consuming class, evidenced in the sheer velocity of the circulation of cultural commodities (6.3 million newspapers; 813 movie theaters), and grandiose department store openings like those of *Mitsukoshi* and *Shirokiya*) becomes intelligible. The appearance of the *mobo* and *moga* (modern boy and modern girl), avant-garde, vaudeville, and domestic and international tourism in the early 1900s all bespoke an increasing consumption of varied and individuated commodities and lifestyles.[39] As Tobin notes,

> By the 1920s, as the Meiji military and industrial sectors accelerated their imitation of and competition with the technological accomplishments of the Western powers, privileged youth in Tokyo and Osaka were playing out their own version of the nihilistic, hedonistic life-style of the West's jazz age. In addition to the Folies Bergere and the tango, the westernized decadent youth of Tokyo embraced jazz, gin, movies, and baseball.... "ero-guro-nonsensu," the erotic-grotesque frivolity associated with the west.
>
> (Tobin 1992: 21–22)

This new cultural style was representative, Maruyama Masao suggests, "of emancipating the individual citizen willingly or unwillingly from the communal ties which have hitherto bound him and which have prescribed to him certain tradition behavior" (cited in Tobin 1992: 22). The privatization and atomization that characterized people, especially intellectuals, at this time was reflected, albeit in more diffuse form, in the attempt by people from the middle class to move out of family households into suburban *bunka jutaku* (cultural residences), the precursor to the *mai homu* (my home) phenomenon of the 1960s.

This modern subjectivity gained a renewed legitimacy, following the attempt in the 1930s to suppress it, in the post-war era in the promotion of *shutaisei* (autonomy and individualistic consciousness). As Victor

Koschmann has so convincingly shown, post-war intellectuals in their effort to come to terms with the fascist debacle and Japan's war-time defeat attempted to delineate, albeit within the parameters of a predominantly Marxian discourse, the subject of a democratic Japan. Arguing that Japan could overcome the vicissitudes of its political and military past only by the creation of a new consciousness based on an individualism that alone could generate and sustain democracy in Japan, the post-war period was marked by a widespread attempt to counter the statist discourse of collectivism. This was most sharply exemplified in the ANPO movement in 1960.

Beginning as a struggle against the renewal of the US–Japan Security Treaty, and culminating in a general strike by 4 million workers, the movement drew upon a wide social base including labor unions, the Socialist party, women's groups, and cultural organizations. It was particularly noteworthy for its strong popular support for rapid economic growth, but also for "individualism, rationalism, consumerism, and the domestic happiness associated with *mai-homu* (my home)." (Koschmann 1993: 406).

This celebration of individuated desire, apparent as shown above, as a discourse of opposition to statist promotions of collectivism, in other instances as the hallmark of a truly modern Japan, took on a sharper, more tangible, expression in the 1970s and 1980s during the economic boom. The opening of the first supermarket *Daiei* in 1957 heralded the beginning of the distribution revolution that was later to compel over 90 percent of all Japanese to identify themselves as middle class based on the goods consumed. With the drive to enhance domestic spending in full swing in the wake of Prime Minister Ikeda's Income Doubling Plan of 1960 – the middle-class life associated with the telephone, refrigerator, and a Japanese style-bath – the television-owning population rose from less than 1 percent in 1956 to 50 percent in 1960. With the consuming lifestyle associated with *mai homu*, there can be no doubt that individuation in Japan was placed squarely within the terrain of consumption.

Several scholars have noted how the middle-class lifestyle served simultaneously to differentiate and homogenize, emphasizing the homogenizing aspects of consumption in Japan in contrast with their individuating consequences elsewhere. Thus Ivy, echoing a view that is fairly widespread in discussions of the meanings attached to consumption in Japan, observes,

> Japanese domestic space . . . became a "concretized metaphorical scene" of social equality: if every household contained the same electrical appliances in similarly constructed domestic spaces, then households were democratically equalized . . . [S]ome view this process as one of. . . . privatization, a dangerous shrinking of social networks and forms of association into the modular confines of "my home" (*mai homu*). The contradiction of privatization lies in this: the more one thinks that a secure private sphere has been constructed – using the home, family, and consumer goods as the basis – the more the bureaucratized, technocratic public sphere has succeeded in consolidating its control
>
> (Ivy 1993: 249–250)

Tomiko Yoda notes, "Although an active consumer society already existed in key areas of urban areas of prewar Japan, it was through the postwar economic growth that it was generalized throughout the nation. The separation of home from work . . . occurred under the ever-increasing importance of domestic life for Japan's economic expansion," and further, "the domestic life of Japanese workers . . . became vital mediums for consumption" (Yoda 2000).

In the wake of the economic miracle of the 1960s and 1970s, the claim that consumption in Japan individuates has come to be widely accepted (Kondo 1990; Kelly 1991; Tobin 1992; Rosenberger 1994; 2001; Ivy 1995). Several scholars have argued that individuation is of recent vintage in Japan, a consequence of the consumer ethos that developed as a result of Japan's rapid economic success.[40] Some recent studies see the *shinjinrui* (the new breed, or consuming class) as emblematic of the nexus between the new consumerism and individuation (Fuchino 1988; Iwao 1988; Nakano 1988; Anderson and Wadkins 1991). A similar claim, repudiating the individuating impulse central to capitalist consumption in general, in the case of Japan, is echoed by Tomiko Yoda who associates the bubble economy of the late 1980s as "marking the completion of the society's shift from the culture of mass consumption (and mass-produced goods) to that of individuated consumption" (Yoda 2000).

> The *shinjinrui* are characterized by personal ambition, an appreciation for the "good life," and an emphasis on individuality and self actualization. A rising level of affluence expanded buying power. But perhaps most significant was the development of limitless demand. A major factor in the proliferation of wants was the linkage of consumer goods with self-hood.
>
> (Anderson and Wadkins 1991: 129)

Central to this analysis of contemporary Japan is the view that "a culture of consumption" shifts the primary basis of identity formation from production to consumption. As Anderson and Wadkins (1991), summarizing this view, put it, "An individual's identity is tied to what one consumes rather than a production culture where an individual's identity is more tied to what one produces." Comparisons with American culture as well as post-modern analyses of the consumer as the social subject of a post-industrial society in which manufacturing and therefore concrete forms of labors lose their constitutive role vis-à-vis identity formation are implicit in this view of Japan.

While this formulation correctly grasps the sense of immediacy surrounding consumption in contemporary Japan, as in other advanced capitalist societies, it mistakenly takes a heightened scale of consumption as indicative of a shift from Japan's alleged socio-centeredness to individualism. By framing consumption as a new phenomenon in Japan, this view fails to take into account the individuating logic inherent in capitalism. The individuating moment appears with the creation of civil society in Japan; the frenetic pace of consumption palpable in contemporary Japan better seen as a heightened expression of a process that has long been underway in Japan rather than a novel phenomenon altogether. Several issues are at stake here. One has to do with mistaking an empirically robust manifestation of the individuating logic of consumption for a theoretically novel phenomenon. The nexus between consumerism and individuation is, however, only a sharper expression of the individuating logic of consumption which is *inherent* in capitalism, and therefore already manifest, albeit in more muted forms, since the creation of capitalist society in Japan.[41] Another is the problematic contrast made between the putative difference in the role of consumption in Japan vis-à-vis other advanced countries. In the latter, consumption is seen to serve individuating purposes, whereas in the former it simply reproduces, albeit in new ways, the "traditional" Japanese proclivity for sameness. The ambiguities in this contrast can be read in several ways, one emphasizing the inadvertent assumption of sameness that has structured not only *Nihonjinron* discourse, but also sociological mappings of performative identity in Japan; the other, the second, a "soft orientalism" that accepts uncritically claims about the homogenizing consequences of consumption in Japan reinscribing essentialized conceptions of Japanese conformity. The tendency to reproduce this binary thus appears in distinctions made between a pre- and a early post-war mass culture in contrast to the nature of consumption associated with the miracle years. Thus Yoda writes of the shift from the culture of mass consumption and (and mass-produced goods) to that of individuated consumption (Yoda 2000) that occurred in the late 1980s. No doubt associated with the "acquisition of prescribed sets of consumer durables" encouraged by the state (recall Ikeda's Income Doubling Plan in1960), this conception of the theoretical location of consumption in Japan's social life rests on a conflation between the logical and the historical. Insofar as mass production and consumption is *intrinsic* to a capitalist order, where the production of standardized goods for *exchange* and their consumption (in use) on a mass scale does not, as argued in the preceding chapter, in itself subvert the link between the necessity of objects (use value) to individuation, claims about the de-individuated location of consumption in social life can be seen as somewhat problematic. In this context, the distinction made between *kosei* (individuality) and *kojinshugisha* (individualism) may be more helpful in shedding light on the question of consumption and its location in Japan's social life. Arguably, claims about consumer*ism* associated with the "miracle economy" years deploy the latter, more negatively valenced term in Japan, the former (*kosei*) more directly relevant to the theoretical argument pursued here.

Similarly, the distinction between an earlier (late-nineteenth-century) use of *jinkaku* as denoting legal personhood and its deployment since the mid-twentieth century as a general category denoting a common humanity, or respect for the individual (Inoue 2001) but within a social nexus, directs attention to the explicit recognition of the conjoined aspects of individual and social in modern conceptions of personhood in Japan.

A third, more problematic issue, has to do with the general claim that consumption, rather than externalizing the self, is simply a mechanism of disciplining and controlling selves. The previous chapter challenges this assumption by emphasizing how the consumption or use of objects enables the expression and externalization of socially self-determined selves: it rejects the dualism in the social/private distinction by showing how in a capitalist society one necessitates the other. The view that consumption simply deepens bureaucratic control of the life-world betrays a one-sided, narrow view of the "private" realm, taking the self-referential, autonomous liberal notion of self as its foundational, though problematic, premise.

In a more controversial argument, Kumazawa (1996) has suggested that the homogenized (de-individuated) lifestyle of Japan's consuming classes has rendered the workplace central to the affirmation of individual desire and competition in Japan. Although his argument is driven more by an attempt to account for the seeming absence of solidarity (and resistance) among Japanese workers, his principal insight about hyper (in the sense of inflated, because displaced) competitiveness among workers (within a work ethos that repudiates merit in favor of seniority) does not vitiate the claim made here about the social ends that production has historically been associated with in modern Japan. That is, while the overt de-individuation of the workplace (in which *shain* (staff) interact as team players in an explicit acknowledgement of their shared ends), the "mass rivalry" that Kumazawa identifies is deployed principally in service of social, not individual ends. Similarly, Osamu Watanabe's (1991) related claim about the consolidation of a corporate ideology and its "ability based competition" (*noryoku kyoso shugi*) throughout Japan, subjecting workers and their families to the logic of achievement and competition associated with the marketplace draws attention to the overarching presence of work and production in framing social life in Japan, not as an individual end of self-seeking, but rather a larger corporatist end.

More recent claims about the role of work/production in relation to self and identity also need to be addressed. The universalization of capitalism on a global scale, the transnational reach of corporations in marketing and selling standardized products, combined with recent developments in cultural theory, has called into question an earlier preoccupation with labor, production, work, and class, generating a turn to consumption as the primary site for identity construction. While it is undoubtedly true that the pace and nature of work is being radically redefined in the post-Fordist era of flexible accumulation, when to use Morris-Suzuki's term "information capitalism" has spawned a new kind of worker, altering the forms of work (in Marx's terms – concrete labor), it is quite another matter to claim that work and individual identity as conceptual categories are being delinked.[42] Although labor in its concrete forms has always been differentiated, the constitutive role of work vis-à-vis identity formation still holds: in the absence of a theoretical reformulation of the relation between labor and identity (as in, for instance, Marx's critique of Hegel), the claim that labor is becoming redundant to individual identity formation appears simply as an ungrounded assertion.

In the case of Japan, although some of the elements that make up the general social milieu related to the workplace show signs of transformation (a loosening of the permanent employment system; increasing instances of company layoffs; new legislation granting paternity leave to fathers as a sign of the weakening of male identification with work;

a gradual increase in the recognition of merit as opposed to seniority in determining wages and so on discussed at greater length in Chapter 5), the pace of change is, at least so far, too incremental and unevenly manifested to qualify as a structural transformation of the culture and political economy of Japan.

Coupled with this general understanding of the temporal or developmental relation between production and consumption in constituting identity is the additional claim that "the absence of moral absolutes and the construction of multiple selves which characterize Japanese culture predispose it to the adoption of a consumer mentality" (Anderson and Wadkins 1991: 129). The related claim that "through the fostering of multiple identities and the emphasis on form over substance...Japan is uniquely adapted to the linking of commodities and self definition" (Anderson and Wadkins 1991: 129–132) uncritically accepts both an a-historical, essentialized notion of the de-centered self as well as the problematic claim that a heightened pace of consumption is tantamount to the emergence of individuated expression.

Instances of the individuating role of consumption in contemporary Japan have been richly documented in recent scholarship – from the purchase of French perfume and handbags, Maine lobsters, Iowa beef, Italian fashion, golf lessons; the proliferation of *depatos* (department stores) to the nostalgic re-appropriation of a uniquely Japanese past via the use of a traditional Japanese bath (*o'furo*); vacations to *furusato* (hometowns), mountains, and seaside resorts; or the occasional "consumption" of a Noh play – the Japanese appear to be engaged in a frenzy of consumption, vividly captured in stereotypes of tourists shopping en masse in the cities of New York, Paris, London, Sydney, or Milan. The rise of service industries, the increased consumption of luxury products, and ever-so subtle advertising appeals to feeling and sensibilities mark the 1980s and 1990s. The "new consumer individualization," in part the result of producers appealing to and fashioning "highly targeted, diversified, and nuanced types of consumer desires" is seen as the quintessential hallmark of Japan's mature capitalism. Consumption in contemporary Japan, in sum, is seen as a liberating force, releasing the individual from the shackles of ascriptive identities, enabling an expressive individuality hitherto unfathomable in the heavily group-oriented context of Japanese society. But as this chapter has attempted to show, the history of the "individual" in relation to consumption in Japan begins not with the affluence of the 1960s and 1970s, but rather with the creation of capitalist social relations in the nineteenth century.

Its accelerated and deepened expression in contemporary Japan simply brings it more easily and more sharply into view.

The alternative view sketched in this chapter rests on the claim that the link between the consumption of commodities and individuation is a modern phenomenon emanating from the transformation of Japan into a capitalist society. Given the historical conditions under which this transition took place, however, the particularity of Japanese capitalism can be grasped in reference to the separation of de-individuated and individuated realms of social life associated with production and consumption respectively. The reason why consumption plays a keener role vis-à-vis individuation has perhaps more to do with the circumscribed zone of individuated expression in modern Japan, rather than some ever-present cultural disposition emanating from "multiple identities and the emphasis on form over substance." As borne out by economic and social historians, consumption as a structuring principle of social life in Japan begins to appear only with the urbanization in the late Tokugawa period with the creation of urban metropolitan centers like Osaka, presaging the final stages of the transition to a capitalist economy and society.

A full account of the animating principle of modernity in Japan must take note of not just its nationalist/productivist orientation, but also the development of a consumption-related process of individuation. In both instances, traditional notions of wealth, polity, and personhood were reworked through the operative logic of capitalism which, once unleashed, could never be fully brought within the control of state managers or the ideological state apparatus.

Indeed, the nature of Japan's welfare state, in terms of discourses on social policy, the nature of goods and services provided by the state, as well as societal attitudes toward different social goods (health care versus monetary public assistance) are incomprehensible in the absence of a fully entrenched notion of the self as individuated being. It is precisely the discourse of individuality, or self-sustaining subjectivity, that the state has periodically deployed to justify its provision of specific goods to the exclusion of others. As Fujtani succinctly puts it, "the state's promotion of the self-disciplined subject, rather than being a continuation of pre-modern form of collectivist subjectivity, constructed a new social subject." The notion of the "self-disciplined subject" would be

> used by the state to explain poverty as the legitimate consequence of a fault in individual moral behavior. In the end, the poor in

> modern Japan became marginalized morally as well as economically – not despite but precisely because of their self-constituting, self-disciplining subjectivity.
>
> (Fujitani 1998: 314)

Those who view Japan's welfare state as distinctive due to its reliance on the family miss an important dimension of its constitutive principle. The state, via the distinction it makes between social and individuated goods, not only reinscribes the social subject of modern Japan as an individuated consumer and polity-oriented producer, but also, in the process, reworks the idea of family as a realm of privatized activity in distinction to the traditional notion of the *ie* as the microcosm of the family-state. The state's own *nihonjinron* rhetoric notwithstanding, the family no longer serves as the repository of a traditional group/state mentality but is rather constructed as an inherently privatized realm of individuated life. Recent attempts to mobilize the family as the proper source of elderly care draws upon a discourse of private relations between individuals in the family to justify familial care, as opposed to simply an older discourse of Confucian filial piety. This cannot be construed as simply the outcome of a continuous reliance on the family and a continuous form of group-centered subjectivity. This would make the creation of a universal system of health care and pensions hard to explain. It is only within the context of this dual determination of subjectivity in modern Japan that the seeming anomaly between a highly developed provision of social need and a minimal provision of individuated need becomes explicable. The construction of the modern subject, partially self-determined via consumption but imbricated in a productivist ethos that both enterprise and state-based welfare system actively foster, is both reflected in and constituted by the institution and social practices of Japan's welfare system. The absence of a normative challenge to welfare statism is then the result of the overlapping and similar ways in which both the state and market-based civil society constitute subjectivity in modern Japan.

4
Social Need and the Welfare State in Modern Japan

Introduction

This chapter examines state-based welfare in relation to the conception of the individual in modern Japan. Unlike analyses that measure a state's welfare role in quantitative terms (as a percentage of GNP), thereby attributing the breakdown of welfare to fiscal overreach or crisis, I have suggested that welfare can be understood as emblematic of the normative structure of subjectivity constituted in the institutions of political economy – the state and a market-based civil society. As such, differences in welfare states may be understood in relation to the underlying conceptions of personhood that inform different institutionalizations of civil society. My objective in this chapter is to demonstrate that the trajectory of welfare in Japan can be readily understood in relation to the ideal of personhood that informs state and civil society. Due to the distinctive nature of Japan's civil society, which has been historically instituted to foster collective forms of consciousness rooted in its productionist ethos, consumption serves as the delimited terrain for individuation.[1] The welfare state reflects and reinscribes this specifically modern notion of personhood by promoting the disbursement of certain welfare goods and limiting others.[2]

The state has historically provisioned welfare goods deemed necessary to propel accumulation, even in instances where its political conservatism would have dictated otherwise, while remaining consistently antipathetic to the provision of goods deemed necessary only from the vantage point of individuated need. It is within this framework that apparent anomalies about Japan's welfare state become explicable.

Notorious as a "welfare laggard," with an alleged emphasis on enterprise and family-based provision of welfare, Japan has developed one of the most enviable health insurance systems in the advanced industrialized world. Japan's ruling conservative Liberal Democratic Party enacted an impressive array of welfare laws virtually doubling its welfare provision in the 1970s in the absence of a significant political challenge. The debates surrounding the "problems" of welfare in Japan, unlike those in the West, do not reveal an anti-welfare sentiment *per se*, but rather highlight the practical difficulties attendant on the continued provision of welfare. Unlike the conservative backlash against welfare in the West, in which the normative validity of welfare has been seriously called into question leading to proposals for the full marketization of welfare, discussions about the problems of welfare in Japan have not taken the form of a normative challenge to the idea of welfare, but have been more narrowly focused on the need for creative financing (altering the tax system, increasing individual contributions due to its rapidly aging population and declining birthrate). What accounts for the absence of the seemingly inevitable ebb and flow of a populist welfare politics in post-war Japan? Why has welfare not captured the socio-political imagination of the Japanese citizenry in the wake of rising unemployment during the economic recession of the 1990s?[3] The chapter that follows focuses on the period of the *Heisei* recession (the 1990s and after); here I attempt to recuperate the pattern of welfare provision historically.

Accordingly, this chapter maps the terrain of welfare in modern Japan. Beginning with a brief discussion of the emergence of welfare policy in Japan that accompanied the crafting of modernity in mid-nineteenth-century Japan, the bulk of the chapter discusses the discourses, laws, and provision of welfare goods in post-war Japan from the vantage point of modern conceptions of the individual and personhood. Rather than providing an exhaustive analysis of the reasons for the development of the welfare state (the subject of much of the debates in the literature), my efforts will be directed more specifically to discerning the logic underpinning the overall pattern of welfare. Specifically, the discussion will show that welfare in modern Japan reveals a distinctive pattern, one that can be readily understood in relation to the ideal of personhood that informs both state and civil society.

To this end, the historical discussion of the discourses, legislation, and disbursement of welfare goods and services will highlight three distinctive elements of welfare policy in Japan: the focus on the provision of needs that enhance collective as opposed to individual well-being (what I have earlier referred to as social need); employment rather than public assistance as a means of enhancing welfare; and societal and state antipathy to the receipt and disbursement of goods that meet individuated need in contrast to the normative legitimation of the receipt and disbursement of goods that meet social need. Social need thus refers to the idea that the ends (or needs) fulfilled are objectively rather than subjectively determined. Because the state's provision of goods that meet the ends of the collectivity has not yet been called into question, the normative appeal of welfare as understood in Japan remains intact.

Due to the nationalist cast capitalist development took in Japan, the state has been inordinately concerned with providing those goods deemed essential to production. Insofar as a healthy and skilled workforce was seen as vital to military and industrial self-sufficiency, Japan's welfare state has been concerned with the provision of health care and education; both are associated in the Japanese socio-political imaginary with a de-individuated productivist ethos. Although education has been historically instituted in Japan to imbue citizens with the habits of mind necessary to contribute to collective as opposed to individuated interest, and would therefore meet the criteria of "social need" as defined here, because it is not typically seen as part of social policy provision, this book does not include an examination of Japan's education policy.

This distinction between the generous provision of social need and the highly restricted scope of provision of individuated need may also help make sense of the wide-ranging assessments offered in the literature on Japan's welfare state. Those who see it as a "welfare superpower" focus on its provision of social need, whereas those who tend to see it as "divisive and controlling" tend to focus on the absence of its provision of individuated need.

Welfare: An historical sketch

Within the distinctive pattern of social relations put in place during the Tokugawa period (1603–1868) in Japan, pre-existing methods of providing assistance to the needy were assimilated and transformed. As in the West, philanthropic and religious organizations had been the main source of institutional care for the sick, aged, and needy. The Political Reformation of the *Taikwa* (646 AD) and the *Taiho* Statues of 701 AD administered by political authorities were the first form of governmental social assistance.[4] Since the beginning of the feudal period in the latter part of the twelfth century, the responsibility for provisioning social assistance fell increasingly on the shoulders of feudal barons. With the increased centralization of administrative activities within feudal domains during the Tokugawa period, however, the burden shifted considerably from Buddhist and Christian centers of welfare provision to the *daimyo* (feudal barons), whose jurisdiction over their respective *han* (fiefs) generated a medley of de-centralized social amelioration schemes. Homes for *ninsoku yoriba* (poor laborers), *hinin-goya* (a home for the outcasts), *tamarino-sei* (medical institutions), and *yojosho* (sanitarium) were some of the more well known centers developed by the "*daimyo*" of *Hitachi, Kaga, and Koishijawa* prefectures respectively.[5]

In particular, the establishment of an office for welfare work in Edo (modern Tokyo) that incorporated the idea of *Sha-so* (the basis of relief work provided by feudal lords) and the creation of a "slush fund" to provide rice in times of emergencies are indicative of a consciousness among the ruling elite of a responsibility for those unable to perform their requisite roles as members of either the producing class, the *eta* (outcasts), or, in the rare instance, the destitute merchant. The detailed documentation of the social welfare programs developed at the level of *han* and in *Edo* challenges the view that the "family clan" system has provided the continuous basis of welfare provision in Japanese history. In light of the *baku-han's* concerted attempt throughout the Tokugawa period to maintain social control and order (in order to ensure its privileged position), efforts to administer welfare at both levels suggest that already before the *Meiji* restoration (1868) there was, at least latent, a consciousness of the need to provision welfare both as a means of maintaining social order and as part of the "state's" obligations.[6] The normative legitimacy of this mutually obligatory structure also had deeper roots, as Harry Harootunian and Bernand Silberman have shown, in the nativist school of thought that equated politics with morality for both ruler and ruled. In return for just rule, the ruled maintained a "reverent quietism toward the social order"[7] that preserved the community as a whole.[8]

The emergence of a recognizably modern social policy occurred with the creation of capitalist exchange relations in modern Japan. Ending over 250 years of Tokugawa feudal isolationism, the *Meiji Ishin* (Restoration) of 1868 marks the beginnings of the creation of a centralized state and industrial economy in Japan. In keeping with its pragmatic need to accelerate modernization by fostering a national consciousness tethered to the figure of the emperor, the making of social policy provided a dual opportunity. By integrating the disparate relief measures of the now abolished administrative units (*han*), it could serve to advance the *Meiji* leaders' efforts at centralization. As an expression of the emperor's mercy toward the disabled and indigent, however, *fukushi* (welfare) could reinforce the postulated deep connection between ruler and ruled. Thus, social policy in the *Meiji* era served the dual purpose of creating a citizenry while at the same time advancing the newly formed state's material interests.

Just as the new, ostensibly democratic, state legitimated the moral authority of imperial power in accordance with dominant social ideals, and capitalist development was intended to serve the national polity (*kokutai*), so too the early social policy measures undertaken by Meiji leaders, although ostensibly modeled on those of Western countries, reinforced existent practices, albeit in new ways. The Poor Relief Regulation promulgated 6 years after the *Meiji* Restoration marks the beginnings of modern Japan's social policy, and is indicative of the individual's relation to both the state, the market, and the individual at the time. Meant to provide relief only to children, the infirm, disabled, or chronically ill for a short period of time (55 days),[9] the notion of public responsibility for individual well-being was circumscribed by what was otherwise a manifestly paternalistic state. Key to the relief provided by this ordinance was the requirement that recipients be registered in the family registry, assuring that community would take up where the state would leave off. Continuation of relief beyond the stipulated period was assessed on a case-by-case basis.[10] Often seen as a "puzzle" explained by the state's explicit reinforcement of an ideology of familism that harnessed the energies of its populace in service of a nationalist ideal, while limiting its responsibility, the role of the state in legislating social policy may be better apprehended in the context of its concurrent efforts to promote capitalist development.

Even as the *Meiji* Poor Law denied access to public relief to the able-bodied poor, encoding the strictures of familial and/or self-help, the rapid rise of mechanized industry created an enormous demand for labor in the 1890s, bringing with it the inevitable problem of urban poverty. With the government's commitment to *shokusan kogyo* (encouraging industry), factory legislation was quickly implemented to create working conditions conducive to rapid industrialization. The discourses on labor legislation at the time provide insight into the purpose social policy was meant to serve.

Central to the debates that ensued at this time was the report on urban poverty (*Nihon no Kaso Shakai* – The lower strata of Japanese society) by a journalist in 1899.[11] Along with the survey of factory workers by the Ministry of Agriculture and Commerce in 1903, the view that poor working conditions in factories were the leading cause of urban poverty generated a wide basis of support for implementing legislation that would target the working poor, rather than the unemployed. It is worth noting here this early origin of what remains a distinctive characteristic of contemporary Japan's welfare state – the focus on the employed rather than the unemployed – a feature that is readily understood in the context of Japan's national project of capitalist development. Despite their obvious admiration for the German model (studied extensively by a number of powerful leaders sent on foreign missions to examine Western institutions), *Meiji* leaders approached the question of labor not simply as an element of production, but, as Sheldon Garon (1987) has shown, a valuable national resource. Thus, a leading politician declared in 1902 that Japan's modern social policies were firmly grounded in the Tokugawa's period's legacy of safeguarding the welfare of the people; leaders of newly created unions avoided confrontations with employers; a social reformer emphasized that

> the state should deal with labor not simply as an element of production, but as a valuable national resource, whose abuse hindered the state's responsibility to maintain public health, domestic order, and a strong military.[12]

Utilitarians like Fukuzawa Yukichi, on the other hand, one of the foremost thinkers of his time, failed to create an alternative Western discourse of "individual happiness" as the basis of welfare, supplanting social order as the *raison d'etre* of social policy. The growing appeal of Marxian ideas among Japanese intellectuals likewise failed to win broad support for the argument that social policy served simply to entrench class interests. Rather, prominent scholars like Kuwata Kumazo emphasized the need for both state-led reforms like the factory law and initiatives by workers to create conditions more conducive to capitalist development.[13] Tozuko Fukuda, another influential critic of Japanese traditionalism and a convert to Marshallian economic thought, was unable to displace the influence of the German historical school in shaping policy on welfare; the language of national interest dominated discussions of how best to institute its provision.

The focus on labor legislation, as opposed to provisioning for the unemployed, placed Japan's emergent welfare policy squarely within the context of industrial policy. The creation of social policy in Japan has been consistently attributed to the *Meiji* state's Confucian-inspired ideology of state socialism. The compulsion to institutionalize egalitarian juridical principles was predicated, however, on the more immediate concerns of creating a national military, and a citizenry committed to the national goal of self-strengthening. This dual compulsion led the new leaders to advocate the well-being of the populace at large, creating a wider basis for social policy. This orientation toward social policy was to impact the development and dynamic of the welfare state in Japan.

The bill on factory workers that ultimately passed in the Diet in 1911, after several years of resistance by industry, reflected the state's effort to promote rapid industrialization and enhance a sense of collective or national consciousness.[14] The 1911 law set limits on the length of the working day and the burden of work for female and under-aged workers, and wages. It came into effect in 1916 and was substantially revised in 1923 with the view to enhancing its effectiveness. Particularly telling in this early stage of the birth of Japan's welfare policy is the distinction that was made between *shakai seisaku*, social policy aimed at protecting the working class, and *shakai jigyo*, social work that was geared toward the improvement of the well-being of those among the less well off in society.[15] While debates between and among intellectuals and policy-makers were, in part, simply a reflection of a fundamental disagreement about what should constitute the proper object of the state's social policy, the notion and institutionalization of welfare in Japan has consistently placed primacy on the production-oriented view, subsuming the idea of the general well-being of the populace within the larger project of national, military, and economic development.

This is evident too in the government's early regulation of private charities and its reformatory (*kanka*) approach to poverty. Unlike Western charitable organizations, which reflected the philanthropic or religious sensibilities of private donors, the Home Ministry (under Inoue Yuichi) adopted a preventive approach to poverty in the local communities, rather than simply providing relief to the poor. The *Chuo Jizen Kyokai* (Central Charity Society) established under the aegis of Inoue Yuichi in 1908 attempted to educate the poor to a better way of life so as to prevent them from becoming a hazard to the social order. At the same time, however, government efforts, for example, were directed at reinforcing the idea that families were primarily responsible for members so as to control the numbers on poor relief.

A broadening of the notion of welfare occurred shortly after the nation-wide rice riots of 1918. The economic and social turbulence wrought by the preceding decades of rapid industrialization created a widespread demand for greater intervention in the lives of those unable to find a niche in the fast-changing economy. The idea that welfare entailed a proactive program of social development for the well-being of the citizenry at large was increasingly advocated to promote social solidarity. But, as Takahashi (1997) citing Yoshimasa Ikeda points out, the notion of social solidarity was itself premised on the idea of state–society as an undifferentiated monolith, an organism in which "individuals and active actors of civil society were neglected."[16] The emphasis on welfare thus derived from a concern with the social order of the whole, rather than the well-being of individuals *per se*.[17]

To this end, a system of district commissioners was set up beginning in 1910. At first with an honorary position without financial remuneration, these *sasei komon* (district commissioners) were to serve as paternalistic guides or counselors to help morally reform the disadvantaged. This system quickly gave way within a decade to the creation of district commissioners who were charged with providing local information about social needs to state officials, maintaining family registries, and especially, tracking migrant labor in cities. As the result of efforts by district commissioners, an amendment was made to the Relief Ordinance of 1874 to the effect that an increased effort on behalf of the disadvantaged was warranted given their status as "children of His majesty the Emperor" (*tenno heika no akago*). The normative justification for social work (*shakai jigyo*) was thus increasingly grounded in the paternalistic *tenno* system whereby the claims citizens could make on the state emanated from the assumed philanthropic largesse of the head of state, rather than as an entitlement due to individuals. Given the deliberate mobilization of *tenno* ideology during the *Meiji* era (Gluck 1985),[18] in service of the nationalist project of industrialization and militarization, it is no surprise that the ideal and practice of welfare developed along similar lines. That the development of Japan's welfare system, episodic and incremental though it was, should reveal a cumulative tendency to provision goods that met social needs in accordance with Japan's productivist ethos is entirely consistent with the constitutive principle that structured modernity in Japan.

This central attribute of Japan's emergent welfare system came into sharp focus during the 1930s. The rise of militarism in Japan coupled with its expansionist drive in Asia beginning with the *Mukden* incident in 1931[19] necessitated the provision of goods deemed vital to Japan's national interest at this time. Of these, public health quickly came to occupy center stage in the newly formed Japanese Ministry of Health and Welfare in 1938. As Johansson and Mosk note,[20] much of the social policy implemented up to the 1930s, including the setting up of the Ministry of Health and Welfare itself, was due to an urgent concern about the poor health of potential recruits. With the Law for National Mobilization brought into effect in 1938, the explicit target of war-time Japan's welfare effort came sharply into focus. Yamaguchi Tadashi, in fact, advocated the renaming of the Health and Welfare ministry to *kosei* (health) rather than *shakai* (social) consistent with the state's obligation to enhance the health of the population in the name of the *tenno*.

The claim that Japan's consistent emphasis on maintaining public health has less to do with its putative Confucian ideology and more with its location in promoting capitalist accumulation is thrown into sharp relief when considering the change in terminology brought into effect during the war years. Between the 1930s and 1940s, the term *kosei jigyo* or "public health" work replaced previous designations for social or welfare policy.[21] That the new Welfare Ministry – *Kosei-Sho* (Public Health work) rather than *Shakai-Sho* (social work) – is, as several historians have pointed out, indicative of its emphasis on the necessity of maintaining public health so as to ensure the availability of a military labor force (Weiss 1993). The exigencies of war-time Japan, in other words, rendered the maintenance of public health vital to the national polity. No matter how one chooses to periodize welfare policy in Japan (before/after war or the "miracle economy" years), the overwhelming emphasis on public health since Japan's emergence as a modern state is striking. As the most vivid expression of the link between production and national consciousness, health policy provides both the leitmotif of Japan's welfare state as well as the key to understanding its primary object – the de-individuated *shimin* (subject) of the emperor-centered nation.

The productionist bent of Japan's social policy at this time was also quite apparent in the number of laws that were enacted to protect mothers and their offspring – the potential labor force. The military lavished praise on the act of mothering *umeya fuyaseyo* (give birth and increase the population), and legislated the Law of Protection of Mothers and Children in 1937, the Law on National Health insurance in 1938, and the Law on Medical protection in 1941, all with the explicit objective of "ensuring productivity of soldiers-to-be" by excoriating women to give birth to as many healthy children as possible.

Similarly, the labor-oriented focus on public health ensured that the rural areas, historically the recruitment ground for the Japanese military (including the current Self Defense Forces), received special attention. In a bid to improve the general physical condition of the people who were to serve in the armed forces, the Law on National Health Insurance aimed at providing medical personnel and clinics in rural areas. As Kyuichi Yoshida points out, the term *kokumin-kai-hoken* (life security for all people), a popular phrase among welfare proponents, was closely linked to *kokumin kaihei* (the people, all to-be soldiers),[22] vivifying the close connection between Japan's war-time needs and perceived welfare needs during the 1930s and 1940s.

The third key development in the pre-war period was the promulgation of the Workers' Pension scheme in 1942 (renamed Labour Pension in 1944). Formed with the explicit intention of enhancing productivity by stabilizing the labor market and reducing labor mobility, the Labour Pension Law illustrated policy-makers' sensitivity to the conditions necessary to ensure rapid capital accumulation. Thus labor became an explicit object of welfare policy, not so much due to its demands for improved working conditions, but rather because certain needs were perceived as vital to the accumulation process.

In sum, the pre-war development of the idea and institutionalization of welfare reveals two distinctive features: (a) unlike the European case where factory legislation was motivated by the concerns of industry, in its inception, social policy in Japan reflected explicitly the national/military agenda of the state as outlined in the previous chapter. The state's role in mandating company welfare benefits, as well as its emphasis on the national provision of health care, was driven primarily by its military/capitalist interests that took precedence over private capital *per se*. Due to this emphasis on ensuring the health of the collectivity, social policy was made an integral part of industrial policy (contra Johnson's bifurcation of the two); (b) the provision of social need was deemed necessary, whereas the provision of Poor Relief served simply the "lesser" purpose of ameliorating individual need. This bifurcation of need becomes explicable only in the context of the exigencies of the military threat Japan faced at the time.

The state's militarist/developmental agenda could not have been quite so easily translated into a social policy that limited the provision of welfare goods to meet social need had it not drawn upon and mobilized prevalent normative understandings of the status of the person in relation to both state and market. I have suggested that the structuring principle of capitalism in Japan was premised upon a distinction between individuated and de-individuated realms of social life. The individuating logic of consumption in a capitalist society coupled with the emphasis on production as a national/collectivist enterprise constructed the modern subject in accordance with this logic. By provisioning goods that promoted the collective interest while leaving individuated need to the realm of market activity, social policy, even in this early stage of modern Japan's history worked to reinscribe a specific notion of subjectivity in Japan. The need to account for the receptivity of the state's developmental agenda within civil society becomes clearer below.

Rejecting both culturalist and bureaucracy-centered statist accounts, the noted historian Sheldon Garon (1997) has suggested that the state's project of social management best accounts for the nature of Japan's welfare system. Arguing that the Japanese state has been more broadly concerned with the cultivation of the "social underpinnings of national economic advance," Garon points to tactics of "moral suasion" deployed by state leaders to shape key aspects of the everyday life of people, including welfare. The state's project of "molding Japanese minds" has not, Garon contends, been forced on a passive, naturally harmonious populace, but has in fact solicited the enthusiastic participation of the vast majority. On this view, the state has restricted the provision of welfare by extolling the virtues of familial and national solidarity and socializing its citizenry accordingly, such that much of the welfare burden continues to be borne by families, especially women. Focusing on state strategies that sought the internalization of a state-sponsored ideology within civil society, Garon attempts to overcome the limits of statist accounts that emphasize the relative autonomy of bureaucrats in shaping society.

Garon offers a persuasive account of how the state has transformed the populace into active supporters of statist projects. Although a focus on the role of ideology is often fruitful to analysis of social order and conflict, in the absence of an account of the social forces underlying a specific ideology, such an approach may unwittingly reproduce the limits of voluntarism identified earlier.[23] The claim that state officials developed and disseminated a specific set of beliefs and values among the populace begs the crucial question of the source of these beliefs and ideas propagated by state leaders. To the extent that ideas are deeply social, that is they exist as "social facts" independent of particular individuals who may lay claim to them at one time or another, they must be properly seen as part and parcel of a social milieu, rather than as singular products of state/official policy-making. In ascribing causal primacy to a state-generated ideology and the state's efforts to cultivate specific ways of thought, this line of thinking is vulnerable to resuscitating the "bureaucratic autonomy thesis" rightly problematized by several historians. Most importantly, the question of why, if it was not already so inclined, the Japanese population has been so receptive to the specific values and beliefs propagated by the state remains unaddressed. What accounts for the state's alleged effectiveness in "molding Japanese minds?"

Central to this formulation is the underlying assumption of causation, associated with linear thinking, that attributes a uni-drectionality of cause and effect. The conceptual problems attendant on such formulation have been addressed in the preceding chapters. Suffice it to say here, a more fruitful approach may be found in treating state and society in mutually constitutive rather than *causal* terms. The notion of mutual constitution can be accessed in this context via the common notion of personhood underpinning both state and society. Institutional arrangements of state and civil society both reflected this notion[24] as well as reinscribed it by objectifying via law and policy an ideal that shaped the social practices of everyday life.

Thus, claims about the state's effectiveness in crafting welfare policy by cultivating in the population "a commitment to diligence, thrift, and other good habits so that families and individuals would avoid relying on public assistance" can be extended to show why *jiei* (self-management) proved to be effective in Japan. The argument developed here – that the abbreviated principle of exchange constituted work as a de-individuated realm of activity, whereas consumption alone provided the terrain upon which a modern (individuated) subjectivity could be fashioned – provides an answer to the question posed above. The state could effectively mobilize a discourse of *jiei* or self-management in service of its own national/military productivist agenda precisely because an individuating logic was operative within civil society. The state, while no doubt actively reinforcing this ideal of personhood through discourse and legislation, as Garon emphasizes, worked not with a static but a dynamic idea of personhood very much prevalent in and enlivened by the social practices of everyday life in modern Japan.

In pre-war Japan, the state's attempt to foster an ethos of self-management was coupled with its explicit attempt to foster a productions ethos in the employable and employed population. An explicit goal of Japan's welfare policy at this time was to preempt labor market failures so as to maximize Japan's productive output. To the extent that all able-bodied Japanese could be commodified, Japan's central goal of promoting the collectivity could be effectively pursued. On the other hand, those unable to be effective participants in market-based relations of production were encouraged to fend for themselves (*jiei*) by relying on the family or community. Individual needs (for income, housing, food, and clothing, in short the necessities of life) remained strictly out of range of public provision. By actively pursuing welfare policies that would enhance social productivity by provisioning goods that were, in a sense, antecedent to individuated well-being (health care and education in particular), coupled with welfare measures targeted specifically at those already employed (labor pensions for instance), the pre-war welfare measures enacted by policy-makers, and as reflected in the dominant social policy discourses of the time, revealed within civil society a ready acceptance of a clear distinction between the state's provision of social need and an active antipathy to the provision of individuated need.

This distinction was entirely consistent with popular notions of personhood at work in Japan at the time. While, on the one hand, the appearance of *mobo* and *moga* (modern boy and modern girl), coupled with a pervasive fascination with Western, especially American, cultural styles (in music, sports, and the arts), was indicative of an expressive individualism at work especially in cultural consumption, the work ethos that developed alongside this expressive individualism betrayed no antipathy to a collectivist, *tenno*-centered system of beliefs and values. Rather, the very idea of modernity embraced these seemingly opposed poles of meaning: to be modern required both the spirit of collectivism deemed essential for Japan's rapid industrialization as well as the cultural hallmarks of an individuated mode of being, exemplified almost exclusively within the realm of consumption and cultural lifestyles.

Japan's imitative zeal embraced both the institutional and the cultural forms of the West, but only by attaching to them social meanings appropriate to Japan's self-understanding at the time.[25] Concretely this translated into the following: Western style individualism could be readily adopted in areas that did not directly threaten the collectivity, especially the nationally driven accumulation drive fostered within the institutions and social practices of both state and civil society. Consumption, to the extent that it was seen as secondary to the productionist ethos that quickly developed in Japan, provided the terrain within which a modern subjectivity could be constituted. The state's periodic exhortions to the population to temper consumption must be seen then not as an attempt to reign in a rampant individualism that threatened to subvert the statist project of development, but rather as an attempt to reinforce the symbolic order underpinning the collectivist orientation within relations of production. Had the individuating impulse of consumption truly threatened to subvert the productionist agenda firmly in place, it is likely the state would have resorted to more enforceable measures (taxation on consumption, specific luxury goods, laws regulating/limiting the sale of specific goods, etc.), rather than episodically deploy a paternalistic discourse of temperance, frugality, and forbearance.

To conclude, the development of social policy from the *Meiji* era up until the defeat of Japan in 1945 was characterized by a focus on improving the social conditions necessary to the successful pursuit of the nationalist project of capitalist development. This meant that welfare took on the explicit meaning of building human capital, a healthy and well-educated workforce, rather than the notion of individual well-being *per se*. Couched explicitly in a discourse of emperor-centered compassion and dispensation, welfare was certainly not an individual right, an entitlement demanded of the state to promote individual happiness, but a social necessity, given the demands of the greater good of the collectivity.

The pattern of welfare in post-war Japan

In tracing the development of the ideal and institutionalization of welfare as it impinges on prevalent notions of personhood in post-war Japan, three conceptually distinct phases are discernable. The first, representing the American Occupation authorities' attempt to democratize Japan (along Western lines) is marked by the effort to link the idea of welfare to individual rights. Despite a spate of legislation that decreed as much, the actual implementation of welfare policy continued to reflect Japan's pre-war productionist/nationalist ethos, clearly distinguishing in normative terms between goods deemed legitimate for state provision and those that were not.

The second phase, spanning the high-point of welfare state expansion in the late 1960s and early 1970s is marked by an astonishingly rapid growth of social spending, the almost overnight creation of universal medical and pension systems, generous benefits for the physically disabled, and children; in short, Japan's veritable transformation into *fukushi kokka* (welfare state) commensurate with those of other advanced industrial societies. Particularly noteworthy in analyzing the types of goods that were provisioned at this time is the continued emphasis on enhancing human capital consistent with Japan's productivist orientation. Unlike Western welfare states in which poverty alleviation has served as the *raison d'etre* of social policy (accounting perhaps for the heavy stigmatization of welfare recipients), the nature of goods deemed de-commodifiable in Japan reveals an alternative "investment strategy"[26] geared to prevent rather than ameliorate the inequities produced by capitalist development. Welfare state expansion during this time emphasized the universal provision of health care, education, and pensions to ensure the well-being of the polity as a whole rather than direct resources to the monetized provision of public assistance to individuals. The legitimation of this bifurcated normative understanding of welfare goods is apparent in the receptivity to goods that meet social need in contrast to an antipathy to the receipt of goods that fulfill individuated need among recipients and non-recipients alike.

This interpretation provides an account of the distinctive pattern of welfare in Japan that moves beyond culture-based claims about familism or enterprise-based welfare. In particular, it draws attention to the unusually generous provision of some goods in contrast to the minimal provision of others to those who fall outside the secure networks of the employment system. As pointed out in the previous chapter, the benefits of the lifetime employment system, which, in principle, would render income support unnecessary, accrue to only a fraction (25–35 percent) of the workforce, predominantly middle and upper management males employed in the big firms (*kaisha*), not to over 70 percent of the workers. Second, the state's repeated attempts to re-invigorate the notion of familial responsibility for those unable to secure a livelihood also points to the contingent nature of familial support in modern Japan: if familism indeed secured individual well-being, the state's periodic attempts to resuscitate this principle would be unnecessary.

Unlike those who suggest that Japan's productivist ethos as reflected in its welfare state is the result of an authoritarian statism or, alternatively, a culture of familism, I argue that the nature of goods disbursed by Japan's welfare state can be better accounted for only when seen in conjunction with the distinctive institutional arrangement of civil society in Japan.

The creation of *fukushi kokka* in the 1960s and 1970s, in which state provision was geared to the provision of social need to the exclusion of individuated need, was entirely consistent with the prevalent notion of personhood insofar as the fulfillment of individuated need was mediated in and through relations of inter-dependency within groups in civil society and family, rather than as preferences exercised by atomistic individuals. As discussed earlier, production serves as the site of reinscribing a collectivist ethos in Japan, in service of the collectivity. However, paradoxically, it is within and through relations at the workplace that the individual both acquires and expresses a sense of self. Thus, rather than the workplace being solely a realm of the formal (*omote*) and outer (*soto*) realms of everyday life, it simultaneously enables an expression of the more informal (*ura*) and inner (*uchi*) aspects of selfhood both through human relations of inter-dependence and benevolent hierarchy (*amae*) as well as the institutionalized provision of individuated need. The practice of employers providing housing, access to recreational facilities, and vacation resorts, dormitories, and wedding and funeral expense payments (even cooks) for single employees – in sum, a range of consumption goods associated with individuation – let alone medical and retirement coverage is, although more typical of big corporations than others, fairly widespread in Japan. The point here is not that this makes income support unnecessary; rather it is to draw attention to how even in the workplace, otherwise associated with collective rather than individual ends, consumption is associated with expressive individualism. That is, the practice of providing consumption goods within the workplace tacitly acknowledges autonomy in consumption even as production continues to be associated with collective rather than individual ends. Similarly, within the family – now transformed into a site of privatized relations (in contrast to the traditional *ie*) – consumption also serves to individuate. Because individuation, as circumscribed by consumption in Japan, is met within the structures of civil society, the state's provision of social need-based goods alone are deemed legitimate.[27]

The nature of goods provided by the Japanese state in relation to questions of personhood makes sense only against the larger context of civil society in Japan. By linking the seemingly narrow compass of Japan's welfare state to the provision of social need and the notion of individuality as manifest within civil society in Japan, I hope to show that accounts that either fault the state for its ideological conservatism, especially in its effort to shift the welfare burden to the family or the corporation, or invoke the traditional culture of familism as explanation of the particularity of Japan's system of welfare provision, fail to see the inter-connections between the organization of Japan's administrative state and civil society, and are consequently unable to account for its seeming success and widespread public support in the face of rising fiscal deficits.

In the absence of a specification of these inter-connections, the apparent lack of welfare advocacy or resistance in the general population eludes explanation. The lack of a populist welfare discourse appears as either the result of a general quietism characteristic of Japanese culture with its alleged emphasis on *wa* (harmony), consensus, and groupism or, in yet another conventional account, the result of Japan's tradition of familism. The quietism charge is quite easily met in light of several social movements, some of them quite militant, in contemporary Japan, including the labor unrest of the 1940s and 1950s, resistance to the renewal of the United States–Japan security treaty in 1960; the decade-long strife against the building of the Narita Airport, environmentalism, the highly visible teachers' union, and the consumer movement led by the *Shufuren* representing ostensibly that most docile of social groups in Japan – housewives. The familism charge, on the other hand, leaves the creation of universal pension and health schemes unexplained. In short, both the nature of Japan's welfare state and the absence of the normative failure of welfare in contemporary Japan can be understood in relation to the idea of personhood that prevails. In provisioning only social need, the welfare state both reinscribes and expresses the particularity of modern subjectivity in Japan.

The third phase covers the period of the 1980s and early 1990s when welfare reform was placed high on the agenda of bureaucrats and politicians alike. Characterized by a singular effort to curtail the cost of financing public assistance for the elderly, the reforms of 1986 have mainly targeted the creation of alternative facilities for the elderly. In the 1990s, even as the state has encouraged the creation of a "participation-oriented welfare society" calling on citizens to contribute voluntary services to enable the creation of communities of care that can supplement state-sponsored welfare service, it has seen fit to improve, rather than curtail, services for the unemployed, aged workers, and parents on child-care leave.

These reforms reflect influential discourses about the need to incorporate within civil society those that remain unincorporated (housewives and the disabled, for instance) indicating that current efforts are directed at further entrenching the provision of individuated need to the institutions of civil society, specifically by enhancing employment opportunities for all, including the elderly, even as the provision of universal health care and education continue to remain at the top of the state's agenda. Once again, the driving force of welfare reform has been to preserve the state provision of goods deemed vital to the productive health of Japan, namely universal coverage for medical care for the working population of Japan.

Welfare as right? The occupation years

Conventional accounts of the creation of a demilitarized, democratic, and eventually advanced capitalist Japan ground its reconstruction and recovery in the reforms undertaken by the American Occupation officials between 1945 and 1952.[28] A similar tendency is discernable in accounts of the development of welfare in post-war Japan. On these views, the Occupation Reforms mark a rupture in social policy, bringing a purportedly "reluctant" welfare provider into the mainstream of appropriate (i.e. Western) welfare thinking. The effort to transform *onkei* (welfare as mercy) to *kenri* (welfare as right) takes center stage in these accounts.[29] Ostensibly reflecting the spirit of the new constitution, drafted under the aegis of Douglas MacArthur, the Supreme Commander of Allied Forces (SCAP), and enforced in 1947, which rendered all Japanese equal in the eyes of the law, welfare in Japan was to reflect the constitutive principle of right and law, rather than divine compassion.

The new constitution, under Article 25 (Clause 1), states, "All people shall have the right to maintain minimum standards of wholesome and cultured living," and further (Clause 2) "the state must make an effort to promote and expand social welfare, social security, and public health services to cover every aspect of the life of the people."[30] To this end, the post-war state has passed seven major welfare laws: the Daily Life Security Law 1946 (revised in 1950); Child Welfare Law, 1947; Law of the Welfare of Physically Handicapped Persons, 1949; Social Welfare Service Law, 1951; Law for the Welfare of Mentally Retarded Persons, 1960; Law for the Welfare of the Aged, 1963; and Law for Maternal and Child Welfare, 1964. The major legislative effort to institute a modern welfare state, whereby the state recognized the rights of citizens to welfare provision, was thus completed under the aegis of SCAP. Its efforts to reframe Japan's social policy within a discourse of public assistance in which the state was to acknowledge responsibility for citizens stands at the center of claims about the putative rupture in social policy.

Yet, as Shindo Muneyuki[31] points out, SCAP's efforts to realign welfare policy in Japan in accordance with equal treatment, state responsibilities, and "no financial limit to assistance for guaranteeing minimum livelihood"[32] were interpreted by those responsible for legislating policy as the extension of state protection (*hogo*) to those most severely disadvantaged. The existent orientation toward a productivist social policy targeting social need, on the Japanese side, remained intact, requiring only the inclusion of the provision of individuated need to those at the very bottom of the economic ladder. This, minimal as it was (like in other countries), still ran counter to societal and state perceptions of the purpose welfare served. As shown later, the strikingly low take-up rates (less than 25 percent) of public assistance, especially by those ostensibly most in need, distinguishes the Japanese case. That the end of the war brought with it the sudden influx of 5.36 million unemployed into the Japanese economy between September 1945 and May 1947 necessitating state support also contributed to this modification in orientation.

Accordingly, the Daily Life Security Law, in principle committed to providing public assistance to all citizens, came into force on October 1, 1946. The Japanese translation of the law, however, it is worth noting, is "Daily Life Protection" implying that the state would extend protection to those most needy but state assistance was not to be seen as *kenri* (right) or an individual entitlement. The notion of welfare as social right in Western countries, on the other hand, although still far from being fully realized, nonetheless provides the ideal that grounds the state provision of welfare. In Japan, on the other hand, welfare has not been justified in the language of citizen right. This interpretation was to guide the legislation of all future social policy laws, although it appeared to some intellectuals at the time to run contrary to the spirit and letter of the new constitution. Specifically, *seizon-ken* (the right to live) enshrined in Article 25 of the constitution was meant to foster the ideal of *fukushi* (welfare) as a citizen right rather than as state beneficence. That the new constitution was subject to two different interpretations, one in Japanese and the other in English, each implying a subtly different conception of welfare is noteworthy. In the English text, Article 25(2) reads, "in all spheres of life, the State shall use its endeavors for the promotion and extension of social welfare and security, and of public health,"[33] including *seizon-ken* (the right to live). I quote,

> As to the right to maintain the minimum standards of wholesome, and cultured living in English, "the wholesome" is expressed as kenko de in Japanese with meaning of healthy. In the process of interpretation, or Japanisation of the GHQ draft – the "wholesome" seems to have been reduced to health, whereas the wholesome can refer not only to health just as a target of medical care but also the sound living in a harmonious state as whole.
>
> (Takahashi 1997: 64)

The discrepancy between the English and Japanese versions of the newly minted occupation social policy reforms can be readily understood in reference to the continued conception of welfare as related to Japan's productivist orientation. The antipathy to the provision of individuated need, evident in debates about the correct interpretation of the "right to live" clause, in the face of a ready recognition of *fukushi* (welfare) as the provision of social need (e.g. medical care) is indicative not simply of a continuation of a war-time mentality, but rather of a fairly well-articulated and entrenched orientation to social policy as a whole in Japan's modern history.

The creation of *fukushi kokka* (welfare state) 1960–1980

This productivist orientation became clearly visible in the first major steps taken toward the creation of a *fukushi kokka* or welfare state in post-war Japan. Thus far, the provision of welfare had targeted, other than labor, specific groups deemed needy by the newly created democratic state (children, people with disabilities, and families of war veterans). In the 1950s, however, the first flush of what was to become known as the economic miracle – coupled with increasing demands by labor unions and Japan's dominant left parties, the Japanese Communist Party (JCP) and the Japanese Socialist Party (JSP) – led to the provision of universal medical care and pension by 1961, enabling Japan to claim its place among the group of advanced industrialized welfare states. In 1960, the year that universal health coverage was first attempted, Japan's social public welfare programs made up only 4.0 percent of Gross National Product (GNP); by 1987 they had increased to 13.3 percent, close to the US equivalent of 14.2 percent with per capita expenditure of $2710 and $2588 in Japan and the United States respectively.[34]

How did Japan go from being a "welfare laggard" to a "welfare super-power" in its universal provision of medical care and pensions? Why, on the other hand, was the provision of fiscally less demanding benefits, like unemployment insurance, aid to people with disabilities, housing, food, and income support not actively pursued by state and citizens alike, despite the need for state assistance? (The absence of any effort, even now, to equip public amenities [public transportation for instance] to accommodate the needs of the disabled is a particularly telling commentary on the state's non-provision of individuated needs). In explaining the phenomenal expansion of Japan's welfare state in the 1960s, attention is usually directed to the economic boom that occurred in that decade or, alternatively, to the "crisis and compensation" (Calder 1988) tactics of the all powerful bureaucrats administering Japan at the time, in conjunction with the support of the ruling Liberal Democratic Party.[35]

While these explanations may help account for the rapid growth in medical and pension coverage, they are less helpful in making sense of why the provision of a range of other goods (what I have called "individuated goods") did not similarly increase, despite the growing need for state support for those outside the supportive networks of both family and civil society. Seen in a comparative light, the development of welfare states in other contexts reveals an increased propensity toward the provision of individuated goods as the *raison d'etre* of social policy (Marshall 1950; Titmuss 1976). Within the United States, Canada, and Scandinavian countries, for instance, the creation of social security schemes, including medical care and pensions, was accompanied by a simultaneous increase in the provision of unemployment insurance, food stamps, housing benefits, and so on. In Japan, to the contrary, the almost overnight creation of universal pension and medical care systems did not reconstitute the idea of welfare to include the provision of individuated need; rather, the pre-1945 commitment to the provision of social need as a means of enhancing productivity was further entrenched. A brief look at the debates that took place around the provision of universal pension and medical care systems is particularly revealing in this regard.

As the objective need to include all citizens in universal welfare schemes began to become apparent with the socio-economic transformation wrought by the era of high-speed growth, the discourses about the traditional provider of a safety net for individuals changed. An increasing demand for wage workers placed a particularly high burden on rural communities to continue to maintain the reproductive structure necessary to supply a labor force, particularly as labor mobility from the agricultural to the manufacturing sector constrained the traditional *ie* (extended household) structure of family life in Japan. The pre-war family system had, by convention, placed the burden of caring for the aged and infirm within households on the elder son, continuing a tradition that had been placed in Japan since the early nineteenth century. In a bid to reconcile the twin pressures of an increasing need to universalize *fukushi* or welfare given the pressures on the *ie* system in the 1950s, while at the same time staying within the parameters of the prevalent conception and institutionalization of welfare as productivist social policy, the Civil Code was revised in the early 1950s. Whereas the former Civil Code had placed the entire burden of caring for the aged or the infirm (including children, the unemployed, or the mentally/physically disabled) squarely on the shoulders of the elder son, the revised Code distributed the burden more equitably; Article 877(1) now specified that "the lineal relatives and brothers and sisters shall be under duty to furnish each other support."

Many have interpreted this attempt to forestall the extension of the state provision of individuated welfare goods to all citizens as an early indication of modern Japan's patriarchal, or "controlling and divisive" state tactics. By legitimating a reconstituted notion of the family imbued with the moral responsibility of caring for members, critics argue, the post-war state succeeded in creating an ideology of care that made the family, particularly women, responsible for the well-being of members.

Two points are worth noting here. First, those who interpret this as an attempt to reinvigorate the traditional idea of the family (*ie*) miss a significant shift in the very idea of the family reflected, albeit subtly, in the revised Civil Code. Rather than promoting continuity in the traditional idea of the family, the revised Civil Code reflects the *reconstitution* of the family that inevitably accompanied the transformation of society into a capitalist one. Capitalism reworks all realms of social life, including the family, principally by privatizing social relations. In regard to welfare, prevalent Confucian notions of family in Japan, in accordance with their recognition of the law of primogeniture, had placed the entire burden of care of aging parents on the elder son. The new Civil Code, by making *all* members of the family equally responsible, implicitly recognized their obligations to each other as ensuing from the inherently *private* nature of inter-personal relations within the familial domain. That is, unlike the earlier Confucian code which held only the elder son accountable, the new Civil Code re-conceived the family on modern lines by recognizing all members as now equally responsible.

Implicit within this too was the subtle recognition of the family as made up of individuals whose patterns of consumption the state would, for the same reason, attempt to mobilize in service of the collective goal of capital accumulation: recall Prime Minister Ikeda's Income Doubling Plan of 1960 and the attempt to promote the consumption of televisions, refrigerators, and electric appliances on the grounds that they enhanced the quality of life, while at the same time attempting to reclaim consumption as the ground of a collectivist project of nation building. Without a recognition of the reconstitution of the family as an individualized realm of activity, the state's disparate attempts over several decades to create a *Nihonjinron*[36] discourse of continuity in the idea of family becomes difficult to fathom. (If the family has indeed continued unchanged in the wake of Japan's transition from feudalism to capitalism, why the periodic attempts to foster a traditional spirit of familism?)

Second, the absence of the provision of goods that meet individual need rather than the provision of social need–based goods provides the focus of these assessments. The very premise of these assessments, however, rests on a prior normative judgment that it is the Kantian ontological subject (self-sustaining, autonomous) that is the proper object of social policy, rendering the state provision of goods that meet individuated need the only viable means of fulfilling the state's welfare obligations to the individual. If, however, the proper object of social policy is the provision of goods that meet *social* rather than individuated need, the expansion and growth of Japan's post-war welfare state strictly in accordance with the provision of social need does not pose a problem from a comparative perspective. Indeed in the context of the institutional arrangement of civil society in Japan, where hierarchies of wealth and status appear, until very recently, remarkably low when compared to other capitalist societies,[37] the state's focus on the provision of social as opposed to individuated need appears to be entirely consistent with the normative structure of civil society.

The remarkably egalitarian distribution of wealth in modern Japan, evident in relatively low disparities in income between senior level managers and workers, the blue-collarization of company benefits (typically reserved for white-collar employees in most advanced industrialized countries), and the similarity in patterns of consumption that leads most (90 percent) Japanese to identify themselves as middle class, renders the state's emphasis on the universal provision of social goods rather than individual needs consistent with the organizing principle of modern Japan's state and civil society.[38]

Thus, among the first steps taken to expand the state's commitment to welfare provision entailed universalizing health care. From being a benefit largely reserved for the military and bureaucratic elite and industrial labor that served Japan's crucial war-time needs, health care reform in the early 1950s extended provision to those employed in the sectors of construction, education, medical, and social welfare, but excluded those working in the agricultural, forestry, fishery, and service sectors. It was only after the second round of reforms in 1961 that all employees received health coverage through a combination of seven divisions of the health insurance program including coverage for (1) those who were employed by a company that had more than five permanent employees; (2) seamen; (3) day-labor; (4) teachers; (5) civil servants; (6) those in local administrations; and (7) public company employees like the Japanese National Railways.[39] For the close to 32 percent of the population that was not covered, the National Health Insurance system was launched in 1961 ensuring that all Japanese, regardless of occupation, income, or age, would be guaranteed access to medical care. As a result, health care in contemporary Japan is provided mostly through job-related insurance, which is, however, underwritten by the state as discussed below. For the 36 percent of population not eligible for work-linked insurance, national health insurance is available directly through local government programs under central government supervision. A brief look at its key features is instructive.

In comparative terms, Japan appears to have achieved an enviable success in providing cost-effective, universal health care. Its gross health indices are the best in the world: infant mortality rate is 0.46 percent, life expectancy for males is 75.09 and 81.1 for females; its expenditure, on the other hand, is 6.8 percent of GDP, virtually half that of the United States.[40] Until the reforms of 1994, the system of universal medical insurance established in 1961 has provided practically free medical care to the elderly since 1972. About half the cost of the national system is funded by an 8.4 percent tax on wages paid by both employer and employee; central and local governments provide about 40 percent of the cost and the remainder is paid by the patient.[41]

Some of the system's more impressive features include universal coverage by employee or government insurance; reimbursement fees for medications, procedures, hospitals stays, and clinic visits are standard throughout Japan, set by a governmental committee of the Ministry of Health, Labor and welfare; hospital stays are longer than those in other OECD countries since the provision of long-term care via hospitalization is the norm (a 1-month hospital stay after surgery is common due to a prevailing norm that focuses on rest as a curative for illness, coupled with the absence of diagnostic-related or reimbursement limits and lack of pressure on the ailing to return to work.).[42]

About 81 percent of Japan's hospitals and 94 percent of its physicians' offices are privately owned, most of them being small, physician-owned family concerns. Larger hospitals within the public sector with high-tech facilities employ physicians on a fixed monthly salary; patients can choose to seek treatment in a clinic or hospital. Fees are standardized, set by the government, regardless of physicians' expertise, facilities, or geographical location. Consumers have no choice but to join the statutory plan offered by their employer; the self-employed must enroll in the scheme provided by their local government and cannot opt out of statutory schemes since private insurance, which is limited to cash payments to cover incidental expenses during hospitalization, is insignificant.[43]

Commentators are struck by the quality of care, low costs, and the level of equity in Japan's health care system. According to a 1988 survey conducted in Tokyo, neither the utilization rate nor the health care expenditure per person was affected by an individual's income.[44] Equity in system is insured because cost or quality of care is non-negotiable due to strict government regulation. Inequities in co-payment rates are mitigated by the provision that any out-of-pocket co-payment faced by a patient in a given month over the amount of 60 000 yen ($480), or $267 for those with a low income is reimbursed regardless of the plan. For those covered by the National Health insurance (insurer for the self-employed, pensioners, and low income groups), the government acts as the insurer and the central government provides a direct subsidy amounting to half the total expenditures.[45] As Naoki Ikegami notes, Japan's health care system

> underscores a socio-philosophical orientation toward collective well-being over individual liberties. The precedence of group welfare is partially reflected in the rather low incidence of medical litigation in Japan.
>
> (Ikegami 1992: 283)

However, comparisons between social spending in Japan and other advanced industrialized countries (Esping-Andersen 1990; Gould 1993) tend to highlight the seemingly wide disparity in the total volume of government expenditure, as evidenced in Table 4.1. Moreover, when juxtaposed with comparisons of per capita income in OECD countries (Table 4.2), social spending in Japan appears deceptively low (Table 4.3).

But, as several scholars have noted (Maruo 1974; Anderson 1993; Goodman and Peng 1996), this indicator is deceptive since, in Japan, the distinctive method of computing government expenditure on social policy (of which health care is the key component) results in understating the state's fiscal role. Funds for the main health care programs that provide universal rights to health care

Table 4.1 Major Industrialized Countries Per Capita National Income

Year	1985	1989	1990
Japan	$9,033	$18,472	$19,035
United States	13,349	16,704	17,379
West Germany	7,830	14,864	17,461
France	7,031	12,752	15,721
Great Britain	6,039	10,820	12,856

Source: "Quality of Life in Japan: is it Affluent or Not?" *Japan Economic Institute Report* Ministry of Labor, # 22A, June 12, 1992: 2.

Table 4.2 General Government Expenditures as a Percentage of Gross Domestic Product

	1989	**1992**
Japan	23.48	23.83
Korea	23.47	25.06
UK	35.80	43.17
Sweden	39.50	46.19

Source: Kwon (1997) 'Comparative Perspectives on East Asian Welfare Systems,' *Journal of Social Policy* 26 (October): 470.

Table 4.3 Trends in Government Social Welfare Spending in Japan (percent of gross national product)

Fiscal year	**Medical care (%)**	**Pensions (%)**	**Other* (%)**	**Total (%)**
1970	2.8	1.1	0.8	4.7
1973	2.9	1.4	0.9	5.2
1975	3.7	2.6	1.4	7.7
1980	4.3	4.3	1.4	10.0
1984	4.4	5.1	1.5	11.1

* Includes unemployment insurance benefits, workers' compensation, and child allowances.
Source: Social Security Research Institute (Cited in *Japan Economic Institute Report* # 12A, March 27, 1987).

> do not go through government accounts and, therefore, this expenditure is not recorded as part of government expenditure. Public agencies, which manage the financing of health care programs, collect insurance premiums through either companies or local authorities, and reimburse health care fees....this being so, a table of government expenditure necessarily misses a significant part of health care expenditure which is still publicly spent.
>
> (Kwon 1997: 470–471)

Social welfare systems contain different combinations of provider and regulator roles for the state. In health care for the aged the Japanese government provides 30 percent of the financial resources. However, the public agencies operating on an insurance basis that reimburse health care fees are regulated by the state in strict accordance with its overall social policy agenda. As such, health care still falls within the ambit of state provision, although the means by which it is disbursed varies from, for instance, the National Health Service in Britain. Thus, contrary to comparative aggregate figures, even though government social expenditure as a share of Japan's GDP appears lower than that of the United States (for instance 17.5 percent in 1981 compared to 20 percent for the United States), the government plays a larger role in the overall social expenditure of Japan (accounting for over 92 percent of overall social expenditure in 1980 compared to 68 percent in the United States).[46] Between 1973 and 1984, Japan's social spending increased at a 15.5 percent average annual pace, rising from 5.2 percent of GNP to 11.1 percent in 1984.[47] As Table 4.4 indicates, health care constitutes the core of the Japanese welfare state, with spending on pensions rapidly catching up due to the fast-aging population.

To illustrate the larger claim advanced here, I briefly consider goods other than health care that were provisioned in this period of welfare state expansion, specifically, pensions, child allowances, and aid to single mothers.

The pension system, universalized by 1961, is a combination of private and public insurance. Thus far, in keeping with Japan's productivist ethos which linked welfare to industrial policy, only workers employed by large companies and the government had received these particular benefits. Given the structuration of the Japanese economy into a relatively small number of export-oriented big companies (*kaisha*) and the predominant sector made up of small companies and sub-contracting firms (some with less than five workers each), in the 1950s, those covered by pension systems accounted for less than one-third of the workforce leaving those engaged in agriculture, the self-employed, and the employed with no coverage. By the 1960s, however, the rapid growth

Table 4.4 Government Social Expenditure in Japan

Year	1980 (%)	2000 (%)	2010 (%)	2025 (%)
Medical Care	4.80	6.5	7.08	9
Pensions	4.20	9.6	12.89	13.40
Education	5.10	4.10	4.60	4.40
Other	1.30	1.30	1.30	1.30
Total	15.40	21.06	25.86	27.16

Source: International Monetary Fund, *Aging and Social Expenditure in the Major Industrial Countries, 1980–2025*, 1986: 56–57 (Cited in *Japan Economic Institute Report*, #16A, April 21, 1989: 7).

of the pension system ensured universal coverage to all, regardless of the nature of employment. The Employees Pension Program (EPP), established in 1941, covers all employees in private sector organizations that have five or more workers (about 44 percent of the population). National and local government employees, teachers at private schools, and workers in farm, forestry, and fishery are covered by separate programs, accounting for 10 percent of all insured persons. The National Pension Scheme (NPS), established in 1961, covers all those who do not come under any other program, covering about 46 percent of the population.[48]

With the pension reforms of 1986, the concept of a basic pension was introduced, requiring all to enroll in the NPS, which serves as a basic floor or safety net, in addition to the pensions based on previous earnings and occupational level. This tiered system of pensions (similar to Europe), combined with the lump-sum severance pay typically given upon retirement in firms with 1000 employees or more, provides a pension package comparable to those of other OECD countries. The introduction of women's pensions in 1986 (all women have compulsory coverage under the NPS regardless of their occupational status) has been instrumental in furthering the goal of universal coverage.[49]

In regard to welfare for children, the comparison between Japan and the United States is also revealing. Unlike the antipoverty strategy adopted in the United States (until the 1996 Welfare Reform Act), in which programs like the Aid to Families with Dependent Children (AFDC) specified maximum family benefits, the equivalent program in Japan, the Child Allowance Program, initiated in 1962, gives flat-amount benefits to all children of the insured worker. Even though the latter uses income ceilings, it is quasi-universal due to its flat-rate provision to families and because its income ceilings are relatively high, especially in comparison to median annual family incomes, thereby enabling the prevention, rather than amelioration, of poverty. Moreover, because these programs are based on "level-income tests" instead of sliding scale income tests (widely used in the United States), they provide identical benefits to all families that fall within a certain range of income. This is consistent with, as Martha Ozawa (1991) points out, Japan's dominant strategy, which is

> an investment strategy, not an anti-poverty strategy...Japanese policy makers seem most interested in the development of the skills, resources, and human capital of every child born in Japan....(they)

> clearly link child welfare policy to social policy for the elderly and to economic policy.
>
> (Ozawa 1991: 19)

Also, unlike the United States where AFDC recipients, mostly female-headed families with children, were heavily stigmatized: "there is little or no stigma attached to receiving allowances and female-headed families with relatively high income can receive allowance" (Ozawa 1991: 19–20). Further, if local welfare departments ascertain that a particular female-headed household is in need of a protected living environment,

> they are housed, at no charge in residential facilities scattered across Japan. A typical facility has apartments, a day-care facility, a playground, and a counseling office. In 1985, 348 such facilities provided services to 7,034 families involving 14,753 persons.
>
> (Ozawa 1991: 13–14)

The treatment of single mothers and children is thus striking in that they are not treated as social pariahs likely to reproduce a cycle of failure and poverty. The contrast with the United States is particularly telling. Unlike the former, where racialized distinctions between the deserving (mentally or physically disabled, elderly) and the un-deserving (able bodied) have contributed to the view that state support generates a culture of "welfare dependency" that can only be stopped by punitive measures that would withdraw support to all, including single mothers with dependent children, state support of single mothers in Japan is not stigmatized. (As the following chapter shows, though, there is a clear distinction made, even among single mothers, the most rapidly growing segment of the "new poor" of the *Heisei* recession era, between general assistance and other forms of state-based aid.) The absence of social stigma is both indicative of the larger societal understanding that single mothers, insofar as they are crucial elements of both biological and social reproduction, constitute a valuable national resource deserving of societal help to get them back into the mainstream of productive life.

This, however, it should be pointed out, is at odds with the general attitude to public assistance among recipients and non-recipients alike. As elaborated further in this chapter, what is striking about public assistance in Japan is the discrepancy between the volume of need and the actual use of state support. As Marr (1997) documents in his anthropological study of the *yoseba* (slums) district, the low take-up rate of public assistance (25 percent) is indicative not of the lack of need but rather of the antipathy to the receipt of state-provisioned monetary aid, in contrast to the willingness to accept non-monetized aid in the form of medical aid, for instance. The continued availability of skid row resources – for example casual labor, affordable single-room housing, and cheap eateries in the *yoseba* – that enable a measure of autonomy, albeit tenuous, on the part of those in need, on the other hand, serves to further augment societal antipathy to public assistance. I develop this point at greater length below. There is, however, an interesting gender dimension to this : this antipathy to the receipt of goods that meet individuated need appears to apply solely to males; as the above discussion makes clear, women, especially single mothers, are excluded from this stigmatization by virtue of their perceived role in biological and, more crucially *social*, reproduction. In other words, it is because public assistance to single mothers falls into the category of social, *not* individuated, need that the absence of stigmatization becomes explicable, further substantiating the broad theoretical claim made here about the organizing principle of Japan's welfare system.[50]

The first oil shock in 1973 coincided with a period of severe inflation in Japan (over 5 percent since 1969). Rather than sending Japan into an immediate recession, however, the annual GDP growth rate of 9.9 percent between 1960 and 1973 slowed to about 3.8 percent between 1974 and 1980. With regard to state budgets on welfare spending, the pace of increase of social budgets was basically maintained throughout the 1970s. In fact, contrary to some recommendations to reduce welfare spending, a widespread support for the expansion of welfare was evident. The year 1973 was officially crowned as *fukushi gannen* (the first year of welfare) by the Japanese government. In December 1973, Finance Minister Fukuda Takeo announced an increase of 36.3 percent in the welfare budget, commensurate with the 36.6 percent increase in the 1962 budget. By this, however, state officials had in mind a distinctive arrangement of welfare provision in which both the public and the private sectors would cooperate to create a "Japanese style" welfare society. In 1975, a research group assigned to provide advice to the Prime Minister and the Social Security Institution Deliberation Council attached to the Prime Minister's office recommended an increase in social security spending, rather than its reduction. A proposal for a tax hike so as to fund increased spending was also made.[51] By 1977 the annual rate of increase of the social budget exceeded that of the general state budgets. The rapid rise in unemployment, 1 million in 1975, no doubt also contributed to the LDP's decision to withhold cutbacks in welfare spending. Noteworthy, however, for our purposes here, was the LDP's quite explicit emphasis throughout the 1970s on the need to continue to improve the medical care system.[52]

Of particular interest in this regard is the influential defense and *raison d'etre* of welfare provided by Miura Funio,[53] a leading expert on welfare. Distinguishing between what he refers to as market and non-market needs, Miura sees the well-being of individuals as constituted within the totality of state, market, and family provision. State provision, for Miura, is necessitated by the inability of the family to provide specific goods (such as medical care, education, and old-age pensions); "support for securing daily life," on the other hand, should remain within the purview of families or neighborhood associations and volunteers. Closely related to this distinction was Miura's insistence on the differential role of monetary and non-monetary support. Emphasizing the state's provision of non-monetary support as the only adequate means of dispensing welfare that met social need, Miura's "need-oriented" approach provided the influential framework within which welfare reforms since the 1970s have been implemented.

Although several scholars, Japanese and Western, have interpreted Miura's need-based approach as a thinly veiled conservative attempt to forestall the creation of a rights-based welfare state, a somewhat different interpretation might help shed light on why it resonated so deeply with both policy-makers and recipients alike. Unlike culture-based arguments that take the individual's reliance on the *ie* as the basic sociological premise of modern Japan, or those who see the state's utilization of views like Miura's as an attempt to create an ideology of "familism," it might be more meaningful to relate the distinction between social and individuated need implicit in Miura's formulation (as well as the specific legislation on welfare) to the social meanings attached to the demarcations made between the more formal, outer, and the informal, inner, aspects of individual identity. As discussed in the previous chapter, individual expression is seen to be highly circumscribed and context dependent, the *omote/honne/uchi* realms signifying the more informal, inner, private realm of expression; the *ura/soto/tatemae*, the more formal, outer realm. The former more informal, private expression, and the latter more formal, disciplined, other-oriented mode of conduct can be seen to have parallels in the demarcation of properly commodifiable (or monetary) and non-commodifiable (non-monetary) goods. Because medical care and education, for instance, are linked to social productivity, they may be seen as representing the outer or social form; individuated need, on the other hand, especially to the extent that it is located within the familial realm, represents the *honne* (inner) or more private dimension of the life-world. Thus, interpretations that see the allocation of individuated need to the self in relation to the family unit as simply manifestation of state manipulation may be missing the deeper undertow of meanings associated with the consumption of different kinds of welfare goods.

It is because the private realm of familial interaction precludes the provision of certain goods that their provision by the state is normatively consistent with the ideal of personhood in modern Japan. On the other hand, it is because the familial context embodies an inner (*honne*) realm of privacy that the state provision of individuated need is socially suspect. Note that arguments against the state provision of individuated need are of an entirely different order in the case of individual rights-based (Western) welfare states. Here, the state provision of individuated need violates an ideal of personhood that posits the autonomous individual as its *primary* referent; in the case of Japan, the state provision of individuated need violates the existent ideal of personhood insofar as the Japanese notion demarcates specific contexts (*uchi-ura-tatemae*) of social life as individuated.

In sum, the 1960s and 1970s saw a rapid expansion of welfare programs, heavily skewed to the provision of goods deemed necessary for the collective well-being of Japan. In keeping with its war-time prioritization of health care, both policy-makers and intellectuals in post-war Japan advocated an enhanced focus on its universal provision. At the height of welfare state expansion in the 1960s and 1970s, much like in pre-war times, the notion of welfare remained closely tied to the dictates of Japan's productivist agenda. The dual emphasis on the universal provision of health care by the state and employment as the primary means of provisioning individuated need was reinforced by the discourses and legislation that prevailed in this period. The emphasis on employment as a mechanism for ensuring the provision of individuated need meant also that welfare did not take on the connotation of poverty alleviation. This dimension of Japan's social policy is addressed at length in the following section.

Welfare reform: 1980–1990

In the aftermath of the economic stagflation of the 1970s, references to the "English disease" (or variously the French or Italian disease) began to be increasingly used to warn of the "crisis" that was fast overtaking Western welfare states. A group of scholars (*Gurupu 1984-nen*) published an article in 1975 called *Nihon no Jisatsu* (Suicide of Japan), in which they warned of the dangers consequent on the state acceding to the "excessive demands of citizens and loss of self-discipline in mass-society due to a misunderstanding of democracy." Despite frequent references to the fear of the welfare disease in academic circles, however, the OECD's report "The Welfare State in Crisis" drew scant attention in Japan, even though it was almost immediately translated into Japanese in 1981. Although references to the English disease continued to pepper official statements, the prospect of reversing the gains made in social policy was never a serious concern.

Distinguishing between *fukushi kokka* (welfare state) and *fukushi shakai* (welfare society), the dominant discourse of this time emphasized the self-help of citizens as the main stay of welfare provision, advocating the state provision of welfare goods only in those areas in which the community or voluntary organizations could not fulfill requisite needs. Several officials suggested that if the pace of the 1970s reforms had continued they would "have resulted in more generous benefits and higher contributions than even the most welfare-oriented European countries."[54] Of particular note was the Life Cycle Plan presented by a working group to the Prime Minister in 1975, which explicitly drew attention to the problems increasingly faced by Western welfare states. Arguing that reliance on the state created "weak" individuals, the authors of the Life Cycle Plan advocated instead the creation of strong individuals whose capacities for self-reliance rather than the welfare state's compensatory provisions should be the proper target of social policy. Recommending a greater focus on the provision of lifetime education, secured pensions, health care, and making available sufficient housing for private ownership, the Life Cycle Plan put forward a notion of welfare that made a clear distinction between state and self-reliance.

Ironically, it was only after the economic slump was over in the early 1980s that advocates of welfare reform began publicly to link the need for welfare with individual failings. Even as debates about the need to cut back on welfare (*fukushi kirisute*) began to emerge in the early 1980s, critics targeted individual recipients of income support such as the unemployed, rather than the universal schemes of health care provision, reinforcing the premise of Japan's welfare state: meeting consumption needs was the responsibility of individuals; the rights of citizens to state-provisioned welfare did not (and could not) extend to the provision of individuated need. In other words, the object of critique was individuated need, thereby reinscribing the productive citizen as the social subject of welfare policy.

This emphasis on self-help was juxtaposed with reports that detailed elaborate criticism of the British and Swedish models of welfare. Professor Koyama Ken'ichi's book *Eikoku-byo no Kyokun* (Lessons of the English Disease) published in 1978, in particular, was used as the basis for an LDP-sponsored report in 1979 to create support for a "Japanese style welfare society" that sought to replace an all-out reliance on the state with *jijo* (self-help) in the context of family and community. This has been interpreted by several critics as an attempt to deflect criticism of the LDP's effort to curtail the exponential growth of social spending.[55] Critics of Japan's welfare state, on the other hand, have seen fit to find in the discourse of "Japanese style welfare society" confirmation of their views that Japan has been unusually successful in resisting the development of a welfare state to the detriment of individual citizens, particularly women. The ideological discourse of *jijo* is seen as regressive, the glorification of the family an attempt at the "invention of tradition" so as to perpetuate a social-political order in which the putative normative authority of family is used as a convenient substitute for responsibilities that strictly belong to the state. (Whether the LDP's attempt to stonewall an increase in welfare spending succeeded, leading to change in the goods the state provided in the 1980s and 1990s, is an issue I take up further along in the discussion.) Suffice it to say here, critics, although correct in their assessment of the LDP's intentions, are too hasty in assuming that the discourse of familism was readily translated into practice. For, as I will show below and in the chapter that follows, contrary to the assumptions underpinning these views, state provision of specific goods in the 1980s and 1990s has been enhanced, rather than curtailed; the discourse of familism appears to have prevailed only in the disbursement of goods that meet individuated need.[56]

Ostensibly meant to foster a new conception of welfare, that of *katsuryoku-aru-fukushi shakai no jitsugen* (realization of welfare society with vitality), proposed in the 1980s, it re-emphasized the discourse of *jijo* or self-help in the context of family, enterprise, and state-based welfare. The central question posed at the time had to do with the necessity of increasing state finance, rather than attempting a drastic rollback of welfare provision. The increase in corporate taxation by 2 percent coupled with the introduction of the 2 percent consumption tax was seen as a way of maintaining current levels of welfare provision without drastically reducing the benefits provided in health care, pension, and education. This is not to say that LDP leaders did not vociferously echo Reagan and Thatcher's arguments in favor of the privatization of welfare in a bid to stem the tide of welfare spending, but that the concrete steps taken sustained the state's commitment to social spending on specific goods. Reflecting the government's increasing concern with Japan's rapidly aging population,[57] an attempt was made in the 1980s reforms to streamline social security spending by redirecting resources to specific services. Japan's rapidly aging population, a result of both a declining birthrate and a radically improved health care has catapulted care for the aged onto the top of the state's welfare concerns.[58] The percentage of those 65 years old and over was 4.9 percent in 1950, 14.8 percent in 1995, and projected to be about 25.8 percent by the year 2025 (Health and Welfare Statistics Association, 1996), placing an enormous burden on the working and tax-paying population of Japan. Interestingly, although the United States has a similar demographic profile (in 1995 the United States had an over-65 population of approximately 12.7 percent while Japan's had approximately 12 percent),[59] the institutional and community-based services, especially for the frail elderly in both countries indicate wide disparity: over 30 percent of non-institutionalized elderly live alone in the United States compared to only 10 percent in Japan. Despite the virtual doubling of public expenditure on social welfare, the Japanese Civil Code, Section 877, stipulates "that those who are in lineal relationships are responsible for supporting and caring for each other" (Emlet 1998: 99).

The piecemeal and incremental reforms undertaken in 1981 placed surcharges on medical treatment for the elderly; partially reduced the level of coverage of health insurance; raised the entitlement age for national pensions (from 60 to 70 for men; 55 to 60 for women); and imposed a 3 percent sales tax to generate greater revenue. The reforms of the early 1980s were meant to increase Old-Age Health Care Facilities (Osawa 1995: 220) designed for bedridden elderly who needed care and supervision, although not hospitalization, for a short period of time. These facilities were meant to compensate for the introduction of a nominal fee for medical care, replacing the earlier system of free medical coverage for the elderly. As many commentators have noted, the main aim of these changes was to discourage a complete reliance on public services and encourage *zaitaku* or stay-home care. But it also reveals a second emphasis, one not so easily discernable in the reforms of the 1980s but clearly developed in the reforms of 1994. This has to do with an ongoing attempt to make work, rather than dependence on the state, the primary source of the provision of the necessities of daily life.

Unlike the case of the United States, however, where the effort to move people from welfare to work has involved federal funding for the creation of non-competitive subsidized jobs (hence the ironic term "work-fare"), in Japan, the effort has not been directed at the creation of an equivalent transitional realm (between welfare and competitive work). Rather, the state has sought to identify existent areas of need within civil society which can utilize the abilities of the elderly (e.g. by employing the elderly in recreational centers for the elderly). Further, in contrast to "work-fare" which involves the close monitoring of "clients" so as to prevent behavioral lapses, the renewed emphasis on work in Japan involves no such state regulation. The call to re-absorb the elderly within the productive activities of civil society simply re-invigorates the social meaning that work carries in the Japanese context. (I consider this point further below.)

The incremental changes that have taken place in elderly care have focused on enacting measures that would lengthen the elderly's active participation in civil society. Current labor force participation among the elderly of Japan is thus much higher than in other OECD countries (over one-third of men aged 65 and above are in the labor force), a situation unique among the developed countries. (In the United States, only 12 percent of those aged 65 and older are in the labor force.)[60] In a bid to re-incorporate the elderly into the mainstream of life via work, since 1980, the Ministry of Labor has instituted over 260 Silver Human resource Centers (SHRC) that provide senior citizens with opportunities for paid work on a part-time temporary basis.[61] Including over 310 000 members by 1994, the SHRCs are open to all aged 60 and above, not just the poor.

In June 1986, the government announced its Policy for the Aging Society, a comprehensive set of policies targeting employment, welfare, education, housing, and environment designed to create a new socio-economic system to meet the needs of a citizenry whose life expectancy was 80 years. Rather than marking a drastic change in the notion of welfare, the changes of the 1980s are better seen as an attempt to re-direct resources into the productive sectors of society so as to offset the objective dictates of fiscal spending on the rapidly growing numbers of elderly citizens. As Roger Goodman and Ito Peng note,

> The Japanese public seems to accept these changes without much resistance. This may be partly because the government has been very effective in raising public awareness about an aging society and potential costs this will entail.... It has to be emphasized (that) the reforms in the 1980s in Japan should not be seen as a neo-liberal assault on the welfare state but were largely reached by consensus,

> with only the left-wing unions (i.e. non-large firms) and the Socialist party being in opposition.
>
> (Goodman and Peng 1996: 204)

This emphasis on employment as a sustained focus of social policy in Japan (now extended to the elderly as well) is worth noting here. Unlike interpretations that view this focus as a conservative attempt to further forestall welfare provision, an alternative explanation may prove helpful.

As previously noted, the claim that welfare states create work disincentives has now become legion in both conservative and, as we have already seen, post-Marxian arguments. State guarantees of income should generate a disincentive to work since an increase in income of even 1 yen (or dollar for that matter) would result in a loss of benefits. The problematic assumption about the disutility of work underpinning the above argument has already been noted. The case of Japan provides an explicit substantiation of this claim. Unlike the dominant view that the motivation to work stems from economic incentives to satisfy deferred needs, the case of Japan reveals otherwise. Work is seen not only as means of ensuring one's place in the collectivity but, as Ozawa notes,

> because they want to be accepted as good members of the group to which they belong. The Japanese, in general, do not see economic incentives as the only motivating factor for work. They work hard because they want to be respected as persons who excel in doing or making certain things... in such an environment, the concern about work disincentives seems remote when it comes to the issue of paying taxes to support (welfare) programs.
>
> (Ozawa 1980: 18)

It is in this context that the state's attempt to mitigate the problems of elderly care by reintegrating them within civil society makes better sense. If indeed family was seen as the solution to the problem of aging, as several critics suggest, the state's investment in these alternative strategies of "re-incorporating" the elderly would be unnecessary. The argument that the state's efforts are instrumentally motivated by electoral concerns fails to carry much weight given the low level of interest-group lobbying on behalf of the elderly in Japan as compared to, for instance, the United States. Rather, the very fact that these initiatives come overwhelmingly from the state (bureaucrats or politicians, as Calder [1988] and Anderson [1993] have argued), explaining the *nature* of these initiatives, requires linking their distinctive logic to the normative principles that undergird Japanese society. The contours of this dominant thinking become clearer in light of the ideas that proved to be most influential in guiding welfare reform.

The reasons for this simultaneous increase and restraint in the provision of welfare goods can be found in Baba Keinosuke's influential book *Fukushi Shakai No Nihon-Teki Keitai* (Japanese Form of Welfare Society) published in 1980.[62] Rejecting both the emphasis on familism sponsored by the LDP as well as the all-out reliance on the state advocated by left-leaning Japanese scholars, Baba argued instead that the distinctive institutionalization of civil society in Japan, with its emphasis on medium level groups (corporations or companies) that mediate life within the family and the collectivity, would better serve as an appropriate locus of welfare provision, in addition to the state provision of needs that could not be met at this interim level. Rather than place all responsibility for the provisioning of individuated need on the atomistic individual (the Western model), or within the family (in accordance with alleged tradition in Japan), Baba called attention to the necessary dispensation of social need (especially health care) by the state, while emphasizing that the needs pertinent to the "sphere of daily life" might be better met by creating *komyunity* (community) that would provide social networks that would compensate family-based care.

It was left to Maruo Naomi to outline the merits of Japan's "enterprise-based" welfare system in 1984.[63] Emphasizing the strength of group solidarity characteristic of market-based behavior in Japan (a collective product of distinctive features like permanent employment, the seniority wage system discussed in the previous chapter), Maruo called for the inclusion of groups traditionally left out of market-based solidarity (for instance, women and the handicapped) in what he referred to as the welfare benefits of Japanese management. In other words, for Maruo, given the institutional arrangement of civil society as well as the socially meaningful ways in which individuals constituted and expressed personhood (in relation to group solidarity), welfare could not be conceptualized (and institutionalized) at either of the two poles of family or state. Rather, the notion of welfare appropriate for Japan required a combination of family, corporation (market), and state-based provision of the well-being of the individual.

What is particularly noteworthy in Maruo's discussion is the implicit connection between the ideal of personhood specific to Japan and the need for institutionalizing welfare provision such that it may be consistent with it, and thereby most effective. While undoubtedly amenable to being put to conservative, even reactionary, usage (by drawing on its bias in favor of the gainfully employed) thus reinforcing, rather than challenging, Japan's productivist orientation (as critics such as Gould (1993) suggest), it is not inconsequential to the outcomes of welfare statism in Japan that societal understandings of individual well-being reflected in Mauro's formulation emphasized the family–corporation–state combination in the provision of welfare.

What some might see as the overly narrow compass of Japan's welfare state, emphasizing health care and pensions over and beyond unemployment benefits, housing, hunger alleviation, and so on, appears as entirely consistent with the normative structure of civil society, family, and state, the LDP's attempt to place all the burden for care on the family unit notwithstanding. It is for this reason that periods of economic slowdown, as in the mid-1970s and early 1990s, have failed to solicit any appreciable "backlash" against the welfare state comparable to what has occurred in Western advanced industrialized societies. Because state provision has been limited to the provision of social need, it has not seriously been called into question even during times of slow economic growth, the threat of curtailing the provision of goods that meet individuated need, the crucial centerpiece of much of the controversy about welfare state reform or cutback, has not arisen in Japan.

One cannot help noticing too the analogy between Maruo's emphasis on providing corporate welfare benefits to all citizens, especially those left unincorporated (like unemployed housewives and the disabled), and Hegel's location of welfare within the corporate structure of civil society. Recall that, for Hegel, poverty connotes not simply the lack of material goods (as is standard) but rather the absence of the possibility for recognition of self that comes from being "incorporated," that is belonging to an estate. Maruo's claim that the problem of welfare can be solved by incorporating all citizens intuitively reflects Hegel's critical claim that individuation can only take place within the institutions and social practices of civil society. That this emphasis on civil society as the proper realm for welfare provision should prevail in Japan can be understood, as argued in this book, in the context of the historical conditions under which capitalism emerged.

Repeated studies find a consistently higher value attached to work in Japan when compared to other countries.[64] Moreover, because work is seen predominantly in non-utilitarian terms, the nexus between work and welfare via "incorporation" in civil society prevails.[65] Although

Maruo does not extend the logic of his argument in favor of "incorporation" to a critique of the family as a site for the provision of welfare, it can be easily seen why, in accordance with Hegel's logic, the family cannot be part of civil society, hence it cannot serve as a proper site for the realization of welfare, understood as particularity.

Public assistance

That Japan's welfare spending has been heavily skewed toward the provision of what I have been calling "social need" can be further substantiated by an analysis of the scope of its public assistance programs and, perhaps more crucially, the societal response to them. As noted earlier, societal dispositions to the receipt of monetized forms of public assistance are marked by antipathy, rather than receptivity. In a curious slant on the allegedly spiraling demands made on welfare states that leads ostensibly to fiscal overreach, demands within civil society, especially those emanating from the potential recipient population, have focused on job-creation, rather than an increase in either cash payments or consumption goods (housing, food, etc.).

To begin with, a comparison of the types of social spending among advanced industrialized countries is especially revealing (Table 4.5). Although Japan's total social spending as a percentage of GDP closely approximates that of Western welfare states, its distribution of resources from the very beginning has been heavily skewed toward the provision

Table 4.5 Government Social Expenditures in the Major Industrial Countries (as percent of gross domestic product)

Country	1980	2000	2010	2025
Japan	15.40	21.06	25.86	27.16
Canada	20.99	17.35	17.40	20.69
France	31.00	32.44	32.61	35.07
Germany	31.08	33.15	35.30	38.77
Italy	25.06	27.67	30.21	34.66
United Kingdom	22.90	22.94	23.96	26.52
United States	17.67	16.44	16.57	19.44

Source: International Monetary Fund, *Aging and Social Expenditure in the Major Industrial Countries, 1980–2025*, 1986: 56–57 (Cited in *Japan Economic Institute Report*, #16A, April 21, 1989: 7).

of health insurance rather than public assistance for the unemployed, social welfare, children, or family allowances. Tables 4.3 and 4.4 provide evidence in support of the thesis advanced here about the productivist orientation of Japan's welfare state that has prioritized the provision of social need in accordance with the nationalist cast capitalist development has taken. The state's contribution to the total income of families, especially low-income families, is strikingly low compared to that of Britain as shown below in Table 4.6.

Japan's social assistance program has been the target of much criticism. Beginning with the Unemployment Insurance Law in 1947, which provided coverage only to employees in large firms, leaving out small enterprises with less than five regular employees and part-time workers, the reforms of 1974 extended coverage to regular employees, thereby protecting older and partially disabled persons. This reflected, as Deborah Milly (1999) documents, an early structural rather than behavioral analysis of poverty in Japan that the lack of jobs, ill health, and the cost of medical treatment were a major source of impoverishment,[66] requiring a greater emphasis on the universal provision of health care, education, and an active labor market policy to ensure full employment, rather than public handouts. As a result the wage replacement ratio has varied between 60 percent and 80 percent depending on the level of the prior income (higher in the case of lower wages). An active labor market policy has meant that the primary effort has been directed at protecting the employment of the core workforce in times of structural

Table 4.6 Contributions of Wages, Self-Employment, State Transfer Payments as a Percentage of Total Income

	Salaries/ Wages	Self employment	Transfer	Other payment
Japan				
Average household	94.5	1.0	2.1	2.4
Low income	81.5	1.4	11.3	5.8
Britain				
Average household	76.5	2.3	20.9	0.3
Low income	21.3	2.3	66.6	9.8

Source: Ito Peng, "*Boshi Katei*: A Theoretical and Case Analysis of Japanese Lone Mothers and Their Relationships to the State, Labour Market, and the Family, with Reference to Britain and Canada." PhD thesis, London School of Economics, 1995 (Cited in Goodman and Peng 1996: 217).

or cyclical difficulties,[67] rather than provisioning a guaranteed source of livelihood for those out of work. As per the directives of the Ministry of Health and Welfare, the implementation of stricter eligibility criteria meant that the able-bodied work-shy were to be denied benefits.

The argument that the non-provision of individuated need is moot in the case of Japan since its rate of unemployment has never exceeded 4 percent is a persuasive one on the face of it. In the throes of the economic recession of the 1990s, Japan's official unemployment rate was 2.8 percent (in November 1993), totaling 1.76 million; it climbed to a record 3.4 percent in 1996, the highest ever since 1953.[68] Insofar as the normative challenge to welfare in most advanced capitalist countries is seen to be inextricably related to the issue of monetary and non-monetary support for the unemployed, justifying the shift to the "work-fare" state, the attempt to move welfare recipients back into the mainstream of market activity, the low level of spending on public assistance in Japan lends itself readily to the above interpretation. But a crucial difficulty remains: if indeed the low demand for public assistance is simply a function of an objectively determined low level of unemployment, how then can one account for the low take-up rate (Soeda, 1990, 1995), that reflects the subjective predisposition toward public assistance?[69]

The claim made here about the social antipathy to the receipt of public assistance in the form of monetary aid, as opposed to non-cash benefits like medical care and education, is echoed by the following observation.

> Although there is a welfare safety-net in Japan, the uptake rate is very low for those who would be expected to benefit most; 5 percent of all elderly households; 0.8 percent of households with a disabled person. The total take-up rate for public assistance is only 1.5 percent or 8 per 1000 population.
>
> (Peng 1995, quoted in Goodman and Peng 1996: 217)

Contrary to the view that the social stigma attached to welfare is an effect of welfare provision, in Japan the clear distinction made between the shame attached to receipt of monetary support to meet individuated need (as in transfer payments for food, clothing, housing, etc.) and, likewise, the social acceptance of non-monetary goods (health care, education) helps provide a more nuanced understanding of the antipathy toward public assistance. Reiterating a similar observation, Huck-Ju Kwon notes,

> The levels of public transfer in Japan are related to the low level of some cash benefits, such as child allowance, public assistance, and invalidity and unemployment benefits.... *Even the majority of those who receive benefits from the Public Assistance Programme get support in the form of medical and education support rather than income support* (emphasis added). (Kwon 1997: 474–475)

A brief look at the attitudes of welfare recipients is helpful here. Although the size of the underclass in Japan is nowhere as big as that of the United States, a fairly visible impoverished, homeless population can be seen in prominent sections (like Shinjuku station in Tokyo) or in the Japanese equivalent of the old poverty-stricken skid-rows of the United States – the *yoseba* (day laborer districts) in most Japanese cities. Mostly male, with a sizable component made up of Japan's ethnic and racial minorities (the *Burakumin*, Korean, and *Ainu*[70]), the four largest – *Kamagasaki* in Osaka, *Sanya* in Tokyo, *Kotobukicho* in Yokohama, and *Sasashima* in Nagoya – are standing testimony to the existence of an underclass in Japan. Totaling about 100 000 in 1994, day laborers find work mostly in the construction industry. The few ethnographic studies available about this marginal population, however, are instructive in that they provide compelling testimony to the broader thesis advanced in this book about the normative distinction made in Japan between the state provision of social and individuated need.

Matthew Marr reports that the main demands made on public administration by laborers have been for the creation of new jobs, rather than an increase in public assistance.[71] Homeless men, once day laborers who have lost their temporary *doya* or rooms in the *yoseba*, consistently reported an antipathy for "free facilities" provided by the city and charitable institutions due to reasons such as "self-pride" (Marr 1997: 238). More crucially, for our purposes here, Marr points out, it is important to note that unlike the increasing "shelterization" and institutionalization of the underclass generated by a "politics of compassion" in most advanced industrial countries, which places primacy on providing services to overcome the pathologies associated with homelessness (such as mental illness, drug abuse, and alcoholism), the continued existence of *yoseba* in Japan, despite the existence of public assistance, minimal though it may be, enables (in Marr's use of the term) a continued "autonomy"[72] (in the sense of freedom from familial or administrative monitoring of daily life) on the part of occupants even in the face of poverty, an attribute highly prized by all those he interviewed. Although autonomy in itself is not sufficient to enable individuation (the latter requires a degree of wealth that those in poverty lack), Marr's interviews time and again highlight the non-pecuniary rewards that work carries in Japan that drive those in need to place a greater value on work over "free facilities." The specificity of the Japanese case (where, because work is tied to collective ends, social worth hinges on the individual's contribution in the realm of work) substantiates the anti-materialist conception of work and poverty developed in this book, in a particularly compelling way.

Reinforcing this observation, Carolyn Stevens' anthropological study[73] of the *Kotobukicho* concludes that the form of public assistance most likely to be utilized by residents is medical, rather than the six other forms of *seikatsu hogo* (welfare) they are entitled to, including livelihood, education, housing, occupational, and funeral expenses assistance. Stevens notes, "between 60 and 70 percent of all welfare cases in *Kotobukicho* involve medical payments" (Stevens 1997: 57). Thus, even for the day laborer, among the group most in need of cash benefits, there is no shame attached to the receipt of medical care, but to accept monetary help betrays whatever sense of self-worth remains in the midst of material deprivation.

This antipathy to the receipt of public assistance in Japan testifies to the success of the state-sponsored ideology of *jiei* or self-management. Insofar as the social meanings attached to the modern ideal of personhood render group-oriented productive work and autonomy in consumption key to the notion of personhood, the rejection of public assistance also draws attention to the distinctive basis of self and social worth in Japan. In this sense, then, not just the heightened pace of consumption discernable in the new consumer culture of the *shinjinrui* but also the construction of selfhood renders consumption far more significant to subjectivity in modern Japan than has been recognized thus far. In this sense, the post-modern claim that the frenetic pace and nature of consumption in Japan provide a textbook example of a hybrid, de-centered subjectivity misunderstands the substantive, indeed very material, way in which consumption serves to create a specifically individuated mode of being, via the use of self-chosen objects in a context in which otherwise consciousness of the collectivity holds a greater claim to individual lives. It is in this sense that the social stigma attached to the receipt of public assistance makes sense.

Indeed, "ordinary citizens have been hesitant to choose any drastic change except for minor protests in elections, though there have been opportunities to do so."[74] Only when the state provision of individuated need is treated as normatively necessary to the very definition of welfare statism (imposing, some might argue, an "imperialism of categories") that the Japanese case appears anomalous, either falling short of the (Western) ideal type or, in a more orientalist construction, suggesting a hyper-exploitative state vis-à-vis society. In Polanyian terms, the double movement (of society against market) need not necessarily take the specific form it has acquired in the West (i.e. political protection by the state against the vagaries of the market); rather the mid-level networks of solidarity that both Baba and Maruo refer to (at the company level) provide an intermediate level of welfare provision that, albeit unevenly distributed (with workers in large companies, 5000+ employees) drawing benefits three times more than those provided by smaller firms (less than 300 workers),[75] enables the fulfillment of individuated need (for housing, vacation and travel allowances, and entertainment, for instance) consistent with (and this is crucial) the notion of personhood that prevails in modern Japan.

The normative repudiation of the provision of consumption goods in Japan and its receptivity to the provision of goods that meet social need reinforce the location of welfare (as subjective particularity) within civil society, albeit in a distinctive way. Social relations within the realm of production both foster a consciousness of the collectivity as well as engender forms of inter-dependence (within the workplace) that repudiate notions of the autonomous individual. Ironically then, the state's appeals in the 1980s and 1990s to a fully marketized provision of welfare, if examined closely, can be seen to stand at odds with the organization of the private sector in Japan.

As already discussed, the relation between labor and capital is cast in terms of inter-dependency, embodied in the social relations and general ethos of the workplace, which emphasizes inter-dependence among *sempai/kohai* (seniors/juniors) and *oyabun/kobun* (boss/subordinate). It mediates, as well, the consumption of what I have called "individuated goods" (from brokering marriages between employees, to providing housing and vacation resorts, arranging tours, etc.), thereby constructing a distinct notion of private and public that is consistent with the fluidity and contextual specificity that these demarcations take in Japanese social life.

In advocating the privatization of welfare, bureaucrats and politicians in Japan are hard put to define the abstract principle of self-reliance in an institutional context where self-reliance carries a radically different connotation in terms of welfare goods. To put it more succinctly, in the 1980s advocates of a welfare society were more successful in highlighting the limitations of a large welfare state based on the experience of

Western welfare states than in outlining structural changes in the institutions and social practices of civil society that would render the idea of self-reliance in the market (in the utilitarian sense) more meaningful. Without changes in the institutions of the market, the suggestion that Japan could successfully imitate Western models of privatization failed to carry weight. Indeed, the central feature of civil society in Japan that couples work to the public rather than private interest (the basis also for the generous welfare packages provided to workers in large companies) works to render meaningless the state's periodic attempts to suggest that *jijo* or self-help should become the basis of a wholly privatized welfare system. The tension inherent in the attempt to simultaneously posit these two claims was not lost on the population at large, as evidenced in their continued support of what has been called "enterprise based welfare" and, more significantly, the absence of any concerted attempt to lobby the government to extend welfare provision into an ever-expanding menu of goods associated with individuated needs.

Ongoing efforts at reform in the 1980s and 1990s have focused on reducing the levels of dependency, especially of the elderly, on institutionalized care and actively fostered self-reliance in the context of community care. The Ministry of Health and Welfare published its White Paper in January 1987, assessing the reforms of the health and public pensions system: "the social security, mainly referring to the public pension and medical care systems in our country has reached standards close to those in the United States and European countries, which means Japan has gained membership of the advanced countries in social security" (MHW 1987: 45). Furthermore, effort has been directed at professionalizing the delivery of social services. As part of the attempt to reform welfare, the law on social workers and care workers was promulgated in May 1987, specifying the qualifications necessary for social welfare specialists. Thus far, social workers had been drawn from the relatively informally constituted group of *minseiin* (welfare workers) with no specified specialization or practical training. The passage of this law in the late 1980s is symptomatic of Japan's recognition of the need for specialized workers, particularly in the context of its rapidly aging society.

The attempt to professionalize the delivery of welfare services even as the need to curtail costs was more publicly articulated did not, however, undermine a parallel emphasis on the need to make the level of the *komyunity* the most appropriate for the provision of welfare to the aged. For this the network of *minseiin*, "people with responsible character," a good "reputation in the local community," and "economically independent," continue to provide the bridgehead between those in need of help and local officials. Acting as a liaison between those in need and welfare experts with professional qualifications, the ration of *minseiin* was 1 for every 270 families in Tokyo and other metropolitan areas in 1990.[76] Receiving only a nominal travel fee, although directly appointed by the Ministry of Health and Welfare, the close inter-personal communication between *minseiin* and local residents mitigates the potentially bureaucratic and alienating environment that welfare recipients have to negotiate with professional social workers.

In the 1980s, with the advent of the "participation-oriented-welfare-society" (*sanka-gata fukushi shakai*), the government's attempt to re-establish voluntary networks as an additional avenue of welfare provision has drawn greater attention to the work *minseiin* have historically performed in Japanese communities. While it is tempting to see this renewed faith in volunteerism as yet another indictment of the hegemony of conservative (not to say anti-feminist) politics in Japan, it is worth noting the parallels between social practice in Japan and contemporary critical social thought pertaining to welfare. In his controversial *Farewell to the Working Class*, Andre Gorz "sketches a grassroots alternative to care that is either commercialized by the market or standardized by the codifying logic of a dependency-promoting state." Gorz writes, "It is not a question of dismantling the welfare state but of relieving it," proposing a "synergy within two-tiers system supported on the one hand by centralized services provided by institutions, and on the other by self-organized, cooperative services staffed by volunteers." In many ways, the recent attempt in Japan to emphasize voluntary work is more appropriately seen as complementing or relieving its existent welfare state rather than an attempt to displace it. Curiously, though, the problems of constructing a "public sphere" in Japan, the space in which volunteer networks could be created is fraught with difficulty, given Japan's historical conflation of the very notion of the "public interest" with production and accumulation.[77]

In the 1990s, another round of welfare law revision took place. The following chapter examines these reforms at greater length. In closing here, I will simply anticipate some of the developments that prepared the ground for the reforms of the mid-1990s. In keeping with its historical legacy of looking pragmatically to the West for ideas and institutions that could be adapted to suit the needs of Japan, welfare bureaucrats set up several study groups in the 1990s to examine the future of welfare policy. Research teams were sent to Britain to study its community care plans, to Brussels and Denmark to learn about reconciling the twin demands of family and work, to Canada to monitor legislation of children's rights and family services, even as scholars and research teams within Japan closely monitored development in the European Union and North America.[78] Revealing, on the one hand, a concerted attempt to complement state-based welfare provision with volunteer social work, the reforms of 1994, on the other, in an interesting contrast with reforms being undertaken in other advanced industrialized countries, increased in some respects rather than rolled back, benefits for the unemployed, aged workers, and parents on child-care leave. The significance of these parallel, seemingly contradictory efforts is worth exploring at some length.

The 1994 amendments to the Unemployment Insurance Law and the Law Concerning the Stabilization of the Employment of Older Workers increased the period of unemployment compensation to those aged 60–64 by 30–60 days over and above the maximum period allowed of 300 days per year. In addition, the 1994 amendments instituted a new procedure that called for the annual adjustment of unemployment benefits rather than, as previously was the case, adjustment only when the wage index increased by 10 percent. The new law stipulated that beginning in 1998 all firms must set the retirement age beyond 60, compensating for the reduced company wage of senior workers by introducing an income supplement to workers aged 60 and between 60 and 64 whose wage had been reduced by more than 15 percent.

What is interesting about these reforms is the effort to reward continued employment. As reported in the *Social Security Bulletin*:

> as a means of encouraging the unemployed to seek jobs and become productive the unemployment insurance program continues to pay benefits even after the worker has found a job. The unemployed person who has found work with at least one-half of the initially certified payment period remaining may continue to receive unemployment benefits for about one third to one half of the remaining days. For example, if the unemployed person finds a new job within the first 101 to 150 days of receiving an unemployment benefit payable for 300 days, he or she will continue to receive unemployment benefits for 70 days while earning wages in the new job.
>
> (*Social Security Bulletin* 1994: 57, 77)

Paradoxically, then, the increase in unemployment benefits has been motivated by an attempt to increase the take-up rate, but with the ultimate goal of reducing reliance on public assistance by re-integrating recipients into the workforce. Prolonging unemployment benefits is thus seen as a way of fast-tracking the unemployed back to work.[79]

Rather than identifying the especially needy and disadvantaged as the objects of social policy, the new law simply referred to those who need welfare services. Especially noteworthy in this new law, however, was the emphasis placed on the provision of non-material, rather than material, needs. Continuing the emphasis on local participation begun in the 1980s, the notion of *nomarizeshon* (normalization) dominated the discourse on welfare in the 1990s. By this, proponents drew attention to the need to postpone the institutionalization of target groups, specifically the elderly and the disabled, by drawing on community resources to enable them to prolong their participation in the mainstream of everyday life.[80] A stated objective in the pursuit of *nomarizeshon* was to strengthen locally based social networks as a potential resource for the provision of welfare, so as to prevent increasingly nuclear families from assuming the burden of care, as well as to curtail rapidly rising welfare costs. In attempting to foster a new, specifically modern, form of *komyunity* government, officials, scholars, and policy activists have made it clear that this is by no means meant as a regressive return to traditional forms of *ie*-based communities. Another way to interpret this might be to see this as an attempt to overcome the anomie of late capitalism that has begun to threaten social life in Japan, as well as an attempt to create a new space which, for lack of a better term, we might call the "public sphere." Paradoxically, in its modern history, the notion of the "public" in Japan has more or less been effectively colonized by an economism that has hindered the emergence of a broader notion of the "public interest," the space within which volunteerism as an alternative or complementary realm of welfare activity might emerge. Precisely because consciousness of the collectivity has been inextricably linked to production, the current attempt by the Japanese government to create new forms of associational life in the "public interest" strikes one as ironic, given the conventional image of Japanese society as being inherently group/community driven.[81] That the call to increase *borantia* (volunteer) activity is not simply a means to roll back state provision of social need was evident in the 1994 proposal to increase the sales tax by 5 percent in fiscal 1995–1996. This tax was intended to function as a form of national welfare tax (Maruo 1994). Further, the government proposal to create a "participation oriented welfare society" makes clear that the "basic needs of social welfare are to be supplied by the public sector (*gyosei*) whereas those activities such as voluntary activities are expected to offer flexibly various services for such welfare demands (*fukushi juyo*) that are difficult for the public sector to respond to."[82] This emphasis in debates about welfare is indicative of the government's attempt to spearhead the creation of modern forms of social capital, rather than, as some are wont to argue, an attempt to resurrect a mythical traditional past of village-based solidarity.[83]

The claim here that the absence of a normative challenge to welfare in contemporary Japan can be understood in relation to the conception of personhood that grounds both state and civil society in Japan is further borne out in the government's recent efforts to deal with the welfare question. Even as incremental reforms since the 1980s have reinforced Japan's productivist orientation in welfare, the government has also reinforced its commitment to the principle of full employment. The 1994 government budget of 333.1 billion yen was aimed at creating 1 million jobs (*Japan Labour Bulletin*, May 1, 1994). In addition, as a result of the reforms in the 1990s, the emphasis on employment as the means to welfare has been further reinforced by wage subsidies to small and medium size companies. It is telling that many of the industries that qualify are in the manufacturing sector.[84] A similar belief in full employment as a welfare policy can be seen in the Labour Ministry's support for firms that retrain and keep on older workers. The emphasis on employment has thus emerged as the dominant leitmotif of current social policy in Japan. Despite a dramatic increase in pensions and health-related expenditure, then, Japan's social spending still stands at an enviable 12 percent of GDP in 1990, low compared to OECD figures.

That Japan's welfare state is geared primarily to the provision of social need in pursuit of its nationally oriented productivist ethos can be finally substantiated by a brief look at the organizing principle of its education system. Its investment in education is comparable with most advanced nations (around 5–6 percent of GDP),[85] once again substantiating the claim made here about the distinction between social and individuated need that structures Japan's social policy. Although Japan is notorious for its highly competitive education system at the college and university levels, where credentials from elite institutions offer a veritable passport to a lifetime of prosperity and status, the school system provides a remarkably equitable product across all of Japan. Using a standardized curriculum across the country, identical standards for the qualification of teachers and expenditures per pupil (subject to cost of living differentials), the Japanese educational system is self-consciously structured to produce citizens who not only enjoy equal opportunity in the realm of education but are also socialized in a remarkably consistent manner, via the standardization of the curriculum. With its primary objective being to produce a diligent and hard-working labor force, in which persistence of effort rather than creativity is of greater value, the larger productivist current of modern Japan ironically works to produce a greater degree of equity in different sectors of social life, including welfare.

How then are we to make sense of Japan's welfare state? Is it, indeed, as many have claimed, a welfare laggard, due to its culture of Confucian-inspired familism that has rendered welfare redundant? If so, its national programs on health care, pensions, education, and so on demand explanation. Or does its distinctive enterprise-based welfare provision provide the necessary and sufficient condition that can account for both Japan's economic development and social policy? I have suggested that Japan's focus on enterprise-based welfare makes sense in the context of its nationally/militarily driven accumulation drive; it is less helpful in sorting out why the state has taken on the additional burden of providing universal provision of social need while corporate welfare schemes have focused on the provision of non-statutory "surplus" goods that meet individuated need.

Lastly, is the current focus on employment simply symptomatic of a larger trend underway? Can Japan's current social policy be read as an Asian counterpart to the shift to the "work-fare" state high on the political and ideological agenda, particularly in the United States and Britain? The analysis of the overall pattern and structure of the goods provisioned by Japan's welfare state suggests otherwise. Key to arguments about the virtues of the "work-fare" state is the claim that individual well-being may be more efficiently provided by the market; the work-fare state focuses on employment as the only mechanism of welfare provision thus advocating the reduction, even dismantling, of the state's welfare role.

In sharp contrast to this line of thinking, the contained emphasis in Japan on the state's provision of social need is indicative of a sustained recognition of the link between the greater good of the collectivity and the state's role in ensuring goods like medical care and education. Its emphasis on paid employment is meant rather to more firmly embed the provision of individuated need in the market. According to the alternative explanation developed here, this can be explained by the continued link between the nature of the goods disbursed in relation to the prevalent notion of personhood in Japan. The analysis of the overall pattern of the goods provisioned by modern Japan's welfare state above thus reveals a distinctive logic: a sustained emphasis on the provision of social goods and an equally strong and consistent antipathy to the receipt of public assistance or goods that meet individuated need.

The absence of a normative challenge to or repudiation of welfare is understood not as the result of a continued ideological discourse of familism or enterprise-based welfare provision, but rather as the result of a conceptualization of welfare to provide goods that enhance collective, rather than individual well-being. Both state and civil society appear to work with similar underlying notions of personhood. Specifically, the antipathy to the provision of individuated goods in the face of a sustained receptivity to the provision of social goods vivifies modern notions of subjectivity that link individuation to the realm of consumption alone, production-related activities laying claim to the good of the social whole.

This antipathy to the receipt of consumption goods in Japan vividly calls into question the left's unexamined assumption that the provision of subsistence need (that basket of consumption goods deemed necessary to survival) is enough to sustain the individual's sense of self-worth. The dominant explanation of this resistance to public assistance in Japan, however, has centered on the high degree of social stigmatization it carries. In most accounts, this is seen as corroborating Japan's status as a welfare laggard; needy individuals are denied their rights to subsistence-based consumption goods due to the perpetuation of negative traditional/cultural attitudes toward welfare or due to the state's success in fostering such societal norms. In contrast to the West, where the provision and ready acceptance of public assistance that fulfills individuated need is upheld as the *raison d'etre* of social and economic rights of the individual, the case of Japan, appears on a linear welfare continuum, putatively "under-developed."

However, as I have tried to show, Japan's pattern of welfare can accordingly, be apprehended only in the context of the distinctive nature of its civil society and the notion of personhood it engenders. The welfare state, by providing goods that facilitate production, finds ready acceptance in a civil society where production realizes the group ideal; consumption, on the other hand, as the delimited terrain of individuation within civil society, remains outside the purview of state provision. Societal antipathy to the receipt of consumption goods and the ready acceptance of the state provision of social need testifies to the bifurcation of the social meanings of exchange relations vis-à-vis individual well-being.

The self in relation to the other constitutes the core of personhood in modern Japan. Because the specificity of this notion ensues so visibly from (indeed is contingent on) the individual's participation in production-related activities within civil society, the antipathy to the receipt of welfare goods that meet individuated need becomes explicable. In sum, welfare in Japan can be more readily understood in relation to the shared ideal of personhood that informs both state and civil society. The distinctive nature of Japan's civil society, discernable in the bifurcated role of exchange vis-à-vis individuation is mirrored in the pattern of welfare in modern Japan.

5
Welfare Reforms in Recessionary Japan

Introduction

The prolonged *Heisei* recession of the 1990s has become something of a boundary marker for Japan's transition to the category of a "mature" capitalist economy beset with all the contradiction of its workings: alienation, inequality, poverty, immiserization, and consumerism.[1] Of the many indicators used to capture the contrast between the "miracle economy" of earlier decades and the stagflation of the 1990s, none, perhaps, is more dramatic than Japan's escalating unemployment rate: in 1990 it stood at 2 percent, the lowest among the OECD countries; by 2003 it had almost tripled to 5½ percent, with a rate of 10 percent for the 15–24 age group (*OECD Economic Surveys Japan* 2005: 174). Contrary to conventional wisdom (Wilensky 1975; Blank 2001; Andren and Gustafsson 2004; Ayala and Perez 2005), however, the rise in the numbers of unemployed in "millennial Japan" (Yoda 2001) and the shift from "miracle to debacle" (Ikeda 2004) has not seen a commensurate increase in unemployment benefit provision or public assistance relief. To the contrary, changes in welfare policy have resulted in a significant decline in both benefits and the total number of individuals in receipt of unemployment benefits. Against the conventional wisdom among scholars and the policy-making elite in Japan that the question of poverty relief was moot in the period of high-speed growth, since a booming economy ensured full employment and high wages, the continuing decline in the numbers of people on public assistance at a time of stagnation and rising unemployment through the 1990s demands explanation.

This chapter examines changes in social policy provision in the 1990s and early 2000s in Japan to see if the structuring principle of welfare state capitalism identified in this study, namely the distinction in the state provision of social needs in contrast to the antipathy to the provision of consumption-related individuated wants, is significantly altered in the recessionary period. Given the centrality of unemployment benefits and public assistance to the theoretical argument advanced in the preceding chapters, the discussion here focuses largely on these two policy domains, placing them in the context of changes in other policy areas (e.g. elderly and child care). Against the prevailing sentiment that tends to explain the absence of increases in unemployment benefit, and evidence of declining public assistance rolls in terms of electoral politics, historical institutionalism and the "varieties of capitalism" approach (Estévez-Abe, Manow, and Ebbinghaus 2001; 2002; Hall and Soskice 2001), or the full-scale embrace of a neoliberal economic growth agenda, the argument advanced here draws attention to the normative structure of Japan's welfare system in understanding the empirical "puzzles," "anomalies," or contradictions of Japan's contemporary welfare system, especially as it pertains to the question of unemployment. As such, it challenges recent claims that changes in unemployment and public assistance policy in the 1990s and early 2000s is indicative of a likely convergence between Japan and other OECD countries (Kasza 2006).[2] It points, rather, to the impediments to this hypothesized convergence grounded in the structuring principle of Japan's normative political economy.

To this end, the chapter is organized as follows. The section that follows provides a brief sketch of the macroeconomic context of rising unemployment since the bursting of the economic bubble in 1990–1991 followed by a discussion of changes in Japan's labor market, principally the rapid increase in the number of temporary and part-time workers and its implications for sustaining policies committed to "commodification" in civil society as the principal means of securing welfare or well-being in modern Japan. The next section provides a detailed discussion of changes in unemployment benefits and public assistance with a view to discerning if there has been any noticeable shift in the normative orientation to the provision and receipt of state-based income support, particularly livelihood or "general assistance." The central finding in this chapter is that while welfare reforms in the 1990s and 2000s indicate a continuity rather than rupture with strategies to enhance participation in exchange relations, and a concomitant antipathy to the receipt of goods that clearly evidence failure relative to the normative ideal of social and self-worth in Japan, an increasing anxiety about the continued salience of the institutions of Japan's political economy, specifically its explicit recognition of the social limits of the market, has injected an incremental erosion of a fundamental commitment to this principle which threatens to de-stabilize, in the long run, the social compact particular to Japanese modernity. Unlike those who advocate an accelerated abandonment of what are seen as "archaic and obsolete institutions," in favor of "American-style management, and economic and political institutions" (as described by Boyer and Yamada 2000: 1), the theoretical argument developed in this book suggests an alternative: the renewal of Japan's explicit (and effective) recognition of the principle of the social limits of the market, if in altered terms, that can, in principle, serve as a globally relevant signifier of a creative resolution to the enabling and disabling attributes of capitalist social and economic organization. This point is developed at greater length in the concluding chapter.

The *Heisei* recession and unemployment

The *Heisei* recession that commenced with the collapse of the speculative financial bubble in 1990–1991 is generally traced back to the high-yen credit surpluses that propelled a real-estate investment boom in the 1980s and the liberalization of capital controls which spurred a flood of overseas investment generating the Japanese equivalent of a "hollowing out" of its manufacturing base. The spiral caused by bad loans that as recently as 1998 amounted to 12 percent of total loans by various banks (Itoh 2001) combined with asset deflation, the inability of small businesses to withstand the deflationary pressure of the credit crunch resulted in a worsening environment for employment and wages.[3] Makoto Itoh, the renowned political-economist, points out that the roots of Japan's de-regulation and privatization efforts in the 1990s and since 2000 must be traced back to escalating debt that resulted from expansive fiscal policy adopted in the 1970s. To lessen debt, the government pursued austerity measures in the 1980s, cutting back on social security and education spending, and the privatization of government-run firms (most notably, Japan National Railways and the Nippon Telegraph and Telephone Public Corporation).

With a decline in real disposable income and real wages, the contraction in domestic demand led firms to compensate for the underutilization of manufacturing capacity by enhanced pressure to compete in the global export market. However, given Japan's structural commitment to one-way trade (what critics sometimes refer to as adversarial trade), enhanced competitiveness globally has vastly exacerbated Japan's trade surpluses generating a stronger yen (making Japanese exports more expensive), leading Japanese manufacturing industry to relocate to low-cost, low-wage areas (in China and SouthEast Asia), increasingly concentrating domestic manufacturing on high value-added sectors and product innovation. This "hollowing out" of the manufacturing industry in Japan in the 1990s has had a direct bearing on the labor force in Japan, not so much via the retrenchment of longtime regular workers as popular misconceptions suggest, but rather by widening the gap between a core, still largely protected, middle-aged male workforce (Schoppa 2006) and the rest, young male and female graduates who join the growing pool of a temporary, part-time workforce, even as the unemployment rate spirals upwards.

In the 1980s, as a growing number of large firms turned to overseas operation, through either direct foreign investment or the acquisition of overseas firms, the annual flow of FDI (foreign direct investment) went from $10 billion in 1984 to $67.5 billion in 1989 (Hasegawa 2005); the growth of manufacturing as a percentage of FDI rose from 17 percent in 1986 to nearly 30 percent in 1988. As cross-border investment increased, the number of transnationals in Tokyo rose from 20 in 1975 to 71 in 1987, the total number of foreign firms in 1989 reaching a figure a little less than 3000 (Itoh 2005). Of this, the share of foreign manufacturing value added increased significantly (from 3 percent in 1985 to 18 percent in 2003).

This increased integration of the Japanese economy with the ebb and tide of globalized production brought with it not only a greater vulnerability to changes in the global economy (particularly the vicissitudes of global finance and global demand for exports), but also the pressures associated with what Stephen Roach has called the "IT-enabled global labor arbitrage" and its negative effect on domestic wages. Income inequality as measured by the Gini coefficient has also risen from 0.271 in 1970 to 0.297 in 1994 and to 0.38 in 2004, indicating the growing economic disparity between haves and have-nots in contemporary Japanese society (http://search.japantimes.co.jp/cgi-bin/ed20060404a1.html. accessed 14/04/2006. See also Tachibanaki 2005 on rising inequality in Japan). While executive salaries and corporate dividends in fiscal 2004 amounted to 1.9 trillion yen more than in fiscal 2000, total wages for workers were 2.5 trillion yen lower (*Japan Times online* 14/4/06). A brief look at changes in average cash earnings is also instructive here. In 1979 the average monthly wage for a male worker in the tertiary sector in Japan was 171 700 yen compared with an average of 181 140 yen in manufacturing, a difference of approximately only 10 000 yen (*Japan Labor Bulletin*, July 1, 1980). In 2004, on the other hand, average monthly cash earnings for workers in construction was 433 235 yen, in manufacturing 419 768 yen, whereas those in wholesale, retail, or food service earned almost 50 percent less – 262 599 yen – a month (*Facts and Figures of Japan*, 2005), evidence of a growing disparity in wages (not assets) that is a new phenomenon in Japan. The year 2002 saw the largest drop in average monthly earnings (by 2.1 percent compared to the previous year), and the number of permanent employees fell by 0.6 percent (*Japan Labor Bulletin*, July 2003: 2). Average monthly cash earnings dropped further to 343 120 yen for fiscal 2002, with the biggest drop recorded in special cash payments (including bonus payments), which fell by 7.4 percent to 64 096 yen, with the mining and construction industries recording the biggest drop (*Japan Labor Bulletin*, July 1, 2003: 3). Manufacturing employment declined from 15 million in 1990 to 11.5 million in 2004, while average monthly cash salaries for regular workers peaked at 480 000 yen in manufacturing, 433 000 yen in services, and 716 000 yen in finance and insurance (2002 figures). Comparable figures for women are 50 percent less (208 000 yen in manufacturing, 178 000 yen in services, and 320 000 yen in finance and insurance) (*Business Facts and Figures Nippon* 2006: 52), vividly illustrating the deeply gendered nature of Japan's political economy. According to a survey by *Nippon Keidanren*, the average pay hike among 185 *kaisha* (large firms) was a mere 5391 yen a month (an annual increase of 1.65 percent). Finally, given the worsened economic climate, the percentage of households with no savings rose from 12.4 percent in 2000 to 23.8 percent in 2005.

It is in the context of these changes in the economic landscape that Japan's shift from a virtually full employment economy to one with an exceptionally high (given its record) unemployment rate of 5½ percent in 2003 garnered much attention.

Japan's low rates of unemployment (hovering around the 2 percent line in the 1970s and 1980s) has been the subject of much discussion among economists and sociologists, and especially influential in constructions of "Japan as Number One" (Vogel 1979). Conventionally explained via reference to the three pillars of the Japanese employment system – enterprise unions, lifetime employment and seniority-based wage system for a core group (30–35 percent of the workforce in the 1980s), and the legal prohibitions set out by Japanese labor law – the state's strategic commitment to commodification as the structuring principle of welfare provision rendered the dismissal of regular full-time employees for anything short of the most dire conditions difficult during the earlier decades. Encouraged to eliminate overtime, suspend new hiring, or temporarily relocate workers to related companies, or, if necessary, buy out senior management through early retirements, the legal and administrative structure within which Japan achieved its famously low rates of unemployment has been kept in place, largely intact, through the "lost decade." It should, however, be noted that claims about Japan's low unemployment rates are not without controversy. Some scholars (Hashimoto 1993; Taira 1983) have suggested that adjusting for differences in the criteria used to measure unemployment (for instance, persons categorized as unemployed in the United States are categorized in Japan as *kyugyosha* (on the payroll but not working), some of whom are *ichiji kyugyosha*, i.e. temporary layoff) yields a much higher figure than is conventionally accepted. Thus, Koji Taira (1983) points out that individuals who would be classified as unemployed in the United States are classified as out of the labor force (i.e. neither seeking work nor employed) based on the measures used in Japan, yielding a lower unemployment rate than would otherwise obtain. After adjusting Japanese figures in accordance with the criteria used to measure unemployment in the United States, Taira's study in the early 1980s recorded an increase in the rate of unemployment for Japan by almost 2 percentage points (from 2 to 4 percent in 1977) (Taira 1983). Having said that, however, it should also be noted that relative to unemployment rates of other advanced industrialized countries in the 1970s and 1980s, Japan's unemployment rates remain low.

In addition to the three pillars of Japanese employment mentioned above, the commitment to commodification as a strategy of optimizing welfare in civil society is evident in the high rate of labor redundancies (the employment of excess labor relative to both productivity and level of output) estimated at between 4.4 and 7.2 percent of labor force (in the late 1970s), exemplifying the premium placed on employment and work in modern Japan. While the surplus revenue generated in the boom years contributed significantly to making labor redundancies financially viable for firms, the high instance of labor redundancies (comprising 10 percent of the labor force in 1977, according to Taira 1983) highlights the emphasis placed on work in Japan. This is evident in the willingness to forego wage increases, work at reduced rates of remuneration, and the active labor market policies adopted in Japan. Claims by senior officials in government that "Japan has an employment, rather than unemployment policy" are quite revealing. For instance, the state's concerted attempt to promote construction in the 1990s was driven as much by the industry's role as an "employment absorbing sector" (Ministry of Labor, Infrastructure and Transport, which includes the earlier Ministry of Construction since 2001) as by efforts to help out banks hit hard by real-estate-related bad loans since the bursting of the bubble economy. As such, active labor market policies, in tandem with the level of labor redundancies sustained not only in the era of high-speed growth, but also during the period of stagflation, as we will see below, reinforce the point made above about the larger commitment of the state to maintaining full employment as a strategy of economic, social, and political management. While this is typically interpreted in purely economistic terms, as a strategy of ensuring fiscally prudent and efficient economic growth, the Hegelian claim about the economy as an ethical or normative realm draws attention to the structure of inter-dependence and social relationality underpinning seemingly atomized transactions of the market. Insofar as the relationality and sociality underpinning economic transactions under a capitalist ordering of social relations is explicitly recognized in Japan, providing the symbolic register within which meanings are shaped, enunciated, and performed (Kondo 1990), the centrality of work/employment serves as the founding pillar not only of economic institutions and social relations *per se*, but of subjectivity as well. Given the specificity of capitalism's development in Japan, I have suggested, specifically production as a mediated realm of sociality oriented to primarily collective ends, in contradistinction to consumption as the de-limited terrain of individuation in Japan, gives modernity and capitalism in Japan its particular hue. It is, therefore, no accident that many of the sociological categories through which Japan is understood (status-based hierarchies, in-group/out-group distinctions, etc.) refer to social contexts in which work or labor provides the central plank of connectivity. In this sense, the conventional wisdom that it is the notion of the family (*ie*) that overlays relations in the workplace may be fruitfully understood in terms of the valuation placed on relationality – the core bridging concept (between *ie* and the workplace) provided not by paternalism/seniority/harmony as the "chrysanthemum club" arguments suggests, but rather by the explicit recognition of social relationality and inter-dependence that is common to both.

The emphasis on employment policy in Japan thus draws attention to the dual aspect of work: one has to do with its income-generating and welfare-enhancing aspect (understood here as the ability to earn a livelihood). The other, however, as suggested in the previous chapters, has to do with the explicit valuation placed on the non-pecuniary aspects of work that are systematically elided in both mainstream and heterodox approaches to labor or work in a capitalist context. Repudiating both neo-classical economic theory's claims about utility-maximizing behavior (by the employer or employee) as well as the class-driven notion of capitalist appropriation of surplus within Marxian social theory, the non-pecuniary, one might say *intrinsic*, quality of work is (1) central to the absence of a structuring distinction between mental and manual work in Japan, and (2) a shared enterprise, key to shaping Japan's collective unconscious (Jameson 1984). As such, and as argued in earlier chapters, labor/work as an embodiment of sociality, a theoretical abstraction vivified in economic and ethical philosophy (as in Chapter 2), attains in Japan the status of an explicitly recognized norm, shaping policy at the objective level, and subjective dispositions toward it.[4] It is within the context of this orientation to work and production that policies and attitudes to employment and unemployment must be understood, including, I attempt to show below, societal and state antipathy to the disbursement and receipt of "general assistance." Suffice it to say here, the negative valuation to state largesse for consumption goods is anchored in a particular orientation to work in which the social relationality intrinsic to work or labor constitutes the pivotal source of value. The antipathy to state largesse for consumption goods is thus conditioned by a prior valuation of the sociality of labor; the shame associated with its receipt stemming from its unearned nature, involving neither social transaction nor social relationality, crucial to the ideal of personhood and modern subjectivity in Japan. As the concluding chapter hopes to show, it is this centrality of work to social and self-worth that must be made central to any efforts to rethink welfare and its provision.

It is in this context that rising unemployment in Japan through the recession years must be placed. The shift from manufacturing to service sectors domestically that accompanied rapidly rising foreign direct investment inevitably entailed a decline in manufacturing employment in Japan – 15 million in 1999 to 11.5 million in 2004 (*Facts and Figures of Japan 2005*) – as well as a precipitous decline in jobs among subcontracting firms (whose employees, because generally outside the lifetime employment system, have been more vulnerable to layoffs to begin with). Part-time employment rose from 2.1 percent in 1992 to 5 percent in 2001, as 83 000 firms went bankrupt. By 2003, part-time and temporary workers made up 34.6 percent of Japan's workforce, up by 7.1 percentage points since 1999. The number of workers dispatched by temp agencies (*haken gaisha*) grew from 0.5 percent in 1997 to 0.7 percent in 2002, while among permanent employees the number of part-time workers grew to 9.5 million (an increase of 3.7 percent over the previous year). Women, however, continue to provide the bulk of the part-time labor workforce, temporary male workers accounting for only 10 percent. Contrary to neo-liberal claims about sweeping corporate layoffs and a rapid dismantling of the pillars of the Japanese employment system, recent studies (Schoppa 2006) suggest that, unlike similar processes in other OECD countries, the brunt of the effect of hollowing-out has been borne by the large sub-contracting sector of the Japanese economy, leaving lifetime employment largely intact for a core, middle-aged, male workforce. Recent surveys, in fact, suggest that the proportion of workers near the end of their careers (age 50–54 years) who are still working with their first employer has actually gone up since the 1980s (http://Japanfocus.org 31/10/2006), although the proportion of men covered by standard employment contracts is at 84.5 percent, far higher than the average which has declined from 80.2 percent in 1991 to 69.6 percent of the workforce, indicating that the brunt of the deterioration in current employment prospects has effected women in non-standard contracts far more (http://Japanfocus.org 31/10/2006). However, Japanese firms continue to display a reluctance to lay off workers even during times of sluggish earning, a view expressed explicitly by no less than the Keidanren chief Mitarai Fujio.[5] As pointed out earlier, it is youth unemployment (nearly 10 percent) and the rising numbers of NEETs (neither in employment, education, or training) and *freeters* (freelancers) whose prospects have dimmed considerably in the wake of the long stagnation in the Japanese economy.

Within a span of a few years, Japan's rate of unemployment, negligible during the miracle years (1 percent for men, 1.3 percent for women in 1965), rose to 5 percent in 2002 (*Annual Report on the Labour Force Survey* 2004; 2005). Of the unemployed today, nearly 2 million are jobless youth (aged 15–19 years); another 800 000 are not even seeking jobs, while another 2–4 million work as "freeters" (freelancers) unable to find regular employment. According to the *Kokumin Seikatsu Kiso Chosa* (*Citizen's Basic Living Survey*) released in mid-2003, the income of the average household fell for the fourth consecutive year to 6.17 million yen, with elderly households averaging 3.19 million, and the poorest, women-headed families, a meagre 2.52 million yen. The number of NEETs aged 15–34 increased from 1.83 million in 1990 to 4.17 million in 2001 according to the Cabinet Office's May 2003 White Paper on National Lifestyle (*Japan Times Online*, accessed 14/04/06). More recent statistics look more promising: the number of employed persons was 63.56 million in 2005, an increase of 27 000 from the previous year (*Annual Report on the Labour Force Survey 2004: 24*). Of these, 5.53 million persons were employed in medical, health care, and welfare-related areas (an increase of 220 000 over the previous year), and indicative of the growing presence of social care as part of the new service economy. Comparable figures for services were 9.16 million; construction, 5.68 million (a decrease of 160 000 from the previous year); manufacturing, 11.42 million (a decrease of 80 000); wholesale and retail trade, 11.22 million; and hotels, 3.43 million (*Annual Report on the Labour Force Survey 2006*: 24–25). Unemployment fell to 2.94 million (1.78 million males and 1.16 million females), a decrease of 19 000 from the previous year, and the third consecutive year recording a decline in the total number of unemployed individuals. The single largest number of unemployed are within the age group of 15–24, recording the highest rate of unemployment (9.9 percent) in the population (*Annual Report on the Labour Force Survey 2006*: 26). Tables 5.1 and 5.2 provide a breakdown of unemployed persons by age and the ratio of the unemployed by age; Table 5.3 provides a comparison of the total number of unemployed and the rate of unemployment among countries.

In this drastically changed economic context, the number of suicides in Japan (always high, relative to OECD countries) reached a record high of 30 000 for the first time in 1998, touching almost 35 000 in 2004, an alarming 7.1 percent increase over the previous years (*Facts and Figures of Japan*, 2005). Economic and livelihood reasons account for 26 percent, failures in work 6 percent, and diseases 45 percent, in which mental diseases such as *karoshi* (death from overwork) are also included (Itoh 2005).

Table 5.1 Unemployed Persons (in tens of thousands) by Age

Year	Total	Years Old									
		15–19	20–24	25–29	30–34	35–39	40–44	45–49	50–54	55–59	60–64
1998	279	15	49	45	26	20	19	22	19	21	33
1999	317	17	55	51	31	22	20	25	26	26	34
2000	320	16	54	51	33	22	20	23	29	26	34
2001	340	16	54	55	38	26	21	25	32	26	35
2002	359	16	53	56	43	29	24	27	36	29	34
2003	350	14	54	54	42	31	24	24	31	31	34
2004	313	13	48	48	39	30	23	21	27	27	27
2005	294	11	44	45	39	29	24	19	23	28	23

Source: Compiled from *Annual Report on the Labour Force Survey 2005*, Statistics Bureau: Ministry of Internal Affairs and Communications, Japan, pp. 130–131.

Table 5.2 Ratio of Unemployed in Labor Force by Age

Year	Total	15–19	20–24	25–29	30–34	35–39	40–44	45–49	50–54	55–59	60–64
1998	4.1	10.6	7.1	5.6	4.0	3.2	2.8	2.5	2.5	3.3	7.5
1999	4.7	12.5	8.4	6.2	4.6	3.5	3.0	3.1	3.2	3.9	7.9
2000	4.7	12.1	8.6	6.2	4.8	3.4	3.1	3.0	3.4	3.9	8.0
2001	5.0	12.2	9.0	6.7	5.3	4.0	3.2	3.4	3.6	4.1	8.1
2002	5.4	12.8	9.3	7.1	5.8	4.4	3.7	3.9	4.1	4.5	7.7
2003	5.3	11.9	9.8	7.0	5.5	4.6	3.6	3.6	3.7	4.5	7.5
2004	4.7	11.7	9.0	6.4	5.0	4.4	3.5	3.1	3.5	3.7	5.7
2005	4.4	10.2	8.4	6.2	5.0	4.1	3.6	2.9	3.2	3.6	4.9

Source: Compiled from the *Annual Report on the Labor Force Survey 2005*, Statistics Bureau: Ministry of Internal Affairs and Communications, Japan, pp. 130–131.

Table 5.3 Unemployed (1000 Persons) Unemployment Rates (%)

	2004	2001	2002	2003	2004
Switzerland	183	2.5	3.0	4.0	4.2
Netherlands	422	2.7	3.2	4.2	5.0
Australia	550	6.7	6.1	5.7	5.4
Korea	813	3.8	3.1	3.4	3.5
Canada	1,234	7.2	7.7	7.6	7.2
UK	1,361	4.8	5.1	4.9	4.7
Italy	1,960	9.6	9.1	8.8	8.1
Spain	2,206	12.9	11.5	11.5	11.0
France	2,727	8.8	9.1	9.9	10.1
Japan	3,130	5.0	5.4	5.3	4.7
Germany	3,920	7.9	8.6	9.3	9.9
USA	8,149	4.7	5.8	6.0	5.5
China	8,300	3.6	4.0	4.3	4.2
EU[(a)]	14,975	7.8	7.9	8.2	8.3

[(a)] Not including Hong Kong and Taiwan.
Source: *Labour Force Statistics 1984–2004*, OECD, Key Indicators 2005, The Asian Development Bank.

The deterioration in the conditions for labor is apparent in the increasing numbers of homeless that gather in the main *yoseba* (day laborer districts) of urban Japan. In the major *yoseba Sanya, Kotobukicho, Sasajima* and, the largest today, *Kamagasaki*, in the Airin district of Osaka, an increasing number of the 6.3 million workers in the construction industry slide into joblessness, as construction work becomes harder to find. This is despite the fact that even in the post-bubble period, construction contributes a little over 10 percent of GDP in Japan, compared to 7.9 percent in Spain, 5.1 percent in the United Kingdom, and 4.0 percent in the United States. The comparable figures for employment are 9.4 percent for Japan and Spain, and 6.7 for the United States. (*Japan Statistical Yearbook* 2003). The slide from joblessness to homelessness among day laborers in the construction industry especially has contributed to a rising instance of homelessness. Official estimates place the number of homeless at 24 000 although advocates insist it is much higher (Gill 2001; Ezawa 2002; Tsumaki 2004; Hasegawa 2005).

In this context, the debate about the direction of welfare reforms to meet the multiple challenges thrown up by changes in the economic and demographic structure of Japan has been particularly sharp. Marked by rising levels of wage inequality, restructuration (*restura* is the katakana term used in Japan), diminished prospects for job creation and employment, and distinctions along the lines of age and gender intrinsic to the institutions of Japan's political economy have been exacerbated by the particular confluence of contradictory trends in contemporary Japan. Its rapidly aging force coupled with the lowest fertility rate among women in the OECD countries (1.26 percent in 2005, Masaki 2006)[6] renders the shortage of labor imminent, its consequences for Japan's tax base ominous in the long run.

The unprecedented increase in the numbers of jobless in the wake of the bursting of the economic bubble, however, called forth rival blueprints for change by politicians and bureaucrats, as well as academics within and outside Japan. Neo-classical economists and business leaders extolled the virtues of de-regulation (Ohmae 1989, 1990; Morita 1993), while criticism of scandals involving bureaucrats in influential ministries (Dore 1997) spurred limited efforts to reform the bureaucratic system and the financial sector by the Hashimoto and Obuchi administrations. It is under the Koizumi leadership (2001–2006), however, that some of the more publicized attempts at reform and de-regulation have gained ground, leading some critics (Dore 2000; 2001; Itoh 2001; Johnson 2001) to vigorously denounce the "Americanization" of the Japanese corporate system and the impending shift from welfare capitalism to "stock exchange capitalism" (Dore 2000) advocated by the reform lobby in Japan as unnecessary, indeed potentially disastrous, for the Japanese economy.

In this changed socio-economic context, Kasumigaseki's embrace of what has been depicted by scholars and media as a neoliberal vision of growth has generated cuts in social welfare and programs on the premise that a leaner/meaner state can deal more efficiently with the exigencies of global competition. But, as Makoto Itoh points out, contrary to the logic of fiscal austerity demanded by neoliberal ideology and repudiating popular wisdom, Japan's historical commitment to a Keynesian-style massive public works program shows no sign of being reduced, constituting even today 5 percent of GDP (4 percent in 1970 and 6.9 percent in 1996),[7] although its centralized disbursement, as Japan's leading "Third-Way" intellectual Kaneko Masaru points out, because subject to pork barrel programs, impedes a more efficient and effective use of available funds. Additionally, an expansion of public expenditure in some policy domains, most significantly elderly and child-care provision, belies sweeping claims about the embrace of a neoliberal conservatism vis-à-vis welfare spending. Changes implemented in unemployment and public assistance benefits appear rather to be consistent with Japan's long-standing commitment to the logic of commodification, principally work and participation in relations of exchange as a mechanism of ensuring welfare or well-being. What appears to be changing, however, with predictably de-stabilizing consequences for social and individual well-being in Japan is a new anxiety and doubt about the continued salience of the social limits long in place on the market in Japan. It is in this context that changes in unemployment benefits and public assistance gain meaning. But before turning to the key issue of unemployment protection and public assistance, I will very briefly map out the changes made in child-care and elderly provision so as to contextualize the former.

Amidst the turbulence of the recessionary years, as the number of part-time and unemployed individuals (including the elderly) and the destitute and homeless grew to record levels, the government's focus on changes in elderly and child-care provision appeared to be, for many critics, futuristic, rather than presentist in orientation. As changes in Japan's demographic structure threaten the fiscal viability of its tax and care system, the need to ensure that adequate care and insurance system is in place, including the labor force necessary to sustain both, by far the more drastic threat of a future crisis, is seen in terms of an imminent labor shortage. Given Japan's declining workforce and aging population, the necessity to fund long-term care is deemed crucial to the long-term economic stability of the country. Estimates by the Ministry of Health, Labor and Welfare (MHLW) suggest that by the year 2030 the number of workers will drop by 10 million from its current level to 56 million: 1 in every 20 will have to be employed in the nursing industry in 2030 to provide the current level of care.[8] In this context, the immediate question of unemployment for new graduates, male and female, is deemed not quite as urgent by government officials tasked with planning for the future health of the economy. Thus, presently, 70 percent of the social welfare budget goes to programs for the aged, such as pensions and medical services, with 4 percent set aside for services to children, child benefits and child-care services, and education-related spending (Masaki 2006).

The Ten-Year Strategy to Promote Health Care and Welfare for the Elderly (commonly known as the Gold Plan) instituted in 1989 was augmented by a public long-term care insurance system begun in April 2000. Under the New Gold Plan (2000), an expansion in the number of home helpers for elderly persons, improvements in the facilities designed for short-stay by elderly citizens, as well as an expansion of at-home services, such as visits by doctors and nurses, have done much to improve the long-term care system for the elderly. A mix of private and public sector provision, the funding of the system is based upon a combination of insurance fees paid by citizens aged 40 and over, with public contributions provided by the central government (25 percent), prefectures (12.5 percent), local municipalities (12.5 percent), and fees from insured individuals (50 percent). In addition to the Silver Resource Centers opened throughout Japan (discussed in the previous chapter), geared to providing both opportunities for re-employment as well as activity centers for the elderly, expenditure on pensions and medical care (a large proportion of which goes to care for the elderly) has increased, even as the number of people aged 60 or older who are employed or looking for jobs rose by 450 000 in 5 years, totaling 9.67 million in 2005.

Despite escalating levels of unemployment in the 1990s and 2000s, it was, paradoxically, the prospect of an imminent labor shortage within the next two decades that drew maximum attention from policy-makers engaged in rethinking welfare provision, focussing attention on the need to draw women back into the workforce, while attempting to increase the fertility rate which fell to an all-time low of 1.29 in 2003. The significance of better, more accessible child care thus emerged as central. The Child Welfare Law, *Jido Fukushi Ho*, enacted in 1947 was revised in 1997 to establish support centers for households with children, *jido katei shien senta*, which work to provide advice and guidance along with staff from child guidance centers. The names of some facilities were changed to emphasize *jiritsu* (self-reliance) rather than custodial care; including the renaming of homes for fatherless families from *boshiryo* to *boshi seikatsu shien shisetsu* (livelihood support facilities for mothers and children), and *kyogoin* (homes for training and education of juvenile delinquents) renamed *jiritsu shien shisetsu* (children's self-reliance support facilities). The Angel Plan of 1994 and the New Angel Plan in 1999 developed programs to encourage people to have more children, and laid out plans to open more nurseries (*hoikuen*) in the 2000–2004 period, with longer opening hours as well as to increase the number of child-rearing support centers *kosodate shien senta* throughout Japan. The plans have been welcomed as a much needed support to enable women to manage their work and family lives, although critics contend progress has been slow and much more needs to be done.

The approach to supporting single mothers, however, has generated considerable debate. Government statistics released in August 2002 claim that lone mothers now constitute the poorest families in Japan.[9] As the Japanese divorce rate continues to rise, the continuation of this trend is all but assured. Furthermore, the Japanese child-care support system is notoriously weak; delinquent fathers (of about 1.2 million families) can be legally compelled to pay only a quarter of the originally agreed monthly amount. Coupled with the high legal costs, this acts as a deterrent to seeking legal redress. Revision of the law in 2003, ostensibly to compel divorced fathers to pay child support, has, paradoxically, lowered the average monthly payment, low to begin with, from 530 000 to 44 660 yen, a decrease of 16 percent (Curtin, Japan Focus.org 30/10/06). Explaining the rationale behind this change, Maya Yoshio notes, to much criticism by progressive and feminist scholars, "in Japan it is easier for this group of mothers to get a part-time job and the level of remuneration they receive for such work is not so bad. Therefore, the living standard of single-mothers is not so poor and they can manage on an adequate economic level" (quoted in Curtin, 30/10/06). The drive to improve child-care provisions so as to enable women to join the labor force appears to have had some effect; 220 000 women have joined the labor force since 2003, bringing the total female labor force to 27.52 million in 2005 (Masaki 2006). In the corporate sector too, recognition that proactive efforts alone will induce women to both bear more children and enter the workforce is evident: Mastsushita Electrical Industrial Company has extended the period of child-care leave to new mothers up to a total of 2 years to care for preschool children; Toshiba allows workers to take paid leave for child care by the hour; Matsushita and Toshima employees are now guaranteed leave to receive fertility treatment under a "child-plan scheme"; Sharp Japan has promised to rehire any female workers who quit after childbirth to care for their child; and finally, Nissan Motors has begun to offer "maternity protection" leave to women with pregnancy-related difficulties (http://Japanfocus.org 08/11/06). The Table 5.4 indicates the emphasis placed on elderly and child-care provision within the current system.

In sum, reforms enacted in the domain of elderly and child-care in the late 1990s expanded, rather than contracted, public spending in these policy domains indicating continuities in (a) the future orientation of government agencies recalling the period of the developmental state's concern with economic management, and (b) the central focus on ensuring the viability of the national economy taken as a whole. When viewed from the perspective of either the neoliberal view (austerity measures and drastic cuts in social spending) or the varieties of capitalism approach with its focus on cultural and institutional path-dependencies, the expansion of welfare provisions for the elderly and the emergent focus on increasing child-care provision (which goes against the grain of Japan's gendered familial norms) and the increased spending this entails appear anomalous. They reflect neither the embrace of neoliberal "best practices" nor a "non-reflexive path-dependency" (Kwon 2005: 236). When viewed, however, from the vantage point of the framework developed here, namely the normative distinction between the state provision of social goods and the provision of consumption goods within civil society, the changes sketched above, insofar as they are driven by a primary concern with the problem of ensuring *future* commodification, affirm and illustrate the continued relevance of this

Table 5.4 Social Welfare Facilities

Social welfare facilities (public and private)	2002
Institutions under the protection of Law	292
Welfare Institutions for the elderly	33,419
Rehabilitation homes for physically handicapped	2,022
Women's guidance homes	50
Children's welfare institutions	33,266
Child and maternal welfare institutions	91
Institutions for protection of the mentally Handicapped	3,650
Social rehabilitation of facilities for the mentally disordered	1,082
Other social welfare institutions	8,398

Source: Ministry of Health, Labor and Welfare.
Japan Fact Sheet, November 2, 2006.

distinction in shaping public policy in Japan. That the present levels of unemployment have been produced within a system geared to prevent their generation, on the other hand, testifies to the contradictions contained within all instances of capitalism, particularized here in relation to the conjoined questions of age and gender in Japan. Insofar as the lifetime employment system was crucial to sustaining an inherently gendered division of labor (where women were solely responsible for the household and for the care of the elderly and children), the continuation of this system both vitiates the possibility of realizing the stated aim of brining more women into the workforce, as well as maintains an age-based seniority system that renders the youth in contemporary Japan (without any prospects of gaining a foothold on the lifetime employment ladder), especially vulnerable to abandoning normative ideals centered on collectivist economic growth.

Changes in unemployment insurance provision

The Revised Employment Insurance Law came into effect on May 1, 2003 with the objective of stabilizing the program's finances. The tax rate in Japan, historically low relative to OECD countries, has risen sharply from 24.3 percent in 1970 to 38.3 percent in 2002. However, its rapidly aging population and declining birthrate (1.29 percent in 2003)[10] and the rapidly shrinking tax base, associated with this depopulation trend, renders the regular payments of social security insurance payments necessary to maintaining the fiscal viability of its social security program. Only 62.6 percent of self-employed people paid the monthly fees (13 000 yen, approximately $130) in 2002 (*Asahi Shimbun Weeky*, September 15, 2003: 6–8). Accordingly, changes in the unemployment insurance program set the premium rate at 1.4 percent for the first 2 years but raised it to 1.6 percent from April 2005. Both the rate and the maximum amount of unemployment benefits have been lowered, and a single system determining the period of payments for both regular and part-time employees put in place. Under the previous system, individuals who found themselves out of work received 60–80 percent of their previous wage (calculated on a daily basis) for a period of 90–330 days. Under the new system, the minimum rate has been lowered to 50 percent, with a reduction in the maximum daily benefit payment. The dual structure of Japan's labor market characterized by hierarchies based on firm size, employment contract, and seniority has created a small core of male, middle-aged "elite" workers, in contrast to the vast majority of peripheral workers (Chalmers 1989); this rationalization of unemployment system is instructive. Comparable figures for the elderly (60 years and over), which were slightly more generous under the previous system (providing 50–80 percent of previous wage) has been lowered to 45 percent under the new law.

Critics justify these changes on the grounds that the previous system was inordinately generous, effectively de-commodifying citizens and acting as a deterrent to re-entry in the labor force. Thus, under the previous system, those who were 60 years and over received the equivalent of the higher of two wages: either the wage they received immediately before giving up their job or the wage at the time they were 60 years old. High earners, on the other hand, were eligible for a level of unemployment remuneration that was higher than the wages they would have likely earned at a new job, recalling Offe's argument about the inadvertent de-commodifying effects of efforts at re-commodification. That empirical evidence to illustrate this claim is forthcoming only in the Japanese case speaks more of the specificity of capitalism in Japan and its encasing within pastoral strategies of political and economic management, than it does about the generalizability of the claim.

The 2003 changes in Law extend the same benefits to part-time workers, who under the previous system were entitled to receive benefits for a shorter duration than regular workers. The integration of both categories of workers (regular and part-time) into one scheme can be seen not only as indicative of a bureaucratic rationalization, but more substantively as recognition of the rapidly changed conditions of labor in the early twenty-first century, specifically the flexibilization of the workforce in the shift from a manufacturing to a knowledge economy. Similarly, the voluntarily unemployed, those who give up their jobs (or reach the mandatory retirement age of 60) are, under the new law, eligible for unemployment benefits for the same period that part-time workers were before the law was revised (i.e. a shorter period). In contrast, workers laid off due to the vagaries of the business cycle (company bankruptcy, dismissal by employers, etc.) are eligible to receive the same benefits as formerly regular employees, that is for a longer period of time.

Like other OECD countries, the increase in the number of part-time workers as a percentage of the total labor force in Japan has increased rapidly in the 1990s, from 10 percent in 1980 to over 21 percent in 1997 (Tamai 2003: 43). Whereas part-time workers and those employed by the vast number of sub-contracting firms that made up Japan's "peripheral workforce" injected an element of flexibility in the Japanese economy (by enabling commitments such as lifetime employment to sustain a core elite workforce in the *kaisha* [big firms]), the main-streaming of part-time work with a decline in the numbers of full-time workers has injected a new dynamic in Japan's labor market. What makes the phenomenon particularly novel in the Japanese context is that this is occurring within the context of a wider panoply of changes that threaten to subvert the normative structure of Japan's political economy, specifically a society- and state-wide commitment to maintaining what I have referred to as the social limits of the market which, until now, have facilitated the pursuit of well-being or, in Hegel's terms, "subjective particularity" within social relations of exchange in the market. In the absence of a renewed commitment to maintaining these limits, the shift to part-time work portends a greater de-stabilization of the social and economic order in Japan.

Changes in the subsidies provided for education and retraining to retool workers to meet the needs of a rapidly changing economy have also been implemented. Under the Education and Training Benefits System established in 1998 by the Ministry of Health, Labor and Welfare, subsidies amounting to 80 percent of costs (up to a maximum of 300 000 yen) were available to individuals who were covered under the employment insurance scheme for 5 years or longer (*Japan Labor Bulletin*, July 1, 2003: 4–5). Under the revised law, the subsidy has been reduced to 40 percent up to a maximum payment of yen 200 000 for those who have been part of the scheme for 5 years. An additional change allows individuals with only 3–5 years' membership to receive 20 percent of educational and training costs up to a maximum of 100 000 yen (*Japan Labor Bulletin*, July 1, 2003, p. 5). The self-employed, part-time workers who work less than 20 hours a week and seasonal workers who work for less than 4 months in a year are not covered by employment insurance schemes; in some sectors – forestry, fisheries, and agriculture, for instance – coverage is optional. A notable exception is the special program for day laborers, which appears anomalous only when compared to OECD countries; given, however, the large role construction plays in the Japanese economy, accounting in large measure for Japan's long-standing commitment to a massive Keynesian public works program (equivalent in value to 5 percent of GDP), the program for day laborers (the vast majority of whom are employed in construction) is internally consistent with the logic of welfare provision in Japan. Tables 5.5 and 5.6 provide a disaggregated view of the principal changes implemented as a result of these reforms, relative to the previous system.

Table 5.5 Daily Unemployment Benefits as Percentage of Previous Salary and Maximum Benefit

Percent of previous wage		**Previous system**	**Revised system**
		59 yrs or less: 80–60 % **60 yrs or more: 80–50 %**	**59 yrs or less: 80–50 %** **60 yrs or more: 80–45 %**
Maximum	upto 30 yrs	8,676	6,580 (−24 %)
	30–44 yrs	9,642	7,310 (−24 %)
	45–59 yrs	10,608	8,040 (−24 %)
	60–64 yrs	9,640	7,011 (−27 %)

Source: Adapted from *Japan Labor Bulletin*, July 1, 2003: 4.

Table 5.6 Revised Period of Eligibility

Workers who Voluntarily left their jobs		**Number of years the person has been a member of the program**				
		Less than one year	**1–4 years**	**5–9 years**	**10–19 years**	**more than 20 years**
	All ages	90 days	90 D	90 D R:−30	120 D R:−30	150 D R:−30
Workers who left jobs due to bankruptcy or dismissal	upto 30 years old	90 days	90 D	120 D P: +30	180 D P: +30	–
	30–34 yrs	90 days	90 D P: +30	180 D P: +30	210 D P: +30	240D
	35–44 yrs	90 days	90 D	180 D P: +30	240 D R: +30 P: +30	270 D R: +30 P: +60
	45–49 yrs	90 days	180 D	240 D P: +30	270 D P: +30	330 D P: +30
	60–64 yrs	90 days	150 D	180 D P: +30	210 D P: +30	240 D P: +30

Note: R = regular workers; P = those who work shorter hours (e.g. part-time workers). D = days; the numbers preceded by + or − signs indicates the change in the number of days one is eligible to receive benefits after the law was revised.
Source: *Japan Labor Bulletin*, July 1, 2003: 4.

Public assistance

Japan devotes less than 1 percent of national income to public assistance. To further confound matters, estimates of the take-up rate for public assistance are also low anywhere from 8 to 10 percent (Taira 1967; Milly 1999; Peng 1995). Amongst those who categorize Japan as a welfare laggard, this alone constitutes an incontrovertible affirmation of their claim. In contrast to other OECD countries, in Europe especially, where proactive strategies to identify those in need in times of economic downturns are seen as having contributed significantly to creating a social safety-net that comes close to the Marshallian ideal of welfare as social citizenship, the absence of commensurate measures in Japan allegedly places it in the category of an "underdeveloped" welfare state. In the 1990s, a period of escalating unemployment in virtually all of the advanced industrialized countries, 17 percent of British citizens received means-tested support compared to 0.7 percent in Japan (Soeda 1991: 41). Unlike medical care and pensions that account for roughly 37 percent and 52 percent respectively of the total social-security-related expenditure, welfare constituted only 11 percent of the budget in 1996 (IPSS 1996 statistics). By 1998, welfare amounted to 14 percent of GDP, 18.9 percent of National Income (MHLW 2001: 128), with only 1.6 percent of GDP going toward welfare services, in contrast to 7 percent for pensions and 4.95 percent for medical care (Takahashi 2004: 285). In sum, assessments that "means-tested public assistance is a necessary, but seemingly minor, component of the welfare system" (Garon 2002: 1) appear hard to refute. When placed, however, in the larger context of the web of social provisioning in modern Japan, including, crucially, its distinctive commitment to making work the centerpiece of social and individual well-being in Japan, the antipathy to the provision of public assistance, at both the objective and the subjective level, as the discussion below hopes to show, appears less as an anachronistic instance of cultural, familial, or statist conservatism, but more as an aspect of Japan's welfare state capitalism that exemplifies and congeals its logic especially in relation to the the specificity of modern subjectivity as constituted within Japan's political economy. This recalcitrance to provide public assistance, in other words, in sharp contrast to expansions in the provision of what I have called "social goods," those deemed necessary to the well-being of the collectivity, distinguishes between the receipts of categories of public assistance, some of which are readily received, while others are not, illustrating both the theoretical argument advanced in Chapter 2 about the necessity of state provision of social goods and civil society and its system of exchange relations to the achievement of social and self-worth (subjective particularity, to recall Hegel's language), as well as its instantiation in the case of Japan.[11]

The fundamental principle of public assistance (*seikatsu hogo*) put in place in 1946 and enshrined in Article 25 of the constitution lays out the basic principle of social security and public assistance provision (revised in 1950) to guarantee a minimum livelihood for people who are living in poverty because of circumstances beyond their control with the aim of helping them achieve self-reliance. Comprised of seven categories, general assistance (for food, clothing, and other items needed to meet daily life requirements), education, housing, medical care, childbearing, work, and funeral expenses, the Livelihood Protection Law devised in 1946 has remained in place following revisions in eligibility criteria and benefit. Public assistance is exclusively financed from tax revenues via a combination of central and local government contributions.

The turn to de-centralization and privatization has resulted in key changes in Japan's social protection provision. The Public Assistance Law of 1950 (*Seikatsu Hogo Ho*), although in principle committed to providing a minimum livelihood for those living in poverty, has, since the late 1980s, been deployed on the basis of strict means-tested criteria. In 1981 the Welfare Ministry issued a notification (n. 123) which laid out stringent means and income-testing guidelines for receipt of *Seikatsu Hogo*, precipitating a 30 percent decline in the number of public assistance recipients from 1.43 to 1.02 million (Ito 1990); by 1993 the number had fallen to 0.88 million. The numbers increased somewhat in the 2000s: the number of people receiving governmental livelihood assistance increased from 751 000 in fiscal 2000 to a little over a million (941 000 households in 2005); the percentage of school children receiving education-related public financial assistance increased from 8.8 percent in fiscal 2000 to 12.8 percent in 2004. A total of 1.34 million Japanese (households) received *Seikatsu Hogo*. Table 5.7 provides a snapshot of the number of recipients relative to total population.

The level of assistance provided varies among recipients. Of those receiving assistance in 1997, 86.6 percent received living allowances, 79.0 percent received medical assistance, and 73.9 percent received housing allowances, while payments subsidizing childbirth, funerals, and finding employment comprised a mere 0.2 percent of the total. The vast majority of recipients, however, are elderly (44 percent) or families with a disabled member (41 percent); whereas single mothers, by the government's own data, the poorest in Japan today, make up only 8.3 percent of the total (Soeda 1995: 297–299). Average aid received by an individual varies from 105 000 yen for an elderly woman to about 195 000 yen for a single mother with two children (Garon 2002: 7–8). These figures, however, are misleading, pertaining as they do only to instances

Table 5.7 Public Assistance under the Revised Daily Life Security Law, 1951–1997

Year	Recipients in thousands	Recipients per 1000 people
1951	1,862	24.4
1955	1,704	21.6
1960	1,425	17.4
1970	1,143	13.0
1980	1,251	12.2
1985	1,431	11.8
1990	1,015	8.2
1991	946	7.6
1995	882	7.0
1997	906	7.2

Source: Adapted from Garon (2002: 2).

of aid given. More telling is the fact that only one-fourth of households living below the poverty line actually receives or takes up public assistance; three-fourths of those who would otherwise meet the criteria to receive aid do not.

Among the reasons given for this wide gap between need and level of provision are a booming economy in the 1970s and 1980s, and the administrative practices associated with determining eligibility and receipt of public assistance. With regard to the former, critics contend, a worsening economic situation through the post-bubble decade has not resulted in improvements in public assistance provision, suggesting that the real explanation for low uptake rates must be found elsewhere. On the latter, negative connotations were associated with those engaged in the praxis of welfare provision, specifically the *minseiin* (district-level welfare commissioners), whose legal authority to determine eligibility and levels of support in place until 1950 is especially singled out for comment.[12] In 1998, volunteer welfare commissioners (mostly women) numbered a little over 200 000, although much of the work of social work has now been professionalized. Unlike the pre-war period, however, welfare commissioners are no longer authorized to assess eligibility; all applications are made directly to the ward office, albeit assisted or guided by the volunteer. The critique of bureaucratization of welfare, however, extends to the lack of any effort on the part of the Ministry of Health and Welfare to devise strategies of actively seeking out the poor and destitute (as, for instance, occurred in the United Kingdom in the 1990s) to enable an increased uptake of available public assistance. Rather, the Ministry's slow response to fast-changing economic conditions has rendered those quite clearly deserving of aid unable to qualify, merely due to outdated practices. For instance, many day laborers rendered homeless and domiciled in the *doya gai* (the temporary accommodation), usually located in the *yoseba*, have not been able to avail of livelihood assistance for much of the 1990s on the ground that they lacked a home address. In *Kamagasaki* in the Airin district of Osaka, for instance, the largest *yoseba* in Japan today, home to some 30 000 day laborers and about 3500 homeless (predominantly male, 67 percent of whom were elderly in 2003), until recent changes that recognized the *doya gai* as a legitimate address, individuals entitled to receive *seikatsu hogo* were unable to avail of it. In 1997, day laborers and families accounted for a mere 1.3 percent of all assisted households. A similarly recalcitrant attitude is evident in anecdotal evidence about the strict application of a bureaucratic guideline about the types of goods that may be purchased under the general assistance scheme: possessions not owned by at least 70 percent of households in the recipient's locale are still deemed luxuries and must be sold (Soeda 1991; *Mainichi News*, 1994).

While all of the above contribute to augmenting a general climate of antipathy to the provision and receipt of general assistance, evidence of subjective dispositions reflective of a similar antipathy have yet to be fully integrated into a theoretical account of the nature of Japan's welfare state capitalism. Construed as an anachronistic holdover from pre-war times or, alternatively, actively produced via the state's successful strategies in moulding Japanese attitudes to public assistance, ethnographic evidence about the sense of "shame" or "the shrinking of personal pride" with regard to the receipt of public assistance vitiates the foregoing as a general stance toward welfare, testifying rather to the significance of a distinction between categories of public assistance made by potential recipients, a factor that is systematically overlooked in both cultural and statist arguments about the sources of antipathy to public assistance in Japan.

Thus, in a widely cited study, Dore (1958) notes that none of the Shitayama-cho residents thought of the state as a source of help for income, although at least more than half of the men and one-fifth of the women in his sample claimed that care for the sick and unemployed was properly the state's responsibility. Not one of the residents interviewed for his study made any mention of public assistance as a source of help when asked where they would turn if they lost their current source of income (Dore 1958: 69–70). "The community tends to regard public assistance as a dependence on charity at the public expense" (Dore 1958: 69–70). Further, Ogawa (1958) confirms the existence of social stigma accompanying public assistance; 45 of 85 ex-recipients interviewed in 1956 mentioned that they "felt a shrinking of their personal pride" during the period they received assistance. Similarly, a sample study of the recipients of medical assistance in Tokyo in 1956 showed that despite considerable deficits in the household economy, a great majority (86 percent) of the recipients of medical assistance did not desire to apply for general assistance in addition. Indeed, Koji Taira notes, "It may be useful to note that the stigma of public assistance varies by kind of assistance. Of the seven kinds of assistance stipulated by the Livelihood Protection Law, the most shameful in the public eye is general assistance. The other 'categorical' assistances at least imply that the recipients are capable of covering their costs of living at a minimum standard" (Taira 1967: 107). My own research in *Kamagasaki* (2003–2005) confirms the distinction made by those in need between the kinds of aid deemed acceptable, specifically medical aid, and those which are not.[13] *Kamagasaki* is described by many as a "city within a city," one square kilometer of concrete, densely populated with overwhelmingly male, and now increasingly elderly (over 67 percent are over 50 years of age), and sick people. *Kamagasaki* serves as a particularly telling instance of the difficulties facing Japan's efforts to "rescale" welfare provision without exacerbating the very problems welfare was initially created to alleviate. Since the *Heisei* recession of the early 1990s, Kamagasaki's conversion from a workers' town to a "welfare-town" threatens to mutate further into a wholly charity-based marginal town. The decline in the numbers of daily job offers relative to the job-seeking population combined with the problems specific to an elderly workforce have aggravated conditions here. While daily wages in transportation and manufacturing are about 13 000 yen and 13 500 yen respectively, the more physically demanding work fetches higher wages (about 18 000 yen for *kikan*). With job offers fewer than 1 million a year, (in 2003), those in need of state/private support have been consistently growing. While the great majority of its population does not have access to state pension and health insurance, which requires regular contributions over a period of time, the two systems that the inhabitants of Kamagaski can rely on are *seikatsu hogo* and *hogai engo* (extralegal assistance). Although the unreasonably rigid restrictions placed on the criteria to receive *Seikatsu hogo* (a permanent address, for instance, by definition not available to the homeless) have been eased with recognition of a room in a doya as adequate proof of residence and a minimal decrease in room rents to enable housing costs to be covered by state payments.

Volunteers with local non-profit groups emphasize the need to avoid approaching residents from the vantage point of charity; the now famous Thursday night patrols are devoted principally to identifying the sick, providing vouchers that will enable individuals to get treatment at the Social Medical Center, rather than the distribution of food or clothing. The shops that provide cheap, affordable consumer durables – from shoes, clothing, and coats, to vegetable, sake, and beer – affirm the independence of spirit, the "refusal of decent civic life" (Tsumaki 2004) that ethnographic studies of the homeless have so thoroughly documented.

Yet another example confirming the specific antipathy to the receipt of consumption goods as either charity or state largesse can be seen in the absence of "soup kitchens," charity-based organizations dispensing free food to the needy. Second Harvest Japan, the largest and the only registered food bank in Japan (*tokutei hieri katsudo houjin*), is run primarily by *gaikokujin* (foreigners) with the help of weekly volunteers. Similarly, despite an increasing number of secondhand stores which sell designer ware at bargain basement prices in some of the more chic neighborhoods of *Shirogane*, *Azabu Juban*, and *Hiroo*, and unlike the local neighbourhood secondhand store for household hoods (both of which suggest that using secondhand, merchandise is indeed an acceptable practice, provided it can be paid for by the consumer), there are virtually no organizations, other than the Salvation Army, that facilitate the re cycling of consumer durables via charitable donations.[14] The point here is not that Japan lacks a history of volunteering, the argument that is typically advanced to account for the paucity of charitable giving in contemporary Japan, but rather that the negative connotations attached to the *receipt* of charity, whether individual- or state-based (as the category of general assistance is typically construed in Japan) is anchored in the repudiation of sociality inherent in the act of accepting charity in Japan. Unlike the West, where charity, individual- or state-based, is seen as exemplifying sociality, understood as the explicitly acknowledgment of an objective realm of individual- or citizen-based relatedness, in Japan, given the centrality of work, labor, and participation in exchange relations as the crucial moment instantiating sociality, the receipt of charity violates the normative construct of social individuation in two ways: because unearned, it instantiates the lack of social relatedness and social worth; because non-agentic (not self-chosen or self-earned) it instantiates the lack of individual worth. That this antipathy is felt most acutely in regard to the receipt of consumer goods even during periods of need, as the examples above indicate, is quite telling. That the "personal (including familial) shame" recounted in ethnographical studies does not extend to state-provisioned medical care, educational or training subsidies, or pensions is especially noteworthy. Had this reluctance manifested itself as a general principle, applicable to all categories of welfare provision, cultural claims about Confucian family-based welfare states or, alternatively, claims about the state's success in shaping attitudes of *jiei*, self-management, and autonomy may well have carried the day; as it is, the distinction in attitudes to the different categories of welfare provision suggest that the link between consumption and sociality exemplified in the antipathy to the receipt of "general assistance" in Japan merits explanation.

The specificity of the link between consumption and sociality in Japan is thrown into sharp relief by the findings of a research project on "social life of low-income households and recipients household" conducted in 2003 in Japan, comparing single-mother recipients with low-income single-mother non-recipients of public assistance, reported in a paper by Reiko Gotoh (2006). Following Amartaya Sen's conception of individual achievements of functioning (as doings and beings) that assesses the individual's valuation of her life, not simply in terms of commodities or utility maximization, the survey indicates a sharp distinction made between the satisfactions associated with social relationality (via work and social relations) and the acquisition of consumer goods, including those deemed "necessities" of everyday life. According to Gotoh, although single-mother recipients of welfare record greater consumption levels (for foodstuffs, housing, lights and water supply, furniture, clothes, and shoes) that exceed that of non-recipients, they record far lower levels of "satisfaction" and social interactions (social activities including readings, cinemas, karaoke, spending time with friends, relatives or neighbors) (Gotoh 2006: 6). In contrast, non-recipient low-income single-mother households record lower levels of commodity consumption but a higher level of satisfaction and social relatedness evidenced in the indicators listed above. While some might claim that the higher rate of commodity consumption made possible by receipt of public assistance vitiates the argument developed here about the distinction between the premium placed on provisioning social needs and the antipathy to the provision of consumption-related individuated wants, it is revealing that a higher level of commodity consumption as indicated in this survey does not generate a commensurately higher level of satisfaction. To the contrary, lower levels of commodity consumption in the case of non-recipient lone mothers, because self-generated, do not impinge on standards of self and social worth leading to higher levels of social relatedness and correspondingly higher levels of reported satisfactions. The normative structure within which the "doings and beings" in modern Japan can be meaningfully apprehended, in other words, reveals not only an *objective* distinction between the provision of social needs and individuated wants, but, as the results of this survey reveal, a parallel *subjective* disposition that betrays a similar impulse.[15]

Thus, changes in welfare provision since the 1990s have alternatively expanded programs for the elderly and child–care provision, and rationalized the system of unemployment insurance for full-time and part-time workers, while streamlining the *seikatsu hogo*. Attempts to make theoretical sense of the various changes ongoing since the late 1980s have yielded a mixed result for competing frameworks. Below, I briefly consider some of the more influential arguments: electoral politics, neoliberalism, varieties of capitalism approach, hyrbidity, and "convergence." For the electoral politics school of thought, claims that levels of social provisioning are shaped by the ruling LDP party's perceived need for electoral support is countered by those who say that by virtue of numbers alone, the 3 million unemployed and on the dole do not constitute a large-enough group to constitute an effective interest group or voting block. For the neoliberal and varieties of capitalism approach, on the other hand, as we have already remarked, changes in Japan's welfare system through the 1990s and 2000s depart from both, conforming neither to the "best-practices" of hyper-marketization that is the hallmark of neoliberalism nor to the traditional practices associated with the path-dependencies emphasized by the latter (Kwon 2005). Consistent with prevailing views about the "hybrid" nature of welfare in Japan, Osawa Mari, a leading scholar of welfare, suggests that changes in Japan's welfare provision in the 1990s have developed in three different directions: a social democratic strand in changes in Japan's child-care provisions, the dominance of neoliberal ideology in the de-regulation of the labor market, and the enhanced stratification of the labor force (between the elite and the peripheral workforce) characteristic of the conservative regime type (Osawa 2001). Contrary to this characterization of Japan's current reform agenda as hybrid, or alternatively, lacking an underlying coherence or logic, the discussion above has attempted to establish the continuities in Japan's normative approach to welfare as the provision of goods deemed necessary to production-related social ends. In this regard, perhaps the key success that post-war Japan has achieved has been in its sustained commitment to optimizing individuals' incorporation into exchange relations, with the sole exception, until the 1990s, of enabling the same entry and exit into system exchange relations for women. The gendered construct of Japan's commitments to commodification, in other words, is incontrovertible. Recent efforts to enhance child-care provision, albeit limited thus far as critics rightly contend, are now compelled by the very same logic; an imminent shortage of labor, given Japan's changing demographic structure and potentially shrinking tax base, renders the optimization of women's skills and labor necessary for Japan's future economic growth. The de-regulation of the labor market, on the other hand, by no means as widespread as popular perceptions would have it, coupled with its inevitable consequences on heightening inequality, does signal an emerging repudiation of Japan's long-standing normative recognition of, and commitment to, placing social limits on the market. The mechanisms of sustaining this commitment must undoubtedly change to incorporate, for instance, not only the growing presence of Japanese women, but also a rising tide of immigrant workers in Japan.[16]

Finally, Gregory Kasza (2006) claims that similarity, indeed convergence, not only characterizes the trajectory of pension and health policies between Japan and other OECD countries, when compared at commensurate levels of industrialization, but also acknowledges a significant divergence in employment policy. Attributing this divergence to a "uniquely long period of high speed growth" (Kasza 2006: 112), rather than "traditional culture" that warrants the label of a "Japanese-style welfare society," Kasza insists on the likelihood of convergence in employment policy as well, as changes introduced in the 1990s accord with "global policy diffusion" as Japan attempts to adopt "best practices" and standards that will, Kasza contends, reshape employment policy in Japan along lines similar to those of other industrialized countries. Two points are worth noting here: (a) the elision of the problem of translatability in claims about global policy diffusion, and (b) the modernization theory bias that underpins this claim insofar as "global policy diffusion" with rare exceptions, entails a one-way movement of policy from West to East. As current work among critical geographers highlights, claims about policy diffusion dependent on "fast-policy transfers," especially in the domain of welfare, inevitably rest on a "thinning out" of policies which, because dependent on highly context-specific contingencies are unlikely to be able to reproduce the effects associated with their originary context. In the Japanese case, specifically, as noted above, evidence on the direction and nature of changes in welfare provision, including welfare policy, repudiates, rather than affirms, claims about Japan's transition to a neoliberal market-based system which constitutes the centerpiece of policy-making within the self-same global epistemic communities that Kasza sees as central to understanding welfare convergence.

Against current sentiment, then, the evidence presented above suggests an emerging tension between the continued emphasis on enabling the commodification of labor (albeit one focused more on the coming crisis of care, given the likelihood of severe labor shortages), and a growing skepticism within certain privileged circles in Japan, the *churyu-nisei* (second-generation middle class), about the social limits placed on the market. I explore the implications of this in the concluding chapter. The antipathy to receipt of consumer goods as part of a basket of welfare provision in Japan, in the context of the collective emphasis placed on work in determining social and self-worth, places the question of welfare squarely within civil society – in relations of exchange through which the individual enters the realm of social self-determination. In the Japanese case, the societal premium placed on work has come at the expense of individuation within social relations in the workplace as the continuing emphasis on hierarchy, seniority, socialization of risk and absence of high rate of returns on risk-taking, and so on, testifies. That this may be gradually changing is pointed out by many observers, even as the structural impediments to change remain high. However, the lesson, as it were, that can be drawn from the Japanese case is not the one conservatives often attempt to highlight – the paucity of welfare provision *per se*, but rather Japan's singular emphasis on employment as the primary mechanism of ensuring the well-being of the majority of its population.

This evidence of the necessity of participation in exchange relations as a measure of social and self-worth, what I have referred to earlier as social individuation, illustrated in the Japanese case, may come as a surprise given the long legacy within comparative studies of viewing Japan through the lens of "groupism," rather than the individual. It may also come as a surprise to students whose dominant frameworks have not considered the theoretical significance of distinctions in the nature of goods provisioned by the welfare state. The framework developed here, however, clearly illustrated via the Japanese case, points to the necessity of the state provision of social (de-individuated) goods, and the equally strong necessity of civil society and its system of exchange relations for the provision of individual wants. That the case of Japan illustrates this claim partially in relation to consumption and not production (where social ends are deemed primary) does not jettison the theoretical claim at stake here. Rather, it suggests that the present constellation of the institutions of political economy, in all its particularizations, cannot be treated as a laboratory or model for other social formations but simply that the necessity of both state and civil society in enabling welfare, from the vantage point of modern notions of personhood, must be made central to any efforts to rethink welfare. This would entail an expansion of the state's provision of social goods (health care, for instance), and the recognition and institutionalization of the social limits of the market within which alone the individual's pursuit of welfare (via work and consumption) may be pursued. Insofar as the Japanese case exemplifies all three (albeit the last in attenuated form), it provides the best example yet of the validity (if not its full realization) of the Hegelian insight into the relation between state, civil society, and welfare, in the context of modern subjectivity. That it is a non-Western, non-individuali*stic* society that offers testimony to the radical insights of an economic philosophy that not only had its origins in the West, but whose claims about property, individuality, and freedom have been deployed as quintessentially *Western* claims in alternatively civilizing, developing, or colonizing the non-West is no small irony. If, however, as mainstream comaparative theory claims,"the strongest possible supporting evidence for a theory is a case that is least likely for that theory but most likely for all alternative theories, and one where the alternative theories collectively predict an outcome very different from that of the least likely theory" (George and Bennett 2005: 121 quoted in Kasza 2006: 173), then the Hegelian interpretation of modern Japan's welfare state capitalism offered here may constitute an unlikely but perhaps persuasive vindication not only of Hegel's radical claim about the necessity of state and civil society to individual well-being, but also of Japan's status within the mainstream of comparative social theory and modernity.

6
Conclusion

The direction of Japan's current economic trajectory has become the subject of much debate within and outside Japan. Its embrace of the "neoliberal turn" globalized by the "Washington Consensus"[1] or, alternatively, the attempt to keep in place a now putatively obsolete and anachronistic institutional economic structure remains a contested field. Discussions of privatization (*minkatsu*), de-regulation (*kisei kanwa*), and marketism (*shijo-shugi*) on the one end, and the conservative defense of the status quo on the other, or alternatively a Japanese "Third Way,"[2] have set the parameters of debate about possible solutions to the long-standing economic malaise since the early 1990s that appears to have consolidated its hold over the "miracle economy". This concluding chapter briefly traverses the theoretical and political terrain with a view toward posing the question: what does the analysis developed in this book contribute to the larger debate about the direction and nature of reform in contemporary Japan? Insofar as its central thematic elaborates an argument about the normative horizon that has shaped Japan's project of modernity, specifically the distinction between the social ends of production and the de-limited terrain of individuated consumption institutionalized via the social limits placed on the market, it is the nature of these limits and their implications for the question of the development of Japan that provides the central thread of the discussion that follows. Re-capping first the theoretical and historical argument developed in the foregoing chapters, these concluding remarks draw attention to some of the antinomies of current thinking on functionalist and neoliberal solutions to the current impasse in Japan from the standpoint of the theoretical framework developed in this book, and the prospects for a renewed commitment to putting in place social limits on a market better suited to the demands of a radically changed world, both inside and outside Japan.

Against conventional interpretations of Japan's welfare system as either a welfare laggard or a superpower, or alternatively a "hybrid" constellation made up of social democratic, liberal, and conservative strands, subject to the multiple and shifting logics associated with each, this book has elaborated an alternative approach to the study of welfare and its location in social and political life in Japan. Challenging accounts that focus on culture, the developmental state, or path-dependency (associated with the varieties of capitalism approach), this book has sought to recover the logic in Japan's pattern of welfare provision by recuperating the link between the institutions of political economy and the nature of the subject specific to modern Japan. Drawing on a neo-Hegelian theorization of this link, in which political economy is seen as "the external structure of subjectivity," an ethical and normative construct, the theoretical framework developed here outlines the process of social individuation contained within the social relations of a market-based civil society, specifically the relations of exchange of production and consumption, and the necessity of both state and civil society to enabling welfare and individual well-being.

Based on this theoretical approach, the investigation of the nature of goods provisioned by Japan's welfare state conducted in this study reveals a homology between the logic of the pattern of welfare provision recuperated here (specifically the generous disbursement of goods associated with the social ends of production, and an antipathy to the provision of consumption goods) and the structure of subjectivity within civil society. What gives modern subjectivity in Japan its specificity, I have argued, contra essentialist and post-modern interpretations, is the distinction made between the social ends of production-related activities and social practices, and those related to consumption as the delimited terrain of individuation. This "structure of subjectivity" is both constituted and realized within the institutions and social practices of Japan's political economy due to the explicit recognition and institutionalization of what I have referred to as the social limits of the market in Japan's modern history. Based on the recognition that "there is no innate tendency within capitalism toward full employment" (Shaikh 2005), the institutionalization of a market-based civil society in modern Japan has sought to harness its power by linking it to a social agenda driven in large measure by the historical contingencies that have shaped Japanese modernity.

The link between the social limits of the market as suggested here is thus seen as crucial to accessing not only the normative structure of subjectivity in modern Japan, but also the larger task of rethinking welfare provision in our times. That both state and civil society bear a necessary relation to individual welfare, or what Hegel calls "subjective particularity," is a claim that the case of Japan helps illustrate. Further, it vivifies the argument made in this book that state and market need not be conceived in inherently antagonistic terms, as the dualism underpinning the dissolution of one into the other (as in state socialism or neoliberal hyper-marketization, for instance) suggests. Rather, the claim elaborated here that this antagonism can be resolved such that a recognition of the social limits of both the state and the market vis-à-vis individual well-being can generate a division between the two that is enabling of welfare is also demonstrated, albeit in a limited way, via a discussion of the Japanese case. The potentialities contained within this division, specifically via the social limits of the market, renders the case of Japan theoretically significant to discussions of welfare, state, and civil society in ways that have perhaps not been fully acknowledged yet.

Dominant accounts of the multiple ills that have plagued the Japanese economy include diagnosis of the crisis as the result of factors endogenous to Japan, and those that anchor an explanation of the crisis within Japan to a set of relations emanating principally outside its national borders. Among the former, and the most widely cited in the press and scholarship, are those of mainstream economists who attribute the crisis to a combination of elements including the absence of efficiency and market discipline, institutional obsolescence, bureaucratic regulation, and neo-classical economic theory's paradigmatic claims about the pathologies associated with "state-intervention" in the economy (Ohmae 1989; Morita 1993; Ozawa 1994; Wolferen 1994; Boyer and Yamada 2000). Others have attempted to explain the Japanese debacle in terms of international regime theory (Gao 2001), globalization (Kwon 2005); as a crisis of capitalist maturity (Burkett and Hart-Landsberg 2003); from a world system perspective (Ikeda 2004); and as indicative of the crisis of capitalist restructuring (Itoh 2005). Linking the two, Anchordoguy (2001), on the other hand, attributes the economic slowdown to the inability of Japan's "communitarian capitalism" (Campbell and Ikegami 1998) to make the necessary institutional transition to a global knowledge economy. Attributing its earlier success to a competitive model built largely around a strategy of reverse engineering and export competitiveness in the context of a liberal external environment, Anchordoguy shares also the skepticism of those who see Japan's "convoy capitalism" (Katz 2003) imperiled by the enhanced competitiveness of a global knowledge economy, and also the lower-cost manufacturing capacity of Japan's neighbors. Still others suggest that the cataclysmic effects generated by the global slowdown have revealed weaknesses endemic to Japan's "developmental state" (Johnson 1982), its "cooperative capitalism" (Schaede 2000), or "referee-free capitalism" (Kaneko 2001), and its inability to regenerate itself in the context of the accelerations of an increasingly globalized economy. Finally, some scholars have drawn attention to the changed context within which Japan must try to re-negotiate its global economic location, not from the standpoint of global economic change *per se* but within the political context of empire and the role of the United States in shaping a new world order. Thus, suggestions that failure to deal with the structural rigidities identified above are internal to economic institutions themselves are countered by those who tend to see this reputed failure as indicative of the politics of the United States–Japan relation, especially under the Koizumi regime, in which the ability of Japan to effectively respond to the crisis (via an aggressive export strategy, for instance) has been forestalled by the far greater urgency placed on assuaging American interests.

It is not my intention here to adjudicate this debate. Suffice it to say that the argument developed in this book sheds a somewhat different light on the question of the roots of the "crisis of capitalism" in Japan and the relative merits of taking either one of the two poles of analysis (endogenous or external) as determinant. Insofar as the theoretical framework developed in this book takes the national economy as its starting point, it shares with the "internalist" arguments a focus on endogenous elements; unlike the behavioral diagnosis of the former, however, it deploys a structural reading of the crisis-prone tendencies innate to Japanese capitalism while remaining attentive to the specificity of the "national" moment eschewed by the latter. Whatever the proximate causes of the bursting of the economic bubble in the early 1990s that ushered in the long decade of slow growth,[3] the analysis pursued here suggests that the larger question of the "crisis" of capitalism in Japan may be better seen not only as a crisis of political economy as is the norm, but more crucially as a crisis of subjectivity. The normative structure of modern subjectivity in Japan, constituted and manifested within the institutions and social practices of the Japan's political economy, congeals a criterion for the division between state and market that can be subverted only at considerable cost to social, economic, and political order in Japan. The development and consolidation of the logic of this normative structure, as this book has shown – the distinction between the social ends of production and the individuated ends of consumption – recuperated here via the study of the pattern of Japanese welfare suggests that it may well constitute the outer limit within which reform may be successfully and legitimately undertaken.

From the vantage point of the theory of social individuation pursued here, the faultlines in the criteria used in advanced capitalist societies to resolve the "boundary question" between state and market are evident. The limits of the criteria of efficiency, the centerpiece of neo-classical economic liberal theory, now redeployed to neoliberal ends are clearly in view, the development of the Keynesian alternative testimony to its limits; the erosion of the Keynesian social compact, in turn, can be seen not as the result of a fiscal crisis of state interventionism *per se*, but due to the absence of a parallel effort to put in place what I have called the "social limits of the market." Communitarian alternatives (in their Keynesian or socialist guise) advocated by those critical of market-based solutions reflect what Walter Mignolo (2002) has described as "the enchantment of enduring oppositions that modernity both reproduces and maintains." However, as the argument pursued in the book has attempted to show, the political and economic ordering of efforts to negotiate this antagonism, between atomism and collectivism, of wealth and want, may perhaps be more fruitfully pursued not as a binary choice, but rather one that can be reconciled by the recognition of market-based civil society's role in enabling social and individual well-being *and* the institutionalization of limits on the market such that its enabling, rather than disabling, role may be facilitated. Insofar as the Japanese case demonstrates precisely such an effort, albeit modified by the historical contingencies that shaped its development, it offers a particularly compelling, if partial, illumination of the potentialities contained within this recognition, a lesson that not only social theorists of welfare, political economy, and subjectivity might profit from, but one that may also help shed light on the question of the direction of reform in Japan.

In this context, then, discussions of resolutions may be of limited use, insofar as they take the "problem-solving" rather than critical approach (Cox 1987), focusing on proximate causes intended to induce behavioral rather than structural reform. Foremost among these and by far the one most widely discussed by policy-makers in government and business in Japan and also by its main backers, the Untied States, is neoliberalism. *Qua* ideology, neoliberalism aims to extend the calculation principle of economic rationality to all domains of social, economic, and political life, subjecting all aspects of life to the logic of the marketplace. The institutionalization of this economic calculus, an inherently political and normative as opposed to ontological project (Brown 2003), entails a re-regulation in accordance with what Gramsci termed "theoretical laissez-faire." Thus, processes of de-regulation (properly renamed re-regulation from a critical standpoint), marketism, privatization, flexibilization of labor markets, and intensification of competition ostensibly geared to revive effective domestic demand have occupied media attention in Japan since the late 1980s. The current pride of place, however, among the neoliberal "market fundamentalists" (Dore 2006) is occupied by the "shareholder revolution"[4] designed to finally accord the private shareholder a level of return on investment and voice (in corporate governance) that has been, critics allege, all too long absent in Japan.

The effects of these reforms on the Japanese economy are far from unambiguous as many critics point out. Greater competition and lower consumer prices in some areas have been offset by a growing divide between those at the top and bottom of the management/labor chain; shareholder dividends have increased manifold even as real wages have declined, generating a sentiment shared across the ideological divide that the central problem in the present day – the question of how to revive effective demand domestically – cannot be solved via the neoliberal solution. Thus Paul Krugman, the noted economist, echoes a view shared by other notables (Jeffrey Sachs and Joseph Stiglitz, for instance) that in the context of rising unemployment, bankruptcies, and heightened economic security, neoliberal reform could further reduce demand and worsen stagnation, rendering policy reform ineffective in the short term. Neoliberalism's sanctification of free trade theory as the engine of trickle-down growth depends, as critics have pointed out (see for instance, Shaikh 2005), on an elision of the theory of competition that underpins it, allowing advocates to claim a Pareto-optimal outcome in international trade that surreptitiously reverses the outcome associated with enhanced competition among regions *within* a closed economy: a growing divide between the strong and the weak, and the split between wealth and want that typically accompanies this stratification.

Analyses of the state's embrace of neoliberalism as a governing technology and its extension into the social domain of family, social care, gender, welfare, and non-profit organizational life (McVeigh 1998; Peng 2002; Ezawa and Fujiwara 2005; Ogawa 2004) also serve as a crucial, albeit critical, discourse on the consolidation of neoliberalism in Japan. Statist arguments, long familiar to students of Japan, are augmented in this case by Foucauldian analyses that suggest that the materialization of neoliberalism depends on the effective deployment of what Sanford Schram (2002) has called a "behaviour modification regime," geared to re-shape subjectivities in Japan in accord with neoliberal desires and social order. On this more reflexive and critical account, the remaking of Japanese citizens into self-reliant and active selves recalls an earlier statist project of promoting *jiei* (self-management) (Garon 1997), and the revitalization of family and *komyunity*, especially in regard to welfare, and is seen as paralleling similar processes of making neoliberal subjects in the rest of the advanced industrialized world. Coupled with the embrace of a neoliberal economic agenda (which dominates mainstream discourse on Japan's ongoing transformation), analyses of the remaking of Japanese subjects via a behavior modification regime and new technologies of government help consolidate the view that what we are witnessing is indeed an irrevocable turn to neoliberalism in Japan. Given the long legacy of statist thinking in Japan Studies, the claim that the end of the Meiji state, evident in efforts at de-centralization since the 1980s, portends the emergence of a new "moment" – a neoliberal one – in the institutions of political economy, and the structure of subjectivity it embodies has all but been universally accepted by those both within and outside Japan.

The absence of evidence testifying to a robust anti-neoliberalism movement in Japan, the decimation of the political left, reduced now to a tiny minority in the Communist Party, the decline of enterprise unions, in the larger context of a largely de-politicized populace that has been remarkably supportive of statist projects through the postwar decades, appear to reinforce the claim about the inevitability of this turn to the market in Japan. Even scholars critical of the "Americanization" of the Japanese economy (Dore 2006; Niwa 2006) and the movement from welfare capitalism to what Ronald Dore (2000) refers to as an "Anglo-Saxon stock-exchange capitalism" concede that many of the current institutions are obsolete, including a lifetime employment system that systematically excludes women, reducing the optimal utilization of available human capital (Schoppa 2006), and Japan's deeply encoded predilection for one-way "adversarial trade." Thus, many scholars make recommendations similar to those supported by market-fundamentalists, but on the grounds that the "old Japan" has run its course. In the context of a new global economy, changes in the demographic structure of Japan renders a rapidly aging population dependent on a shrinking tax base: as Japan's fertility rate becomes the lowest in the advanced industrialized world, the changes advocated by the ideologically neutral (we might say "functionalists") emphasize the need to incorporate women, minorities, and immigrant labor in the workforce, by a series of changes that include, above all, abolishing the dual structure of the Japanese economy embodied in the lifetime employment system and seniority wages. The structural reform of the Japanese economy in the areas of banking, shareholder-sovereignty, corporate governance, lifetime employment protections for a minority elite male workforce are thus deemed central. Similarly, many feminists (Ueno 2005; Peng 2002; Schoppa 2006; Ezawa 2002; Ezawa and Fujiwara 2005) rightly criticize the government's woefully inept efforts to encourage women to have more children, while failing to put in place the systems of support (child care, family-friendly corporate policies, etc.) necessary to sustain a simultaneous increase in both the rate of fertility and the rate of female participation in the labor force.

In this context, claims about the consolidation of a "neoliberal turn" in Japan appear hard to refute, the shift in Japan from a centralized "Meiji state" committed to a developmental agenda in which society was a pliant partner, to a post-Meiji de-centralized, marketized social order in which Japan attempts to renegotiate its standing in the New World Order by adopting the best practices and "global standards" better suited to a global economy, all but assured. The analysis offered in this book, however, suggests otherwise.

From the vantage point of the theoretical framework developed in this book, the link between state and market and the specificity of the boundary between the two has been seen as pivotal to, indeed constitutive of, the nature of subjectivities constituted in relation to both. Further, welfare, as the embodiment of the boundary between state and market, has been seen as a particularly acute access point for the recuperation of the structure of subjectivity shaped by, and in relation to, the specific ways in which state and market are bounded. This approach, which sees political economy as the external structure of subjectivity, offers then an alternative reading of the present historical juncture in Japan. It suggests that the success of the neoliberal turn depends not so much on the positive demonstration effects of reforms undertaken in its name – larger dividends for shareholders, or greater profits for firms currently weighed down by costs, (for instance labor, deemed in excess, based on the criteria of efficiency) – but rather on the successful re-shaping of subjectivities that would in turn provide its constitutive conditions of possibility (Dean 1995; Rose 1996; Schram 2002). That is, the success of the neoliberal economic agenda depends pivotally on the successful fashioning of neoliberal subjectivities necessary to its materialization. (For example, without risk-taking entrepreneurial capitalists oriented to the task of valorizing capital, capitalism as an economic and social order is untenable.) Here, the structure of modern subjectivity recuperated via an analysis of its pattern of provision vitiates claims about a potential shift from the pastoral strategies of care that structure the institutions and social practices of a system of production geared to meet social ends to a normative structure of neoliberal subjectivity via the constitution of self-reliant autonomous selves.

In the Western context, the "conduct of neoliberal conduct" attempts to revitalize the institutions of direct sociality – the family, religious charities, and private philanthropic social networks – as the appropriate containers of extra-market dependency, while advocating a return to the pre-Keynesian a-social domain of the "free" (unregulated) market. In the case of Japan, however, the terrain of an unmediated sociality has included not only the family, but also the *kaisha* (firm), neighborhood associations, and social groups marked by the thick affinities of shared in-group (*uchi*) sameness, and a mode of conduct – interdependence, hierarchy, deference, and care – that is more accurately described as pastoral (*bokuminkan*). In this context, claims about the fashioning of a neoliberal subjectivity from within a moral economy in which one pole – production and labor – remains saturated by the logic of strategies of pastoral care evidenced in the strong reluctance to dismantle long-standing lifetime employment schemes, for instance (see, Ono 2005 and Schoppa 2006 especially), are tenuous at best. That is, unlike the West, where the mapping (and shaping) of subjectivities has entailed a progression from pastoral strategies of power specific to feudalism to disciplinary forms of power specific to liberalism, and only then techniques of government associated with the shaping of neoliberal subjectivity, a parallel argument in the case of Japan elides the necessity of the middle term – the liberal subject – to the consolidation of *neo*liberal subjectivity in Japan. In the absence of the "liberal moment" as a feature of social life as a whole, seen in the relation between civil society, welfare, and the modern subject examined in this book, efforts to release the normative limits of the culturally coded institutions of Japan's political economy may prove to be self-defeating, signaling a crisis not only of political economy, as mainstream scholarship suggests, but, equally as the theoretical framework elaborated in this book postulates, a crisis of subjectivity.

Signs of this unfolding crisis of subjectivity in contemporary Japan are already apparent and can be accessed at multiple levels. A couple of examples here may suffice. At one extreme are the *hikikomori*,[5] once restricted to the 15–20 age group but now including those in their early 1930s, whose inability to maintain the modicum of autonomy necessary to negotiate the social world of schools, jobs, and so on has resulted in a pathologized withdrawal into isolation – a hyper-autonomy that ostensibly brooks no connections with others, family, friends, or caregivers, but which paradoxically depends on the indefinite extension of pastoral care provisioned by the family. The antinomies of this diremption in subjectivity is equally evident in the breakdown of the "maternal principle" (Asada 1989; Yoda 2000) of Japanese society, a crisis of gender that is seen by many to be the most pivotal to Japan's ongoing transformation. And finally, at the other end, is the crisis of national subjectivity manifest in recent years by signs of a revived militarism, evidenced in the *Yasukuni* shrine controversy and its grounding in the crisis of national identity (Tamamoto 1994, 2001; Ollman 2001; Takahashi 2006). In this context, the neoliberal turn in Japan and its embrace of hyper-autonomized forms of subjectivity do not hold out much promise, not only on the grounds well chartered by those critical of the economic effects of a neoliberal growth agenda – the growing gap between wealth and want – but also, as the argument developed in this book suggests, on the grounds of the normative horizon and structure of subjectivity currently in place in Japan. To the extent that a reform agenda's potential success remains tied to its legitimation within an existent normative horizon, the project of rethinking the political economic institutions of civil society, welfare, and the market in Japan can profit from an attentiveness to "the deep history of the subject" (Chakrabarty 1998) as constituted within political economy. This history can be repudiated only at considerable cost, psychic, social, political, and economic, to the vast majority of the population of Japan, a cost the ruling elite in Japan may indeed be willing to impose; that is a question that the politics of reform will determine. It cannot, however, be rationalized on functional terms as the above discussion has hopefully demonstrated.

In this context, then, alternatives proposed by thinkers and activists committed to a progressive vision of Japan – including the new associationist movement initiated by Kojin Karatani, worker-communities by Marxist critics, non-profit "integrated communities" (along the lines of Futagami Nouki's organization, New Start), Niwa Uichiro's focus on the tax system as the principal means of redistributing income, and

Kaneko Masaru's "Third Way" proposals (reform of economic institutions, including asset taxes that can fund an expansion of a state-provisioned safety-net to enable a more comprehensive coverage of risk) – suggest that the opportunity to put back into play Japan's distinctive commitment to a social agenda has not yet been undone by the neoliberal turn. At a time when no clear alternatives to neoliberal globalization present themselves, Japan's history of maintaining a commitment to social protection and economic growth by maintaining the connectivity between economy and public authority can serve as a powerful and distinctive framework from within which institutions and social practices more hospitable to alterity of *ethnie*, race, and gender in Japan's "diasporic space" (Kang 2001) can be re-made. And if, following Hegel, "the extraordinary and unexpected can only arise from the prose of the well-known and familiar" (Malabou 2005: 190), progressives and intellectuals in present-day Japan may be extraordinarily well positioned to offer a creative response to the challenge of rethinking the relationship between state, civil society, and welfare under conditions of late capitalism.

Notes

1 Introduction: civil society, welfare, and Japan in comparative studies

1. There is a vast and growing literature on alternative modernities and civil society, some of it referenced in the sections that follow on civil society and comparative studies.
2. The argument that Japan is simply a welfare laggard, given its situational characteristics as a Gerschenkronian "late industrializer" lends itself too easily to the logic of the convergence thesis: as late developers "catch up" the social problems, and solutions they encounter will more likely resemble those of already developed societies. The shortcoming of this claim is not that it mis-specifies the common structural characteristics that typify late industrializers, but that it fails to take into account the full implications of the alternative logic set into motion by the distinctive institutionalization of both state and market. Institutions created to deal with the problems typical of late industrializers do not simply lose their distinctiveness once those goals are met, but may indeed by virtue of their institutional organization, memory, and constitutive role continue to develop goals and implement policies in distinctive ways. Japan may not simply be a "welfare laggard," but may indeed have institutionalized the provision of welfare differently.
3. The point here is that the assumption of uniformity of welfare needs across nations may be untenable. If this is right, then welfare regime theory, the bedrock of contemporary scholarship, which takes this assumption as its starting point in order to classify different states along a welfare continuum, may be questionable.
4. Michael Hardt's claim that 'the society we are living in today is more properly understood as a postcivil society' makes the case that due to changes in the sphere of wage labor, but also 'desiring production, intellectual creativity, caring labor, kin work," (Hardt 1995: 41), in sum the nature of labor itself, what is often loosely described as the post-modern condition, is better understood as a 'postcivil society' (Hardt 1995). Hardt's argument is a provocative one and merits close attention; because, however, it applies, as Hardt himself suggests, to what Jameson in another context refers to as late capitalism, not the historical period that is primarily the focus of this study of Japan, I do not engage this argument here.
5. Dipesh Chakrabarty, the noted historian points to the legitimate and effective deployment of the language of rights in the Indian context, in anti-colonial national struggle and by oppressed minorities against the Indian state, in contrast to and the dissonance generated by the use of this language of rights to negotiate the gamut of family and kin connections. His point is that while the language of rights works in certain areas of social life in non-Western contexts, it does not, indeed cannot, encapsulate others. He is right

on this but, and this is crucial, not as a particularistic claim relevant to the case of India alone, but equally, I would suggest, in the case of Western societies as well. To the extent that the language of rights has entered the realm of the family in the West, it has done so in violation of a relationality that is deemed the 'ethical domain' of family life. Chakrabarty is, however, right in his insistence on recovering what he calls the "deep history" of the subject of non-Western, in this case, Japanese modernity. This entails, he suggests, an "effort to recover the richer, older, more complex histories of the training of the senses . . . the history of embodied practices of subjectivity" (1998: 285–296). See his afterword to Vlastos (1998) for an insightful engagement with the essays on Japanese modernity.

6. Post-colonial critique that the categories of nation-state and capitalism render other (non-Western) histories outside the temporal and spatial ordering of modernity is a powerful one, highlighting the alienation and anxiety producing effects of the hierachialization of forms of being that have accompanied the spread of capitalism via colonialism. What they may have perhaps overlooked is the categorical imperative of 'alienation' that is internal to capitalism and at play in all capitalist societies. The experiential forms alienation takes are, arguably, different, depending on one's location in the West or non-West, the one seen as culturally consistent, a product of one's own lived time, the other experienced as an external (cultural) imposition.
7. That many of the more well-known civil society associations (the End Poverty campaign or the anti-globalization movements) take as their platform and mandate an essentially reformist agenda (of humanizing rather than repudiating capitalist structures of social organization), focuses critical attention again on the underlying disregard of material processes of civil society in the Tocquevillean celebration of civil society *qua* associational life and, help account in large measure for its success in capturing the political imaginary of policy-makers, politicians, academics, and activists alike.
8. Birnbaum's identification of the paradox at the heart of de Tocqueville's thesis on associational life is also instructive here: the individual, the basis of the free social and political associations, is both the object and subject of associational life (Birnbaum 1977). See also Woldring (1998) for a good discussion of this tension.
9. In Japan, Tsujinaka (1998, 2002), Yamamoto (1999, 2002), and Amenomori (1997) are especially relevant on the growth of interest-groups and the non-profit sector. Tsujinaka Yukata's landmark research project "Civil Society, the State and Culture in Comparative Perspective" at the University of Tsukuba, 2005–2010, which empirically investigates civil society structure and conducts comparative surveys of civil society organizations in various countries, provides the template within which civil society studies of Japan are typically located. Collaboration with partner institutions like the Civil Society in Asia project organized by the East–West Center (Hawaii) have also yielded important studies, influential in framing questions about civil society in Asia for a new generation of researchers (see Alagappa 2004). Keio University's Center for Civil Society with Comparative Perspective has also been active in organizing symposia around its project, "Designing toward the ordering of political society in a multicultural and pluri-generational world"

under the government's twenty-first-century Center of Excellence funding scheme. Numerous government-funded efforts to establish links between social activism and voluntary groups between Japan and other countries have been gaining visibility. The Japan Foundation Newsletters regularly carry featured articles and announcements about these links. See especially its July 2002 issue (see also Yamamoto and Ashizawa 1999, 2001). A singularly influential collection of essays on civil society in Japan, Schwartz and Pharr's edited volume (2003) includes essays by leading Japan specialists Sheldon Garon, Andrew Barshay, and Susan Pharr, among others. Pekkanen (2006, 2004), focuses exclusively on the Tocquevillean approach, reflecting a new generation of Japan scholars working on the non-profit sector and volunteering in Japan. See also Ogawa (2004); Shipper (2002); Hirata (2002; 2004); Sorensen (2001). Maclachlan (2002) is an exception here since she focuses on the relationship between market and civil society (as the plurality of voices and identities). Funding agencies such as the Japan Foundation, the Japan–United States Friendship Commission have been especially active in promoting workshops and symposia on civil society in Japan. See especially the civil society project directed by the Center for Global Partnership. Papers by Deguchi (1999), Imata (1999), Chanin (1999), and Bestor (1999) are also accessible online at http://www.us-japan.org/dc/cs.objectives.htm.

10. In contrast to the literature on civil society in the non-West briefly discussed above, where critiques of the 'NGOization of civil society," the presumed hegemony of liberal organization of civil society effectively elides (and delegitimates) what Nancy Fraser has referred to as subaltern counter-publics, the uncritical view of civil society qua associational life effectively domesticates and manages the question of an oppositional politics in the Asian context.
11. The term *shimin shakai* combines *shimin* meaning either city (*shi*) inhabited by people (*min*) or simply people as used in social movement of people (*shimin undou*) or revolution (*shimin kakumei*). As a transliteration of the English term 'civil society," *shimin shakai* points to the gap between the set of meanings signified by the English and Japanese terms.
12. This distinction between internationally oriented NGOs and domestically oriented small groups (NPOs) is distinctive to Japan, and significant, as discussed further along in this chapter; in the West all NPOs are included in the wider group of NGOs.
13. Fujitani (1992) offers an excellent mapping of the *tennosei* discourse in Japan, as well as a critique, suggesting that rather than the transhistorical "empty center" notion formulated by Roland Barthes, post-1989 productions of the "symbolic emperor system" depends rather on its mediaization. Tokyo University's T. Tetsuya suggests that the deeper roots of the "*Yasukuni* controversy" are to be found in the profound reluctance to separate church and state within significant sections of the political elites as well as the powers-that-be at the *Yasukuni jinja* (shrine). To what degree this reluctance shadows the collective unconscious in contemporary Japan is open to debate. The point here is not to discount the significance of the changes in the tenor of political life in post-war Japan, but rather to inject a note of caution in attributing determinacy to claims about a neat rupture between imperial

subjecthood of pre-war Japan and a *sui generis* citizen-based subjectivity post 1946.

14. In the context of the *Yasukuni* shrine controversy, this claim merits serious attention.
15. This informal sector provided the bulk of the 17 billion yen in charitable donations in the aftermath of the Kobe earthquake, compared with the institutionalized non-profit sector that provided only 3 million yen in contrast.
16. Keishi Saeki, a staunch critic of the current civil society boom in Japan articulates the gap that structures celebrations of civil society on the one hand, and its potential to propel a real transformation in Japan on the other. He suggests that calls for civil society in Japan are superficial, lacking substance, and driven by a heightened sensitivity to political correctness in the absence of any real commitments to resolving social and economic problems. This sensitivity to international discourse echoes a long-standing theme in Japanese history, namely an acute vulnerability and attentiveness to its image in the world, especially in relation to the United States.
17. Pekkanen categorically rejects all claims about what he terms "civil society modernization theory," suggesting that the path dependencies associated with the dual structure of civil society he identifies forecloses any convergence between Japan and Western (especially North-American) civil society.
18. In Japan, an important distinction is made between NGOs, non-profit organizations with legal status, monitored by the government largely concerned with overseas development, human security, and human rights issues, and NPOs unincorporated not-for-profit-organizations made up of citizens groups, neighborhood associations, and so on concerned mostly with domestic issues. No such distinction is made in the West, where the language of NGOs includes all of these groups.
19. In the case of Japan, it is debatable whether the short-lived New Associationist Movement, formed by Karatani Kojin Nishibe Makoto, Kuchiki Sui, and Asada Akira in 2000, with its strategy of "counter-act" (*taiko*) (anti-state and anti-capital, although not workerist as in socialism) would meet the criteria to be included as a civil society social group in the Schwartz and Pharr volume.
20. See Hirata's (2005) review of the Schwartz and Pharr (2003) collection.
21. The term *bokuminkan* (shepherds of the people) is a term that pre-war bureaucrats invoked to describe their position vis-à-vis the people. Arguably, this inherently pastoral orientation, with its associated co-dependencies between shepherd and flock can be seen to be at work in post-war Japan as well.
22. This is not to be confused with Fred Hirsch's (1977) famous thesis on the *Social Limits to Growth* that addressed the question of positional goods, social scarcity, and its implications for economic growth. In deploying the term "social limits of the market," I mean to invoke the idea, rooted in a Hegelian understanding of political economy, that the market's capacity to facilitate and impinge on well-being requires limits placed on it in accordance with the criteria appropriate to the ideal of social individuation, not efficiency as in neo-classical economic theory, or equal distribution as in socialist critiques, but justice, seen here as social self-determination. See Levine (1995).

23. See for instance Anderson (1993), Emi (1983: 1–10), Fujita (1982), Garon (1987), Gould (1983:57–67), Hoshino (1988: 241–69), Lee (1982), and Campbell (1992).
24. Takayama (1982) and Yamada (1990: 327–63).
25. Most of the literature on Japan's post-war welfare state concurs with this description including the following: Andersen (1993), Shinkawa (1990), Fujita (1982), Shiratori (1985: 200–23), and Matsuura (1981: 3–17).
26. In addition to the literature already identified above, see also Campbell (1992), Esping-Andersen (1990), Lee (1987), Pinker (1986), Bennett and Levine (1976: 391–438), and Chubachi and Taira (1976: 439–92).
27. Roger Goodman and Ito Peng echo a similar sentiment: "These debates in North American and Western Europe about Japanese social welfare tell us more about those countries – and their own concerns – than they do about Japan.... In most cases, analyses have sought to fit Japan into one of a variety of pre-existing social welfare models conceptualized from a Western framework rather than examining it in its own terms." See their chapter in Esping-Andersen (1996a:192–224).
28. Consider, for instance, the debate about the difficulties attendant on creating a standardized system of welfare provision in the European Union (EU). The central claim that variations in the provision of a range of welfare goods within the different states that make up the EU defy standardization due to the "irreversibility" of welfare gains made by distinct groups of people fails to notice that the irreversibility claim resonates not so much because of institutional rigidity, but rather as the result of differential antecedent underlying normative understandings of what counts as an appropriate measure of individual welfare. At the heart of these normative judgments are the meanings attached to personhood and social worth that vary in different societies, rendering societal understandings of personhood central to considerations of welfare state failure, reform, or restructuring. I develop this argument further in the following chapter.
29. Hoshino (1988); Nakagawa (1979:5–51); Gould (1993); and Reed (1989). Nakagawa Yatsuhiro suggests the success of this mix has earned Japan the status of a welfare superpower, whereas Arthur Gould faults it for being "divisive and controlling." Steven Reed on the other hand suggests this mix should not be judged by European standards as it serves the distinctive welfare needs of Japan.
30. Distinguishing between a system that is "plan-rational" and one that is "market-rational," Johnson suggests that the latter "concerns itself with the forms and procedures... the rules... of economic competition, but it does not concern itself with substantive matters." The plan rational developmental state, on the other hand, sets substantive social and economic goals via industrial policy. Taking the opposite view, Shinkawa (1990) has argued that the development of social policy in the 1970s was the result of a "crisis of social integration" in the late 1960s that compelled the state to briefly shift its focus from the needs of capital accumulation to social integration.
31. A similar point can be made with regard to Garon (1997).
32. Halliday (1975); Dower (1975); Morris-Suzuki and Seiyama (1989); Moore (1983); and Itoh (1990).
33. Esping-Andersen (1997: 179–89).

34. There is by now a fairly robust and ongoing discussion of the reconstitution of area studies. On Japan and Asia specifically, see Johnson (1974; 2005); Gibson (1994); Fowler (1996); Gordon (2004); Reader (1995); Steinhoff (1993); Bowen (1989); Tansman (2003); Cumings (1997); and Miyoshi and Harootunian (1993).
35. Alan Tansman (2003) offers a comprehensive survey of this debate and a persuasive argument about prioritizing the archive over theory for the scholar of Japanese literature especially. What deserves greater attention, however, is how in many instances English-language scholarship by the Japanese-speaking scholar, as in other language-intensive areas (Arabic or Chinese for instance), depends on the translation of ideas, insights, debates, and arguments produced within the Japanese scholarly community, valorized now as the contributions of Western "area experts" to the field of Japan Studies. Unlike projects of direct translation (of books, articles, etc. produced in one language translated for consumption in another, heavily weighted, in this case to the translation of non-Japanese language books into *Nihongo*), this is a more perilous enterprise where mastery of language enables appropriation and authorization of ideas that would otherwise never enter the commoditized circuits of academic exchange. This is not simply a claim about originality or due acknowledgment of sources, but rather one that gestures toward the fundamentally colonial mode of knowledge transfer that is implicit in even the most *intentionally* benign acts of translation, given the larger objective structure of power and knowledge. See Conrad (1999) for an astute discussion of the ramifications of this larger problem in the construction of Japanese historiography.
36. As noted in the acknowledgements, a Long-Term Postdoctoral Fellowship from the Social Science Research Council and the Japan Study for the Promotion of Science enabled me to spend 2 years in Tokyo (November 2003–December 2005). During this time I had the opportunity to meet with a number of people working on social policy, immigration, and citizenship-related issues, including activists, welfare workers and recipients, bureaucrats, academics, officials in government at the national and ward-office levels, and especially, officials, social workers, and student activities in the *Kamagasaki yoseba* (day laborers) in the Airin district of Osaka.

2 Theoretical contestations: state, market, and the individual

1. Challenging the claim that appears now to have become orthodoxy in the policy-making circles of the OECD countries as well as international economic institutions like the IMF and World Bank that welfare states constitute a drag on the economy, and concomitantly that drastic cuts in public expenditure are positively correlated with economic growth, comparative data suggests otherwise. In fact the OECD has had to acknowledge in one of its reports that 'there is not an immediate link between unemployment rates and unemployment benefit entitlements' (cited in Navarro

1998: 639). Similarly, the neoliberal claim that countries with comprehensive programs of social protection are more likely to register decelerated economic growth rates is called into question by data that suggest that indeed the opposite is true: Germany, Denmark, Ireland, and Norway, all with extensive social protection programs registered a higher annual growth rate of total output per capita between 1979 and 1997 than those that instituted neoliberal economic policies, including reductions in public expenditures, especially the United States and Britain.

2. Christopher Nock (1988) points out that 'in order to meet Friedman's criteria of freedom, persons should be free to enter or not enter market transactions. To accomplish as much, individuals should have access to a means of livelihood that alone can make the decision to enter the market an authentically voluntary one. To the extent that the welfare state, in theory, can do this, welfare states can be seen as necessary rather than inimical to market-centered conception of freedom' (1988: 757–769).
3. Mitchell Dean points out that the OECD's study *The Future of Social Protection* (1988) notes a 'growing syndrome of deprivation' which leads to a 'ghetto existence' 'with no stake in official society and as heavily dependent on welfare and prone to illegalities as to exhibit a marked behavioral contrast with the mainstream' (Dean 1995: 579).
4 For a good overview of conservative arguments against the welfare state, see Furniss and Tilton (1977: 51–66).
5. See especially Sanford Schram (1995) for an exhaustive critique of the dependency argument along these lines. In detailing how poverty and what are deemed 'pathological behaviors' are more appropriately seen as the results of the structural problems of a capitalist economy, he rightly draws attention to the ideological undertow of neoliberal analyses of welfare.
6. The French Regulation School that developed in the 1970s attempted to use Marxian categories to show how specific constellations of institutional forms and social norms create 'regimes of accumulation' that enable structural reproduction and transformation. By taking Marxian theory, as David Kotz (1990) puts it, 'to a lower level of abstraction,' Regulation theorists hope to show how forms of capitalism, especially the institutional/accumulation nexus, change, even as the structure of capitalism remains the same. While seemingly departing from the economic determinism of orthodox Marxian theory, Regulation theorists betray a similar propensity to assume that the changes necessary to facilitate capital accumulation (as it enters a putatively new phase) will automatically ensue, thus ascribing an economistic inevitability to what are in fact social and, more importantly, political processes, contingent on the collective agencies exercised in favor of alternatives to existent institutional arrangements. For good critical discussions of the Regulation school, see Kotz (1990: 5–28) and Bonefeld (1993: 113–121). For representative works, see Lipietz (1988: 7–35; 1989); Aglietta (1979); and Jessop (1983: 89–112; 1995: 307–333).
7. For the difficulties of theorizing the individual within a Marxian theoretical framework, see Leonard (1983).
8. The worker has nothing to sell but his labor-power when he becomes free in the double sense: as a free man he can dispose of his labor-power as his

own commodity and he has no other commodity for sale; and he is short of everything necessary for the realization of his labor-power (*Capital*, Vol. I, 1867, 1967a: 169). Labor-power refers to the capacity to labor. Since, for Marx, capitalism is a system of production for exchange, it results in the commodification of all elements brought into exchange. Since the worker sells his capacity to labor in exchange for wages, his labor-power is itself a commodity (albeit a fictitious one as Polanyi points out) that its owner, the worker, is compelled to sell.

9. This distinction is drawn by Caporaso and Levine (1992: 61). This section draws on their chapter on Marxian Political Economy in the same book (1992: 55–78).
10. Marxists distinguish between a class-in-itself and a class-for-itself; the former exists *qua* class due to an objective reality, the latter subjectively in the minds of those who objectively belong to the class. In the first case, a worker belongs to the proletariat class even though she may not be conscious of it; in the second, the worker is now conscious of her class location and is therefore now a class agent. Given this distinction, a matter of great controversy for Marxist political theory has been to account for the transformation of a class in itself into a class for itself. In the welfare state literature, for instance, working-class consciousness is seen to have been the basis for a collective demand for state-sponsored welfare, and the subsequent emergence of the welfare state in several countries. As discussed below, the social democratic version of class politics has been particularly influential in studies of the emergence of welfare states.
11. My purpose here is not to assess the role of subsistence in economic theory *per se*, but to examine how the idea of subsistence lends itself to a particular notion of the individual and welfare, and the implications of this for the relation between state and individual posited by Marxian theories of welfare state capitalism.
12. Sherover (1979), comparing Hegel's and Marx's notion of the poor, points out that, for Marx, the poor carry an ontological and moral significance that both grounds Marx's view of the proletariat as the subject of history, as well as introduces a tension in it. This is worth a brief comment, however, since it helps shed light on Marx's problematic use of the idea of subsistence. As Sherover describes it, Marx takes the view that the poor are the "elemental class of human society" in that, like for Hegel, they do not belong to civil society. For Hegel, this exclusion is not simply material but constitutes a denial of the poor's participation in the modern human community and therefore denies them "civil honor," or the social relations of mutual recognition necessary to be counted as somebody. For Marx, on the other hand, the poor, precisely because they remain outside the sphere of civil society, remain untouched by the false conceptions and artificial values, fetishism, and the corruption of private property. By virtue of being untouched by civil society, the poor display a moral insight that is inherently superior to that of members within civil society; their very existence amounts to an immanent critique of civil society. Marx's notion of the poor as a naturalized site of revolutionary consciousness can illumine, in part, his central focus on the idea of subsistence. Not only does the idea of subsistence ground his theory of exploitation (via the production of surplus value), but it helps

make better sense of how, for Marx, the proletariat constitutes the revolutionary subject. To the extent the poor "seem to have the correct (morally right) [i.e. revolutionary] perceptions and values *a priori* simply by virtue of their poverty," workers, in so far as they subsist on the bare necessities of life, come closest to approximating Marx's ontological view of the poor. In other words, Marx is able to transpose his ontological-moral and eventually political view of the poor (non-members in civil society) to the proletariat (members of civil society) in part as the result of attributing to the latter the fixity of subsistence need based. This is by no means to suggest that Marx romanticized the actual living conditions of the proletariat, but rather to point to the continuities between the poor and the proletariat via the idea of subsistence need in Marx's ontology. To the extent that Marx's notion of the poor provides the antecedents of his conception of the proletariat, it reveals a tension. In the former instance, the proletariat is by virtue of their very nature and existence the revolutionary subject; in the latter, they acquire revolutionary consciousness only via a long process of education and praxis.

13. Some recent attempts at developing a Marxian theory of the state actually argue for such a position, even though, for Marx, capitalists are characterized by the pursuit of their private-interest and remain by and large unaware of their structural or objective identity as a class *qua* class. Miliband's notion of the state as an instrument of the ruling class, or Poulantzas's idea that the state rules on behalf of the ruling class, though not at its behest, attributes agency to capitalist *qua* class that Marx himself did not claim. The only collective interest among capitalists that Marx visualizes was a shared systemic interest in maintaining a capitalist social order. Jeopardizing a capitalist social order (right to private property and its alienation, for instance) would threaten the very existence of the capitalist.
14. See Levine (1995) for a compelling argument that because they consume, rather than use objects, it is the capitalist rather who fails to individuate.
15. For discussions of problems of state interventionism in the economy broadly sympathetic to a Marxian vantage point, see the following: Barrow (1993); Berger (1990: 103–122); Blanke *et al.* (1976: 68–126); Gough (1975: 53–91); Holloway and Picciotto (1978); Lindberg *et al.* (eds) (1975); O'Connor (1973); and Urry (1981).
16. Offe (1984: 257). Despite Marxian claims about the stabilizing activities of the state in deferring the crisis tendencies of the capitalist economy, it is clear that Marxists remain skeptical about the long-run impact of social policy. As one critic writes, 'the practice of social policy and administration can only be seen in the logic of Marxian social theory as a snare and delusion or as a heresy,' cited in Carrier and Kendall (1986: 327). Offe takes issue with the standard Marxian view in that he makes the case that the structural contradiction of the capitalist state's welfare role is *political*, not economic, at root. Thus, he takes political intervention, ostensibly the temporary solution to economic crisis on most Marxian accounts, to be the principal source of crisis in late capitalist democracies.
17. In other words, the commodification of labor (i.e. the laboring capacity of healthy and appropriately skilled workers exchanged for wages) provides the central dynamic of capitalist accumulation. Only the exchange of labor

power for wages can simultaneously sustain the worker and the process of capital accumulation. Offe thus makes exchange-relations, specifically the 'commodification' of labor, pivotal to the idea of a 'market' (or capitalist economy).

18. Marx (1976: 1005).
19. Offe writes, "State policies which attempt to reproduce the commodity form (i.e. the profitable exchange of labor and capital) through decommodified means have the unintended effect of undermining both the institutionalized power and legitimacy of commodified processes" (Offe 1984: 25).
20. Offe's claim about de-commodification applies principally to labor. That is, the state's efforts to bring the 'paralysed commodity-form of labor' back into the realm of exchange as a commodity inadvertently create conditions that no longer compel the worker to commodify her capacity to labor.
21. It should be noted that while others have employed the language of "de-commodification" to analyze the consequences of welfare statism, Offe's conceptualization differs from most in its emphasis on the erosion of the normativity of exchange as the analytical cornerstone of "de-commodification." For other, more descriptive, uses of the term, see Esping-Andersen (1990), Kolberg (1992: 77–111), and Western (1989: 200–221).
22. Offe (1983) clarifies this: 'Collectively binding decisions cannot be reached if a logically prior decision has not already been made. This prior decision concerns the procedures according to which the decisions shall be made.... The fundamental procedural rules of collective decision making acquire a curious double status: On the one hand, they must be presupposed as unquestionably valid whenever decisions have to be made; on the other hand, their validity can be presupposed only if their validity claims can withstand questioning' (Offe 1983: 709–11).
23. Offe (1984: 19).
24. The environmental movement in particular has drawn some criticism for overreaching its claim to being a critical paradigm. By laying emphasis on behavioral change (patterns of consumption, etc.) environmentalists not only ignore the structural basis of inequality both within and between countries, but also do not give primacy to the eradication of extremes of wealth and poverty. A predominantly single-issue movement, environmentalism must be seen, these critics argue, as yet another expression of an essentially liberal (not radical) politics.
25. On the dual nature of capitalist exchange relations, see Hirschman (1982: 1463–1484) and Hirsch (1977).
26. This is by no means to point to a celebration or vindication of existent vast inequities of wealth that typically characterize capitalist societies but simply to draw attention to the dual nature of capitalist social relations.
27. On a related note, Offe's inclination to see the relationship between the economic and the non-economic aspects of capitalist social relations in mutually exclusive terms stems, in part, from his use of systems analysis. Thus, the dominance of the exchange principle in late capitalism is eroded to the extent that the non-economic sub-systems no longer remain "subordinate" to it (as, he argues, was the case in the period of liberal capitalism).

28. This is, of course, the general theme of Habermas modernist rejoinder to those who reject as false the Enlightenment's privileging of the "Promethean self." See Benhabib 1992.
29. Recall Adam Smith's statement that 'the only sensible question worth pursuing is the division of labor between state and market' (cited in Katznelson [1988: 521]).
30. O'Malley and Palmer (1996: 139).
31. This phrase is taken from the title of Nikolas Rose's article (1996: 327–356). For related arguments, see Dean (1995: 559–583) and Hunter (1993: 123–136).
32. See Schram (1995); Fraser and Gordon (1994: 309–336); Reed (1992: 21–38); and Fox Piven and Cloward (1983).
33. Benhabib's (1992) sustained critique of the Foucauldian position is that it develops an "overly constructed view of the self." See also Newton (1998: 415–447).
34. For critical discussions of postmodernism's notion of the death of the subject and its consequences for social theory, see in particular Callinicos (1989); Glass (1994); Gitlin and Norris (1990); and Roseneau (1992).
35. Agency refers to the source of action: to speak of the subject as an agent is to see the individual as having intrinsic purpose. Insofar as humans are self-interpreting beings, capable of reflecting on their desires and transforming their desires and action on the basis of this evaluation, the notion of agency refers essentially to reflexivity. See Taylor (1985).
36. Patterson (1989) offers a similar view: 'If there is no foundation or "one true account" of a social practice against which to measure the worth of competing claims for the logic of the enterprise, then everything is up for grabs, and practical reasoning – that is, arguments about what we as a society or group should be doing–cannot and will not be resolved. In short, the debate will be interminable' (Patterson 1989: 1667).
37. In my attempt to understand the structure of Hegel's thought, I have found the following particularly helpful: Beiser (1993); Brod (1992); Kincaid (1991: 28–47); Kolb (1986); Lamb (1987); MacGregor (1992); Plant (1983); Rose (1981); Smith (1987: 99–126); Stillman (1987); Taylor (1975) (1979) and (1985); Stace (1955); and Westphal (1992).
38. I have relied here on the work of social theorists who have taken as their particular focus this specific claim: Levine (1988) and (1995); Pelczynski (1984); and Winfield (1988) (1990) and (1991).
39. Monological conceptions of the individual, on the other hand, cannot provide an account of differentiation. Richard Winfield puts it well:

    > Monologically defined, the will is something all selves possess as such, which means that it cannot serve to differentiate their agencies or actions from one another. So conceived, the free will is automatically reduced to a solely universal faculty containing no element of particularity that could individuate one will from another through its own freedom.
    >
    > (Winfield 1988: 162)

    The monological self, on the other hand, as a desiring subject confronts a world of objects it has had no role in shaping. Because its will lacks content and is only abstract, content can only be given to it from the external world. In confronting the world of objects (the world of culture or meaning), the desiring empty self can only take in the meanings that exist independent of him. Like the natural self, the monological self cannot act, but remains acted upon.

40. The post-structural view also subscribes to a deterministc view of persons. On this view, subjects are variously seen as contingent effects, a position in language, or simply constructs of particular spatial-temporal political and historical contexts. For a critique of conceptions of the subject as a 'preconstituted center of the experience of culture and history,' see in particular Callinicos (1989); Glass (1994); Gitlin and Norris (1990); and Roseneau (1992).
41. Brod puts it thus, 'consciousness of oneself as an individual can never be an initial given but can only emerge as a result of a process of differentiation from the starting point of one's own environment' (Brod 1992: 64).
42. Hegel's For an extended discussion of this, see David P. Levine (1997) *Self-Seeking and the Pursuit of Justice* Brookfield VT: Ashgate (Avebury Series).
43. Maletz refers to this as the source of the inherent directedness that characterizes persons (1989: 33–50).
44. This does not mean, literally, that actually existent markets fulfill the demands of the ideal of freedom *in principle* possible only through the system of exchange relations. Hegel's work relates to the logic of the market principle and this is what concerns us here. That existent markets institute the principle of exchange such that it is debilitating of the freedom and welfare of many leading to vast inequalities of poverty and wealth is a question about the history of different embodiments of the market principle, not its immanent logic.
45. For the classic statement on this, see the section on master–slave relation in Hegel's *Phenomenology of Mind* #178–196. For helpful discussions of this idea, see Kojeve (1969); Taylor (1975); and Kelly (1972).
46. Hegel's distinctive conception of labor was one that Marx was to later take and re-work into a theory of the exploitation of labor, but which would also provide the basis for an alternative socialist conception of the freedom of all men. It should also be noted that, for Hegel, labor was crucial to reconciling what was merely particular with the universal. Insofar as individual labor takes shape only within the context of a social division of labor, the activity of laboring manifests in concrete form the interconnectedness of the social world from which it springs. The significance for Hegel, of course, is that this overcomes the otherness of the objective world, thereby actualizing freedom. Labor is a central category of the system of needs, but it is far more than that for Hegel. It is central for self-consciousness and for knowledge of objects in the natural world. "It was labor, with its twin dimensions of developing the subject's consciousness and manipulating external objects, that helped to solve this problem for Hegel. It was in labor that the reconciliation between subject and object was overcome for him" (Plant 1977: 104). Thus, for Hegel, Labor is a personally liberating facet of human activity.
47. Quoted in Scholz (1993: 359).
48. Hegel writes, 'The shape does not become something other than himself through being made external to him for it is precisely this shape that is

his pure being-for-self, which in this externality is seen by him to be the truth. Through this rediscovery of himself by himself the bondsman realizes that it is precisely in his work wherein he seemed to have only an alienated existence that he acquires a mind of his own' in *Phenomenology of Spirit*, #196.

49. A feminist reading of Hegel has tended to discount Hegel's treatment of civil society as the realm of self-formation and self-seeking due to his distinction between the public and the private realms, and his relegation of the woman's ethical role to the family. The thrust of the critique is that in ascribing a familial role to women, Hegel conceives women as being subject to natural forces, capable only of passive (because it is not self-created) reproduction. See Butler (1987); Easton (1987); Scholz (1993); and Pateman (1988). For a sympathetic reading of Hegel from a feminist standpoint, see Brod (1992). Brod correctly notes, '...bringing feminist theory to bear on Hegel means more than simply looking at Hegel's writings on women' (Brod 1992: 177). A feminist reading of Hegel, by focusing narrowly on his explicit statements on women, is much too hasty in dismissing his theory as being altogether incompatible with a feminist agenda and social theory. Hegel's work, insofar as it provides a compelling argument for a conception of justice in which social self-determination and mutual regard are the very foundation of a social order, may be singularly conducive to a feminist standpoint committed to the idea of the self-determination of women.
50. In this context, Raymond Plant writes, 'The conception of human nature which Hegel brings to bear on the sphere of need is not one in which man is prey to need, or subject to need; rather, man is if anything the sovereign of need, developing needs as a result of the growth of his own self-consciousness' (Plant 1977: 92).
51. Baker (1992: 61).
52. To suggest that commodification, participation in civil society, the use of property, and capacity to engage in "exchange" in the market are necessary to individual welfare, the process of self-formation, self-seeking, and self-expression is not to claim, as critics of Hegel do, that individual creativity, expression, or worth are exhaustively realized in the market. It is simply to argue that the economy is, as Hegel put it, a necessary "moment" of human creativity, expression, and freedom. As Hegel's writings clearly articulate, human expression in the family, art, religion, and so on is vital to the full realization of man's creative knowledge and experience of the world.
53. Linking property rights to the use of objects in accord with the realization of individuality renders the capitalist production process (production for exchange) as opposed to a system of production for use, especially appropriate to the realization of individuality. In artisanal production the producer leaves her mark on the object produced (a painting, for instance) thus limiting the use of the object in a way that makes manifest *only* the personality of the consumer. In a capitalist economy, however, "machine-based mass production occurs independent of the will or personality of any particular individual" since only those objects that fulfill a social need are produced. As Baker puts it, 'An object produced in a capitalist production process is freed to meet a set of social needs that is totally unrelated to the

particular personalities of the individuals involved in its production' (Baker 1992: 76).

54. Although taking the argument in a direction markedly different than the one developed here, Baudrillard makes a similar point, that is that consumption is not simply an economic or material act but also symbolic. It is symbolic since by consuming or using an object the consumer identifies with a set of meanings or values that are associated with the object. Bocock (1993), discussing Braudillard's view, observes, 'Consumption is to be conceptualized as a process in which a purchaser of an item is actively engaged in trying to create and maintain a sense of identity through the display of purchased goods' (Bocock 1993: 67).

Of course the difference between the personality theory of property developed here and Baudrillard's is that whereas the latter sees identity as the creation of objects of consumption, Levine, elaborating Hegel, sees consumption as an expression of identity. The difference is a subtle though crucial one and merits attention, especially in light of recent attempts to employ Hegelian theory in service of an argument that is the antithesis of Hegel's core claim about the link between individuality and consumption. For Baudrillard (and others who argue in the same vein), people consume commodities not in order to realize or express who they are, but in effect to become that which is symbolized by the object itself. Quoting Bocock's commentary on Baudrillard again, 'Baudrillard suggests that consumers do not purchase items of clothing, food, body decoration, furniture or a style of entertainment, for instance, in order to express an already existing sense of who they are. Rather, people create a sense of who they are through what they consume' (Bocock 1993: 68). The thrust of Baudrillard's argument, like much of postmodernism, is that the individual's sense of self is wholly contextual; the subject does not exist as an integrated idea of self that is then externalized, but is, in effect, a composite, reductively determined by different contexts. This emphasis on an external determination of the self of an individual not only denies the very idea of a subject *qua* agent, but also conceives the individual as necessarily enslaved by the process of consumption. The consumer, on this view, does not use or consume the object, but insofar as she is determined by the object, is consumed or made use of by the object instead. Baudrillard writes, "This suggests that there are no limits to consumption. If it was that which it is naively taken to be, an absorption, a devouring, then we should achieve satisfaction. If consumption appears to be irrepressible, this is because it is a total idealist practice, which has no longer anything to do (beyond a certain point) with the satisfaction of needs nor with the reality principle. (Baudrillard 1975: 24–25). While providing a valid critique of biologically or naturally determined needs, Baudrillard's attempt to link the individual to the signification of objects of consumption goes too far. If individuals are simply produced by the meanings associated with objects of consumption, the essence of what it means to be an individual (a self-determined, self-conscious being) is lost.

Hegel's original argument, elaborated by Levine in his theory of consumption, both anchors the idea of individuality within the self (in a notion of agency implying an independent, self-sustaining autonomous will) and embeds the idea within a social context. Unlike utilitarian theories of consumption that require an atomistic, pre-social notion of the individual, Hegel and Levine's argument that the individual externalizes the self via consumption preserves the idea of individuality while at the same time grounding it in an inter-subjective world of meanings denoted by the idea of social determination. Hegel and Levine's consumer is not necessarily one enslaved by objects of consumption, as the consumer on Baudrillard's definition must be. Unlike Baudrillard's consumer for whom there cannot be any limits to consumption (since the individual is simply the set of meanings signified by the objects he/she consumes), Hegel and Levine's consumer's pattern of consumption is necessarily self-limiting. Only insofar as objects externalize a particular (self-limited or bounded) mode of life can a claim to objects of consumption be legitimated. Whereas, for Baudrillard, consumption must incessantly change, given the speed and rapidity of the proliferation of new products dictated by technological innovations, gripping the consumer in an unending immediacy of consumption, Hegel and Levine's consumer, insofar as she externalizing a self, mediates and (changes) her selection of objects in accord with the self-conscious development of personality.

55. David Levine (1995) 'On Justice and the Economy: the Limits of Distributive Justice,' Unpublished paper, 1995.
56. The collapse of communism in the Soviet Union and the rise of market socialism in China speaks to this point. Among the many contributing factors, the denial of the expressive and constitutive role of the market vis-à-vis the individual contributed to the loosening of state control over society. That in both cases today, civil society appears denuded of a secure juridical/legal base, a terrain of rampant consumerism and lawlessness, resilient to he social seen either as civility, law, or mutual recognition, points to the force of this need as much as to its unmediated, and hence untempered expression in erstwhile state-led communist societies.
57. Even within neo-classical economics, traditionally hostile to anything other than a pure-market understanding of capitalism, the idea of basic needs has gained prominence through the work of noted economist Amartaya Sen (1985).
58. Communitarian theorists (including among others, Alasdair McIntyre, Michael Walzer, and Michael Sandel) lament the decline of moral and political communities in advanced capitalist democracies and urge instead the creation of institutions that would recognize the primacy of the social community, rather than the autonomous individual of political liberalism. While an extended discussion of communitarian thought is beyond the scope of the present endeavor, suffice it to say here that by failing to interrogate the nature of communities, whereby the organizing principle of different communities may be held up to scrutiny, communitarians tend to assume *a priori* the virtue of community *per se*, without questioning the demands different communities make upon individuals, or whether, more crucially, they impinge upon or enable individuality. While the challenge of "building community" may indeed offer a way out of the moral dilemma faced by contemporary advanced industrialized societies (how can alienated, atomized, un-connected, "morally impoverished" individuals solve social

problems), communities that require the subsumption of individual self-determination to group agency end up repudiating rather than enabling social individuality. Without careful attention to the nature of communities, the danger of simply replacing the disembedded atomized individual with communities that subordinate the individual would simply substitute one set of problems with another.

3 Self, state, and civil society in modern Japan

1. Fujitani (1998: 307).
2. Benedict (1964).
3. Nakane (1970).
4. On a different note, by comparing the Japanese and Western self in dichotomous terms, this approach lends itself easily to the charge of orientalism (constructing and valorizing a view of self by making the other the repository of disavowed parts of the self). The dualisms of individual/society, modern/tradition, reason/intuition, and so on thus serve to construct Japan as the "other" group-self so as to posit a view of the Western self as self-determined.
5. MacIntyre (1990: 490).
6. Doi (1981). For recent applications of his theory about the relation between individual and society based on differences in ways of relating, see Bachnik and Quinn (1994).
7. Lebra (1976).
8. Richard Winfield (1991) has also shown how the notion of inter-subjectivity, in fact, presupposes subjectivity: without an account of the latter, inter-subjectivity is rendered purely abstract, ill suited to ground substantive accounts of identity formation.
9. Bourdieu (1973).
10. Najita (1993: 13–30).
11. Eisenstadt (1996: 192).
12. Eisenstadt (1996: 25).
13. Garon (1987: 10).
14. Rozman (1973) cited in Ramseyer.
15. Miyoshi (1991: 150).
16. The controversy over the nature of pre-war capitalism in Japan, whether it retained feudal remnants (Kozha school of thought) or not (the Rohnoh school) continues to inform neo-Marxian debates about the nature of contemporary capitalism. For a detailed description of this debate, see Germaine Hoston (1985). For a good overview of the debate, see Shibagaki (1988: 29–56). See also Albritton (1980) and Itoh (1988; 1990). Baba (1985: 26–53).
17. Kaichiro Oishi (1971).
18. This is Kazuo Shibagaki's term (1973: 70–87).
19. Shozaburo Fujino (1966: 59).
20. Kuniko Fujita (1982: 59).
21. Sheldon Garon (1987:10).
22. As the result of its victory in its wars with China in 1894–1895 and with Russia in 1904–1905, Japan gained territorial concessions in both China and

Korea, which were to prove to be an important source of labor, raw material, and markets in the pre-war years.

23. Ikegami (1995: 185–221).
24. Eisenstadt (1996: 30).
25. Eisenstadt (1996: 37).
26. Miyoshi (1991: 151).
27. In what may constitute one of the most subtle portrayals of the individuating moment unleashed by the spread of exchange relations, Kawabata's *Master of Go* captures the transmutation of a quintessentially traditional Japanese game into a modern one, one bearing, nonetheless, the specific face of Japanese modernity. Kawabata tells the story of how in a game widely watched and reported in the newspapers in 1938, the master was caught off-guard by a challenger who changed the game. Rather than playing the game in the traditional Japanese way, in which the symmetrical co-construction of the pieces on the board brought the two players into a cooperative venture, the young challenger plays a game in which winning is all. In an attempt to demonstrate and be recognized for his individual prowess, the young challenger disregards the age of his opponent and substitutes competitiveness for deference. For Kawabata this was a metaphor for the transformation of Japan, one in which modernity did not assault directly the structures of tradition but, by resisting the re-contextualizing strategies of an existent cultural rationality, subsumed all other forms into the rationality of exchange.
28. Silverberg (1993: 116).
29. For a more abstract rendering of the nature of modern Japan's collective consciousness, see Samuel N. Eisenstadt. For a more detailed exposition of this argument, see Eisenstadt (1996). He notes that Japan's collective consciousness has been constructed on the basis of a 'scared particularity,' not on the basis of a transcendental universalistic mission (1996: 29).
30. For an exhaustive description of the system of permanent employment, see especially Clark (1979); Dore (1973); and, more recently, Harcourt (1996: 177–202).
31. The modern family-corporation traces its lineage to the *dozoku*, commercial household confederations.
32. Tanaka (1982: 24).
33. Morishima (1995: 611).
34. Weiss (1993: 325–354).
35. Andrew Gordon (1997: 245–283).
36. Although Kondo's argument about the relational self in Japan serves to substantiate a claim about the de-centered nature of subjectivity, consistent with post-modern understandings, I draw upon her work simply to substantiate an empirical claim about the social meanings attached to work, to elaborate an alternate (modernist) account of personhood.
37. Silverberg (1993: 121).
38. Silverberg (1993:121).
39. See especially Ivy (1993: 239–258).
40. See William Kelly (1991); Rosenberger (1994); and Tobin (1992). See also Anderson and Wadkins (1991: 129–134). Anderson and Wadkins find a parallel between the *shinjinrui* and the culture of consumption that emerged in the United States at the turn of the century in which selfhood becomes

tied to consumption rather than production. This heightened emphasis on consumption, however, is to be understood in the context of the multiplication of need that advanced capitalism makes possible (the seemingly limitless choices produced as a result of technological innovation and increased productivity generates what appears as limitless demand or consumerism). It does not, however, indicate a reverse process – the diminishing role of production in constituting selfhood. In this vein, Francis Fukuyama's claim that in the late twentieth century work no longer affords the means for recognition due to the incessant demands to constantly reinvent oneself professionally, given the economic velocity of these times, also mistakes changes in the conditions of capitalism as a subversion of its logic.

41. The linkage between the multiplication of wants, constitution and expression of the self, and wealth is certainly a valid one, central in fact to the theory of social self-determination that grounds this study. Where the consumerism/individuation thesis falters, however, is in working through the conceptual inter-connections between these three elements. The multiplication of wants necessitates a dynamic notion of individuation which makes the idea of subsistence highly problematic to notions of individuality. However, affluence *per se* also repudiates the idea of individuation depending on the *nature* of consumption. I can use an object (to enable expression of a part of myself) or I can be used by the object (who I am is simply determined by the social status accorded to that object). By failing to probe the notion of individuation implicit in the alleged connection between consumerism and individuality, scholars tend to take what is very often tantamount to a disavowal of self through the consumption of commodities for its very expression. What is missing in the postulated nexus between consumerism and individuation is a conceptualization of individuality.
42. Of course, Marx had made a similar claim but in the context of the specific notion of alienated labor.

4 Social need and the welfare state in modern Japan

1. Makoto (1999) makes a similar observation: '... [O]fficialdom monopolizes the public realm while the people, the masses, are permitted the pursuit of private gain, personal welfare, and individual happiness insofar as these things lie within the legal and political frameworks dictated by the government. This tradition has largely demarcated the realms of public and private in Japanese society' (Makoto 1999: 51).
2. Brian McVeigh (1998) offers a provocative account of how the modern Japanese state subjects focuses on the creation of the 'bureaucratized self,' but takes as its empirical focus the education system's role in shaping subjectivities.
3. Hiwatari Nobuhiro (1993), a noted political scientist at the University of Tokyo notes, "Drastic reforms in health care and public pensions, the two major public welfare programs in Japan took place in the mid 1980s. Such measures did not ignite strong protests nor did it polarize the political spectrum... instead of being penalized, the ruling party responsible for the reforms was awarded, while the major opposition party, the Socialists, could

not attract those discontent with the reforms to turn around their declining electoral fortune." See his paper, "Sustaining the Welfare State and International Competitiveness in Japan: The Welfare Reforms of the 1980s and the Political Economy," presented at the Annual Meeting of the American Political Science Association, Washington, D.C., September 2–5, 1993. Similar observations (about the absence of advocacy or resistance to welfare among the population at large) have been noted by Goodman and Peng (1996).

4. Japanese Joint Organizing Committee, *Social Services in Japan* (1958: 26–27). See also Linhart (1983: 703–715).
5. See the detailed description provided by "The Development of Social Welfare Services in Japan," *Social Services in Japan* (1958), Akimoto (1989), and Anderson (1993).
6. For good overviews of the historical origins of Japan's welfare system, see Kyung (1982).
7. Eisenstadt (1996).
8. Cited in Eisenstadt (1996).
9. Takahashi (1997).
10. Takahashi (1997: 35).
11. Takahashi (1997: 36).
12. Garon (1997: 11).
13. Takahashi (1997: 36).
14. Komatsu (1992: 128–147).
15. Takahashi (1997: 37).
16. Takahashi (1997: 40).
17. Ishida (1989: 270–271).
18. Gluck (1985).
19. For a persuasive argument that links the state's active attempt to foster industrialization to the needs of the military, see Weiss (1993: 325–354).
20. Johansson and Mosk (1986: 415–440).
21. Takahashi (1997: 43).
22. Yoshida (1994).
23. The classic formulation on the role of ideology in crafting social order is, of course, Antonio Gramsci's. In his account, though, the source of hegemony in civil society (social consent with regard to a specific belief structure) is class-based. Thus, a specific class in society garners consent for its class-derived interests by penetrating the myriad avenues of civil society. The components of the ideology, in other words, have social, not individual, roots. Similarly, fascism and Nazism as ideologies were deeply social, with firm roots in the material and ideational reality of mid-twentieth-century Italy and Germany, not merely the artifacts of states or individual leaders.
24. Mary Douglas (1987) suggests that institutions gain legitimacy by 'the naturalization of social classification' and further 'There needs to be an analogy by which the formal structure of a crucial set of social relations is found in the physical world or in the supernatural world. So long as it is not seen as a socially contrived arrangement. Being naturalized (institutions) are part of the order of the universe and so ready to stand as the ground of argument' (1987: 35).
25. This is the thrust of Samuel Eisenstadt's argument in his monumental *Japanese Civilization* (1996:25).

26. This term is borrowed from Ozawa (1991).
27. By this I do not mean to suggest that, analytically, family and civil society are identical. Where the one treats individuals as members of a group, the other enables the constitution and actualization of a self-determined mode of being. However, to the extent that the self-chosen wants that enable individuals to create a self-chosen mode of life via the objects they use are central to constructing the home as a private realm of expression, consumption within the home must be seen as central to individuation. This is especially so in the case of Japan since it is primarily consumption rather than production-related activities that individuate.
28. For a comprehensive review of changes that were initiated see the report, *Japanese Social Insurance Systems Through 30 June 1950*, Rohrlich and Metterst (1951).
29. Takahashi (1997: 55–69).
30. Quoted in Takahashi (1997: 63–64).
31. Shindo (1994: 55–62). Tokyo: University of Tokyo Press, 1994.
32. Takahashi (1997: 60).
33. Quoted in Takahashi (1997: 64).
34. Ozawa (1991: 4). Statistics on welfare expenditure in the United States typically include expenditures on education, thereby suggesting a wider disparity in welfare expenditures between the two countries. Once the US figures are corrected to exclude spending on education, the two countries show a much greater similarity in quantitative terms; the real difference, then, in the welfare programs of the United States and Japan has to do with the nature of goods provisioned with the former providing a much larger number of what are referred to as individuated goods, whereas the latter directs the larger percentage of its resources to the provision of goods that meet social need.
35. The sweeping transformation of Japan into *fukushi kokka* (welfare state) with the reforms of 1961 has been variously interpreted as the result of the ruling Liberal Democratic Party's approach of "crisis and compensation," a response to a crisis in accumulation, or as the result of the prescience of leading LDP politicians, especially Prime Minister Ikeda. Debates among Japanese scholars of welfare reveal differing interpretations of the notion of welfare that was brought into play with the health and pension reforms of 1961. Ichibangase Yasuko, interpreting Article 25 as guaranteeing the right to life (*seikatsu kenri*) along Western lines, is critical of the 1961 reforms as being insufficient to the realization of self-fulfillment on the part of all citizens. Takashima Susumu taking a class struggle approach to the development of social policy sees the 1961 reforms as an attempt by the capitalist class to ensure the reproduction of labor.
36. *Nihonjinron,* literally, "discussions of the Japanese," is a form of discourse about Japan that attempts to 'define the specificity of Japanese identity' by emphasizing its uniqueness, in cultural and racial terms. As a self-conscious practice of 'cultural nationalism,' *Nihionjinron* emphasizes, even creates, the myth of an unbroken cultural continuity between Japan's past and present; among the categories through which an ever present past is evoked, *ie* or the Japanese family figures prominently. See Dale (1986).

37. In contrast to the taxable average income of American chief executives (estimated at $645,000 in 1986), top businessmen in Japan earned an average of $186,000 in 1985. Moreover, the upper level income tax in Japan is much heavier than the upper level US tax rate, reaching 50 percent for taxable income greater than $148,148 in Japan, whereas in the United States. the top marginal rate is approximately 31 percent. *Japan Economic Institute*: 5–6. Among OECD countries, Japan has consistently recorded the lowest Gini coefficient score (the standard measure for distribution of income), indicating that the distribution of income is most equitable in Japan. In an interesting extension of Chalmers Johnson's notion of the "developmental state," Bai Gao has recently argued that the state was able to solicit support for its developmental agenda within civil society by providing not only an increase in standards of living but rather by ensuring that this was equitable; that is, equity in Japan is a necessary correlate of the "developmental state."
38. Murakami, a theoretical economist, first advanced the homogeneity thesis using data from a social attitude survey conducted by the Prime Minister's office in which over 90 percent of Japanese responded that their standard of living was in the middle income level. The homogeneity thesis is quite widely accepted in studies on Japan despite criticism, mostly by Marxian scholars like Kishimoto who argued that "increased consumption and homogeneity of life style are surface phenomena and the basic principle of the society as a whole is the 'bipolarity' between capitalists and workers." For a good review of this debate, see Ishida (1989: 66).
39. For good overviews of Japan's Health Care System see the following: Steslicke (1989); Campbell (1992); Kobayashi (1994: 197–208); Ikegami and Campbell (1995: 1295–1299); Iglehart (1988: 807–812); Campbell and Ikegami (1998); Levin and Wolfson (1989: 311–323); Norbeck and Lock (1987); Powell and Masahira Anesaki (1990); and Sonoda (1988).
40. Ikegami (1992: 614).
41. *Japan Economic Institute Report,* #12A, March 27 (1987: 5).
42. Tierney and Tierney (1994: 210).
43. Ikegami (1992: 614–618).
44. Ikegami (1992: 615).
45. Ikegami (1992: 615).
46. *Japan Economic Report,* #12A, March 27, 1987: 3. See also Gould (1983: 57–67).
47. *Japan Economic Report*, #12A, March 27, 1987: 2.
48. Ozawa (1985: 476–495); Takayama (1982: 71–91).
49. For discussions of the pensions system, see in particular Noguchi (1983: 43–68); Fujita (1986: 15–27); Hiwatari (1996); and *Outline of Social Insurance in Japan, 1990.*
50. This may be seen as a central reason why a feminization of poverty has not occurred in Japan, in contrast to other cases of welfare state capitalism. For a general comparative assessment on this theme, see Axinn (1990).
51. Mikanagi (1997:15).
52. Takahashi (1997: 127).
53. I have relied on Takahashi's rendering of Miura's thought. See Takahashi (1997: 131–136).
54. Goodman and Peng (1996: 218).

55. Takahashi (1997: 142–154).
56. For an assessment of the family-as-provider argument, see Ogawa and Retherford (1997: 59–94).
57. For analysis of the problems of elderly care in contemporary Japan, see especially Hoshino (1996: 37–55) and Campbell (1998).
58. For overviews of Japan's policies on elderly care, see the following: Palley and Usui (1995: 241–257); Miyajima (1994: 3–23); Emlet (1998: 97–113); Lawrence (1985: 677–697); and Okamoto (1992: 305–403).
59. Emlet (1998: 98).
60. Clark and Ogawa (1996: 449). See also Bass (1996: 57–58).
61. Centers provide work for members by contracting with businesses or individuals in the community (for service such as baby-sitting, cleaning, weeding, tourist assistance, housework, etc.) or with the city for public service work (such as maintaining parks, cleaning public offices, doing calligraphy for award certificates, and generate their own income-producing activities by making souvenirs, etc.). Members are paid dividends (*haibunkin*) according to the hours they have worked. See Roberts (1996: 115–132).
62. For a good discussion of Baba's ideas, see Takahashi (1997: 157–158).
63. See Maruo (1974).
64. Findings from research supported by the Commonwealth Fund reveal that in five countries, namely the United States, Canada, Britain, West Germany, and Japan, older people are more interested in work than their counterparts in the three other nations. Reported in Scott Bass (1996: 65).
65. The close connection between work, self-mastery, and its role in constituting the self in relation to society, by creating a sense of belonging to the workplace an individual shares with coworkers is vividly highlighted in films such as *Takarazuka*, in which one of the main tasks of new entrants is to meticulously clean every nook and corner of the dance hall. See also Ian Buruma's insightful essay (1995: 246–257).
66. Milly (1999).
67. Seeleib-Kaiser (1995: 276). For a general overview of the development of unemployment assistance, see Woodsworth (1977).
68. *New Statesman and Society*, January 21, 1994:10.
69. See also, Seeleib-Kaiser (1995: 269–293).
70. Japan's minorities include over 200 000 Korean immigrants and descendants not given citizenship rights, 300 000 former outcasts or *eta*, and 10 000 *burakumin* or "hamlet people"; the *Ainu*, the original proto-Caucasian inhabitants of Hokkaido, and foreign laborers in Japan also stand in need of social services that the government has been reluctant to provide.
71. For a dense, early history of poverty in Japan, see Chubachi and Taira (1976).
72. Marr (1997: 229–250).
73. Stevens (1997).
74. Goodman and Peng (1996: 164).
75. Goodman and Peng (1996: 218).
76. Takahashi and Hashimoto (1997: 309).
77. The implications of this for re-visiting claims about civil society as associational life may be significant.
78. Goodman and Peng (1996: 212).

79. The Manpower Development Research Corporation of New York studied a similar effort that was made in Minnesota, United States. Its early reports indicate greater levels of improvements in children's behavior and school performance, an increased marriage rate, enhanced marital stability, decreased domestic abuse, and enhanced prospects for self-reliance among recipients.
80. See Kimura (1996: 177–189).
81. Takahashi (1997) notes, "the increased interest in *komyuniti* since the late 1960s seems to indicate that in the term *komyuniti* it is expected to create a new type of community on the basis of non-hierarchical solidarity and spontaneous participation… neither the pre-war type of rural communities nor pre-war type of family institutions are available in contemporary Japan" (Takahashi 1997:195).
82. Cited in Takahashi (1997:197).
83. The response to the Great Kobe earthquake of January 1995, which killed over 5000, is instructive in this regard. The claim that volunteerism could never take root in Japanese society due to the selfishness of Japanese youth (in contrast to the selflessness of older generations) was seriously challenged as close to 1 million individuals came forward to participate in the task of reconstruction and support for the 320 000 left homeless by the earthquake.
84. In August 1994, 244 000 companies with a total of 5.75 million employees qualified for this subsidy. See Seeleib-Kaiser (1995: 280).
85. Esping-Andersen (1997: 180–181).

5 Welfare reforms in recessionary Japan

1. There is an interesting counterargument to claims about the self-generated causes of stagflation and deflation in Japan developed in Ikeda (2004). Countering what he dubs 'essentialist' claims based on the national economy as a the unit of analysis, Satoshi Ikeda outlines a world-system perspective based on Immanuel Wallerstein's work: Emphasizing the global economic crisis triggered by global financial deregulation and liberalization, with the United States at its epicenter, Ikeda suggests that the roots of the problems of the Japanese economy are to be found in the 'limits of capitalist development on a world scale' (Ikeda 2004: 382). For a good discussion of theoretical frameworks that offer competing explanations about theHeisei recession, see Yoda's comprehensive essay on millennial Japan (Yoda 2001).
2. Gregory Kasza not only makes a strong case demonstrating the similarity, indeed 'convergence' in pension and health policies between Japan and other OECD countries, but also acknowledges a significant divergence in employment policy. Attributing this divergence to a 'uniquely long period of high speed growth' (Kasza 2006: 112), rather than 'traditional culture' that warrants the label of a 'Japanese-style welfare society,' Kasza insists on the likelihood of convergence in this policy domain as well, as changes introduced in the 1990s shape employment policy in Japan along lines long familiar in other industrializing countries.

3. A provocative alternative explanation is offered by Kwon (2005), who suggests that the Japanization of American and German management practices, specifically a move from mass to lean production systems via industrial restructuring, contributed significantly in altering the global competitive environment for Japanese firms and led directly to worsened economic conditions domestically for Japan.
4. The notion of 'work-ethic' often advanced to capture the sense of diligence, duty, and perfectionism that characterizes all manner of labor in Japan – from the early acculturation of children to sweeping classroom floors, the honing of window-sill-cleaning skills by trainees in the wildly popular *Takarazuka* dance academy, to the quality circles of production teams in Japan's leading export industries. The lack of wide gaps in wages between workers in the tertiary, service, and manufacturing sectors, until very recently, also underscores the absence of distinctions between mental and manual work in Japan.
5. Leonard Schoppa suggests that, paradoxically, it is globalization that has made possible the continuation of what he terms an 'obsolete' life-time employment system, since the declining cost of investment and conducting business overseas has 'thrown Japanese manufacturers a lifeline.'
6. The comparable fertility rates were 2.04 for the United States, 1.89 for France, 1.32 for Germany, and 1.29 for Italy (Masaki 2006). In a recent Cabinet Office Survey, only about 40 percent of Japanese parents said they would like to have more children, the lowest among five countries' survey. The large majority cited financial reasons for their reluctance to have larger families.
7. Itoh suggest that if public corporation costs of purchasing necessary land are added to the highway construction total investment in public utilities, the total amounts to a staggering 50 trillion yen. His view, however, is that this heavy capital injection was not just to restore macro demand, as per conventions of Keynesian demand management, but because a large portion of bad loans were related to real estate, construction, public expenditure outlays were driven by a political intention to help offset losses.
8. Suggestions by the Koizumi government that Japan should open its doors to allow entry to foreign workers in fields not currently open to them (nursing for instance and as indeed has already occurred in the case of IT software programmers from India), and as indeed has already occurred in the case of IT software programmers from India, was met with resistance from the HLW Minister Kawasaki Jiro, who cautioned against allowing more foreign workers into Japan.
9. Newspapers in Japan have only intermittently reported on tragedies that highlight the plight of single mothers. Among these, the death of a baby who died of starvation in Utsonomiya city in Tochigi prefecture in February 2000 was reported by the *Yomiuri Shimbun* and the *Mainichi Shimbun*. For a discussion of these events and their representation in the media, see Sean Curtin (2002).
10. Japan's population, currently 127.7 million, is estimated to shrink to a third in 100 years; children below 14 years of age comprise only 14 percent of the population.
11. Garon observes the contrast between Japan's 'modest program for lower-income Japanese... and the expanding programs of universal entitlements'

but does not attribute this distinction to the logic of the institutions of modern Japan's political economy but rather to continuities in the state's management of the problem of poverty and its role in shaping societal mores in relation to it (Garon 2002: 1).

12. See Dore's (1958) influential study of a Tokyo ward in 1951, where he describes the experience of dealing with *minseiin* recounted to him by interviewees as both personally demeaning and dis-empowering, as the details of an individual's personal circumstances were to be fully bared, subject to the judgment of the individual welfare commissioner who dispensed or withheld assistance not as a legally sanctioned right, but as a 'favor' to be acknowledged with an appropriate level of gratitude and indebtedness.
13. During 2003–2005, I visited the Kamagasaki *yoseba* several times on visits that ranged from 7 to 10 days each to speak with officials in the Kamagasaki Job Placement Office, volunteers with the Kamagasaki Night Patrol, and local non-profit groups and people living in the *doya-gai*. This research was conducted under the auspices of an SSRC/JSPS fellowship award for a project on changes in the modalities of citizenship under conditions of globalization in Japan.
14. My own efforts, at the end of a 2-year stay in Tokyo, to locate an organization willing to accept a stroller, toys, and two suitcases filled with sweaters, jackets, shoes, and miscellaneous items of clothing for adults and children for distribution among the 'needy' failed quite abysmally. I recruited the help of the Director of my son's *hoikuen* (day-care center) as well as the teachers at my daughter's elementary school and our combined efforts suggested my best option was to travel at least an hour and a half by train to the Salvation Army's warehouse to drop off the bags. In the end, I donated many items to the *hoikuen* itself and to friends of my children whose mothers were not averse to making use of 'hand-me-downs' in good condition.
15. Gregory Kasza points out that these numbers are based on pure anecdotal estimates and range from 10 to 45 percent. 'If these estimates were far wrong,' he writes, 'the MHLW could easily correct them by publishing authoritative figures. It has not' (Kasza 2006: 99–100).
16. Paradoxically, demographic changes in Japan, specifically a rapidly aging population and a declining birthrate and workforce, have rendered the prospect of a severe labor shortage imminent, despite the slowdown of the economy. With Japanese workers reluctant to undertake low-paid, unskilled work (euphemistically called the 3Ks: *kiken*, dangerous; *kitanai*, dirty; and *kitsui*, stressful), the twin compulsion to loosen restrictive immigration policy while keeping out unskilled laborers poses a real problem for state managers. Due to Japan's citizenship policy, however, which is based on the principle of *jus sanguinis* (citizenship by descent, i.e. birth), large numbers of native-born Korean and Chinese residents of Japan do not qualify for citizenship. In addition to legal migrants, comprised mainly of 'oldcomers' *zainichi* (Japan-born Korean and Chinese), *nikkeijin* (foreign-born, mostly Brazilian–Japanese), trainees from Asia (about 1.2 million in all), illegal workers (visa-overstayers or illegal entrants) are currently estimated to number 232 000 (Ministry of Justice Immigration Bureau, 2001), made up predominantly of East Asians from China, South Korea, Thailand, Philippines, Iran, and

South Asia (Bangladesh and Pakistan), bringing the total foreign population in Japan currently to over 2 million. The surge in the numbers of legal 'documented' *nikkeijin* is largely the result of the Immigration Reform Act of 1990, which allowed second-generation foreign-born Japanese and 'trainees' (mainly from China and South Korea) legal entry as unskilled 'trainees.' The majority of foreign residents in Japan are thus Asian (Koreans 32 percent, Chinese 24 percent, and Philippines 99 percent), with Brazilian *nikkeijin* constituting 14 percent of the population. A small percentage is North American (United States 2.5 percent, Canada 0.6 percent, and United Kingdom 1 percent) (*Shutsunyukoku kanri tokei* – Annual Report of Statistics on Legal Migrants, 2004). Finally, there are the refugees. Japan's rate of acceptance of refugees is notoriously low. Despite having ratified the 1951 Convention on Refugees in 1981, Japan was compelled to amend its Immigration Control and Refugee Recognition Act in 2004, following harsh criticism of its treatment of asylum seekers. Between 1982 and 2004, Japan received 3544 applications for refugee status but granted only 330 requests, accepting a total of 15 refugees in 2004 (in contrast to almost 13 000 by the United Kingdom and 21 000 by the United States). Against recommendations from the UNHCR, the practice of holding asylum seekers in detention centers continues in Japan, harsh publicity from the attempted suicide of several Afghani asylum seekers and changes in the Immigration Control and Refugee Recognition Act in 2004 notwithstanding. Vulnerable to exploitative labor conditions (withholding of wages, confiscation of passports, etc.) 'denizen' rights (by virtue of residency) do not apply to this group, since public services are closed to all but legally registered migrants, leaving them exposed to the demands of full payment of services including high medical fees (400 000 yen for delivery of a new born, for instance). Although the total foreign population in Japan is still comparatively low (2 percent), the concentration of ethnic communities in specific areas has generated a varied response in localities, bringing the 'migrant' more sharply into view in some places as compared to others as the object of racialized otherness.

6 Conclusion

1. Discussions about the vested interests of the United States in privatizing capital-rich sectors of the Japanese economy are now commonplace. Thus speculations about where Japan's postal savings and insurance funds – some $3 trillion and more – would end up included discussions of their potential role in financing the US budget deficit that has resulted from excessive military spending related to the Iraq War coupled with the tax cuts made by a two-term Republican administration in the United States. The Washington Consensus refers to the tacit political agreement between the IMF, the World Bank, and the US Treasury to rationalize global markets.
2. Kaneko Masaru, a leading critic of the government's neoliberal reforms, is often referred to as Japan's Third Way intellectual. His criticisms of the Koizumi administration, especially the reform strategy of Takenaka Heizo, the Minister of State for Economic and Fiscal Policy, have been reported widely in the media.

3. Much of the debate, it bears noting, especially among those focused on endogenous explanations, is essentially a contestation about proximate causation.
4. As indication of this shift Dore (2006) points out that the Stock Analyst's Association in Japan which had a mere 1000 members when it instituted its professional examination in 1981 now boasts 21 000 qualified members. And even more striking is the change in emphasis from the good of the social whole to private profits are indicated by the following examples: in the late 1980s, as Japan entered a period of recovery after a brief recession, wages increased by 19 percent and dividends only by 2 percent. In contrast, in the 2001–2005 recovery period wages have gone down by 6 percent while dividends have increased by 175 percent (Dore 2006).
5. The term *hikikomori* refers to 'those suffering acute social withdrawal' defined by the government as youths who confine themselves to a room in their parents' home for 6 months or more. Estimates of the total number vary from many thousands to over a million. Along with NEETs, *hikikomori* represent a growing social problem among the young that has given rise to a new class of social workers devoted to offering counsel and care.

Bibliography

Abegglen, J.C. (1958) *The Japanese Factory: Aspects of its Social Organization*, Glencoe, Il: Free Press.

Aglietta, M. (1979) *A Theory of Capitalist Regulation: The US Experience*, London: New Left Books.

Akimoto, T. (1989) "Workers' Welfare and Labor Administration in Japan: Towards the Establishment of a Concept of Workers' Welfare", Ph.D. diss., City University of New York.

Alagappa, M. (ed.) (2004) *Civil Society and Political Change in Asia: Expanding and Contracting the Democratic Sphere*, Stanford: Stanford University Press.

Alber, J. (1988) "Continuities and changes in the idea of the welfare state", *Politics and Society* 16: 451–468.

Albo, G., Langille, D., and Panitch, L. (eds) (1993) *A Different Kind of State? Popular Power and Democratic Administration*, Toronto: Oxford University Press.

Albritton, R. (1980) *A Japanese Reconstruction of Marxist Theory*, London: St. Martin's Press.

Alvares, C. (2005) "On white mythologies: detotalising the legacy of modernity", *Culture, Theory & Critique* 46(2): 93–113.

Anchordoguy, M. (2001) "Whatever happened to the Japanese miracle?" *Japan Policy Research Institute Working Paper No. 80*. http://www/jpri.org/publications/workingpapers/wp80.html.

Anderson, L. and Wadkins, M. (1991) "Japan – A culture of consumption?" *Advances in Consumer Research* 18: 129–134.

Anderson, S.J. (1993) *Welfare Policy and Politics in Japan: Beyond the Developmental State*, New York: Paragon House.

Andren, T. and Gustafsson, B. (2004) "Patterns of social assistance receipt in Sweden", *International Journal of Social Welfare* 13(1): 55–68.

Annual Report on the Labour Force Survey (2004) Statistics Bureau: Ministry of Internal Affairs and Communications, Japan.

—— (2005) Statistics Bureau: Ministry of Internal Affairs and Communications, Japan.

—— (2006) Statistics Bureau: Ministry of Internal Affairs and Communications, Japan.

Aoi, K., Morioka, K., and Suginohara, J. (1985) *Family and Community Changes in East Asia*, Tokyo, Japan: Japan Sociological Society.

Arai, K. (1988) "The cost of living and the seniority-based wage system in Japan", *Hitotsubashi Journal of Economics* 29: 21–35.

Aoki, H. (2000) "The underclass in Japan: a case study of homeless men in Kamagasaki and their winter struggles", *The International Scope* 2(4): 1–20.

Arai, T. (1999) "1999 Revision of employment security law and worker dispatching law", *Japan Institute of Labour* 38: 9.

Armstrong, B. (1988) "Racialisation and nationalist ideology: the Japanese case", *International Sociology* 3: 329–343.

Arnason, J.P. (1987) "The modern constellation and the Japanese dilemma Part I", *Thesis Eleven* 17: 4–39; Part II *Thesis Eleven* 18/19: 56–84.
Arneson, R.J. (1990) "Liberalism, distributive subjectivism, and equal opportunity for welfare", *Philosophy and Public Affairs* 19: 158–194.
Arthur, C.J. (1987) "Hegel on political economy", in D. Lamb (ed.) *Hegel and Modern Philosophy*, London: Croom Helm.
Asada, A. (1989) "Infantile capitalism and Japan's postmodernism: a fairy tale", in M. Miyoshi and H.D. Harootunian (ed.) *Postmodernism and Japan*, Durham, N.C.
Asahi Shimbun Weekly (2003), September 15: 6–8.
Ashford, D.E. (1991) "Bringing the welfare state back in", *Comparative Politics* 23: 351–375.
Atherton, C.R (1989) "The welfare state: still on solid ground", Social *Service Review* 63: 167–179.
—— (1990) "Adam Smith and the welfare state", *Arête* 15: 24–31.
Atkinson, M.M. and Coleman, W.D. (1988) "Strong states and weak states: sectoral policy networks in advanced capitalist economies", *British Journal of Political Science* 19: 47–67.
Austin, L. (ed.) (1976) *Japan: The Paradox of Progress*, New Haven: Yale University Press.
Avineri, S. (1972) *Hegel's Theory of the Modern State*, Cambridge: Cambridge University Press.
Axinn, J. (1990) "Japan: a special case", in G. Schaffner, Goldberg, and E. Kremer (eds) *The Feminization of Poverty: Only in America*, New York: Greenwood Press, 1990.
Ayala, L. and Perez, C. (2005) "Macroeconomic conditions, institutional factors and demographic structure: what causes welfare caseloads?", *Journal of Population Economics* 18(3): 563–581.
Baba, H. (1985) "Changing the paradigms of Japanese Marxist economics", *Annals of the Institute of Social Sciences* 27: 26–53.
Bagchi, A.K. (1987) "East Asian capitalism: an introduction", *Political Economy Studies in the Surplus Approach* 3: 115–132.
Baker, D. (1992) "The right to income", *Journal of Income Distribution* 2: 59–89.
Balaban, O. (1989) "The positivistic nature of the critical theory", *Science and Society* 53: 442–458.
Barrow, C.W. (1993) *Critical Theories of the State: Marxist, Neo-Marxist, Post-Marxist*, Madison, WI: University of Wisconsin Press.
Barry, N. (1990) *Concepts in Social Thought: Welfare*, Minneapolis: University of Minnesota Press.
Barshay, A. (1998) "'Doubly cruel' Marxism and the presence of the past in Japanese capitalism", in Vlastos S. (ed.) *Mirror of Modernity: Invented Traditions of Modern Japan*, Berkeley: University of California Press.
Bass, S.A. (1996) "An overview of work, retirement, and pensions in Japan", *Journal of Aging and Social Policy* 8: 57–78.
Baudrillard, J. (1975) *The Mirror of Production*, trans. M. Poster, New York: Telos Press.
—— (1981) *For a Critique of the Political Economy of the Sign*, trans. with an Introduction by C. Levin, St. Louis, MO: Telos Press.
—— (1996) *The System of Objects*, trans. J. Benedict, London: Verso.

Baynes, K. (1992) *The Normative Grounds of Social Criticism: Kant, Rawls, and Habermas*, Albany, NY: State University of New York Press.
Bean, P. and MacPherson, S. (eds) (1983) *Approaches to Welfare*, London: Routledge & Kegan Paul.
Befu, H. (1980) 'A critique of the Group Model of Japanese Society,' *Social Analysis 5/6*: 29–43.
—— and Kreiner, J. (eds) (1992) *Othernesses of Japan: Historical and Cultural Influences on Japanese Studies in Ten Countries*, Munich: Judicium Verlag.
Beiser, F.C. (ed.) (1993) *The Cambridge Companion to Hegel*, Cambridge: Cambridge University Press.
Bell, D. (1976) The *Cultural Contradictions of Modern Capitalism*, New York: Basic Books.
Ben-Ari, E., Moeran, B., and Valentine, J. (eds) (1990) *Unwrapping Japan: Society and Culture in Anthropological Perspectives*, Manchester: Manchester University Press.
Benedict, R. (1946) *The Chrysanthemum and the Sword: Patterns of Japanese Culture*, Boston, MA: Houghton Mifflin.
Benhabib, S. (1992) *Situating the Self: Gender, Community and Postmodernism in Contemporary Ethics*, New York: Routlege.
—— (1999) "Sexual difference and collective identities: the new global constellation", *Signs* 24: 335–361.
Bennett, J. and Levine, S.B. (1976) "Industrialization and social deprivation: welfare, environment, and the postindustrial society in Japan", in H. Patrick (ed.) *Japanese Industrialization and Its Social Consequences*, Berkeley: University of California.
Berger, J. (1990) "Market and state in advanced capitalist societies", *Current Sociology* 38:103–132.
Berger, J. and Offe, C. (1982) "Functionalism vs. rational choice: some questions concerning the rationality of choosing one or the other", *Theory and Society* 11: 521–526.
Bernstein, I. (1991) *The Crooked Timber of Humanity: Chapters on the History of Ideas* New York: Alfred A. Knopf.
Bernstein, R. (1975) "The politics of the crisis theory", *Telos* 23: 3–52.
Bernstein, R.J. (1978) The *Restructuring of Social and Political Theory*, Philadelphia: University of Pennsylvania Press, Harcourt Brace Jovanovich.
Bestor, V.L. (1999) "Reimagining 'civil society' in Japan", *Washington – Japan Journal* (special issue, Spring): 1–10.
Birnbaum, N. (ed.) (1977) *Beyond the Crisis*, London: Oxford University Press.
Blank, R.M. (2001) "What causes public assistance caseloads to grow?", *Journal of Human Resources* 36(1): 85–118.
Blanke, B., Jurgens, U., and Kastendiek, H. (1976) "The relationship between the political and economic as a point of departure for a materialist analysis of the bourgeois state", *International Journal of Politics* 6: 68–126.
Blau, J. (1989) "Theories of the welfare state", *Social Service Review* 63: 26–38.
Block, F. (1977) "The ruling class does not rule: notes on the Marxist theory of the state", *Socialist Revolution* 1: 6–28.
—— (1985) "Postindustrial development and the obsolescence of economic categories", Politics *and Society* 14: 71–104.
Bobbio, N. (1988) "Gramsci and the concept of civil society", in J. Keane (ed.) *Civil Society and the State*, London: Verso.

Bocock, R. (1993) *Consumption*, London: Routledge.
Boling, P. (1998) "Family policy in Japan", *Journal of Social Policy* 27: 173–179.
Bonefeld, W. (1993) "Some notes on the theory of the capitalist state", *Capital and Class* 49: 113–121.
Bottomore, T. and Bryn, R.J. (eds) (1973) "Cultural reproduction and social reproduction", in R. Brown (ed.) *Knowledge, Education, and Cultural Change*, 71–112, London: Tavistock.
—— (1989) *The Capitalist Class: An International Study*, New York: Harvester Wheatsheaf.
Bourdieu, P. (1973) "Cultural reproduction and social reproduction", in R. Brown (ed.) *Knowledge, Education, and Cultural Change*, London: Tavistock.
Bowen, R. (1989) "Japanology and Ideology: A Review Article", *Comparative Studies in Society and History* 31(1): 185–190.
Bowles, S. and Gintis, H. (1986) *Democracy and Capitalism*, New York: Basic Books.
Boyer, R. and Yamada, T. (2000) "Introduction: A puzzle for economic theories", in R. Boyer and T. Yamada (eds) *Japanese Capitalism in Crisis: A Regulationist Interpretation*, London: Routledge.
Brennan, T. (2000) "The illusion of a future: 'Orientalism' as traveling theory", *Critical Inquiry* 26(3): 558–583.
Briggs, A. (1961) "The welfare state in historical perspective", *European Journal of Sociology* 2: 221–258.
Broadbent, J. (1988) "State as process: the effect of party and class on citizen participation in Japanese local government", *Social Problems* 35: 131–144.
Brod, H. (1987) "The 'Spirit' of Hegelian politics: public opinion and legislative debate from Hegel to Habermas", in P. Stillman (ed.) *Hegel's Philosophy of Spirit*, Albany, NY: State University of New York Press.
—— (1992) *Hegel's Philosophy of Politics: Idealism, Identity, and Modernity*, Boulder: Westview Press.
Brown, R. (ed.) (1973) *Knowledge, Education, and Cultural Change*, London: Tavistock.
Brown, W. (2003) "Neo-liberalism and the end of liberal democracy", *Theory and Event* 7(1).
Buchanan, J. (1987) *The Political Economy of the Welfare State*, Stockholm, Sweden: The Industrial Institute for Economic and Social Research.
Burkett, P. and Hart-Landsberg, M. (2003) "The economic crisis in Japan: mainstream perspectives and an alternative view", *Critical Asian Studies* 35(3): 339–372.
Buruma, I. (1995) "Work as aform of beauty", in M.I. White and S. Barnet (eds) *Comparing Cultures: Readings on Contemporary Japan for American Writers*, Boston: Bedford Books.
Business Facts and Figures, Nippon 2006, WEIS: Japan.
Butler, J. (1987) *Subjects of Desire: Hegelian Reflections in Twentieth-Century France*, New York: Columbia University Press.
—— (1997) "Merely cultural", *Social Text* 52/53: 265–277.
—— (2001) "Giving an account of oneself", *Diacritics* 31(4): 22–40.
Cahoun, C. (ed.) (1992) *Habermas and the Public Sphere*, Cambridge, MA: MIT Press.
Calder, K.E. (1988) *Crisis and Compensation*, Princeton: Princeton University Press.
—— (1990) "Linking welfare and the developmental state: postal savings in Japan", *Journal of Japanese Studies* 16: 31–59.

Calichman, F. (2000) "Nothing resists modernity: On Takeuchi Yoshimi's *Kindai Towa Nanika*", *Positions: East Asia Cultures Critique* 8(2): 317–348.
Calichman, R.F. (2005) *Contemporary Japanese Thought*, New York: Columbia University Press.
Callinicos, A. (1989) *Against Postmodernism: A Marxist Critique*, New York: St. Martin's Press.
Cameron, C.D. (1982) "On the limits of the public economy", *Annals of the American Academy of Political and Social Science* 459: 46–62.
Cameron, D. (1978) "The expansion of the public economy: A comparative analysis', *American Political Science Review* 72:1243–61.
Campbell, J.C. (1992) *How Policies Change: Japanese Government and the Aging Society*, Princeton: Princeton University Press.
—— and Ikegami, N. (1998) *The Art of Balance in Health Policy: Maintaining Japan's Low Cost, Egalitarian System*, Cambridge: Cambridge University Press, 1998.
Campbell, J.L. and Lindberg, L.N. (1990) "Property rights and the organization of economic activity by the state", *American Sociological Review* 55: 634–647.
Caporaso, J.A. (ed.) (1987) *A Changing International Division of Labor*, International Economy Yearbook, Vol. 2., Boulder, CO: Lynne Rienner.
—— (ed.) (1989) *The Elusive State: International and Comparative Perspectives*. Newbury Park, London: Sage.
—— and Levine, D. (1992) *Theories of Political Economy*, Cambridge: Cambridge University Press.
Carrier, J. and Kendall, K. (1986) "Categories, categorizations and the political economy of welfare", *Journal of Social Policy* 15: 315–335.
Carrithers, M., Collins, S., and Lukes, S. (eds) (1985) *The Category of the Person: Anthropology, Philosophy, History*, Cambridge: Cambridge University Press.
Castles, F. (ed.) (1986) *Working Class and Welfare: Reflections on the Political Development of the Welfare State in Australia and New Zealand*, London: Allen and Unwin.
—— (1989) *The Comparative History of Public Policy*, Cambridge, UK: Polity Press.
Chakrabarty, D. (1994) "Categorical theory: a response to Aijaz Ahmad", *Middle East Report* No. 187/188, Intervention and North-South Politics in the 90s. (March – June): 54–55.
—— (1998) "Afterword: Revisiting the tradition/modernity binary", in S. Vlastos (ed.) *Mirror of Modernity: Invented Traditions of Modern Japan*, Berkeley: University of California Press.
—— (2000) *Provincializing Europe: Postcolonial Thought and Historical Difference*, Princeton: Princeton University Press.
Chalmers, N.J. (1989) *Industrial Relations in Japan: The Peripheral Workforce*, London: Routledge.
Chanin, C. (1999) "Voice of the people: the development of NGOs in Japan", *Washington – Japan Journal* (special issue, Spring): http://www.us-japan.org/dc/cs.channin.paper.htm 10/10/06.
Chatterjee, P. (1997) *A Possible India: Essays in Political Criticism*, Delhi: Oxford University Press.
—— (1998) *Possible India Essays in Political Criticism*, Oxford University Press Due/Published.
Cheng, M.T. (1991) "The Japanese permanent employment system: empirical findings", *Work and Occupations* 18: 148–171.

Chiba, A. (1980) "The aged of Japan", *Across the Board* 17: 30–31.

Cho, Y.H. (1996) "The growth of enterprise welfare in Japan", *Economic and Industrial Democracy* 17: 281–300.

Chou, M. (1975) "Japan", in D. Yokelson (ed.) *Collected Papers on Poverty Issues*, Vol. 4, in P. Karsten (ed.) *International Poverty and Social Welfare Policies: A Study of Seven Countries*, New York: Hudson Institute.

Chubachi, M. and Taira, K. (1976) "Poverty in modern Japan: perceptions and realities", in H. Patrick (ed.) *Japanese Industrialization and its Social Consequences*, Berkeley: University of California Press.

Clark, R. (1979) *The Japanese Company*, New Haven: Yale University Press.

Clark, R.L. and Ogawa, N. (1996) "Public attitudes and concerns about population aging in Japan", *Aging and Society* 16.

Clarke, J., Cochrane, A., and Smart, C. (eds) (1987) *Ideologies of Welfare: From Dreams to Disillusion*, London: Hutchinson Education.

Clarke, S. (1987) "Capitalist crisis and the rise of monetarism", in R. Miliband, L. Panitch, and J. Saville (eds) *Socialist Register*, London: The Merlin Press.

—— (1989) "The basic theory of capitalism: a critical review of Itoh and the Uno school", *Capital and Class* 37: 133–149.

—— (1990–91) "The Marxist theory of overaccumulation and crisis", *Science and Society* 54: 442–467.

Cochran, B. (1984) *Welfare Capitalism – and After*, New York: Schocken Books.

Cohen, J. (1988) "Discourse ethics and civil society", *Philosophy and Social Criticism* 14: 315–337.

—— and Arato, A. (1992) *Civil Society and Political Theory*, Cambridge, MA.: MIT Press.

Collick, M. (1988) "Social policy: Pressure and responses", in J.A.A. Stockwin, A. Rix, A. George, J. Horne, D. Ito, and M. Collick (eds) *Dynamic and Immobolist Politics in Japan*, Basingston: Macmillan.

Collingwood, R.G. (1971) *The Idea of History*, London: Oxford University Press.

Comaroff, J. and Comaroff, J. (eds) (1999) *Civil Society and the Political Imagination in Africa: Critical Perspectives*, Chicago: University of Chicago Press.

Connolly, W. (ed.) (1984) *Legitimacy and the State*, New York: New York University Press.

Conrad, S. (1999) "What time is Japan? Problems of comparative (intercultural) Historiography", *History and Theory* 48: 67–83.

Corrigan, P. and P. Leonard (1978) *Critical Texts in Social Work and the Welfare State: Social Work Practice Under Capitalism: A Marxist Approach*, London: Macmillan Press.

Cox, R. (1987) *Production, Power and World order: Social Forces in the Making of History*, New York: Columbia University Press.

Cummings, (1997) "Boundary displacement: area studies and international studies during and after the cold war", *Bulletin of Concerned Asian Scholars* 29(1): 6–26.

Curtin, J.S. (2006) "Women and Japan's new poor", *Japan Focus* http://japanfocus.org/products/details/1641.

Dale, P.N. (1986) *The Myth of Japanese Uniqueness*, New York: St. Martin's Press.

Dalley, G. (1983) "Ideologies of care: a feminist contribution to the debate", *Critical Social Policy* 8: 72–81.

Dalton, G. (1971) *Economic Anthropology and Development: Essays on Tribal and Peasant Economies*, New York: Basic Books.

Dean, M. (1995) "Governing the unemployed self in an active society", *Economy and Society* 24: 559–583.
Deguchi, M. (1999) "A comparative view of civil society", *Washington – Japan Journal* (special issue, Spring): 11–20.
Dennett, D. (1976) "Conditions of personhood", in A.O. Rorty (ed.) *The Identities of Persons*, Berkeley: University of California Press.
DeSario, J.P. (ed.) (1989) *International Public Policy Sourcebook:* Vol. 1, *Health and Social Welfare*; Vol. 2 *Education and Environment*, New York: Greenwood Press.
Desmond, W. (ed.) (1989) *Hegel and his Critics: Philosophy in the Aftermath of Hegel*, Albany: State University of New York Press.
De Vos, G. and Wagatsuma, H. (1967) *Japan's Invisible Race: Caste in Culture and Personality*, Berkeley: University of California Press.
Dobb, M. (1946) *Studies in the Development of Capitalism*, London: Routledge and Kegan Paul.
Doi, T. (1981) *The Anatomy of Dependence*, trans. J. Bester, Tokyo; New York: Kodansha International.
Dore, R. (1958) *City Life in Japan*, London: Routledge & Kegan Paul and Berkeley, University of California Press.
—— (1973) *British Factory-Japanese Factory*, London: Allen and Unwin.
—— (1997) "The distinctiveness of Japan", in Crouch, C. and Streeck, W. (eds) *Political Economy of Modern Capitalism*, London: Sage.
—— (1999) "Japan's reform debate: Patriotic concern or class interest? Or both?", *Journal of Japanese Studies* 25(1): 65–89.
—— (2000) *Stock Market Capitalism: Welfare Capitalism: Japan and Germany versus the Anglo-Saxons*, New York: Oxford University Press.
—— Social Evolution Economic Development and Culture: what it means to take Japan seriously: selected writings of Ronald Dore (with H. Whittaker)", Aldershot, E. Elgar, 2001.
—— (2006) "Japan's new miracle economy: neoliberalism and the poverty of wealth", *JapanFocus* http://www.japanfocus.org/products/details/2267.
Douglas, J.D. (1989) *The Myth of the Welfare State*, New Brunswick, NJ: Transaction.
Douglas, M. (1987) *How Institutions Think*, Syracuse: Syracuse University Press.
Dower, J.W. (1975) "E.H. Norman, Japan and the uses of History", in J.W. Dower (ed.) *Origins of the Modern Japanese State: Selected Writings of E.H. Norman*, New York: Pantheon.
Doyal, L. and Gough, I. (1984) "A theory of human needs", *Critical Social Policy* 10: 6–38.
Duus, P. and Okimoto, D.I. (1979) "Fascism and the history of pre-war Japan: the failure of a concept", *Journal of Asian Studies* 39: 65–76.
Easton, S.M. (1987) "Hegel and feminism", in D. Lamb (ed.) *Hegel and Modern Philosophy*, London: Croom Helm.
Ehrenberg, J. (1999) *Civil Society: The Critical History of an Idea*, New York: New York University Press.
Eisenstadt, S.N. (1989) "Cultural premises and the limits of convergence in modern societies: An examination of some aspects of Japanese society", *Diogenes* 147: 125–147.
—— (1996) *Japanese Civilization: A Comparative View*, Chicago: The University of Chicago Press.
—— (1998) "Modernity and the construction of collective identities", *International Journal of Comparative Sociology* 39(1): 1381–402.

—— and Ahimeir, O. (eds) (1985) *The Welfare State and its Aftermath*, London: Croom Helm, Jerusalem Institute for Israel Studies.
Emi, K. (1983) "Increasing medical expenses and the social insurance system", *Hitotsubashi Journal of Economics* 24: 1–10.
Emlet, C.A. (1998) "The graying of our global village: an analysis of social welfare systems for the aged in the United States and Japan", *Journal of Applied Social Sciences* 22: 97–113.
Employment and Employment Policy (1988) The Japan Institute of Labour, Tokyo: Japanese Industrial Relations Series, #1.
Esping-Andersen, G. (1983) "After the welfare state", *Public Welfare* 41: 28–35.
—— (1985) *Politics Against Markets*, Princeton: Princeton University Press.
—— (1989) "The three political economies of the welfare state", *The Canadian Review of Sociology and Anthropology* 26: 10–35.
—— (1990) *The Three Worlds of Welfare Capitalism*, Princeton: Princeton University Press.
—— (1996a) *Welfare States in Transition: National Adaptations in Global Economies*, London: Sage.
—— (1996b) "After the golden age? Welfare state dilemmas in a global economy", in G. Esping-Andersen (ed.) *Welfare States in Transition: National Adaptations in Global Economies*, London: Sage.
—— (1997) "Hybrid or unique: the Japanese welfare state between Europe and America", *Journal of European Social Policy* 7: 180–181.
—— and Kolberg, J.V. (1991) "De-commodification and work absence in the welfare state", *International Journal of Sociology* 21: 77–111.
Estévez-Abe, M. (2003) "State-society partnerships in the Japanese welfare state", in F.J. Shwartz and S.J. Pharr (eds) The State of Civil Society in Japan, Cambridge, UK and New York: Cambridge University Press.
—— (2005) "Gender bias in skills and social policies: the varieties of capitalism perspective on sex segregation", *Social Politics: International Studies in Gender, State and Society* 12(2): 180–215.
——, Iversen, T, and Soskice, D. (2001) "Social protection and the formation of skills: a reinterpretation of the welfare state", in P.A. Hall and D. Soskice (eds) *Varieties of Capitalism: The Institutional Foundations of Comparative Advantage*, Oxford: Oxford University Press'
—— (2002) 'Negotiating Welfare Reform: Actors and Institutions in Japan', in S. Steinmo and B. Rothsetin (eds) *Institutionalism and Welfare Reforms* Palgrave: Basingstoke.
Evans, P., Rueschemeyer, D., and Skocpol, T. (eds) (1985) *Bringing the State Back In*, Cambridge: Cambridge University Press.
Ezawa, A. (2002) "Japan's new homeless", *Journal of Social Distress and the Homeless* 11(4): 279–291.
—— and Fujiwara, C. (2005) "Lone mothers and welfare-to-work policies in Japan and the United States: towards and alternative perspective", *Journal of Sociology and Social Welfare* 32(4): 41–63.
Facts and Figures of Japan (2005), Foreign Press Center, Japan.
Fallows, J. (1988) "The other Japan: the lower class", *Current Issues* 304: 32–36.
Feenberg, A. (1994) "Alternative modernity? Playing the Japanese game of culture", *Cultural Critique* 107–137.
Fischer, N. (1979) *Economy and Self: Philosophy and Economics from the Mercantilists to Marx*, Westport, CT: Greenwood Press.

Flora, P. (1985) "On the History and Current Problems of the Welfare State", in S.N. Eisenstadt and Ora Ahimeir (eds) *The Welfare State and it's Aftermath*, 11–30, London: Croom Helm.

—— (ed.) (1986) *Growth to Limits: The Western European Welfare States since World War II*. Vols 1 and 2, New York: Walter de Gruyter.

Forbes, I. (1990) *Marx and the New Individual*, London: Unwin Hyman.

Fowler, E. (1996) "Reflections on hegemony, Japanology, and oppositional criticism", JJS 22.2: 401–412.

Fraser, N. (1989) "Talking about needs: interpretive contests as political conflicts in welfare-state societies", *Ethics* 2: 291–313.

—— (1992) "Rethinking the public sphere", in C. Calhoun (ed.) *Habermas and the Public Sphere*, Cambridge: MIT Press.

—— and Gordon, L. (1994) "A genealogy of *Dependency*: tracing a keyword of the U.S. welfare state", *Signs* 19: 309–36.

Friedman, D. (1988) *The Misunderstood Miracle: Industrial Development and Political Change in Japan*, Ithaca: Cornell University Press.

Friedman, M. (1962) *Capitalism and Freedom*, Chicago: University of Chicago Press.

Fuchino, K. (1988) "Wage earners' changing attitudes", *Japan Echo* 15:17–23.

Fujino, S. (1966) "Business cycles in Japan 1868–1962", *Hitotsubashi Journal of Economics*, (June): 53–62.

Fujita, G. (1986) "Japanese corporate pensions: the current issue", *Hitotsubashi Journal of Social Studies* 18: 15–28.

Fujita, K. (1982) "State Economic Intervention and Struggle over the State in Japan", Ph.D. diss., Michigan State University.

Fujitani, T. (1992) "Electronic pageantry and Japan's 'Symbolic Emperor' ", *The Journal of Asian Studies* 51(4): 824–850.

—— (1998) "*Minshushi* as critique of orientalist knowledge", *Positions* 6: 301–322.

Fujiwara, S. (1989) "Foreign trade, investment, and industrial imperialism in postwar Japan", in T. Morris-Suzuki and T. Seiyama (eds) *Japanese Capitalism Since 1945: Critical Perspectives*, Armonk, New York: M.E. Sharpe.

Fukui, M. (1992) "Helping Japan grow old", *Business Tokyo*, February 18.

Fulcher, J. (1988) "The Bureaucratization of the State and the Rise of Japan", *British Journal of Sociology* 2: 228–254.

Furniss, N. and Tilton, T. (1977) *The Case for the Welfare State: From Social Security to Social Equality*, Bloomington: Indiana University Press.

Gao, B. (1998) "The search for national identity and Japanese industrial policy, 1950–1969", *Nations and Nationalism* 4: 227–245.

—— (2001) *Japan's Economic Dilemma: The Institutional Origins of Prosperity and Stagnation*, New York: Cambridge University Press.

Garon 2003. 'From Meiji to Heisei: The state and civil society in Japan,' in F.J. Schwartz and S.J. Pharr (eds) The state of civil society in Japan (Cambridge: Cambridge University Press), pp. 42–62.

Garon, S. (1987) *The State and Labor in Modern Japan*, Berkeley: University of California.

—— (1994) "Rethinking modernization and modernity in Japanese history: a focus on state–society relations", *The Journal of Asian Studies* 53(2): 346–366.

—— (1997) *Moulding Japanese Minds: The State and Everyday Life*, Princeton: Princeton University Press.

—— (2002) *Japanese Policies toward Poverty and Public Assistance: A Historical Perspective*, Washington, DC: World Bank Institute.

Gellner, E. (1985) *Relativism and the Social Sciences*, Cambridge: Cambridge University Press.

Genda, Y. and Rebeick, M. (2000) "Japanese labour in the 1990s: stability and stagnation", *Oxford Review of Economic Policy* 16: 2.

George, A. and Bennett, A. (2005) *Case Studies and Theory Development in the Social Sciences*, Boston: MIT Press.

George, V. and Howards, I. (1991) *Poverty Amidst Affluence: Britain and the United States*, Aldershot, UK: Edward Elgar.

—— and Wilding, P. (1985) *Ideology and Social Welfare*, London: Routledge & Kegan Paul.

Gibson, M. (1994) "Easter contexts/Western theory—Cultural studies and Japan", *Southeast Asian Journal of Social Science* 22: 14–20.

Giddens, A. (1973) *The Class Structure of the Advanced Societies*, London: Hutchinson.

Gilbert, N. (1983) *Capitalism and the Welfare State: Dilemmas of Social Benevolence*, New Haven: Yale University Press.

—— and Gilbert, B. (1989) *The Enabling State: Modern Welfare Capitalism in America*, New York: Oxford University Press.

Gilder, G. (1981) *Wealth and Poverty*. New York: Basic Books.

Gill, T. (2001) *Men of Uncertainty: The Social Organization of Day Laborers in Contemporary Japan,* Albany Ny: Suny Press.

Ginsburg, N. (1979) *Class, Capital and Social Policy*, London: Macmillan.

Gitlin, T. and Norris, C. (1990) *What's Wrong with Postmodernism: Critical Theory and the Ends of Philosophy*, Baltimore: The Johns Hopkins University.

Glass, J. (1994) *Shattered Selves: Multiple Personality in a Post-Modern World*, Ithaca: Cornell University Press.

Glazer, N. (1988) *Limits of Social Policy*, Cambridge: Harvard University Press.

Gluck, C. (1985) *Japan's Modern Myths: Ideology in the Late Meiji Period*, Princeton: Princeton University Press.

Gold, D.A., Clarence, Y.H., and Wright, E.O. (1975) "Recent developments in Marxist theories of the state", *Monthly Review* 27: 29–43; Part 2, 27 (November): 36–51.

Goldberg, G.S. and Kremen, E. (eds) (1990) *The Feminization of Poverty: Only in America?* New York: Greenwood Press.

Goldthorpe, J.H., Lockwood, D., Bechhofer, F., and Platt, J. (1969) *The Affluent Worker in the Class Structure*, Cambridge: Cambridge University Press.

Gooby, P. Taylor (1986) "Privatisation, power and the welfare state", *Sociology* 20: 228–246.

Goodman, R. and Peng, I. (1996) "The East Asian welfare states: peripatetic learning, adaptive change, and nation-building", in G. Esping-Andersen (ed.) *Welfare States in Transition: National Adaptations in Global Economies*, London: Sage.

Gordon, A. (ed.) (1993) *Postwar Japan as History*, Berekeley: University of California Press.

—— (1997) "Managing the Japanese household: the New Life movement in postwar Japan", *Social Politics* 4: 245–283.

—— (2004) "Rethinking area studies, once more", *The Journal of Japanese Studies* 30(2): 417–429.

Gordon, D.M. (1988) "Can we pay the piper? Linkages between the macroeconomy and the welfare state", *Politics and Society* 16: 487–501.
—— and Katznelson, I. (1988) "Reflections on the welfare state: Introduction", *Politics and Society* 16: 447–50.
Gordon, L. (1990) "The welfare state: Towards a socialist-feminist perspective", in R. Miliband, L. Panitch, and J. Saville (eds) *The Socialist Register*, London: Merlin.
Gotoh, R. (2006) "Basic Capability, Work Incentive and Public Reciprocity – towards Realization of Basic Income in Japan", Paper presented at the 20th IPSA World Congress, Fukuoka, July 9–13.
Gough, I. (1975) "State expenditure in advanced capitalism", *New Left Review* 92: 53–91.
—— (1979) *The Political Economy of the Welfare State*, London: MacMillan.
Gould, A. (1993) *Capitalist Welfare Systems: A Comparison of Japan, Britain and Sweden*, London: Longman.
Gould, C.C. (1978) *Marx's Social Ontology: Individuality and Community in Marx's Theory of Social Reality*, Cambridge: The MIT Press.
Gould, F. (1983) "Public expenditure in Japan: a comparative view", *Hitotsubashi Journal of Economics* 23: 57–67.
Green, D.G. (1993) *Reinventing Civil Society: The Rediscovery of Welfare Without Politics*, Civitas: Institute for the Study of Civil Society.
Griffith, D.C. (1987) "Nonmarket labor processes in an advanced capitalist economy", *American Anthropologist* 89: 838–852.
Grimmer-Solem, E. (2005) "German social science, Meiji conservatism, and the peculiarities of Japanese history", *Journal of World History* 16(2).
Habermas, J. (1973) "What does a crisis mean today? Legitimation problems in late capitalism", *Social Research* 40: 643–667.
—— (1975) *Legitimation Crisis*, Boston: Beacon Press.
—— (1983) "Modernity: An incomplete project", in H. Foster (ed.) *The Anti-Aesthetic: Essays on Postmodern Culture*, Port Townsend, Washington: Bay Press.
—— (1989) *The Structural Transformation of the Public Sphere; An Inquiry into the Category of Bourgeois Society*, trans. T. Burger and F. Lawrence, Cambridge: MIT Press.
—— (1996) *Between Facts and Norms: Contributions to a Discourse Theory of Law and Democracy* trans., W. Rehg, Cambridge, Mass.: MIT Press.
Hadenius, A. (1986) *A Crisis of the Welfare State? Opinions about Taxes and Public Expenditure in Sweden*, Sweden: MiniMedia.
Hall, J.A. (ed.) (1995) Civil Society: Theory, History, Comparison. Cambridge, England: Polity Press.
Hall, P.A. (ed.) (1989) *The Political Power of Economic Ideas: Keynesianism Across Nations*, Princeton: Princeton University Press.
Hall, P.D. (1987) "A Historical overview of the private nonprofit sector", in W.W. Powell (ed.) *The Nonprofict sector: A Research Handbook*, New Haven, CT.: Yale University Press.
Hall, P.A. and Soskice, D. (eds) (2001) *Varieties of Capitalism: The Institutional Foundations of Comparative Advantage*.
Halliday, J. (1975) *A Political History of Japanese Capitalism*, New York: Monthly Review Press.

Ham, C. and Hill, M. (1984) *The Policy Process in the Modern Capitalist State*. Sussex: Wheatsheaf Books.

Hansen, F.R. (1985) *The Breakdown of Capitalism: A History of the Idea in Western Marxism, 1883–1983*, London: Routledge & Kegan Paul.

Hara, M. (2005) "Where will Japan's postal funds end up? The money trail and the future of reform", Japanfocus.org.

Harcourt, J.M. (1996) "Unemployment reduction in Canada: lessons from Japan and Sweden", *Industrial Relations* 52: 177–202.

Hardt, M. (1995) "The withering of civil society", *Social Text* 45, 14(4): 27–44.

Harootunian, H. (2000) *History's Disquiet: Modernity, Cultural Practice, and the Question of the Everyday Life*, New York: Columbia University Press.

—— (2001) *Overcome by Modernity: History, Culture, and Community in Interwar Japan*, Princeton: Princeton University Press.

Harootunian, H. and Sakai, N. (1999) 'Dialogue: Japan Studies and Cultural Studies', *Positions* 7(2): 593–647.

Harris, D. (1987) *Justifying the Welfare State: The New Right Versus the Old Left*, New York: Basil Blackwell.

Hart-Landsberg, M. and Burkett, P. (1998) "Contradictions of capitalist industrialization in East Asia: A critique of 'Flying Geese' theories of development", *Economic Geography* 74(2): 87–110.

Hartmann, K. (1984) "Towards a new systematic reading of Hegel's *Philosophy of Right*", in Z.A. Pelczynski (ed.) *The State and Civil Society: Studies in Hegel's Political Philosophy*, Cambridge: Cambridge University Press.

Harvey, D. (1990) *The Condition of Postmodernity*, Cambridge, Mass.: Blackwell.

Hasegawa, M. (2005) "Economic globalization and homelessness in Japan", *The American Behavioral Scientist* 48(8): 989–1013.

Hashimoto, M. (1993) "Aspects of labor market adjustments in Japan", *Journal of Labor Economics* 11(1): 136–161.

Hastings, S.A. (1980) "The Government, the Citizen and the Creation of a New Sense of Community: Social Welfare, Local Organization and Dissent in Tokyo 1905–1937", Ph.D. diss., University of Chicago.

Hattori, S. (1980) "Absolutism and historiographical interpretation", *The Japan Interpreter* 13: 15–35.

Havel, V. (1985). *The Power of the Powerless: citizens against the state in central eastern europe*, (J. Keane, ed.). Armonk, NY: M.E. Sharpe.

Hay, C. (1986) "Globalization, welfare retrenchment and the 'Logic of No Alternative': Why second-best won't do", *Dissent* 33: 351–356.

Hayek, F. (1960) *The Constitution of Liberty*, London: Routledge and Kegan Paul.

Healey, P. (1990) "Policy processes in planning", *Policy and Politics* 18 (April): 91–103.

Hearn, J. (1982) "Radical Social Work: Contradictions, Limitations and Political Possibilities", *Critical Social Policy* 2 (Summer): 19–34.

Hechter, M. (1981) "Karl Polanyi's Social Theory: A Critique", *Politics and Society* 10: 399–429.

Hegel, G.W.F. (1967) *Philosophy of Right*, trans. with notes by T.M. Knox. Oxford: Oxford University Press.

—— (1977) *Phenomenology of Spirit*, trans. by A.V. Miller, Oxford: Oxford University Press.

Heidenheimer, A. (1983) *Comparative Public Policy* 2nd edn, New York: St. Martin's Press.

Held, D. (1980) *Introduction to Critical Theory: Horkheimer to Habermas*, Berkeley: University of California Press.

Heller, P.S., Hemming, R., and Kohnert, P.W. (1986) *Aging and Social Expenditure in the Major Industrial Countries 1980–2025*, Washington, DC: International Monetary Fund.

Higgins, J. (1981) *States of Welfare: A Comparative Analysis of Social Policy*, New York: St. Martin's Press.

Hill, D.M. (1978) "Political ambiguity and policy: the case of welfare", *Social and Economic Administration* 12 (Summer): 89–119.

Himmelstrand, Ulf (1986) "The Future of the Welfare State: A Question of Holistic Diagnosis and Structural Reforms", in Else Oyen (ed.) *Comparing Welfare States and their Futures*, 33–128, Aldershot, England: Gower.

Hinrich, K., C. Offe, and H. Wiesenthal (1988) "Time, Money and Welfare-State Capitalism", in John Keane (ed.) *Civil Society and the State*, 221–244, London: Verso.

Hiraishi, N. (1980) *Social Security*. Japanese Industrial Relations Series #5. Tokyo: The Japan Institute of Labour.

Hirata, K. (2002) *Civil Society in Japan: The Growing Role of NGOs in Tokyo's Aid Development Policy*, Palgrave Macmillan: New York.

Hirsch, F. (1977) *Social Limits to Growth*, London: Routledge and Kegan Paul.

Hirschman, A.O. (1970) *Exit, Voice, and Loyalty: Responses to Decline in Firms, Organizations, and States*, Cambridge, M.A.: Harvard University Press.

—— (1982) "Rival interpretations of market society: civilizing, destructive, or feeble?" *Journal of Economic Literature* 20(December): 1463–1484.

Hiwatari, N. (1996) "Sustaining the welfare state and international competitiveness in Japan: The welfare reforms of the 1980s and the political economy", Paper presented at the Annual Meeting of the American Political Science Association, Washington DC 1993.

Hollingsworth. J.R. (1982) "The Political-structural basis for economic performance", *Annals of the American Academy of Political and Social Science* 459: 28–45.

Hollis, M. and Smith, S. (1990) *Explaining and Understanding International Relations*, Oxford: Clarendon Press.

Holloway, J. and Picciotto, S. (1978) *State and Capital: A Marxist Debate*, Austin: University of Texas Press.

Horiuchi, A. (1999) "Financial fragility and recent developments in the Japanese safety net", *Social Science Japan Journal* 2(1): 3–21.

Hoshino, S. (1988) "Perspective of the Japanese welfares", in R. Morris (ed.) *Testing the Limits of Social Welfare: International Perspectives on Policy Changes in Nine Countries*, Hanover, England: University Press of New England.

Hoshino, S. (1996) "Paying for the Health and Social Care of the Elderly", Journal for Aging and Social Policy 8: 37–55.

Hoston, G. (1985) *Marxism and the Crisis of Development in Prewar Japan*, Princeton: Princeton University Press.

Houlgate, S. (1995) "The unity of theoretical and practical spirit in Hegel's concept of freedom", *Review of Metaphysics* 48: 859–881.

Hueglin, T.O. (1987) "The politics of fragmentation in an age of scarcity: a synthetic view and critical analysis of welfare state crisis", *Canadian Journal of Political Science* 20: 235–264.

Hunter, I. (1993) "Subjectivity and government", *Economy and Society* 22: 123–136.
Iglehart, J.K. (1988) "Health policy report: Japan's medical care system", *The New England Journal of Medicine* 319: 807–812.
Ikeda, S. (2004) "Japan and the changing regime of accumulation: A world-system study of Japan's trajectory from miracle to debacle", *Journal of World-Systems Research* 10(2): 363–394.
Ikegami, E. (1995) "Citizenship and national identity in early Meiji Japan", *International* Review of Social History 3: 185–221.
Ikegami, N. (1992) "The economics of health-care in Japan", *Science* #5082: 614–618.
—— and Campbell, J.C. (1995) "Medical care in Japan", *New England Journal of Medicine* 333: 1295–1299.
Imata, K. (1999) "Civil society in the US and Japan: polar opposites", *Washington – Japan Journal* (special issue, Spring): 21–28.
Inamoto, Y. (1989) "Restriction of private rights to landed properties and the role of the 'Public': a note on the ongoing discussion about landownership and the public welfare", *Annals of the Institute of Social Science* 31: 1–15.
Inoguchi, T. (2000) "Social capital in Japan", *Japanese Journal of Political Science* 1(1): 73–112.
Inoue, K. (2001) *Individual Dignity in Modern Japanese Thought: The Evolution of the Concept of Jinkaku in Moral and Ediucational Discourse*, Ann Arbor: University of Michigan Press.
IPSS Statistics (1996) *The Cost of Social Security in Japan FY 1996, Summary of 1996 Statistics*, Institute of population and social security research. http://www.ipss.go.jp/ss-cost/e/IPSS/P2-4 e.html 8/10/2006.
Ishi, H. (1988) "Historical background of the Japanese tax system", *Hitotsubashi Journal of Economics* 29 (June): 1–20.
—— (1990) "Taxation and public debt in a Growing economy: the Japanese experience", *Hitotsubashi Journal of Economics* 31 (June): 1–22.
Ishida, H. (1989) "Class Structure and Status Hierarchies in Contemporary Japan", *European Sociological Review* 5 (May): 65–80.
—— (1993) *Social Mobility in Contemporary Japan: Education Credentials, Class and the Labor Market in a Cross National Perspective*, Stanford: Stanford University Press.
Ishida, T. (1983/84) "Rethinking political development: The Japanese case", *Annals of the Institute of Social Science* 25: 1–8.
—— and Krauss, E.S. (eds) (1989) *Democracy in Japan*, Pittsburgh: University of Pittsburgh Press.
Ito, Y. (1995) "Social work development in Japan", *Social Policy and Administration* 29: 258–268.
Itoh, M. (1988) *The Basic Theory of Capitalism: The Form and Substance of the Capitalist Economy*, Basingstoke, Hampshire: Macmillan.
—— (1990) *The World Economic Crisis and Japanese Capitalism*, New York: St. Martin's Press.
—— (2001) "The Japanese economic crisis reconsidered", *la rivista del manifesto* 19 http://www.larivistadelmanifesto.it/originale/19A20010713.html.
—— (2005) "The Japanese economy in structural difficulties", *Monthly Review* 56(11) http://www.monthlyreview.oirg/0405itoh.htm.

Ivy, M. (1993) "Formations of mass culture", in A. Gordon (ed.) *Postwar Japan as History*, Berkeley: University of Californaia Press.
—— (1995) *Discourses of the Vanishing: Modernity, Phantasm, Japan*, Chicago: University of Chicago Press.
Iwao, S. (1988) "The Japanese portrait of change", *Japan Echo* 15: 2–6.
Jameson, F. (1984) "Postmodernism, or the cultural logic of late capitalism", *New Left Review* 146(July–August): 53–92.
Janoski, T. and Hicks, A.M. (1994) *The Comparative Political Economy of the Welfare State*, Cambridge: Cambridge University Press.
Japan 2006: An International Comparison (2005), Tokyo: Keizai Koho Center.
Japan Economic Institute Report (1987) #12A, March 27.
Japan Economic Institute Report #16A (1989) "Challenges to Japan's Health Insurance System", Washington, DC, April 21.
Japan Labor Bulletin (2003) Japan Institute of Labour 42(7): 1–12.
Japan Labor Bulletin (1994), Statistical Aspects, 33(5), May 1. www.jil.go.jp/jil/bulletin/year/1994/vol33–0.5htm.
The Japan Labor Flash (e-mail journal) Japan Institute of Labor 26 (November 1, 2004), online at http://www.jil.go.jp/foriegn/emm/bi/26.htm (accessed March 23, 2006).
Japan: Social Security Bulletin (1994), Tokyo.
Japan Statistical Yearbook (2003), Ministry of Public Management, Home Affairs, Post and Telecommunications.
The Japan Times Online (2006) "Editorial: a divide over the income gap", http://search.japantimes.co.jp/cgi-bin/ed/20060404a1.html.
Jay, M. (1973) *The Dialectical Imagination: A History of the Frankfurt School and the Institute of Social Research 1923–1950*, Boston: Little Brown.
Jessop, B. (1977) "Recent theories of the capitalist state", *Cambridge Journal of Economics* 1: 353–73.
—— (1982) *The Capitalist State*, Oxford: Martin Robertson.
—— (1983) "Accumulation strategies, state forms, and hegemonic projects", *Kapitalstate* 10/11: 89–112.
—— (1995) "The regulation approach, governance and post-Fordism: Alternative perspectives on economic and political change", *Economy and Society* 24: 307–333.
Jiro, A. (1989) "Quieting social security nightmares", *Japan Quarterly* 36: 141–145.
Johansson, S.R. and Mosk, C. (1986) "Income and mortality: evidence from modern Japan", *Population and Development Review* 12: 415–440.
Johnson, C. (1974) "Political science and East Asian area studies", *World Politics* 26(4): 560–575.
—— (1982) *MITI and the Japanese Miracle: The Growth of Industrial Policy, 1925–1975*, Stanford: Stanford University Press.
—— (1988) "The Japanese political economy: a crisis in theory", *Ethics and International Affairs* 2: 79–97.
—— (2001) "Japanese 'Capitalism' " Revisited', *Japan Policy Research Institute (JPRI) Occasional Paper*, No. 22.
—— and Ijiri, H. (2005) "About area studies and Japan", *Japan Policy Research Institute* #34.
Johnson, N. (1988) *The Welfare State in Transition: the Theory and Practice of Welfare Pluralism*, Amherst: University of Massachusetts Press.

Jordan, B. (1987) *Rethinking Welfare*, Oxford: Basil Blackwell.

Kamagasaki Resource Center (KRC) (1999) Information from homepage, Osaka, KRC.

Kamata, S. (1987) "The impact of social security on capital accumulation and labor supply", *Oikomomika* 23: 81–90.

Kaneko, M. (2001) "No more games in Japan's referee-free capitalism", *EJCJS* (*Electronic Journal of Contemporary Japanese Studies*) #4. http://www. japanesestudies.org.uk/discussionpapers/Kaneko.html.

Kang, S. (2001) "Post-colonialism and diasporic space in Japan", *Inter-Asia Cultural Studies* 2(1): 137–144.

Kangas, O. (1991) "The bigger the better? On the dimensions of welfare state development: Social expenditure versus social rights", *Acta Sociologica* 34: 33–44.

—— (1991) "Tax Reform in Japan: A Model of Strategic Behavior of Bureaucrats", Paper Presented at the Annual Meeting of the Association for Asian Studies, New Orleans, L.A., April 13.

Kasza, G. (2006) *One World of Welfare: Japan in Comparative Perspective*, Ithaca and London: Cornell University Press.

Kato, J. (1991) "Public pension reforms in the U.S. and Japan: A study of comparative public policy", *Comparative Political Studies* 24: 100–126.

Katz, R. (2003) *Japanese Phoenix: The Long Road to Economic Revival*, Armonk, NY: M.E. Sharpe.

Katznelson, I. (1988) "The welfare state as a contested institutional idea", *Politics and Society* 16(December): 517–531.

Kaviraj, S. and Khilnani, S. (eds) (2001) *Civil Society: History and Possibilities*, Cambridge: Cambridge University Press.

Keane, J. (1978) "The legacy of political economy: Thinking with and against Claus Offe", *Canadian Journal of Political and Social Theory* 2 (Fall): 49–92.

—— (1984) *Public Life and Late Capitalism: Toward a Socialist Theory of Democracy*, Cambridge: Cambridge University Press.

—— (ed.) (1988) *Civil Society and the State*, London: Verso.

—— and Owens, J. (1986/87) "The future of full employment", *Critical Social Policy* 18: 4–14.

Kelly, G.A. (1972) "Notes on Hegel's Lordship and Bondage", in Alasdair MacIntyre (ed.) *Hegel: A Collection of Critical Essays*, Garden City, NJ.: Doubleday and Co.

Kelly, W. (1991) "Directions in the anthropology of contemporary Japan", *Annual Review of Anthropology*, 395–431.

Kenney, M. and Florida, R. (1988) "Beyond mass production: production and the labor process in Japan", *Politics and Society* 16 (March): 121–158.

Kimura, T. (1996) "From transfer to social service: A new emphasis on social policies for the aged in Japan", *Journal of Aging and Social Policy* 8: 177–189.

Kincaid, H. (1991) "Hegel on external relations and partial understanding", *Idealistic* Studies 21 (January): 29–47.

King, D.S. (1987) "The State and the Social Structures of Welfare in Advanced Industrial Democracies", *Theory and Society* 16 (November): 841–868.

Kitamura, H. (1976) *Choices for the Japanese Economy*, London: The Royal Institute of International Affairs.

Kobayashi, Y. (1994) Health expenditures for the elderly and reforms in the health care system in Japan", *Health Policy* 29: 197–209.

Kojeve, A. (1969) *Introduction to the Reading of Hegel*, New York: Basic Books.
Kolb, D.A. (1986) *The Critique of Pure Modernity: Hegel, Heidegger and After*, Chicago: The University of Chicago Press.
Kolberg, J.E. (ed.) (1992) *The Study of Welfare State Regimes*, Armonk, NY: M.E. Sharpe.
Komatsu, R. (1992) "The state and social welfare in Japan", in P. Close (ed.) *The State and Caring*, 128–147, London: Macmillan.
Kondo, D. (1990) *Crafting Selves: Power, Gender, and Discourses of Identity in a Japanese Workplace*, Chicago: University of Chicago.
Koschmann, V. (1993) "Intellectual and Politics", in A. Gordon (ed.) *Postwar Japan as History*, Berkeley: University of California Press.
—— (1996) *Revolution and Subjectivity in Postwar Japan*, Chicago: Chicago University Press.
Kothari, R. (1988) The State Against Democracy: In Search of Human Governance. Delhi: Ajanta.
Kotz, D.M. (1990) "A Comparative Analysis of the Theory of Regulation and the Social Structure of Accumulation Theory", *Science and Society* 54 (Spring): 5–28.
Krasner, S.D. (1987) *Asymmetries in Japanese–American Trade: The Case for Specific Reciprocity*. Policy Papers in International Affairs, 32. Berkeley: Institute of International Studies, 1987.
Krause, L.B. (1991) "Japanese capitalism: a model for others?" *International Economic Insights* 2: 6–10.
Kuhn, T.S. (1962) *The Structure of Scientific Revolutions*, Chicago: University of Chicago Press.
Kumar, K. (1993) "Civil society: an inquiry into the usefulness of an historical term", *British Journal of Sociology* 44(3): 375–395.
Kumazawa, M. (1996) *Portraits of the Japanese Workplace: Labor Movements, Workers, and Managers*, trans. A. Gordon and M. Hane, Boulder, Co.
Kurokawa, T. (1989) "Problems of the Japanese Working Class in Historical Perspective", in T. Morris-Suzuki and T. Seiyama (eds) *Japanese Capitalism Since 1945: Critical Perspectives*, 131–165, Armonk, New York: M.E. Sharpe.
Kwon, H.-K. (2005) "National model under globalization: The Japanese model and its internationalization", *Politics and Society* 33(2): 234–252.
Kwon, H.J. (1997) "Beyond European welfare regimes: comparative perspectives on east Asian welfare systems", *Journal of Social Policy* 26 (October): 467–484.
Kyung, L.H. (1982) "Develeopment of Social Welfare Systems in the US and Japan: A Comparative Study", Ph.D. diss., University of California, Berkeley.
The Labour Year Book of Japan (1969) Ohara Institute for Social Research Tokyo, Japan: Hosei University.
—— (1973) Ohara Institute for Social Research, Tokyo: Hosei University.
—— (1988) Ohara Institute for Social Research, Tokyo: Hosei University.
—— (1989) Ohara Institute for Social Research, Tokyo: Hosei University.
Lamb, D. (1987) "Sense and meaning in Hegel and Wittgenstein", in D. Lamb (ed.) *Hegel and Modern Philosophy*, London: Croom Helm.
Lash, S. and J. Friedman (eds) (1992) *Modernity and Identities*, Oxford: Blackwell.
—— and J. Urry (1987) *The End of Organized Capitalism*, Cambridge, London: Polity Press.
Lawrence, T.L. (1985) "Health Care Facilities for the Elderly in Japan", *International Journal of Health Services* 15: 677–696.

Lebra, T.S. (1976) *Japanese Patterns of Behavior*, Honolulu: University of Hawaii Press.

Lee, H.K. (1982) "Development of Social Welfare Systems in the United States and Japan: A Comparative Study", Ph.D. diss., University of California, Berkeley.

—— (1987) "The Japanese Welfare State in Transition", in Robert Friedman, Neil Gilbert, and Moshe Sherer (eds) *Modern Welfare States*, 243–263, New York: New York University Press.

Lee, P. and C. Raban. (1988) *Welfare Theory and Social Policy: Reform or Revolution?* Newbury Park: Sage.

Lee, S.-J. (1989) "The Limits of the Welfare State: Liberalization and Industrial Reorganization of the 1960s", Ph.D. diss., Harvard University.

Leonard, P. (1983) "Marxism, the Individual and the Welfare state", in Philip Bean and Stewart MacPherson (eds) *Approaches to Welfare*, 64–82. London: Routledge & Kegan Paul.

Levin, P.J., J. Wolfson, and H. Akiyama (1987) "The Role of Management in Japanese Hospitals", *Hospital and Health Services Administration* 32 (May): 249–261.

Levin, P.J. and Wolfson, J. (1989) "Health Care in the Balance: Japanese Eurythmy", *Hospital and Health Services Administration* 34 (Fall): 311–323.

Levine, D.P. (1978) *Economic Studies: Contributions to the Critique of Economic Theory*, London, Henley, and Boston: Routledge, Kegan & Paul.

—— (1988) *Needs, Rights, and the Market*, Boulder, C.O.: Lynne Rienner.

—— (1995) *Wealth and Freedom: An Introduction to Political Economy*, Cambridge: Cambridge University Press.

—— (1997) *Self-Seeking and the Pursuit of Justice*, Brookfield VT: Ashgate (Avebury Series).

Levine, D.P. (1998) *Subjectivity in Political Economy: Essays on Wanting and Choosing* (London: Routledge: 1998), pp. 8–30.

Levine, S. (1958) *Industrial Relations in Postwar Japan*, Urbana: University of Illinois Press.

Lewis, P. (1981) "Family, Economy, and Polity: A Case Study of Japan's Public Pension Policy", Ph.D. diss., University of California, Berkeley.

Libby, R. (1988) "Japan's ailing health care system", *Tokyo Business Today*, February, 12.

Lie, J. (1987) "The discriminated fingers: The Korean minority in Japan", *Monthly Review* 8 (January): 17–23.

—— (1987) "Reactionary Marxism: the end of ideology in Japan?" *Monthly Review* 11 (April): 45–51.

Lincoln, E.J. (1984) *Japan's Industrial Policies: What are they, Do they Matter and are they Different from those in the United States?* Washington, DC: Japan Economic Institute of America.

Lindberg, L.N. (1982) "The problems of economic theory in explaining economic performance", *Annals of the American Academy of Political and Social Science*, 459 (January): 14–27.

——, Alfod, R., Crouch, C., and Offe, C. (eds) (1975) *Stress and Contradiction in Modern capitalism: Public Policy and the Theory of the State*, Lexington, MA.: D.C. Heath and Company.

Linhart, S. (1983) "Social security versus family ideology. The State's reaction to the consequences of early industrialization in Japan", *Rivista Internazionale Di Sceinze Economiche e commerciali* 30: 703–715.

Lipietz, A. (1988) "Reflections on a tale: the Marxist foundations of the concepts of regulation and accumulation", *Studies in Political Economy* 26: 7–36.
—— (1989) *Towards a New Economic Order: Post-Fordism, Ecology and Democracy*, Cambridge: Polity Press.
Logue, J. (1979) "The welfare state: victim of its success", in S.R. Graubard (ed.) *The State*, New York: W.W. Norton.
—— (1986) "Can welfare states survive in the global economy?" *Dissent* 33: 351–356.
Lord, A. and Mellor, M. (1996) "Women and the cooperative provision of care: the example of the '*Fukushi* Club' in Japan", *Economic and Industrial Democracy* 17: 199–220.
MacDonald, L. (1994) "Globalising civil society: interpreting international NGOs in central America", *Millennium: Journal of International Studies* 23: 267–285.
MacGregor, D. (1992) *Hegel, Marx and the English State*. Boulder: Westview Press.
MacIntyre, A. (1971) *Against the Self Image of the Age: Essays on Ideology and Philosophy*, New York: Schocken Books.
—— (1990) "Individual and social morality in Japan and the United States: rival conceptions of the self", *Philosophy East and West* 40(4): 489–497.
Maclachlan, P.L. (2002) "Japanese civil society in the age of deregulation: The case of consumers", *Japanese Journal of Political Science* 3(2): 217–242.
Makoto, I. (1999) "Japan's Civil Society", in Yamamaoto, T. (ed.) *Deciding the Public Good: Governance and Civil Society in Japan*, New York: Japan Center for International Exchange.
Malabou, C. (2005) *The Future of Hegel: Plasticity, Temporality and Dialectic*, trans. L. During, London and NY: Routledge.
Maletz, D.J. (1989) "Hegel on right as actualized will", *Political Theory* 17: 33–50.
Margolis, J. (1983) "The nature and strategies of relativism", *Mind* 368: 548–567.
Markovits, A.S. (1990) "Capitalism and its contradictions: a review of two recent works by Claus Offe", *Critical Sociology* 17: 131–136.
Marr, M.D. (1997) "Maintaining autonomy: the plight of the American skid row and Japanese *yoseba*", *Journal of Social Distress and the Homeless* 6: 229–250.
Marshall, T.H. (1950) *Citizenship and Social Class and Other Essays*, Cambridge: Cambridge University Press.
—— (1972) "Value problems of welfare capitalism", *Journal of Social Policy* 1: 15–32.
Maruo, N. (1974) "Measurement of welfare in Japan: a new basis for social planning", in H. Simonis and U.E. Simonis (eds) *Japan: Economic and Social Studies in Development*, Otto Harrassowitz and Wiesbaden: Institute of Asian Affairs in Hamburg.
—— (1979) "The levels of living and welfare in Japan reexamined", *Japanese Economic Studies* 8: 42–93.
—— (1982) "The development of the welfare state in Japan", *The Journal of Economics* 3: 1–25.
—— (1986) "The development of the welfare mix in Japan", in R. Rose and R. Shiratori (eds) *The Welfare State East and West*, New York: Oxford University Press.
—— (1994) "The future of the social security system", *Economic Eye* 15: 9–10.
Maruyama, M. (1982) "Kindai nihon no chishiki-jin" (Modern Japanese Intellectuals), *Toei no ichi kara* (From afar), Tokyo: Miarai-sha.

Marx, K. *Capital*, Volume 1.
—— (1970) *Critique of Hegel's "Philosophy of Right"*, trans. A. Jolin and J. O'Malley and J. O'Malley (ed.), Cambridge: Cambridge University Press.
—— (1976) *Capital: A Critique of Political Economy*, Vol. 1, intro. E. Mandel, trans. B. Fowles, London: Penguin Books.
Masaki, H. (2006) "Japan stares into a demographic abyss", Japanfocus.org.
Mathews, G. (1995) *What Makes Life Worth Living? How Japanese and Americans Make Sense of Their Worlds*, Berkeley: University of California Press.
Matsuura, T. (1981) "The development of the welfare state in Japan", *Giornale Degli Economisti E Annali Di Economia* 40: 3–17.
Mauss, M. (1967) *The Gift: Forms and Functions of Exchange in Archaic Societies*, New York: W.W. Norton.
McBride, S. (1987) "The state and labour markets: towards a comparative political economy of unemployment", *Studies in Political Economy* 23: 141–154.
McVeigh, B. (1998) *The Nature of the Japanese State: Rationality and Rituality*, London: Routledge.
—— (2005) Review of Frank J. Schwartz and Susan J. Pharr (eds) *The State of Civil Society in* Japan, H-US-Japan, H-Net Reviews, March. http://www.h-net.msu.edu/reviews/showrev.cgi?/path+48121119465994.
Melling, J. (1991) "Industrial capitalism and the welfare of the state: the role of employers in the comparative development of welfare states: a review of recent research", *Sociology* 25: 219–239.
Mendl, W. (1989) "Independence and interdependence: Japan in a changing international environment", in "The Advanced Industrial Societies in Disarray: What are the Available Choices?" Special issue of *Annals of the Institute of Social Science* (University of Tokyo): 25–39, 1989.
Mignolo, W.D. (2002) "*The* enduring enchantment: (Or the epistemic privilege of modernity and where to go from here", *The South Atlantic Quarterly* 101(4): 927–954.
Mikanagi, Y. (1997) "Japan's Gender-Biased Social Security Policy", Paper presented at the 38th Annual Convention, International Studies Association, Toronto, Canada, March 18–22.
Miliband, R., Panitch, L., and Saville, J. (eds) (1990) *The Socialist Register*, London: Merlin Press.
—— and Saville, J. (eds) (1978) *The Socialist Register 1978*, London: The Merlin Press.
Miller, R.F. (ed.) (1992) *The Development of Civil Society in Communist Systems, Sydney*, Sydney, Australia: Allen and Unwin.
Miller, R.W. (1978) "Methodological individualism and social explanation", *Philosophy of Science* 45: 387–414.
Milly, D.J. (1999) *Poverty, Equality, and Growth: The Politics of Economic Need in Postwar Japan*, Cambridge, Mass.: Harvard University Asia Center.
Mainichi News (1994) "Welfare Guidelines Deprived Woman 79 of Air Conditioner", September 7.
Ministry of Health and Welfare (1998–1999) *Annual Report on Health and Welfare*.
—— (2000) *Hoiku saabisu no jikyu – tokki no jokyo* (April 1).
Ministry of Health, Labour, and Welfare, 2001.
Ministry of Internal Affairs and Communications, Statistics Bureau *Jutaku tochi tokei chosa – Heisei 10-nen*.

Mishra, R. (1977) *Society and Social Policy: Theoretical Perspectives on Welfare*, Atlantic Highlands, NJ: Humanities Press.

—— (1990) *The Welfare State in Capitalist Society: Policies of Retrenchment and Maintenance in Europe, North America and Australia*, New York: Harvester Wheatsheaf.

Miyajima, H. (1994) "Japan's aging society", *Japanese Economic Studies* 21: 3–23.

Miyamoto, T. (2003) "Dynamics of the Japanese welfare state in comparative perspective: Between 'three worlds' and the developmental state", *The Japanese Journal of Social Policy* 2(2): 12–24.

Miyanaga, K. (1991) *The Creative Edge: Emerging Individualism in Japan*, New Brunswick, NJ: Transaction Publishers.

Miyazawa, K. (1975) "Income redistribution: prescription for a welfare society", *The Japan Interpreter* 9: 257–275.

Miyoshi, M. (1991) *Off Center: Power and Culture Relations Between Japan and the United States*, Cambridge, Mass.: Harvard University Press.

—— and Harootunian, H. (eds) (1993) *Japan in the World*, Durham: Duke University Press.

Mizoguchi, T. (1968) "On the high personal saving ratio in Japan", *Hitotsubashi Journal of Economics* 8: 59–70.

Moore, J. (1983) *Japanese Workers and the Struggle for Power 1945–47* Madison: University of Wisconsin.

Morioza, K. (1989) "Japan", in T. Bottomore and T. Bryn (eds) *The Capitalist Class: An International Study*, New York: Harvester Wheatsheaf.

Morishima, M. (1995) "Union loyalty among white-collar workers in Japan", *Journal of Organization Behavior* 16: 611.

Morita, A. (1993) "Shin jiyu keizai e no teigen (Suggestions for a new free economy)", *Bungeishunju*, Februrary 71(2): 94–109.

Morris, R. (1988) (ed.) *Testing the Limits of Social Welfare: International Perspectives on Policy Changes in Nine Countries*, Hanover: Brandeis University Press.

Morris-Suzuki, T. and Seiyama, T. (eds) (1989) *Japanese Capitalism Since 1945: Critical Perspectives*, Armonk, New York: M.E. Sharpe.

Mosher, M. (1998) "Machiavellian politics and Japanese ideals: the Enigma of Japanese Power eight years later", *JPRI occasional* Paper#10, Japan Policy Research Institute http://www.jpri.org/publications/occasionalpapers/op10.html.

Mouer, R. and Sugimoto, Y. (1986) *Images of Japanese Society: A Study in the Social Construction of Reality*, London: KPI.

Mulholland, L.A. (1989) "Hegel and Marx on the human individual", in W. Desmond (ed.) *Hegel and his Critics: Philosophy in the Aftermath of Hegel*, Albany, NY: State University of New York Press.

Murakami, K. (1981) *Retirement Benefits and Pension Plans in Japan*, Socio-Economic Institute, Bulletin No. 79, Tokyo: Sophia University.

Murray, C. (1986) *Losing Ground: American Social Policy 1950–1980*, New York: Basic Books.

—— (1988) *In Pursuit of Happiness and Good Government*, New York: Simon and Schuster.

Myles, J. and Quadagno, J. (1988) "Decline or impasse? The current state of the welfare state", *Studies in Political Economy* 26: 73–107.

—— (1991) *States, Labor Markets, and the Future of Old-Age Policy*, Philadelphia: Temple University Press.

Myrdal, G. (1958) *Beyond the Welfare State: Economic Planning and its International Implications*, London: University Paperbacks.
Najita, T. (1993) "Japan's industrial revolution in historical perspective", in M. Miyoshi and H.D. Harootunian (eds) *Japan in the World*, Durham and London: Duke University Press.
Nakagawa, Y. (1979) "Japan, the welfare super-power", *Journal of Japanese Studies* 5: 5–51.
Nakane, C. (1970) *Japanese Society*, Berekely: University of California Press.
Nakano, O. (1988) "The surrogate family", *Japan Echo* 15: 48–52.
Nandy, A. (1983) *The Intimate Enemy: Loss and Recovery of Self Under Colonialism*, Delhi: Oxford, 1983. Oxford: Oxford, 1988.
Nandy (1980) "The political culture of the Indian State" *Daedalus* 118(4): 1–26.
Navarro, V. (1991) "Production and the welfare state: the political context of reforms", *International Journal of Health Services* 21: 585–614.
—— (1998) "Neoliberalism, 'Globalization,' unemployment, inequalities, and the welfare state", *International Journal of Health Services* 28: 608–682.
Neary, I. (2006) "State and civil society in Japan", *Asian Affairs* 34(1).
Neocleous, M. (1995) "From civil society to the social", *The British Journal of Sociology* 46(3): 395–408.
New Statesman and Society, January 21, 1994.
Newton, T. (1998) "Theorizing subjectivity in organizations: the failure of Foucauldian Studies?" *Organization Studies* 19: 415–447.
Nishida, Y. (1990) "Reassessment of welfare services and the trend of welfare policy for the disabled", *Annals of the Institute of Social Sciences* 32: 115–154.
Niwa, U. (2006) "The 'Second Plateau': Japan's Economy and Structures of Inequality", in JapanFocus.org accessed 12/29/2006.
Niwata, N. (1986) *The Theory of Insurance and Social Security in Japan*, Tokyo: The Insurance Institute of Keio University.
Nock, Christopher J. (1988) "The Welfare State: An Affront to Freedom?" *Canadian Journal of Political Science* 21(4): 757–769.
Noguchi, Y. (1983) "Problems of public pensions in Japan", *Hitotsubashi Journal of Economics* 21: 43–68.
—— (1986) "Overcommitment in pensions: the Japanese experience", in R. Rose and R. Shiratori (eds) *The Welfare State East and West*, New York: Oxford University Press.
Norbeck, E. and Lock, M. (eds) (1987) *Health, Illness, and Medical Care in Japan*. Honolulu: University of Hawaii Press.
O'Connor, J. (1973) *The Fiscal Crisis of the State*, New York: St. Martin's Press.
—— (1987) *The Meaning of Crisis*, New York: Basil Blackwell.
—— and Robert, B. (1981) "The meaning of crisis", *International Journal of Urban and Regional Research* 5: 301–329.
—— (1988) "Public welfare expenditure in OECD countries: towards a reconciliation of inconsistent findings", *British Journal of Sociology* 37: 47–68.
O'Malley, P. and Palmer, D. (1996) "Post-Keynesian policing", *Economy and Society* 25: 137–155.
OECD Economic Surveys Japan (2005) OECD Publishing.
Offe, C. (1972) "Advanced capitalism and the welfare state", *Politics and Society* 2: 479–488.
—— (1972) "Political authority and class structures: an analysis of late capitalist societies", *International Journal of Sociology* 2: 73–108.

—— (1973) "The abolition of market control and the problem of legitimacy (I) & (II)", *Kapitalistate* 1: 109–116; 2: 73–75.

—— (1974) "Structural problems of the capitalist state: class rule and the political system: on the selectiveness of political institutions", in L.V. Beyme (ed.) *German Political Studies*, Vol. 1, Beverly Hills: Sage.

—— (1975) "The theory of the capitalist state and the problem of policy formation", in L. Lindberg (ed) *Stress and Contradiction in Modern Capitalism*, Lexington, Mass.: D.C. Heath.

—— (1976) *Industry and Inequality: The Achievement Principle in Work and Social Status*, trans. by J. Wickam. London: Edward Arnold.

—— (1983) "Political legitimation through majority rule", *Social Research* 50: 709–756.

—— (1984) *Contradictions of the Welfare State*, Cambridge, Mass.: M.I.T. Press.

—— (1985a) *Disorganized Capitalism: Contemporary Transformations of Work and Politics*, John Keane (ed.) Cambridge: MIT Press, 1985.

—— (1985b) "New social movements: challenging the boundaries of institutional politics", *Social Research* 52: 817–868.

—— (1987) "Challenging the boundaries of institutional politics: social movements since the 1960's ", in C.S. Maier (ed.) *Changing Boundaries of the Political*, Cambridge: Cambridge University Press.

—— (1996) *Modernity and the State: East, West*, London: Polity Press.

—— (1997) "The utopia of the zero-option: modernity and modernization as normative political criteria", *Praxis International* 7: 1–24.

Offe, C. and Heinze, R.G. (1992) *Beyond Employment*, trans. A. Braley, Philadelphia: Polity Press.

—— and Wiesenthal, H. (1980) "Two logics of collective action: theoretical notes on social class and organisational form", *Political Power and Social Theory* 1: 67–115.

Ogawa, A. (2004) "The Failure of Civil Society? An Ethnography of NPOs and the State in Contemporary Japan", Ph.D. diss., Cornell University.

Ogawa, N. and Retherford, R.D. (1997) "Shifting Costs of Caring for the Elderly back to Families in Japan: Will It Work?" *Population and Development Review* 23: 59–94.

Ohmae, K. (1989) *Heisiei Ishin*, Tokyo: Kodansha.

—— (1990) *Heisei Ishin* (*Heisei* Restoration), Tokyo: Kodansha.

Ohnuki-Tierney (1987) *The Monkey as Mirror: Symbolic Transformations in Japanese History and Ritual*, Princeton: Princeton University Press.

Oishi, K. (1971) "The differentiation of the peasantry and peasants' movements in the process of integration of feudal and seigneurial land property in Japan", *Annals of the Institute of Social Science*.

Okachi, K. (1973) *Workers and Employers in Japan*, Tokyo: University of Tokyo Press.

Okamoto, Y. (1992) "Health care for the elderly in Japan: medicine and welfare in an aging society facing a crisis in long term care", *British Medical Journal*.

Okimoto, D. (1989) *Between MITI and the Market: Japanese Industrial Policy for High Technology*, Stanford: Stanford University Press.

Okumura, H. (1992) "Corporate capitalism: cracks in the system", *Japan Quarterly*, March: 54–61.

Ollman, B. (1986) "The meaning of dialectics", *Monthly Review* 38: 42–55.

—— (2001) "Why does the emperor need the *Yakuza*? Prolegomenon to a Marxist theory of the Japanese state", *New Left Review* 8: 73–98.
Olson, M. (1968) "Economics, sociology, and the best of all possible worlds", *Public Interest* 12: 96–118.
Olsson, S.E. (1990) *Social Policy and Welfare State in Sweden*, Lund, Sweden: Arkiv.
Onis, Z. (1991) "The logic of the developmental state", *Comparative Politics* 24: 109–126.
Ono, H. (2005) "Whither Japan's lifetime employment system?" Japanfocus.org.
Osawa, M. (1995) "Nihongata fukushi kokka" in Totsuka, H. and Tokunaga, S. (eds) gendai Nihon no Rodo Mondai, Tokyo: Minerva Shobo
Ostrom, D. (1997) "Prospects for economic reform in Japan: where is the safety net?" *JEI Report* 37A.
—— (1999) "Unemployment in Japan: How serious is the problem", *JEI Report* 2A (January 15).
Outline of Social Insurance in Japan, 1990, Social Insurance Agency, Japanese Government. Tokyo, March 1991.
Oyen, E. (ed.) (1986) *Comparing Welfare States and their Futures*, Aldershot, England: Gower.
Ozawa, I. (1994) *Blueprint for a New Japan: the Rethinking of a Nation*, Tokyo: Kodansha International.
Ozawa, M. (1985) "Social security reform in Japan", *Social Service Review* 59: 476–495.
—— (1991) "Child welfare programs in Japan", *Social Service Review* 65: 1–21.
Ozawa, T. (1980) "Japanese world of work: an interpretive survey", *MSU Business Topics* 28: 45–55.
Palme, J. (1990) "Models of old-age pensions", in A. Ware and R.E. Goodin (eds) *Needs and Welfare*, London: Sage.
Palley, H.A., and Usui, C. (1995) "Social policies for the elderly in the republic of Korea and Japan: a comparative perspective", *Social Policy and Administration* 29: 241–257.
Pampel, F.C. (1987) "Capitalist restructuring and labor strategies", *Studies in Political Economy* 24: 131–149.
—— and Williamson, J.B. (1989) *Age, Class, Politics and the Welfare State*, Cambridge: Cambridge University Press.
——, Williamson, J.B., and Stryker, R. (1990) "Class context and pension response to demographic structure in advanced industrial democracies", *Social Problems* 37: 535–547.
Pateman, C. (1988) *The Sexual Contract*, Stanford: Stanford University Press.
Patey, D.L. (1992) "Hegel on causality: toward an understanding of the absolute relation", *Idealistic Studies* 22: 179–188.
Patrick, H. (ed.) (1976) *Japanese Industrialization and it's Social Consequences*, Berkeley: University of California Press.
Patterson, D.M. (1989) "Hegel and postmodernity", *Cardozo Law Review* 10: 1665–1672.
Pekkanen, R. (2004) "Japan: Social capital without advocacy", in M. Alagappa (ed.) *Civil Society and Political Change in Asia: Expanding and Contracting the Democratic Sphere*, Stanford: Stanford University Press.
—— (2006) *Japan's Dual Civil Society: Members Without Advocates*, Stanford: Stanford University Press.

Pelczynski, Z.A. (ed.) (1984) *The State and Civil Society: Studies in Hegel's Political Philosophy*, Cambridge: Cambridge University Press.

Pempel, T.J. (1989) "Japan's creative conservatism: continuity under change", in F.G. Castles (ed.) *The Comparative History of Public Policy*, New York: Oxford University Press.

—— (ed.) (1990) *Uncommon Democracies: The One-Party Dominant Regimes*, Ithaca: Cornell University Press.

Peng, I. (1995) "*Boshi Katei*: A theoretical and Case Analysis of Japanese Lone Mothers and their Relationships to the State, the Labour Market, and the Family, with Reference to Britain and Canada", Ph.D. diss., London School of Economics.

—— (2002) "Social care in crisis: gender, demography, and welfare states restructuring in Japan", *Social Policy* 411–443.

Pharr, S. (1990) *Losing Face: Status Politics in Japan*, Berkeley: University of California Press.

Pharr, S. (2003) "Conclusion: Targeting by an Activist State: Japan as a Civil Society Model", in *The State of Civil Society in Japan* Edited by Frank J Schwartz and Susan J Pharr Cambridge University Press, Cambridge 2003, pp.316–336.

Pierson, C. (1984) "New theories of state and civil society: recent developments in post-Marxist analysis of the state", *Sociology* 18: 563–571.

—— (1990) *Beyond the Welfare State?* University Park, Pennsylvania: Pennsylvania State University Press.

Pierson, P. (1994) *Dismantling the Welfare State?: Reagan, Thatcher, & the Politics of Retrenchment*, Cambridge: Cambridge University Press.

Pinker, R. (1979) *The Idea of Welfare*, London: Educational Books.

—— (1986) "Social welfare in Japan and Britain: a comparative view", in E. Oyen (ed.) *Comparing Welfare States and their Futures*, Aldershot, England: Gower.

Piore, M.J. (1987) "Historical perspectives and the interpretation of unemployment", *Journal of Economic Literature* 25: 1834–1850.

Piper, A. (1980) "Property and the limits of the self", *Political Theory* 8: 39–64.

Piven, F.F. and Cloward, R.A. (1983) *Regulating the Poor: The Functions of Public Welfare*, undated ed., New York: Vintage.

Plant, R. (1977) "Hegel and political economy", *New Left Review* 103: 79–92; 104: 103–113.

—— (1982) "Jurgen Habermas and the idea of legitimation crisis", *European Journal of Political Research* 10: 341–352.

—— (1983) *Hegel: An Introduction* 2nd ed., Oxford: Basil Blackwell.

—— (1984) "Hegel on identity and legitimation", in Z.A. Pelczynski (ed.) *The State and Civil Society: Studies in Hegel's Political Philosophy*, Cambridge: Cambridge University Press.

——, Lesser, H., and Taylor-Gooby, P. (1980) *Political Philosophy and Social Welfare: Essays on the Normative Basis of Welfare Provision*, London: Routledge & Kegan Paul.

Plath, D. (1980), *Long Engagements: Maturity in Modern Japan*, Stanford: Stanford University Press.

Plath, D.W. (ed.) (1983) *Work and Lifecourse in Japan*, Albany, NY: State University of New York Press.

Polanyi, K. (1957) *The Great Transformation: The Political and Economic Origins of our Time*, Boston: Beacon Press.

Poulantzas, N. (1975) *Classes in Contemporary Capitalism*, London: New Left Books.
—— (1978) *Political Power and Social Classes*, London: New Left Books.
—— (1978) *State, Power, Socialism*, London: New Left Books.
Powell, M. and M. Anesaki. (1990) *Health Care in Japan*, London: Routledge.
Prychitko, D.L. (1990) "The welfare state: what is left?" *Critical Review* 4: 619–632.
Przeworski, A. (1985) "Marxism and rational-choice", *Politics and Society* 14: 379–409.
—— and Wallerstein, M. (1988) "Structural dependence of the state on capital", *American Political Science Review* 22: 11–29.
Putman, R.D. (1993) *Making Democracy Work. Civic Traditions in modern Italy*, Princeton, NJ: Princeton University Press.
Putman, R.D. (2000) Bowling Alone. The collapse and revival of American community, New York: Simon and Schuster.
Quadagno, J.S. (1984) "Welfare capitalism and the social security act of 1935", *American Sociological Review* 49: 632–647.
—— (1987) "Theories of the welfare state", *Annual American Review of Sociology* 13: 109–128.
Rajagopal, B. (2003) *International Law from below: Development, Social Movements and Third World Resistance*, Cambridge: Cambridge University Press.
Reader, I. "Studies of Japan, area studies, and the challenges of social theory", *Monumenta Nipponica* 53(2): 237–255.
Reed, A. Jr (1992) "The underclass as myth and symbol: the poverty of discourses about poverty", *Radical America* (January): 21–38.
Rein, M., Esping-Andersen, G., and Rainwater, L. (1987) *Stagnation and Renewal in Social Policy: The Rise and Fall of Policy Regimes,*. Armonk, New York: M.E. Sharpe.
—— and Rainwater, L. (1987) "From welfare state to welfare society", in M. Rein, G. Esping-Andersen, and L. Rainwater (eds) *Stagnation and Renewal in Social Policy: The Rise and Fall of Policy Regimes*, Armonk, New York: M.E. Sharpe.
Reischauer, E. (1988) *The Japanese Today*, Cambridge: Harvard University Press.
Riedmuller, B. (1977) "Crisis as crisis of legitimation: a critique of J. Habermas's concept of a political crisis theory", *International Journal of Politics* 7: 83–117.
Rieger, E. and Liebfried, S. (1998) "Welfare state limits to globalization", *Politics and Society* 26: 363–390.
Riley, P. (1982) *Will and Political Legitimacy: A Critical Exposition of Social Contract Theory in Hobbes, Locke, Rousseau, Kant, and Hegel*. Cambridge, MA: Harvard University Press.
Rix, A. (1985) "Marxism in Japan: Theory Versus Tradition", in Mackerras, C. and Knight, N. (eds) *Marxism in Asia*, 176–201, London: Croom Helm.
—— (ed.) (1986) *Public/Private Interplay in Social Protection: A Comparative Study*, Armonk, New York: M.E. Sharpe.
Roberts, G.S. (1996) "Between policy and practice: Japan's silver human resource centers as viewed from the inside", *Journal of Aging and Social Policy* 8: 115–132.
—— (2002) "Pinning hopes on angels: reflections from an aging Japan's urban landscape", in *Family and Social Policy in Japan: Anthropological Approaches 54-91*. ed. Roger Goodman Cambridge: Cambridge University Press.
Rohlen, T.P. (1974) *For Harmony and Strength: Japanese White Collar Organizations in Anthropological Perspective*, Berkeley, CA: University of California Press.
Rohrlich, G.F. and Metterst, M. (1951) "Japanese Social Insurance System Through 3 June 1950", Report by General Headquarters, Supreme Commander For

the Allied Powers, Public Health and Welfare Section, Programs and Statistics Division, Tokyo.
Rosa, J.-J., (ed.) (1982) *The World Crisis in Social Security*, San Francisco: Institute for Contemporary Studies.
Rose, G. (1981) *Hegel Contra Sociology*, London: The Athlone Press.
Rose, N. (1996) "The Death of the Social? Re-figuring the Territory of Government", *Economy and Society* 25 (August): 327–356.
Rose, R., and R. Shiratori. (ed.) (1986) *The Welfare State East and West*, New York: Oxford University Press.
Rosen, S. (1988) "The Economy and the Welfare State", *Social Policy* 19 (Fall): 56–61.
Rosenberger, N.R. (ed.) (1994) *Japanese Sense of Self*, Cambridge: Cambridge University Press.
—— (2001) *Gambling with Virtue: Japanese Women and Sense of Self in a Changing Nation*, Honolulu, HI: University of Hawaii Press.
Roseneau, P.M. (1992) *Post-Modernism and the Social Sciences: Insights, Inroads and Intrusions*, Princeton: Princeton University Press.
Rozman, G. (1973) *Urban Networks in Ch'ing China and Tokugawa Japan*, Princeton: Princeton University Press.
Ryan, A. (1987) *Property*, Minneapolis: University of Minnesota Press.
Said, E. (1978) *Orientalism*, New York: Pantheon Books.
Sakakibara, E. (1995) "Towards alternative models of capitalism", *Internationale Politik und Gesellschaft* 4: 394–398.
Sakuma, T. (2006) "Japanese officials try to woo civil society reps", http://www.focusweb.org/publications/1999/.
Samuels, R. (1987) *The Business of the Japanese State: Energy Markets in Comparative and Historical Perspective*, Ithaca: Cornell University Press, 1987.
Sato, Y. (1968) [1991] *"Zaiseiteki sokumen kara mita sekatsu hogo kijun hikiage no shomondai"* quoted in Y. Soeda (1990) "The development of the public assistance system in Japan 1966–73", in "Japanese 'welfare state' today", *Annals of the Institute of Social Science* 32. Tokyo: Institute of Social Science, University of Tokyo.
Sayer, D. (1975) "Method and Dogma in Historical Materialism", *Sociological Review* 23 (November): 779–810.
Scase, R. (1977) *Social Democracy in Capitalist Society: Working Class Politics in Britain and Sweden*, London: Croom Helm, 1977.
—— (ed.) (1980) *The States in Western Europe*, New York: St. Martin's Press.
Schaede, U. (2000) *Cooperative Capitalism: Self-Regulation, Trade Associations, and Antimonopoly Law in Japan*, Oxford: Oxford University Press.
Schaff, A. (1970) *Marxism and the Human Individual*, New York: McGraw-Hill.
Schmitter, P.C. (1988) "Five reflections on the future of the welfare state", *Politics and Society* 16 (December): 503–515.
Scholz, S.J. (1993) "Reproductive labor: the impact of the patriarchal family on Hegel's Phenomenology", *Clio* 22 (Summer): 357–368.
Schoppa, L.K. (2006) *Race for the Exits: The Unraveling of Japan's System of Social Protection*, Ithaca: Cornell University Press.
Schram, S. (1991) "Welfare spending and poverty: cutting back produces more poverty, not less", *American Journal of Sociology* 2 (April): 129–141.
—— (1995) *Words of Welfare: The Poverty of Social Science and the Social Science of Poverty*, Minneapolis: University of Minnesota Press.

—— (2002) *Praxis for the Poor: Piven and Cloward and the Future of Social Science in Social Welfare*, New York and London: New York University Press.
Schwartz, F. (2002) "Civil society in Japan reconsidered", *Japanese Journal of Political Science* 3(2): 195–215.
—— and Pharr, S. (eds) (2003) *The State of Civil Society in Japan*, Cambridge, UK and New York: Cambridge University Press.
Seeleib-Kaiser, M. (1995) "The development of social assistance and unemployment insurance in Germany and Japan", *Social Policy and Administration* (29): 269–293.
Seligman, A. (1992) *The Idea of Civil Society*, Princeton: Princeton University Press.
Sen, A.K. (1985) *Commodities and Capabilities*, Amsterdam: North-Holland.
Shaikh, A. (2005) "The economic mythology of neoliberalism", in A. Saad-Filho and D. Johnston (eds) *Neoliberalism: A Critical Reader*, London: Pluto Press.
Shapiro, S. (1990) *Between Capitalism and Democracy: Educational Policy and the Crisis of the Welfare State*, New York: Bergin & Garvey.
Sheingate, A.D. and Yamagishi, T. (2006) "Occupation politics: American interests and the struggle over health insurance in postwar Japan", *Social Science History* 30(1): 137–164.
Sherover, E. (1979) "The Virtue of Poverty: Marx's Transformation of Hegel's Concept of the Poor", *Canadian Journal of Political and Social Theory* 3 (Winter): 53–66.
Shibagaki, K. (1973) "The Logic of Japanese Imperialism", *Annals of the Institute of Social Science* 14: 70–87.
—— (1988) "Studies in Japanese capitalism: a survey with emphasis on the contributions of the Marx-Uno school", *Annals of the Institute of Social Science* 30: 29–56.
Shimazu, N. (ed.) (2006) *Nationalisms in Japan*, London: Routledge.
Shindo, M. (1994) "The history of local government", in Hitoshi A. (ed.) trans. J.W. White *The Government and Politics of Japan*, 55–62, Tokyo: University of Tokyo Press.
Shinkawa, T. (1990) "The Political Economy of Social Welfare in Japan", Ph.D. diss., University of Toronto.
Shipper, A.S. (2002) "The political construction of foreign workers in Japan", *Critical Asian Studies* 34(1): 41–68.
Shiratori, R. (1985) "The experience of the welfare state in Japan and it's problems", in S.N. Eisenstadt and O. Ahimeir (eds) *The Welfare State and it's Aftermath*, London: Croom Helm.
Shweder, R.A. and Bourne, E.J. (1984) "Does the concept of the person vary cross-culturally?" in R.A. Shweder and R.A. Levine (eds) *Culture Theory: Essays on Mind, Self, and Emotion*, Cambridge: Cambridge University Press.
Silberman, B.S. (1993) *Cages of Reason: The Rise of the Rational State in France, Japan, the United States, and Great Britain*, Chicago: The University of Chicago Press.
Silverberg, M. (1993) "Constructing Japanese cultural history", in M. Miyoshi and H.D. Harootunian (eds) *Japan in the World*, Durham and London: Duke University Press.
Simonis, H. and Simonis, U.E. (eds) (1974) *Japan: Economic and Social Studies in Development*,Otto Harrassowitz, Wiesbaden: Institute of Asian Affairs in Hamburg.

Skocpol, T. (1980) "Political response to capitalist crisis: neo-Marxist theories of the state and the case of the new deal", *Politics and Society* 10: 155–201.
Skocpol, T. and Amenta, E. (1986) "States and social policies", *Annual Review of Sociology* 12: 131–157.
—— and Finegold, K. (1982) "State capacity and economic intervention in the early New Deal", *Political Science Quarterly* 97: 255–278.
Skocpol, T. and Fiorina, M.P. (eds) (1999) *Civic Engagement in American Democracy*, Washington, DC: Brookings Institution Press.
Smith, K. (2002) "The Showa hall: memorializing Japan's War at home", *The Public Historian* 24(4): 35–64.
Smith, R. (1983) *Japanese Society: Tradition, Self, and the Social Order*, Cambridge, New York: Cambridge University Press.
Smith, S.B. (1987) "Hegel's idea of a critical theory", *Political Theory* 15: 99–126.
—— (1989) "What is right in Hegel's *Philosophy of Right?" American Political Science Review* 83: 3–18.
Social Services in Japan (1958) Japanese Joint Organizing Committee, Ninth International Conference of Social Work.
Soeda, Y. (1990) "The development of the public assistance system in Japan, 1966–1983", *Annals of the Tokyo Institute of Social Science* 32: 31–66.
—— (1991) 'The Development of Public assistance system in Japan, 1966–73". In "Japanese 'Welfare State' Today", *Annals of the Institute of Social Science* 32 (1990): 31–65, Tokyo: Institute of Social Science, University of Tokyo.
(1995) *Seikatsu hogo seido no shakaishi*, Tokyo. Tokyo daigaku shuppankai (A Social History of Public Assistance in Japan, Tokyo: University of Tokyo Press).
Sonoda, K. (1988) *Health and Illness in Changing Japanese Society*, Tokyo: University of Tokyo Press.
Soper, K. (1995) *What is Nature?: Culture, Politics and the Non-Human*, Cambridge, Massachusetts: Blackwell.
Sorensen, A. (2001) "Urban planning and civil society in Japan: Japanese urban planning development during the 'Taisho democracy' period (1905–31)", *Planning Perspectives* 16(4): 383–406.
Spivey, W.A. (1985) "Problems and paradoxes in economic and social policies of modern welfare states", *The Annals of the American Academy of Politics and Social Science* 479: 14–30.
Stace, W.T. (1955) *The Philosophy of Hegel: A Systematic Exposition*, Toronto: Dover Publications, Inc.
Statistics Bureau of the Management and Coordination Agency *Kakei chosa nenpo* (Family Income and Expenditure Survey –FIES).
Steinberger, P.J. (1977) "Hegel as a social scientist", *American Political Science Review* 71: 95–110.
Steslicke, W.E. (1989) "Japan", in J.P. DeSario (ed.) *International Public Policy Sourcebook. Vol. 1, Health and Social Welfare*, New York: Greenwood Press.
Steven, R. (1983) *Classes in Contemporary Japan*, London: Cambridge University Press.
—— (1988) "The high yen crisis in Japan", *Capital and Class* 34: 76–149.
Stevens, C.S. (1997) *On the Margins of Japanese Society: Volunteers and the Welfare of the Urban Underclass*, London: Routledge.
Stillman, P.G. (1980) "Hegel's civil society: a locus of freedom", *Polity* 12(4): 622–646.

—— (ed.) (1987) *Hegel's Philosophy of Spirit*, Albany, NY: State University of New York Press.

Stryker, R. (1990) "Science, class, and the welfare state: a class-centered functional account", *American Journal of Sociology* 96: 684–726.

Sumiya, T. (1989) "The structure and operation of monopoly capital in Japan", in T.M. Suzuki and T. Seiyama (eds) *Japanese Capitalism Since 1945: Critical Perspectives*, Armonk, New York: M.E. Sharpe.

Suzuki, K. (1995) "Women rebuff the call for more babies", *Japan Quarterly* 42(1).

Suzuki, T.M. and Seiyama, T. (eds) (1989) *Japanese Capitalism Since 1945: Critical Perspectives*, Armonk, New York: M.E. Sharpe.

Sweezy, P.M. (1980) "Japan in perspective", *Monthly Review* 31: 1–14.

—— (1981) *Four Lectures on Marxism*, New York: Monthly Review Press.

—— (1987) "Some problems in the theory of capital accumulation", *International Journal of Political Economy* 17: 38–53.

Tabata, H. (1990) "The Japanese welfare state: it's structure and transformation", *Annals of the Institute of Social Science* 32: 1–30.

Tachibanaki, T. (2005) *Confronting Income Inequality in Japan*, Cambridge, Mass: MIT Press.

Taira, K. (1967) "Public assistance in Japan: development and trends", *Journal of Asian Studies* 27(1): 95–109.

—— (1968) "Ragpickers and community development: 'Ants' Villa' in Tokyo", *Industrial and Labor Relations* 22(1): 3–19.

—— (1983) "Japan's low unemployment: economic miracle or statistical artifact", *Monthly Labor Review* (July): 3–10.

Takahashi, M. (1997) *The Emergence of Welfare Society in Japan*, Aldershot, UK: Avebury.

—— (2004) "Beyond crisis and dissonance- the restructuring of the Japanese welfare state under globalisation", *Social Policy and Society* 3(3): 283–290.

—— and Hashimoto, R. (1997) "*Minsei-in* between public and private: a local network for community care in Japan", *International Social Work* 40.

Takahashi, T. (2003) "The emperor Showa standing at ground zero: on the (re-) configuration of a national 'memory' of the Japanese people", *Japan Forum* 15(1): 3–14.

—— (2006) "The national politics of the *Yasukuni* shrine", trans. by P. Seaton in N. Shimazu (ed.) *Nationalisms in Japan*, London: Routledge.

Takayama, No. (1982) "Japan", in J.J. Rosa (ed.) *The World Crisis in Social Security*, San Francisco: Institute for Contemporary Studies.

Tamai, K. (2003) "Development of Social Policy in Japan," in M. Izuhara (ed.) *Comparing Social Policies: Exploring New Perspectives in Britian and Japan*. Bristol: Policy Press.

Tamamoto, M. (1994) "The ideology of nothingness: a mediation on Japanese national identity", *World Policy Journal* 11(4): 89–99.

—— (1995) "Reflections on Japan's postwar state", *Daedalus* 124(2): 1–23.

—— (2001) "A land without patriots: the Yasukuni controversy and Japanese nationalism", *World Policy Journal* 18(3): 33–40.

Tanaka, F.J. (1982) "Lifetime employment in Japan", *Challenge* 24 (July–August): 23–29.

Tanner, M.D. (2003) *The Poverty of Welfare: Helping Others in Civil society*, Washington, DC: Cato Institute.

Tansman, A. (2003) "Japanese studies: the intangible act of translation", *UCIAS Vol.3*, University of California International and Area Studies Digital Collection http://repositories.cdlib.org/uciaspubs/editedvolumes/3/5.

Taylor, C. (1975) *Hegel*, Cambridge: Cambridge University Press.

—— (1979) *Hegel and Modern Society*, Cambridge: Cambridge University Press.

—— (1985) *Human Agency and Language: Philosophical Papers I*, Cambridge: Cambridge University Press.

—— (1985) "The person", in M. Carrithers, S. Collins, and S. Lukes (eds) *The Category of the Person: Anthropology, Philosophy, History*, Cambridge: Cambridge University Press.

—— (1990) "Modes of civil society", *Public Culture* 3(1): 95–118.

Therborn, G. (1980) *What Does the Ruling Class do When it Rules?* London: Verso.

—— (1986) "Neo-Marxist, Pluralist, Corporatist, Statist Theories and the Welfare state", in Ali Kazancigil (ed.) *The State in Global Perspective*, 204–231. Brookfield, VT: Gower.

Therborn, G. and Roebroek, J. (1986) "The irreversible welfare state: its recent maturation, its encounter with the economic crisis, and its future prospects", *International Journal of Health Services* 16: 319–338.

Thomas, J.A. (2001) *Reconfiguring Modernity: Concepts of Nature in Japanese Political Ideology*, Berkeley and Los Angeles: University of California Press.

Tierney, M.J. and Tierney, L.M. (1994) "Nursing in Japan" *Nursing Outlook* 42.

Titmuss, R.M. (1976) *Essays on "The Welfare State"* 3rd edn, introd. B. Abel-Smith, London: Allen & Unwin.

Tobin, J. (ed.) (1992) *Remade in Japan: Everyday Life and Consumer Taste in a Changing Society*, New Haven: Yale University Press.

Trimberger, E.K. (1977) "State power and modes of production: implications of the Japanese transition to capitalism", *Insurgent Sociologist* 7: 85–98.

Tsujinaka, Y. (1998) "A Comparative Analysis of Korean and Japanese Interest Associations: Korean Civil Society and its Political Regime since 1987." *Leviathan* 24: 19–50.

—— (ed.) (2002) Gendai Nihon no Shimin Shakai–Rieki Dantai (Civil Society in Modern Japan: Interest Groups). Tokyo: Bokutaskusha.

—— (2003) "Japan's civil society organizations in comparative perspective", in F.J. Shwartz and S.J. Pharr (eds) *The State of Civil Society in Japan*, Cambridge, UK and New York: Cambridge University Press.

Tsumaki, S. (2004) "Preference for Homelessness Categorized as 'Refuse of a Decent Civic Life': A Critical Perspective", Paper presented at the Eighth Asian Studies Conference Japan, Sophia University, June 19.

Ueno, C. (2005) "In the feminine guise; A trap of reverse orientalism", in R. Calichman (ed.) *Contemporary Japanese Thought*, New York: Comumbia University Press.

Ujihara, S. (1981) "Employment and income of elderly workers in Japan", *Annals of the Institute of Social Sciences* 22: 94–123.

Urry, J. (1981) *The Anatomy of Capitalist Societies: The Economy, Civil Society and the State*, London: Macmillan Press.

—— (1982) "Some themes in the analysis of the anatomy of contemporary capitalist societies", *Acta Sociologica* 25: 405–418.

Valocchi, S. (1991) "The class basis of the state and the origins of welfare policy in Britain, Sweden, and Germany", in S. McNall, R. Levine, and R. Fantasia (eds) *Bringing Class Back In*, Boulder: Westview Press.

Venable, V. (1966) *Human Nature: The Marxian View*, Cleveland and New York: Meridian Books.

Verba, S., Kelman, S., Orren, G.R., Miyake, I., Watanuki, J., Kabashima, I., Feree, G.D.F (1987) *Elites and the Idea of Equality: A Comparison of Japan, Sweden, and the United States*, Harvard: Harvard University Press.

Vlastos, S. (ed). (1998) *Mirror of Modernity: Invented Traditions of Modern Japan*, Berkeley: University of California Press.

Vogel, E. (1963) *Japan's New Middle Class: The Salary man and His Family in a Tokyo Suburb*, Berekeley: University of California.

—— (1979) *Japan as Number One: Lessons for America*, Massachusetts: Harvard University Press.

Wada, J. (1999) "Civil society in Japan through print and statistical data", in T. Yamamoto (ed.) *Deciding the Public Good: Governance and Civil Society in Japan*, Tokyo: Japan Center for International Exchange.

Wade, R. (1985) "The Role of Government in Overcoming Market Failure: Taiwan, South Korea and Japan", Paper Presented to School of Pacific Studies, Australian National University, Canberra, 10–12 September 1985.

—— (1991) "The idea of civil society" *Dissent* 38. n2: 293–305.

—— (1998) "The concept of civil society", in M. Walzer (ed.) *Towards a Global Civil Society*, Providence, RI.: Berghahn Books.

Ward, A. (1992) "Hegel and the search for epistemological criteria", *Idealistic Studies* 22: 189–202.

Ware, A. and Goodin, R.E. (eds) (1990) *Needs and Welfare*, London: Sage.

Waswo, A. (1989) "Modernism and cultural identity in Japan", *Asian Affairs* 20: 45–56.

Watanabe, M. (1991) "Marx's category of service labour", *Hitotsubashi Journal of Social Studies* 23: 23–36.

Watanabe, O. (1991) *Kigyo shihai to kokka* (Corporate Domination and the State) Tokyo.

Watanabe, S. (1987) "On Socio-institutional conditions of Japan's modernisation", *Studies in Political Economy: The Surplus Approach* 2: 181–199.

Weaver, F.S. (1992) "Toward an Historical understanding of industrial development", in R.E. Galli (ed.) *Rethinking the Third World: Contributions toward a New Conceptualization*, New York: Crane Russak.

Weiner, S.E. (1987) "Why is Japan's unemployment rate so low and so stable?" *Economic Review: Federal Reserve Bank of Kansas City*, April 3.

Weir, M., Orloff, A., and Skocpol, T. (eds) (1988) *The Politics of Social Policy in the United States*, Princeton: Princeton University Press.

Weiss, L. (1993) "War, the state, and the origins of the Japanese employment system", *Politics and Society* 21: 325–354.

Welfare Pension Insurance Law (1986) # 115, May 1954. Tokyo: Eibun-Horei-Sha, Inc.

Westergaard, J. (1978) "Social policy and class inequality: some notes on welfare state limits", in R. Miliband and J. Saville (eds) *The Socialist Register*, London: Merlin Press.

Western, B. (1989) "Decommodification and the transformation of capitalism: welfare state development in seventeen OECD countries", *Australian and New Zealand Journal of Sociology* 25: 200–221.

Westphal, M. (1992) *Hegel, Freedom and Modernity*, Albany, NY: State University of New York Press.

Wetherly, P. (1988) "Class struggle and the welfare state: some theoretical problems considered", *Critical Social Policy* 22: 24–40.

White Paper on Japanese Economy (1991) Tokyo: Business Intercommunications Inc.

Wilensky, H.L. (1975) *The Welfare State and Equality: Structural and Ideological Roots of Public Expenditures*, Berkeley: University of California.

—— and Lebeaux, C.N. (1965) *Industrial Society and Social Welfare*, New York: The Free Press.

——, Luebbert, G.M., Hahn, S.R., and Jamieson, A.M. (1985) *Comparative Social Policy: Theories, Methods, Findings*, Berkeley: Institute of International Studies, University of California.

—— and Turner, L. (1987) *Democratic Corporatism and Policy Linkages: The Interdependence of Industrial, Labor-Market, Incomes, and Social Policies in Eight Countries*, Berkeley: Institute of International Studies, University of California.

Williams, D. (1983) *Beyond Political Economy: A Critique of Issues Raised in Chalmers Johnson's MITI and the Japanese Miracle*, Berlin: Free University Berlin.

Williams, K. (1975) "Facing reality: a critique of Karl Popper's empiricism", *Economy and Society* 4: 309–358.

Winfield, R.D. (1988) *Reason and Justice*, Albany: State University of New York Press.

—— (1990) *The Just Economy*, New York: Routledge.

—— (1991) *Freedom and Modernity*, Albany, NY: State University of New York Press.

Woldring, H.E.S. (1998) "State and civil society in the political philosophy of Alexis de Tocqueville", *International Journal of Voluntary and Nonprofit Organizations* 9(4): 363–373.

Wolferen, K.V. (1994) "Nihon kaishakozo nazo (Japan: the Puzzle of the corporate structure)", *Shukan Toyo Keizai*, July 23: 6–7.

Wong, P. and M. Daley (1990) "Long run development versus crisis management in welfare states", *Social Policy and Administration* 1: 2–12.

Wood, A.W. (1990) *Hegel's Ethical Thought*, Cambridge: Cambridge University Press.

Wood, E.M. (1981) "The separation of the economic and the political in capitalism", *New Left Review* 127: 66–95.

—— (1997) "Capitalism, globalization, and epochal shifts: an exchange", *Monthly Review* 48: 21–32.

—— (1997) "Labor, the state, and class struggle", *Monthly Review* 49: 1–17.

Woods, D. (1992) "Civil society in Europe and Africa: limiting state power through a public sphere", *African Studies Review* 35(2): 77–100.

Woodsworth, D.E. (1977) *Social Security and National Policy: Sweden, Yugoslavia, Japan*, Montreal: McGill-Queens's University Press.

Workmen's Accident Compensation Law # 5 April 7, 1947 (1984) Tokyo: Eibun-Horeisha, Inc., 1984.

Wright, E.O. (1978) *Class, Crisis and the State*, London: New Left Books.

Yaffe, D. (1973) "The Marxian theory of crisis, capital and the state", *Economy and Society* 2 (May): 186–232.

Yamada, T. (1990) "The effects of Japanese social security retirement benefits on personal saving and elderly labor force behavior", *Japan and the World Economy* 2: 327–263.

Yamamoto, K. (1990) "The Japanese-style industrial relations and an 'Informal' employee organization: a case study of the Ohgi-Kai at T electric", *Annals of the Institute of Social Science* 32: 155–215.

Yamamoto, T. (1989) "Reform of the Japanese foster care system", *Child Welfare* 68: 215–20.

—— (ed.)(1999) *Deciding the Public Good: Governance and Civil Society in Japan*, New York: Japan Center for International Exchange.

Yamamoto, T. and Ashizawa, K.G. (1999) Corporate-NGO Partnership in Asia Pacific Tokyo: Japan Center for International Exchange 1999.

—— (2001) "Oberviero", in T. Yamamuto and K.G. Ashizawa (eds) Governance and Civil Society in a Global Age, pp. 9–29. Tokyo: Japan Center for International Exchange.

Yamamura, K. and Yasuba, Y. (eds) (1987) *The Political Economy of Japan: The Domestic Transformation*, Stanford: Stanford University Press.

Yamazaki, H. (1990) "The employees pension system in Japan: past and present", *Annals of the Institute of Social Science* 32: 67–114.

Yang, M.M. (1994) *Gifts, Favours, and Banquets: The Art of Social Relationships in China*, Ithaca, NY: Cornell University Press.

Yasuba, Y. (1975) "Anatomy of the debate on Japanese capitalism", *Journal of Japanese Studies* 2(1).

Yoda, T. (2000) "The rise and fall of maternal society: gender, labor, and capital in contemporary Japan", *The South Atlantic Quarterly* 99(4): 865–902.

Yoda, T. (2001) "A road map to millennial Japan", *The South Atlantic Quarterly* 99(4): 629–668.

Yoshida, K. (1994) *History of Social Service in Japan*, Tokyo: Keiso Shobo

Yoshitomi, M. (1990) "Keiretsu: an insider's guide to Japan's conglomerates", *International Economic Insights* 1: 10–17.

Index